Arabic Today

Second Edition

Arabic Today

A student, business and professional course in spoken and written Arabic

Second Edition

John Mace

EDINBURGH UNIVERSITY PRESS

Edinburgh University Press Ltd
22 George Square, Edinburgh

First published in 1996
This edition 2008

Reprinted 2011

Typeset by the author in Palatino, Times and Arial
and in Traditional Arabic, Giza and Ruq'a,
and printed and bound in Great Britain by
CPI Antony Rowe, Chippenham, Wilts

A CIP record for this book is available from the British Library

ISBN 978 0 7846 3557 3 (hardback)
ISBN 978 0 7846 3558 0 (paperback)

The audio material accompanying this book is available to
download from our website at
www.euppublishing.com/page/ArabicToday/audio

Contents

Part II: Written Arabic

Introduction

You can learn Arabic.

This course is designed to help people visiting the Arab world – whether for work, study or other reasons – who wish to communicate at first hand with the people and the institutions of the region. It is written in a manner suitable either for self-tuition or for use in a classroom.

One problem facing teachers and students of Arabic is the divergence between the written language and the many regional forms of speech. Teachers and students feel forced to make a choice, and this sometimes highlights or even exaggerates this divergence.

This course attempts to cut through the dilemma. **Part I** offers, in a simple and reliable Roman-letter transcription, a form of educated spoken Arabic which leads without strain to the written language explained in **Part II**. Here the Arabic letters are learned in groups, the most useful ones first, while the written language is presented not as a contrast but as a complement to the spoken.

Grammatical terms, kept to a minimum, are explained in the text.

Part I is based on the speech of the Levant, Egypt and the Arabian Peninsula which is also widely understood from Morocco to Oman. The reasons for this choice lie in the cultural, political and economic importance of the region. Not only will this form of speech enable you to understand and be understood in the Arab Middle East, among rich and poor alike, as well as among educated people in North-west Africa, but it also serves as a base on which the bridge to standard written Arabic is easily built.

At the same time, you will find in Part I important regional speech variations.

You may choose to stop at the end of Part I, if you have no time, or no need, for reading and writing. Or you may, after a time if not immediately, go on to Part II, building on what you learned in Part I.

This course rejects the premise that Arabic is very difficult, remote or mysterious, accessible only to specialists. It recognises the need for our better understanding of the Arabs, and offers some help in achieving it. True, it is possible to live and work in an Arab country with no knowledge of the language. But it is rather like listening to Bach with your head under a pillow. You always feel you are missing something.

For the pronunciation, you should make full use of the audio material accompanying this book. Some Arabic sounds are not easy, and, while they are described in the following chapter, the best result is achieved by hearing a native produce the real thing. Everything marked 🎧 is available on the website.

References in the lessons and indexes indicate: lesson no./paragraph no.

I take this opportunity to express my gratitude to Dr Julia Bray of the University of Paris VIII for many valuable suggestions and corrections made for an earlier edition, and to Professor Carole Hillenbrand of the University of Edinburgh for her support and encouragement in this venture. I am likewise indebted to Marilyn Moore for her tireless help in checking the text of both editions, and to

Jihad Haddad for checking the Arabic text. My thanks also go to Dolly Saba, Alain Chbeir and Jihad Haddad for recording parts of the text. Willem Herpels gave me valuable and unstinting help with the computer technology, for which I am also very grateful. Any shortcomings remaining in the book are my responsibility.

I dedicate this book to the memory of my teacher, and to the many other Arab refugees who have contributed to development in the Middle East and elsewhere.

Pronunciation

1. General

Throughout this book, the Arabic sounds are transcribed in a simple system of symbols. The following description of the sounds represented by the symbols refers by comparison to standard English pronunciation. It does not replace the disc available with this book; good Arabic pronunciation can be learned only by listening to a native voice.
Bearing this in mind, pronounce the symbols of the transcription (in italic type) as shown below. Every symbol should be pronounced wherever it occurs; none is silent as is the case with some letters in English spelling.

2. Vowels and diphthongs

a as a in English 'man': *bada* 'to begin'.
ā as a but long: 'ma-a-an': *kān* 'to be'.
i as i in English 'pit': *min* 'from'.
ī as i in English 'machine': *kīs* 'bag'.
u as u in English 'put': *zurt* 'I visited'.
ū as u in English 'rule': *bidūn* 'without'.
aw as ou in English 'loud': *law* 'if'.
ay as ay in English 'day': *bayn* 'between'.
ou as ou in English 'soul': *youm* 'day'.

3. Consonants similar to English

b, d, f, k, m, n, s, t, v, w, z much as in English.
dh as th in English 'that': *kadha* 'so'.
g as g in English 'good': *gārāj* 'garage' (see under *j* below).
h as h in English 'head': *hum* 'they', *lahja* 'accent'.
j as j in English 'jam': *jamb* 'beside'; in Egypt this sound is replaced with *g*, see above.
l as light or front l in English 'leaf': *li* 'for'; not as dark or back l in English 'wall'.
r always rolled: *rama* 'to throw', *yirmī* 'he throws'.
sh as sh in English 'she': *masha* 'to walk'.
th as th in English 'thin': *thalātha* 'three'.
y as y in English 'year' (i.e. a consonant): *yamīn* 'left'.

4. Consonants different from English

kh as ch in German 'Buch', Welsh 'bach' or Scots 'loch': *khamsa* 'five'; if you have difficulty, first form *k*, but before pronouncing it, release the closure slightly. The result will be *kh*.
gh as r in the French pronunciation of 'Paris': *ghāz* 'gas'; this is the voiced counterpart of *kh*. Proceed as for *kh*, but starting with *g* instead of *k*
ḥ as h but pronounced far back in the throat: *ḥāl* 'condition', *baḥr* 'sea'; *ḥ* is the sound produced when you breathe on glass to clean it

’ glottal stop: *sa’al* ‘to ask’; this is the sound heard before each word in the expression “absolutely awful”, which we could transcribe as *[’absolutely ’awful]*. In the text we often refer to the glottal stop as *hamza*, which is the sign marking it. There is more about *hamza* in paragraph 9 below.

q as *k* but pronounced far back in the throat: *qāl* ‘to say’; for *k* the closure is at the rear of the palate, while for *q* the closure is as low in the throat as you can make it.

9 a sound like a gulp: *sā9ad* ‘to help’. Proceed as follows. Repeat several times the name Maggie; as you say it, try to stop making contact in the throat for the sound -gg-; let this middle consonant become progressively more vague until it is no more than a gulp, with no contact. The result is near to the Arabic word *ma9ī* ‘with me’. Probably the most difficult sound in Arabic. Listen carefully to the disc.

5. Deep (‘velarised’) consonants

ṭ, ḍ, ṣ, ð̣ and ***ẓ*** are the deep or velarised counterparts of ***t, d,*** *s*, ***dh*** and *z*. The difference is important. In pronouncing *t, d* and *dh,* the end of the tongue touches the top front teeth or teeth-ridge. For *s* and *z* the contact is between the middle of the tongue and the teeth-ridge. In both cases the rest of the tongue follows the curve of the palate. For each of the velarised counterparts, the point of contact is unchanged, but the rest of the tongue is dropped as far as possible, forming a deep cavity. Prepare, for example, to pronounce *t*. Now, maintaining the contact between the tip of the tongue and the top front teeth-ridge, create a cavity by dropping the rest of the tongue as low as possible. Say *t* with this position. It will sound something like *ṭ*.

Proceed in like manner for each of the other velarised consonants. Prepare the unvelarised sound, then, holding the point of contact, drop the body and base of the tongue to make the cavity for the velarised counterpart. Feel the cavity clearly when pronouncing the velarised consonants, which are unmistakable on the disc.

ð̣ and *ẓ* are the velarised counterparts of *dh* and *z* respectively. But Arabs use either *ð̣* for both velarised sounds, or *ẓ* for both velarised sounds. *ð̣* is the ‘classical’ pronunciation and is especially common in the Arabian Peninsula and the Gulf. Both forms are correct.

6. Vowel-attraction: velarised *a* and *ā*

Next to a velarised consonant (*ṭ, ḍ, ṣ* or *ð̣/ẓ,* see above), the vowels *a* and *ā* automatically acquire a deeper sound because of the cavity. They are ‘attracted’. This happens also when *a* or *ā* occur next to *q* because of the latter’s depth, and very commonly with *kh* and *r*, especially when the vowel is stressed (see below). Distinguish carefully, and listen for the difference on the disc. In the following examples, and at certain other points in the book, we mark the velarised *a*’s as *ạ* and *ạ̄* for clarity.

ạ sounds like u in English ‘but’: *mạṭạr* ‘rain’; *ạ̄* sounds like a in English ‘calm’: *ṭạ̄r* ‘to fly’. Compare the *a*’s in the two columns:

tamm	to end	*ṭạbīb*	doctor

'afād	to benefit	*fạḍī*	empty
hādha	this	*ðạll*	to remain
sāda	plain	*ṣạr*	to become
mazrū9	planted	*mạẓbūṭ*	correct
kānat	she was	*qạlat*	she said
dākhil	inside	*khạrij*	outside

Vowel-attraction also occurs with *a* before the combination *9ṭ* or *9ḍ*; the velarised consonant appears to exercise the attraction through the *9*:

'ạ9ṭū	they gave	*bạ9ḍ*	some

The two diphthongs *aw* and *ay* are also attracted when next to a velarised consonant, and often after *q*, *kh* or *r*. The *a* of the diphthong deepens to *ạ*:

ṣạwt	voice	*ḍạyf*	guest

In the vocabularies and text we will show the velarisation as *ạ* and *ạ̄* only when drawing attention to it.

7. Stress

In an Arabic word of several syllables, one syllable is stressed, i.e. spoken with more force than the others. In the first three lessons we show the stress with an acute accent, ..́. . There are simple rules:

- Stress the last heavy syllable when there is one. A heavy syllable is one consisting of either:
  - a diphthong or long vowel + consonant, or
  - a short vowel + two consonants or a doubled consonant*

lubnā́n	Lebanon	*dábbar*	to arrange
dabbárt	you arranged		

- Stress the first syllable when there is no heavy syllable:

'ána	I	*kátabat*	she wrote

* See below for doubled consonants.

In the first three lessons the stress is fully marked. For four special cases, the stress is marked throughout the book:

- on words carrying a stressed ending in the form of a long vowel. These are explained as they arise:

dabbartū́	you arranged it	*warā́*	behind him

- on words ending *-iya*, which always carry the stress on the previous syllable; this is to avoid confusion with the ending *-ī́ya* which is always stressed on its long *-ī-* :

thā́niya	second	*qáriya*	village

- on certain verb forms having irregular stress:

insáḥabū	they withdrew	*ittáṣal*	to contact

  (not *[íns-, ítt-]* as the rule states)
- where certain words carry the stress of the whole expression:

fī́ shī	there's something	*mā́ fī shī*	there's nothing

8. Hyphens

A hyphen is sometimes shown in the transcription, for grammatical or phonetic clarity. It should be ignored in pronunciation:

al the + *bayt* house → *al-báyt* the house

Pronounce the expression without a pause: *albáyt.*

To avoid confusion with the consonants *dh, kh, sh* and *th,* the consonants *d, k, s* and *t* followed by *h* are shown with a hyphen: *d-h, k-h, s-h, t-h.* Ignore the hyphen in pronouncing, but be sure to sound two separate consonants:

t-hímmnī it concerns me *náfs-ha* herself

9. Weak vowels

A vowel beginning a word is called a weak vowel. It is dropped when the preceding word in the same phrase ends with a vowel:

li to + *al-bálad* the town → *li l-bálad* to (the) town

húwa he + *ibtáda* began → *húwa btáda* he began

Pronounce each combination without a pause: *lilbálad, húwabtáda.*

This rule applies only when the second word begins with a *vowel,* not when it begins with *hamza* (see paragraph 4 above) + a vowel, since *hamza* itself is a *consonant*:

húwa he + *'ársal* sent → *húwa 'ársal* he sent

Further, when a long vowel at the end of a word is followed by a word which has lost its initial weak vowel and now begins with two consonants, the long vowel becomes short:

shā́fū they saw + *al-báyt* the house

→ *shā́fu l-báyt* (pronounced *shā́fulbáyt,* short *-u-*) they saw the house

10. Doubled consonants

Consonants transcribed double must be pronounced double, i.e. held longer than single consonants:

dáras	to study	*dárras**	to instruct
zamī́l	colleague	*az-zamī́l*	the colleague

* pronounce as if it were transcribed *dár-ras.*

We have the phenomenon also in English, in the pronunciation of words such as 'unknown' and of expressions such as 'eight times'.

11. Written pronunciation

In the text, reference is made to 'written pronunciation'. This is not nonsense; it is the pronunciation used in reading from a prepared text. We study it in Part II. It differs in a few respects from the pronunciation of unscripted speech, which we study in Part I.

Part I

Spoken Arabic

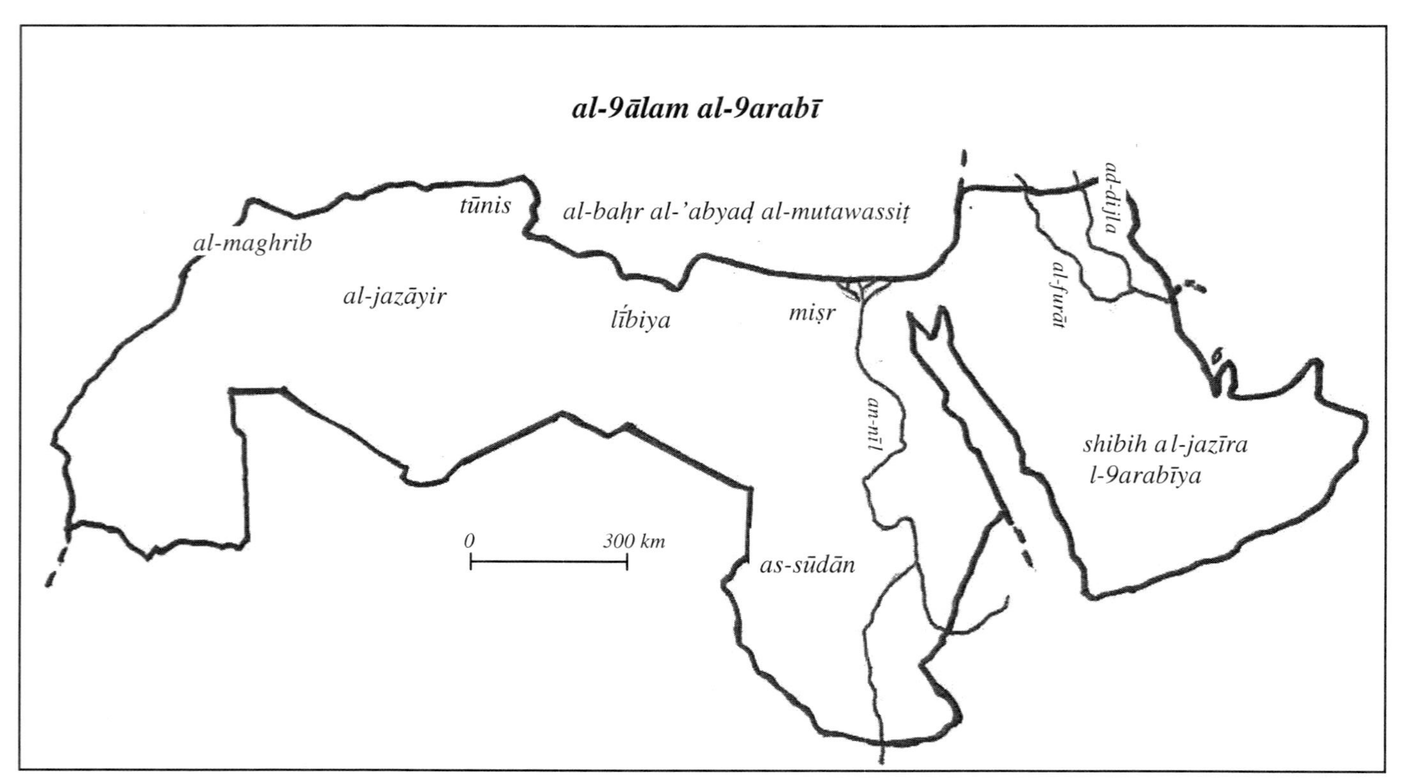
al-9ālam al-9arabī
al-maghrib
tūnis
al-baḥr al-'abyaḍ al-mutawassiṭ
al-jazāyir
lībiya
miṣr
an-nīl
as-sūdān
ad-dijla
al-furāt
shibih al-jazīra l-9arabīya
0
300 km

ad-dárs al-'áwwal – Lesson 1
taḥīyā́t – Greetings

1. *al-ḥiwā́r* – Dialogue

(Peter Brown, an engineer from Cambridge, boards a flight to Amman. He sees a passenger, Dr Fuad Sharif *(fu'ā́d sharī́f)* reading an Arabic newspaper, sitting next to an empty seat.)

	mása l-kháyr	good afternoon/ evening
	mása n-nū́r	good afternoon/ evening (in reply)
Peter:	mása l-kháyr.	Good evening.
fu'ā́d:	mása n-nū́r.	Good evening.
	'ísmaḥ lī	permit me; (here:) excuse me
	hā́dha l-maḥáll	this place
	fā́ḍī	empty, free
	min fáḍlak	please
Peter:	'ísmaḥ lī, hā́dha l-maḥáll fā́ḍī, min fáḍlak?	Excuse me, is this place free, please?
	ná9am	yes
	tfáḍḍal	please (offering something)
fu'ā́d:	ná9am, fā́ḍī. tfáḍḍal.	Yes, it's free. Help yourself.
	shúkran	thank you
	9áfwan	don't mention it
Peter:	shúkran.	Thank you.
fu'ā́d:	9áfwan.	Don't mention it.
	'ísmī	my name
	'ána	I
	muhándis	engineer
	kayf	how
	ḥā́lak	your condition
Peter:	'ísmī Peter Brown. 'ána muhandis. kayf ḥā́lak?	My name is Peter Brown. I'm an engineer. How are you?
	u	and
	ṭabī́b	doctor
fu'ā́d:	u 'ána fu'ā́d sharī́f, ṭabī́b.	And I'm Fuad Sharif, a doctor.
	mabsū́ṭ	pleased; (here:) well
	(al-)ḥamdílla	God be praised; (here:) thank you
	'int	you
	mabsū́ṭ, al-ḥamdílla	I'm well, thank you.

	kayf ḥā́lak 'int?	How are you?
	kamā́n	also, too
	'amáyrkī	American
Peter:	'ána mabsū́ṭ kamā́n, ḥamdílla.	I'm well too, thank you.
fu'ā́d:	'int 'amáyrkī?	Are you American?
	la'	no
	'inglī́zī	English, British
	wa	and
	'úrdunī	Jordanian
Peter:	la', 'ána 'inglī́zī.	No, I'm British.
	wa 'int 'úrdunī?	And you're Jordanian?
	min	from
	al-'úrdun	Jordan
	9ammā́n	Amman
fu'ā́d:	ná9am, 'ána min al-úrdun, min 9ammā́n.	Yes, I'm from Jordan, from Amman.
	'áhlan	welcome
	bīk	to you
	'áhlan.	Welcome.
Peter:	'áhlan bīk.	Welcome to you.
	al-muḍī́fa	the stewardess
	márḥaba	hello
	yā	(a particle of address)
	sā́datī	gentlemen
	marḥabtáyn	hello (in reply)
al-muḍī́fa:	márḥaba, yā sā́datī.	Hello, gentlemen.
Peter:	marḥabtáyn.	Hello.
	qáhwa	coffee
	wílla	or (in questions)
	shā́ī	tea
	sáyyid	gentleman, Mr
al-muḍī́fa:	qáhwa wílla shā́ī, yā sáyyid Brown?	Coffee or tea, Mr Brown?
	law samáḥtī	please
	dúktur	Dr, doctor
	min fáḍlik	please
Peter:	qáhwa, law samaḥtī.	Coffee, please.
al-muḍī́fa:	wa 'int, yā dúktur?	And you, Doctor?
fu'ā́d:	qáhwa kamā́n, min fáḍlik.	Coffee too, please.
	tfáḍḍalū	please (offering something)
	jazī́lan	abundantly; (here:) very much
al-muḍī́fa:	tfáḍḍalū.	Here you are.
fu'ā́d:	shúkran jazī́lan.	Thank you very much.
al-muḍī́fa:	9áfwan.	You're welcome.

	ṣabā́ḥ al-kháyr	good morning
	ṣabā́ḥ an-nū́r	good morning (reply)
	al-yóum	today
fu'ā́d:	ṣabā́ḥ al-kháyr, yā sáyyid Peter.	Good morning, Mr Brown.
Peter:	ṣabā́ḥ an-nū́r, yā dúktur.	Good morning, Doctor.
	kayf ḥā́lak al-yóum?	How are you today?
	mish baṭṭā́l	not bad
	jíddan	very
	nushkurálla	thank God; (here:) thank you
fu'ā́d:	mish baṭṭā́l, shúkran.	Not bad, thank you.
	kayf ḥā́lak 'int?	How are you?
Peter:	mabsū́ṭ jíddan, nushkurálla.	Very well, thank you.

2. *mufradā́t 'iḍāfī́ya* – Additional vocabulary
al-míhan wa l-buldā́n – Professions and countries

mu9állim	teacher (man)	*mu9állima*	teacher (woman)
ṣúḥufī	journalist	*muḥā́mī*	lawyer
mudī́r shárika	company director	*mudī́r bank*	bank manager
diblumā́sī	diplomat	*tā́jir*	businessman, trader
muḥā́sib	accountant	*mu'állif*	writer
ṭā́lib	student (man)	*ṭā́liba*	student (woman)
muwáẓẓaf ḥukū́ma	civil servant	*'ingíltra*	England, Britain
'amáyrka	America	*'almā́niya*	Germany
faránsa	France	*'īṭā́liya*	Italy
al-yābā́n	Japan	*al-hínd*	India
miṣr	Egypt	*sū́riya*	Syria
lubnā́n	Lebanon	*al-9irā́q*	Iraq
as-sa9ūdī́ya	Saudi Arabia	*sa9ū́dī*	Saudi
al-kuwáyt	Kuwait	*lī́biya*	Libya
tū́nis	Tunisia, Tunis	*al-jazā́yir*	Algeria, Algiers
al-mághrib	Morocco	*as-sūdā́n*	Sudan
filasṭī́n	Palestine	*9árabī*	Arab
'urúbba	Europe		

an-náḥū – Grammar
3. Greetings

Many polite expressions in Arabic are in two parts: a 'greeting' and a 'response'. Sometimes the first speaker makes a further response. Examine:

Greeting		→	Response	
ṣabā́ḥ al-kháyr	Good morning		*ṣabā́ḥ an-nū́r*	Good morning
'ísmaḥ lī	Excuse/Permit me		*tfáḍḍal*	Please do/Go ahead
min fáḍlak	Please (requesting)		*tfáḍḍal*	Here you are/Go ahead
tfáḍḍal	Please (offering)		*shúkran*	Thank you

(further response:) *9áfwan* Don't mention it/You're welcome

kayf ḥā́lak?	How are you?	*mabsū́ṭ, al-ḥamdílla* *mabsū́ṭ, nushkurálla* *mabsū́ṭ, shúkran* *mish baṭṭā́l*, shúkran*	Fine, thank you

* informal response

áhlan	Welcome	*áhlan bīk*	Welcome yourself
márḥaba	Hello	*marḥabtáyn*	Hello
mása l-kháyr	Good afternoon/evening	*mása n-nū́r*	Good afternoon/evening

Greetings may be repeated during the day, as a sign of courtesy.

4. Gender and number

Some greetings and responses change according to whether they are said to a male person (masculine, m.), a female person (feminine, f.), or a group (plural, pl.). Examine:

to a male person (m.)	to a female person (f.)	to a group (pl.)	
'ísmaḥ lī	*'ísmaḥī lī*	*'ísmaḥū lī*	Excuse/Permit me
tfáḍḍal	*tfáḍḍalī*	*tfáḍḍalū*	Please (offering)
law samáḥt	*law samáḥtī*	*law samáḥtū*	Please (requesting)
'áhlan bīk	*'áhlan bī́ki*	*'áhlan bī́kum*	Welcome
min fáḍlak	*min fáḍlik*	*min fáḍilkum*	Please (requesting)
kayf ḥā́lak?	*kayf ḥā́lik?*	*kayf ḥā́lkum?*	How are you?

This looks more complicated than it really is; we shall learn simple rules later. The distinction between masculine, feminine and plural runs right through the language and is important.

5. Pronouns

The personal pronouns (I, you, he etc.) are:

1st person:	*'ána*	I	*'íḥna/níḥna*	we
2nd person:	*'int*	you (m.)	*'íntū*	you (plural)
	'ínti	you (f.)		
3rd person:	*húwa*	he, it (m.)	*hum*	they (animate)
	híya	she, it (f.)	*híya*	they (inanimate)

Note:

- The two forms for 'we' are equally common.
- The 'you' form varies for gender in the singular, but not in the plural.
- There is no neuter gender; we express 'it' with the masculine (m.) *húwa* or the feminine (f.) *híya* according to the gender of the corresponding noun (i.e. person, place, creature, thing or idea).
- The 'they' forms are not distinguished for gender, but there is one form used for people (the *animate* form ['an.', 'anim.']) and an *inanimate* form ('inan.') used elsewhere, i.e. for other creatures, and for places, things and ideas. The distinction between animate and inanimate is important in Arabic. The inanimate plural has the same form as the feminine singular.

Inanimate plural rule: For all parts of speech except nouns, the inanimate plural has the same form as the feminine singular.

The personal pronouns are used only when needed for extra emphasis, since other parts of the sentence usually indicate who or what is intended.

6. The verb 'to be'

The equivalent of the verb 'to be' in present time ('am, is, are') is omitted in Arabic, being inferred from the context:

'ána mabsū́ṭ. I('m) well. *kayf ḥā́lak?* ('How [is] your condition?') How are you?

When both verb and pronoun are omitted we may get a one-word sentence:

mabsū́ṭ. (I'm) well. *mabsū́ṭ?* (Are you) well?

7. Article

There is no indefinite article ('a, an') in Arabic:

'ána muhándis. húwa ṭabī́b. I'm (an) engineer. He's (a) doctor.

8. Interrogative

Questions can be indicated by making the voice rise momentarily on the stressed syllable of the word questioned:

hā́dha l-maḥall fā́ḍī? Is this place free?

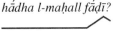

kayf ḥā́lak? How are you? *mabsū́ṭ?* Are you well?

9. *nísba* adjectives

Adjectives are words which describe or qualify nouns or pronouns. Many adjectives are formed from nouns by adding the ending *-ī*. We call such adjectives *nísba* ('relationship') adjectives. The prefix *al-* attached to some nouns, and the endings *-a* and *-iya*, are dropped before *-ī* is added:

miṣr	Egypt	*míṣrī*	Egyptian
al-hínd	India	*híndī*	Indian
ḥukū́ma	government	*ḥukū́mī*	governmental
'īṭā́liya	Italy	*'īṭā́lī*	Italian
'urúbba	Europe	*'urúbbī*	European

A few are otherwise modified before *-ī* is added:

faránsa	France	*faransā́wī*	French

10. Agreement of adjectives

Adjectives are made m. or f., and singular ('s.') or pl., to agree in gender and number with the noun or pronoun which they qualify. Most *nísba* adjectives, and some others, are 'sound', i.e. they form their f. and pl. regularly, as follows:

	m.s.	f.s./inan. pl.	an. pl.	
nísba:	*-ī*	*-ī́ya*	*-īyī́n*	
examples:	*'úrdunī*	*'urdunī́ya*	*'urdunīyī́n*	Jordanian
other adj.:	final consonant	*-a*	*-ī́n*	pleased,
examples:	*mabsū́ṭ*	*mabsū́ṭa*	*mabsūṭī́n*	well

A few adjectives ending in *-ī* are not *nísba* adjectives; they have a different stress pattern in the feminine singular/inanimate plural form:

	-ī	***´-iya***	*-īyī́n*	
example:	*fā́ḍī*	***fā́ḍiya***	*fāḍīyī́n*	empty, free

(hum) kuwaytīyī́n? Are they Kuwaiti?
– *la', húwa 'úrdunī u híya miṣrī́ya.* – No, he's Jordanian and she's Egyptian.
'íntu fāḍīyī́n? híya mabsū́ṭa?

A few *nísba* adjectives have a 'broken' (irregular) plural:

'inglī́zī	*'inglīzī́ya*	*'inglī́z*	British, English
'amáyrkī	*'amayrkī́ya*	*'amayrkā́n*	American
9árabī	*9arabī́ya*	*9árab*	Arab
híndī	*hindī́ya*	*hunū́d*	Indian

Adjectives used in greetings and responses must also agree:

kayf ḥā́lak? – mabsū́ṭ. – I'm well. (male person responding)
kayf ḥā́lik? – mabsū́ṭa. – I'm well. (female person responding)
kayf ḥā́lkum? – mabsūṭī́n. – We're well. (responding for a group)

11. Word-order; qualifying words

Qualifying words such as adjectives and adverbs* usually follow the word or expression which they qualify:

muhándis 'inglī́zī a British engineer
mabsū́ṭ jíddan very well, very pleased

*An adverb is word describing or modifying an adjective, a verb or another adverb. In the expression 'very well', 'very' is said to modify the adjective 'well'.

Qualifying word rule: A qualifying word follows the word which it qualifies.

12 Vocative

When addressing a person we use the vocative particle *yā* before the name or title. Arabs often use the first name, preceded, for politeness, by *sáyyid* 'Mr' or *sitt* 'Mrs/Miss/Ms' or another title:

tfáḍḍal, yā fu'ā́d. Here you are, Fuad.
kayf ḥā́lak, yā sáyyid Peter? How are you, Mr Brown?
shúkran, yā dúktur. Thank you, Doctor.

13 'Please'

Distinguish between the expressions for 'please':

min fáḍlak (etc.), *law samáḥt* (etc.)	(enquiring or requesting)
tfáḍḍal/-ī/-ū	(offering or proposing)

14 *u* 'and'

Although consisting only of a weak vowel (see Pronunciation, paragraph 9), the word *u* 'and' is never elided:

shā́ī u qáhwa	tea and coffee

15. *júmal mithālī́ya* – Model sentences

'int min kuwáyt? – la', 'ána sa9ū́dī.	Are you from Kuwait? – No, I'm Saudi.
híya ṭā́liba? – ná9am, híya ṭā́liba miṣrī́ya.	Is she a student? – Yes, she's an Egyptian student.
fu'ā́d mudī́r bank? – la', húwa ṭabī́b.	Is Fuad a bank manager? – No, he's a doctor.
'int fā́ḍī? – ná9am, al-yóum fā́ḍī, tfáḍḍal.	Are you free? – Yes, today I'm free. How can I help you?

16. *at-tamārī́n* – Exercises

1. Give the response to the greeting:
e.g.: mása l-kháyr. – mása n-nū́r.
(a) kayf ḥā́lak? (b) tfaḍḍal. (c) ṣabā́ḥ al-kháyr.
(d) kayf ḥā́lik? (e) márḥaba.

2. Repeat the following greetings or responses, speaking to a woman:
e.g.: tfáḍḍal. – tfáḍḍalī.
(a) kayf ḥā́lak? (b) law samáḥt. (c) 'int mabsū́ṭ?
(d) márḥaba. (e) 'áhlan bīk.

3. Repeat Ex. no. 2, speaking to a group:
e.g.: tfáḍḍal. – tfáḍḍalū.

4. Repeat the following greetings or responses, speaking to a man:
e.g.: min fáḍlik. – min fáḍlak.
(a) kayf ḥā́lkum? (b) 'áhlan bī́ki. (c) ṣabā́ḥ al-kháyr.
(d) tfáḍḍalī. (e) 9áfwan.

5. Make the expression feminine singular:
e.g.: húwa 'inglī́zī. – híya 'inglīzī́ya.
(a) mu9állim míṣrī (b) 'int 'amáyrkī?
(c) mabsū́ṭ jíddan, shúkran. (d) 'ána 'inglī́zī.
(e) húwa min al-'úrdun.

6. Repeat Ex. no. 5, making the expression plural:
e.g.: húwa 'inglī́zī. – hum 'inglī́z.

7. Make the expression masculine singular:
e.g.: ’ána mabsū́ṭa. – ’ána mabsū́ṭ.
(a) hum sūrīyī́n. (b) mu9állima ’inglīzī́ya
(c) ’íntī lubnānī́ya? (d) fā́ḍiya (e) fāḍiyī́n

8. Answer the question:
e.g.: Peter muhándis? – ná9am, húwa muhándis.
Peter míṣrī? – la’, húwa ’inglī́zī.
(a) fu’ā́d muḥā́sib? (b) fu’ā́d ’úrdunī wílla míṣrī?
(c) Peter mabsū́ṭ? (d) hā́dha l-maḥáll fā́ḍī? (e) kayf ḥā́lak?

9. Mark the stress:
e.g.: muhandis –muhándis
(a) nushkuralla (b) fāḍī, fāḍiya, fāḍiyīn (c) mabsūṭīn
(d) 9arabī, 9arabīya, 9arab (e) ṭālib ’inglīzī

ad-dárs ath-thā́niya – Lesson 2
fi l-maṭā́r – At the Airport

1. *al-ḥiwā́r* – Dialogue

	fī, fi	in
	al-muhā́jara	immigration
	fi l-muhā́jara	in Immigration
	al-ma'mū́r	the official
	ḥáḍirtak	you (deferential form)
	wayn	where
	jawā́z sáfarak	your passport
(fi l-muhā́jara		In Immigration)
al-ma'mū́r:	ḥáḍirtak min wayn?	Where are you from?
Peter:	min 'ingíltra	From England.
al-ma'mū́r:	jawā́z sáfarak, min fáḍlak	Your passport, please.
Peter:	tfáḍḍal.	Here you are.
	kam	how much, how many
	waqt	time
	tíbqa	you stay
al-ma'mū́r:	kam waqt tíbqa fi l-'úrdun, yā sáyyid Brown?	How long are you staying in Jordan, Mr Brown?
	shahr	month
	wā́ḥid	one
	taqrī́ban	approximately
	kwáyyis	good
	hay	here is, here are
	jawā́zak	= *jawā́z sáfarak*
Peter:	shahr wā́ḥid taqrī́ban.	One month approximately.
al-ma'mū́r:	kwáyyis. tfáḍḍal, hay jawā́zak	Good. Here you are, here's your passport.
	al-júmruk	Customs
	hunā́k	there
	wára	behind
	an-nā́s	the people
Peter:	shúkran. wayn al-júmruk, min fáḍlak?	Thank you. Where's Customs, please?
al-ma'mū́r:	hunā́k, wára n-nā́s. tfáḍḍal.	There, behind the people.
Peter:	shúkran.	Thank you.

–

(fi l-júmruk		In Customs)
	áhlan wa sáhlan	welcome
	shánta	suitcase. case
	9índak	you have
al-ma'mū́r:	'áhlan wa sáhlan.	Welcome.
Peter:	'áhlan bīk.	Thank you.

al-ma'mū́r:	kam shánta 9índak?	How many cases do you have?
	thalā́tha	three
	kīs	bag
	ṣghīr	small
Peter:	thalā́tha, wa kīs ṣghīr.	Three, and a small bag.
	shū	what
	fī́	there is, there are
	fi sh-shánta	in the bag
	mashrūbā́t	drinks (here:) liquor
	'aw	or
	sīgā́ra	cigarette (here:) cigarettes
al-ma'mū́r:	shū fī́, fi sh-shánta?	What is there, in the case?
	fī́ 9índak mashrūbā́t 'aw sīgā́ra?	Have you got any liquor or cigarettes?
	'aghrā́ḍ	things, possessions
	shákhṣī	personal
	bas	only
Peter:	la', 'aghrā́ḍ shakhṣī́ya bas;	No, only personal things;
	malā́bis	clothes
	kam	(also:) some
	kitā́b	book
	kádha	thus, so; (here:) such
Peter:	malā́bis, kam kitā́b u kádha.	clothes, some books and the like.
	ziyā́rtak	your visit
	ṭawī́la	long
	fáqaṭ	only
al-ma'mū́r:	ziyā́rtak ṭawī́la?	Is your visit long?
Peter:	shahr wā́ḥid fáqaṭ.	Only one month.
	ṭáyyib	good
	ma9 as-salā́ma	goodbye
	'álla yisállimak	goodbye (response)
al-ma'mū́r:	ṭáyyib. ma9 as-salā́ma.	Very well. Goodbye.
Peter:	'álla yisállimak.	Goodbye.

2. *9ibārā́t* – Expressions

ḥáḍirtak ('your presence') you. A polite way of addressing a stranger. It is in no way servile. It varies with the person(s) addressed: *ḥáḍirtik* to a woman, *ḥaḍrā́tkum* to a group. For referring to such a person or persons, we can use *ḥáḍirtu* (m.), *ḥaḍrít-ha* (f.), *ḥaḍrā́t-hum* (pl.) The apparent irregularities in the stress are explained later.

'áhlan wa sáhlan Welcome (invariable greeting). The response is *'áhlan bīk/bī́ki/bī́kum.*

ma9 as-salā́ma (['Go] with safety') Goodbye (invariable greeting).

'álla yisállimak ('God save you') Goodbye (response). This response agrees with the person or group addressed, thus:

(to a male person)	*'álla yisállimak*
(to a female person)	*'álla yisállimik*
(to a group)	*'álla yisallímkum*

3. *mufradā́t 'iḍāfī́ya* – Additional vocabulary. *as-safarā́t* – Travel

musā́fir	traveller	*rā́kib*, pl. *rukkā́b*	passenger(s)
tádhkara	ticket	*táksī*	taxi
sayyā́ra	car	*'utubī́s, bāṣ*	bus
ṭayyā́ra	aeroplane	*'újra*	fare
vī́za	visa	*'iqā́ma*	stay, residence
maṭā́r	airport	*ṣandū́q*	box, trunk
mughā́dara	departure	*wuṣū́l*	arrival
ta'khī́r	delay	*muta'ákhkhir*	late, delayed
jádwal	timetable	*fulū́s* (pl.)	money
jináyh	pound (£)	*dīnā́r*	dinar
riyā́l	rial, riyal	*lī́ra*	lira
doulā́r	dollar	*'ū́ro, yū́ro*	euro

an-náḥū **– Grammar**

4. Gender of nouns

Nouns (see 1/5) are either masculine or feminine.

Feminine are:

- nouns denoting females;
- nouns denoting double parts of the body, which we shall point out as they occur;
- nouns ending in *-a* and not denoting males;
- a very small number of other nouns, which we shall point out as they occur.

All other nouns are masculine.

Examples: f.: *mu9állima, ṭā́liba, shánta, sayyā́ra*
m.: *mu9állim, ṭā́lib, kīs, 'ism*

There are a few exceptions to these rules; for example, *mása* is masculine. Such exceptions will also be noted as they occur.

Some words like *dúktur* are masculine but refer also to women.

5. Article

The definite article in English is 'the'. The Arabic definite article is used more than its English counterpart. It takes the form of a prefix, i.e. it is attached before the word which it defines. The article is invariable for gender or number. In transcription it is usual to show the attachment of the article with a hyphen.

It has the form *al-* before most words: *al-mu9állim, al-muḍī́fa, al-maṭā́r*; but before words beginning with sounds pronounced with the tip or near-tip of the tongue, i.e. *t, d, ṭ, ḍ, th, dh, s, ṣ, sh, z, ẓ, ǭ, r, l* and *n*, the *-l-* of the article assimilates, i.e. assumes the sound of that letter, which is then pronounced double:

as-sayyā́ra, ash-shánta, az-ziyā́ra, ad-dúktur, an-nā́s

The *-a-* of the assimilated article is always deepened (see Pronunciation) when next to the velarized consonants *ṭ, ḍ, ṣ* and *ð̣/ẓ*; and is often deepened next to *r*. In the examples shown below the deepened *a* is shown dotted, for clarity:

ạṣ-ṣúḥufī, ạṭ-ṭạyyā́rạ, ạr-rukkā́b

The vowel of the article is always weak and unstressed.

6. Agreement of adjectives

When an adjective is the complement (i.e. completes the sense) of a verb, including an implied verb 'to be', it agrees in gender and number with the noun or pronoun which it qualifies:

aṭ-ṭabī́b míṣrī. *híya lubnānī́ya.* *ar-rukkā́b mabsūṭī́n.*

But when it is not a complement, the adjective must in addition be definite if its noun is definite. The definite adjective takes the prefixed article, under the same rules as for nouns:

aṭ-ṭabī́b al-míṣrī hunā́k. *wayn al-mu9állima s-sūrī́ya?*

The inanimate plural rule (see 1/5) holds for adjectives, definite or not:

(ar-)rukkā́b (al-)'amayrkā́n but: *(as-)sayyārā́t (al-)'amayrkī́ya*

7. Prepositions

Here are common prepositions ('in', 'on' etc.), some known to you:

fī	in	*9ála*	on
dā́khil	inside	*khā́rij*	outside
wára	behind	*'amā́m, quddā́m*	before, in front of
ma9	with (accompanied by)	*bi*	with (by means of), in
bidū́n	without	*9ind*	at, in the presence of
'íla, li	to, for	*min*	from
ba9d	after	*qabl*	before
fouq	above	*taḥt*	under
ḥawl, ḥawā́lī	around, about	*9an*	from, about
bi sábab	because of	*bi r-raghm min*	despite
ḥatta	until, as far as	*mundh, min*	since
khilā́l	during	*ṭūl*	for the whole (duration) of
bi khuṣū́ṣ	concerning	*jamb*	beside
'ílla	except	*bayn*	between, among
mithl	like	*ḍidd*	against

A preposition governing a noun precedes that noun, as English:

dā́khil al-maṭā́r inside the airport *fī 9ammā́n* in Amman

8. Possessive suffixes; Pronouns with prepositions

The possessive adjective ('my', 'your' etc.): takes the form of a suffix, i.e. it is attached after the noun denoting the person or thing 'possessed':

-ī	my	*-na*	our
-ak	your (m.)	*-kum*	your (pl.)

-ik	your (f.)		
-u	his/its	*-hum*	their (animate)
-ha	her/its	*-ha*	their (inanimate)

These possessives correspond in person and use exactly to the personal pronouns given in 1/5.

After a noun ending in a consonant, the suffix has the form shown above:

mu9állimī my teacher; *kitā́bu* his book; *ṭabī́bna* our doctor

After final *-ī*, the suffixes *-ī, -ak, -ik* and *-u* become *-ya, -yak, -yik, -yu*:

muhāmī́ya, muhāmī́yak, muhāmī́yik, muhāmī́yu my, your, his lawyer

The noun-ending *-a* becomes *-t* before a suffix beginning with a vowel, and *-ít* before a suffix beginning with a consonant:

sayyā́rtī, sayyā́rtak/sayyā́rtik, sayyā́rtu/sayyārít-ha;

sayyārítna, sayyārítkum, sayyārít-hum my, your, his (etc.) car

For ease of pronunciation, nouns ending in two consonants + *-a*, or in *-ta, -da, -ṭa, -ḍa* keep their final vowel and add *-t-* before all the suffixes: *shántatī*

A noun with a possessive suffix is definite; its adjective, when not a complement, must therefore also be definite:

kitā́bak al-9árabī *shántatu l-fā́ḍiya*

A possessive suffix is also added to a preposition to express the pronoun governed by it. The meaning is then 'me', 'you', 'him' (etc.):

má9ī	with me	*dā́khilu*	inside it
'amā́mna	in front of us		

When the suffixes *-ha* and *-hum* are added after *t, d, k* or *s* we shall transcribe with a hyphen to make the pronunciation clear:

sayyārít-ha *fulū́s-hum*

With some prepositions, either the preposition or the suffix, or both, may be modified:

- *min* and *9an* double their *n* before a suffix beginning with a vowel:
  mínnī, mínnak/mínnik, mínnu *9ánnī, 9ánnak/9ánnik, 9ánnu*
  but: *mínha, mínna (min + na), mínkum, mínhum*
  9ánha, 9ánna (9an + na), 9ánkum, 9ánhum
- *bayn* meaning 'between' governs two concepts. If one is a pronoun, *bayn* is repeated: *bayn miṣr u lubnā́n*
  but: *báynhum u bayn al-mudī́r; báynī u báynak*

The prepositions ending in a vowel have the following forms when the suffixes are added; at the same time the suffix itself may be modified:

wára:	*warā́ī, warā́k/warā́ki, warā́/warā́ha;*
	warā́na, warā́kum, warā́hum
bi:	*bī́ya* or *bī́nī, bī́k/bī́ki, bī́*/bī́ha;*
	bī́na, bī́kum, bī́hum
9ála:	*9aláyy* or *9aláyya, 9aláyk/9aláyki, 9aláy/9aláyha;*
	9aláyna, 9aláykum, 9aláyhum

fī follows the pattern of *bi; 'ila* and *ḥawā́lī* follow the pattern of *9ála.*

* Throughout this book we show the accent on the last syllable of words like *bī́* 'with it/him', *fī́* 'in it/him', *9aláy* 'on it/him' (etc.), for clarity.

The modified ending (long vowel *-ā* or *-ī*, or vowel-combination *-ay*) of the preposition always carries the stress before a suffix; the 3rd person m. sing. has no suffix, but the stress remains, as shown.
Note that *li* has two forms: *lī, lak/lik, lu/láha; lána, lákum, láhum*
and: *'ilī, 'ilak/'ilik, 'ilu/'ílha; 'ílna, 'ílkum, 'ílhum*
ḥatta and *'ílla* are not commonly used with pronouns.

9. *kam*

The adjective *kam* has two meanings. In statements, 'some', 'a little'. In questions: 'how much/many?'
In both uses, it precedes the noun which it qualifies, which is always in the singular, even when a plural (animate or inanimate) is intended:

kam waqt	some/a little time
kam waqt?	how much time/how long?
kam rā́kib	some/a few passengers
kam rā́kib?	how many passengers?

In its interrogative use, it may also be a pronoun, i.e. stand without a noun:

kam?	how much? how many?

10. Final long vowel

See Pronunciation, paragraph 9. A long vowel at the end of a word is shortened when followed by two consonants or a doubled consonant in the next word of the same phrase. This most commonly happens when the second word has the article. (The hyphen of the article is disregarded in pronunciation; it is purely a transcription device.) In this circumstance final *-ā*, *-ī* and *-ū* become respectively *-a*, *-i* and *-u*. Examine:

kitā́bī hunā́k.	but:	*kitā́bi l-9árabī hunā́k.*
fī 'ingíltra	but:	*fi l-'úrdun; fi ṭ-ṭayyā́ra*

> Long vowel rule: A final long vowel is shortened before two consonants or a double consonant in the same phrase.

11. *fī́*

fī́ 'in it' (2/8 above) also means 'there is', 'there are', or the corresponding interrogatives 'is there?', 'are there?':

fī́ nās khā́rij al-maṭā́r.	There are people outside the airport.
shū fī́, fi sh-shánta?	What is there, in the suitcase?

12. 'to have'

The concept 'to have' is not normally expressed with a verb in Arabic. We use the preposition *9ind* 'with', 'in the possession of':

9índī, 9índak/9índik, 9índu/9índ-ha; 9índna, 9índkum, 9índ-hum
'in my, your, his, her, its; our, your, their possession'

9índī waqt.	I have time.
9índu shánta.	He has a suitcase.

9índ-hum 'aghrā̍ḍ shakhṣī̍ya. They have personal effects.

The expression with *9ind* may be reinforced with *fī̍* 'there is/are':

fī̍ 9índak waqt? *kam shánta (fī̍) 9índak?*

The negative of this expression is *mā̍ fī 9ind* (*fi* is obligatory here; note also that the stress shifts to *mā̍*):

mā̍ fī 9índ-hum vī̍za. They have no visa.

mā̍ fī 9índak waqt? Have you no time?

We avoid using *9ind* in this possessive meaning directly with a noun. If a noun is to be used, we restate with a pronoun suffix:

al-musā̍fir, 9índu vī̍za. 'The passenger, he has a visa.'

13. *júmal mithālī̍ya* – Model sentences

al-musā̍fir, kam ṣandū̍q 9índu?	How many boxes has the traveller got?
wayn 'aghrā̍dak? – hunā̍k, wára s-sayyā̍ra.	Where are your things? – There, behind the car.
ar-rukkā̍b al-miṣrīyī̍n, kam tádhkara 9índ-hum?	How many tickets have the Egyptian passengers got?
malā̍bisik fī shántatik? – ná9am, wa hay ash-shánta. híya ṣghī̍ra bas.	Are your clothes in your case? – Yes,and here's the case. It's only small.
fī̍ kam musā̍fir khā̍rij al-júmruk.	There are some travellers outside Customs.

14. *at-tamārī̍n* – Exercises

1. Make definite with the article:

e.g.: maḥáll fā̍ḍī – al-maḥáll al-fā̍ḍī; sayyā̍ra – as-sayyā̍ra

(a) maṭā̍r (b) ziyā̍ra ṭawī̍la (c) rā̍kib 'amáyrkī
(d) kīs ṣghīr (e) ṭabī̍b míṣrī

2. Make the suffix plural:

e.g.: maḥállī – maḥállna; fī̍ki – fī̍kum

(a) sayyā̍rtu (b) shántatik (c) 9índu
(d) warā̍ī (e) ṣandū̍qak

3. Make indefinite:

e.g.: ar-rā̍kib al-lubnā̍nī – rā̍kib lubnā̍nī

(a) fi s-sayyā̍ra (b) al-'aghrā̍ḍ ash-shakhṣīya
(c) tadhkártak (d) shantátkum

4. Make a sentence:

e.g.: ána, sayyāra – 9índī sayyāra.

(a) hum, tádhkara (b) híya, shánta ṣghī̍ra (c) 'ínti, fulū̍s
(d) aṭ-ṭā̍lib, kam kitā̍b (e) aṭ-ṭabī̍b, waqt

5. Make the suffix singular:
e.g.: ziyārítkum – ziyā́rtak, ziyā́rtik
(a) kitā́bna (b) tadhkarít-hum (c) fulū́skum
(d) ’amā́mhum (e) warā́hum (f) fī́na
(g) ’iláyhum (h) 9aláykum (j) 9ánhum
(k) mínkum

6. Make the adjective agree:
e.g.: sayyā́ra (’almā́nī) – sayyā́ra ’almānī́ya
(a) rukkā́b (lubnā́nī) (b) ṭayyā́ra (muta’ákhkhir)
(c) al-mu9állim (sū́rī) (d) ṣúḥufī (9árabī) (e) dīnā́r (kuwáytī)

ad-dárs ath-thā́lith – Lesson 3
fi l-'utáyl – In the Hotel

1. *al-ḥikā́ya wa l-ḥiwā́r* – Narrative and Dialogue

(Peter recounts his arrival at the hotel.)

	lámma	when
	kharájt	I came/went out
	binā́ya	building
Peter:	lámma kharájt min binā́yat al-maṭā́r,	When I came out of the airport building,
	wajádt	I found
	musāfirī́n	travellers
	kthī́r, ikthī́r	much/many
	sayyārā́t	cars
	wajádt musāfirī́n ikthī́r u sayyārā́t ikthī́r.	I found many travellers and many cars.
	9iríft	I knew
	'utáyl	hotel
	walā́kin	but
	mā 9iríft	I did not know
	ṭarī́q (m./f.)	road
	bálad	town
	9iríft 'ism al-'utáyl, walā́kin mā 9iríft ṭarī́q al-bálad.	I knew the name of the hotel, but I didn't know the road to town,
	ṭalábt min	I asked, I requested
	sawwā́q	driver
	'ínnu	that he
	yākhúdhni	he takes me
	u ṭalábt min sawwā́q táksī 'ínnu yākhúdhni 'íla l-'utáyl.	and I asked a taxi driver to take me ('that he takes me') to the hotel.
	rikíbt	I mounted, got in
	tarákna	we left
	wa rikíbt at-táksī u tarákna l-maṭā́r.	I got into the taxi, and we left the airport.
	–	
	yā́ sī́dna	sir
	filadílfiya	Philadelphia
	tíkram	certainly
as-sawwā́q:	li wayn, yā́ sī́dna?	Where to, sir?
Peter:	li 'utáyl filadílfiya, min fáḍlak.	To the Philadelphia Hotel, please.
as-sawwā́q:	tíkram.	Certainly
Peter:	shúkran.	Thank you.

wiṣílna	we arrived
bāb	door
kbīr, ikbī́r	big
ba9d kam waqt wiṣílna quddā́m bāb 'utáyl ikbī́r.	After some time we arrived in front of the door of a big hotel.
nizílt	I went/got down
dafá9t	I paid
dakhált	I entered
shantā́t	suitcases, cases
nizílt min at-táksī u dafá9t 'újratu u dakhált al-'utáyl ma9 shantā́tī.	I got out of the taxt, paid the ('its') fare and went into the hotel with my suitcases.
istiqbā́l	reception
muwáẓẓaf	employee, clerk
sa'álnī	he asked me, enquired of me
9ind al-istiqbā́l, al-muwáẓẓaf sa'álnī 'ísmī	At Reception, the clerk asked me my name
ṭálab	he asked for, requested
'áyḍan	also
ḥammā́l	porter
yā́khudh	he takes
fouq	(also:) up
ghúrfa	room
u ṭálab mínnī jawā́z sáfarī. ṭálab 'áyḍan min ḥammā́l al-'utáyl 'ínnu yā́khudh shantā́tī fouq 'ila ghúrftī.	and asked me for my passport. He also asked the hotel porter to take ('that he takes') my cases up to my room.
ba9d mā	after
kátab	he wrote
9unwā́n	address
ba9d mā kátab muwaẓẓaf al-istiqbā́l 'ísmī wa 9unwā́nī,	After the reception clerk wrote my name and ('my') address,
'akhádht	I took
miftā́ḥ	key
ṭilí9t	I went up
'óuḍa	= *ghúrfa*
fatáḥt	I opened
'amárt	I ordered
fuṭū́r	breakfast
'akhádht miftā́ḥ ghúrftī u ṭilí9t 'íla l-'óuḍa u fatáḥt shantā́tī	I took my room key, went up to my ('the') room, opened

u 'amárt al-fuṭū́r.	my cases and ordered breakfast.

2. *9ibārāt* – Expressions

tíkram Certainly. Varies with the person(s) addressed: *tíkramī* to a woman, *tíkramū* to a group. There is no prescribed response.

ba9d kam waqt after some time

3. *mufradāt 'iḍāfīya* – Additional vocabulary – *al-'utáyl*

ḍayf	guest	*ḥisāb*	bill, account
bawwāb	doorman	*máṭ9am*	restaurant
ghadā'	lunch	*9ashā'*	dinner
fársha	bed	*baṭṭānīya*	blanket
mukhádda	pillow	*shárshaf*	sheet
ḥammām	bath	*mínshafa*	towel
'asansáyr	lift	*másbaḥ*	swimming-pool
maftūḥ	open	*musákkar*	closed
'óuḍat noum, ghúrfat noum			bedroom
'óuḍat ḥammām, ghúrfat ḥammām			bathroom

***an-náḥū* – Grammar**

4. Construct

Examine the expressions

bināyat al-maṭār	the airport building
'ism al-'utáyl	the name of the hotel
ṭarīq al-bálad	the road to town
miftāḥ ghúrftī	my room key
shantāt Peter	Peter's cases

In each of these expressions, the two nouns are associated; the association is often possession, but not always so. Such an expression is called a *construct*. For convenience we can call the first noun of the construct the *theme*, and the second noun the *attribute*. In the constructs shown here both nouns are definite; the attribute is obviously definite because it has an article or a possessive suffix, or because it is a proper noun (e.g. Peter); the theme looks indefinite but is deemed to be made definite by the attribute. These are definite constructs.

Indefinite constructs also exist; in these, both nouns have the indefinite form:

muwáẓẓaf ḥukūma	a government employee
miftāḥ ghúrfa	a room key

Nouns ending in *-a* add *-t* when used as the theme of a construct:

'újrat táksī	a taxi fare
'újrat at-táksī	the taxi fare
sayyārat ad-dúktur	the doctor's car

We may have a 'string' construct with more than two nouns, each noun but the last being defined by its successor:

miftāḥ ghúrfat aṭ-ṭabīb	the doctor's room key

It is a most important rule that only the last noun of a construct may have a definite 'marker', i.e. a definite article or a possessive suffix, or be a proper noun.

Construct rule: Only the last noun in a construct may be explicitly defined.

An adjective cannot interrupt a construct. It must follow it, whichever noun it qualifies:

'ism al-'utáyl al-'úrdunī *mudīr al-bank al-míṣrī*

The second of these expressions has two possible meanings: 'the Egyptian bank manager' or 'the manager of the Egyptian bank'. We shall learn later how to avoid the ambiguity.

5. The triliteral verb – roots and root letters

A verb is a word denoting an action which is performed or a situation which is experienced: 'arrived, knows'.

Most Arabic verbs are *triliteral,* i.e. built on a *root* consisting of three letters. The root is not a word; it is simply the theoretical base. A typical triliteral root is *k t b;* the three letters are its root letters, which remain through all forms of the verb.

Spoken Arabic has five classes of triliteral verb, of which we deal with two in this lesson.

In English we quote a verb by its so-called *infinitive* form, e.g. 'to write'. Arabic has no such form; it denotes its verbs by their simplest or basic form, which is the *húwa* form of the past tense, e.g. *kátab.* In a sentence this means 'he wrote', but in the vocabulary we quote it as 'to write', following English practice.

6. Past tense of sound verbs

Sound verbs are so called because their three root letters – initial, middle and final – are all consonants and are all 'stable', i.e. invariable. We add the following personal endings to the basic form to make the past tense ('I did', 'I have done'):

('ána)	*-t*	I	*('íḥna)*	*-na*	we
('int)	*-t*	you (m.)	*('íntū)*	*-tū*	you (pl.)
('ínti)	*-ti*	you (f.)			
(húwa)	- (no ending)	he, it	*(hum)*	*-ū*	they (animate)
(híya)	*-at*	she, it			

Thus, for *kátab* ('he wrote'), 'to write', root *k t b*:

('ána)	*katábt*	*('íḥna)*	*katábna*
('int)	*katábt*	*('íntū)*	*katábtū*
('ínti)	*katábti*		
(húwa)	*kátab*	*(hum)*	*kátabū*
(híya)	*kátabat*		

I, you, he, she; we, you, they wrote/have written/has written

The pronouns are used only for emphasis or extra clarity.

So also: *kháraj* to come/go out, root *kh r j*:

kharájt, kharájt/kharájti, kháraj/khárajat; kharájna, kharájtū, khárajū

I, you, he, she; we, you, they came/went out

I, you, he, she; we, you, they have/has come/gone out

The vowels vary from verb to verb; *a-a* is the commonest pattern.

You can now understand the following sound verbs in the text:

Root *9 r f*, basic form *9írif* to know; *9iríft* I knew
Root *r k b*, *ríkib* to mount, get in: *rikíbt* I mounted, got in

so also: *tarákna*	we left	*nizílt*	I got down/out
dafá9t	I paid	*dakhált*	I entered
ṭilí9t	I went up	*fatáḥt*	I opened
ṭalábt	I requested	*ṭálab*	he requested

To the persons shown above we can add the inanimate 'they' form, which is always the same as 'she' (inanimate plural rule, see 1/5); it is used only where it can make sense, e.g. *(híya) khárajat* 'they (animals, things) went out', *(híya) ṭíli9at* 'they went up'. Since it is completely regular, it is not shown separately in the verb tables in this book.

The past tense is also called, in some books, the *perfect* tense.

7. Verbs with root letter *hámza*

Verbs which have as initial or middle root letter *hámza* (*'* – see Pronunciation) count as sound verbs in spoken Arabic. We have encountered in the past tense:

Root *' m r*, basic form *'ámar* to order:

'amárt, 'amárt/'amárti, 'ámar/'ámarat; 'amárna, 'amártū, 'ámarū
I, you, he, she; we, you, they (have/has) ordered

Root *' kh dh*, basic form *'ákhadh* to take:

'akhádht, 'akhádht/'akhádhti, 'ákhadh/'ákhadhat;
'akhádhna, 'akhádhtū, 'ákhadhū
I, you, he, she; we, you, they took, have/has taken

Root *s ' l*, basic form *sá'al* to ask, enquire:

sa'ált, sa'ált/sa'álti, sá'al/sá'alat; sa'álna, sa'áltū, sá'alū
I, you, he, she; we, you, they (have/has) asked, enquired

To these we can add the common verb *'ákal* 'to eat', root *' k l*:

'akált, 'akált/'akálti, 'ákal/'ákalat; 'akálna, 'akáltū, 'ákalū
I, you, he, she; we, you, they ate, have/has eaten

Verbs with *hámza* as final root letter behave differently. We study them later.

8. Initial-*w* verbs

Verbs with initial root letter *w* ('initial-*w* verbs') follow the sound-verb pattern in the past tense. Examine:

Root *w ṣ l*, basic form *wíṣil* to arrive:

wiṣílt, wiṣílt/wiṣílti, wíṣil/wíṣilat; wiṣílna, wiṣíltū, wíṣilū
I, you, he, she; we, you, they (have/has) arrived

Root *w j d* basic form *wájad* to find:

wajádt, wajádt/wajádti, wájad/wájadat; wajádtna, wajádtū, wájadū
I, you, he, she; we, you, they (have/has) found

9. Negative of the past tense

Any verb in the past tense can be made negative by putting the particle *mā* before it:

mā 9iríft	I didn't know	*mā wíṣilū?*	haven't they arrived?
mā 'akálna	we didn't eat		

10. Use of the past tense.

The past tense is used in Arabic for any completed action or situation:

mā wíṣilū 9ála l-waqt. They didn't arrive/haven't arrived on time.
'akhádht al-fulū́s? Did you take/Have you taken the money?
mā 9írif al-9unwā́n. He did not know the address.

It can be used for pluperfect actions ('I had done'):

ba9d mā kátab 'ísmī, 'akhádht al-miftā́ḥ.
After he wrote/had written my name, I took the key.

A pluperfect tense exists, but it is little used. We learn it later.

11. Long vowel

The long vowel rule (2/10) applies to the endings of verbs, as it does everywhere else:

tárakū	they left	but:	*táraku l-maṭā́r.*	They left the airport.
'akáltū	you ate	but:	*'akáltu l-fuṭū́r?*	Have you eaten breakfast?

12. Word-order

The subject of a verb (i.e. the person or thing performing the action or experiencing the situation) usually precedes its verb, as in English:

ar-rukkā́b wíṣilū. The passengers have arrived.

But the verb may precede the subject in two possible circumstances; either to emphasise the verb:

wíṣilu r-rukkā́b. The passengers (really) have arrived.

or when the subject is much longer than the verb:

ba9d mā kátab muwáẓẓaf al-istiqbā́l 'ísmī u 9unwā́nī ... After the reception clerk wrote my name and address ...

This word-order is borrowed from written Arabic, in which it is common.

13. Sound plurals of nouns

In 1/10 we studied the sound masculine plural pattern of certain adjectives. Some masculine nouns denoting people ('sound masculine animate nouns') also make their plural on this pattern:

- for sing. ending *-ī*, add *-yī́n*:

ṣúḥufī	a journalist	*ṣuḥufīyī́n*	journalists
míṣrī	an Egyptian	*miṣrīyī́n*	Egyptians

- for any other sing. ending, add *-ī́n*:

muhándis	an engineer	*muhandisī́n*	engineers
al-musā́fir	the traveller	*al-musāfirī́n*	the travellers

Sound masculine *inanimate* nouns, and all sound feminine nouns whether animate or inanimate, make their plural on the so-called sound feminine pattern. This pattern is found only with nouns:

- for f. sing. ending *-a*, substitute *-ā́t*:

ṣuḥufī́ya	a journalist (f.)	*ṣuḥufīyā́t*	journalists
miṣrī́ya	an Egyptian lady	*miṣrīyā́t*	Egyptian ladies
ash-shárika	the company	*ash-sharikā́t*	the companies

as-sayyā́ra	the car	*as-sayyarā́t*	the cars

- for the (very rare) m. sing. ending *-a*, add *-yā́t*:

al-másа	the evening	*al-masayā́t*	the evenings

- for any other sing. ending, add *-ā́t*:

maṭā́r	airport	*maṭārā́t*	airports

All sound plurals, masculine and feminine, are stressed on the ending.

The following nouns learned so far (in addition to those given above) have sound plurals, animate or inanimate:

- all *nísba* adjectives used as nouns, except *'amáyrkī, 'inglī́zī, híndī* and *9árabī* in the masculine (plurals *'amayrkā́n, 'inglī́z, hunū́d* and *9árab*);
- all nouns ending in *-a* except *ghúrfa, 'óuḍa* and *tádhkara;*
- all nouns beginning with *mu-*, except *mudī́r;*
- *'asansáyr, 'utáyl, bawwā́b, doulā́r, ḥammā́l, ḥammā́m, ḥisā́b, jawā́z, jináyh, ma'mū́r, riyā́l, sawwā́q, ṣabā́ḥ, táksī, vī́za.*

The other nouns learned so far have so-called 'broken' (= irregular) plurals, which we shall study later.

The only difference between sound noun plural and sound adjective plural endings is that nouns also have the sound feminine ending *-āt.*

In Arabic the plural noun does not denote more than *one* but more than *two* of a kind; for two of a kind we use not the plural, but the dual form of the noun, which is studied in Lesson 4.

14. Verbs with plural subjects

The inanimate plural rule (1/5) holds for the third person of verbs:

al-musāfirī́n dákhalu l-maṭā́r.	The travellers	entered the airport.
as-sayyārā́t dákhalat al-maṭā́r.	The cars	

15. Time expressions

mundh and *min* are used with present time-sequence for a situation beginning in the past and lasting into the present:

húwa hunā́k mundh/min waqt ṭawī́l. He's been there ('since') a long time.

qabl before an expression of time means '... ago' for a past action or situation:

wíṣilū qabl shahr . They arrived a month ago.

16. 'to ask'

Distinguish between the two verbs meaning 'to ask':

sá'al	to ask a question, to enquire
ṭálab min	to ask for something, to request

sá'al takes two direct objects*; *ṭálab* has one direct object (the thing sought), and one prepositional object* (the person asked) after *min*:

sa'ált ar-rā́kib 'ísmu. ṭálab at-tádhkara min ar-rā́kib.

* a direct object is the person or thing directly affected by the action of the verb; a prepositional object is indirectly affected, i.e. through a preposition such as 'to, with, from'.

17. ***kthīr* 'much, many'**

This adjective has a regular feminine but a 'broken' plural: f. *kthīra*, pl. *kthār*. But it is common to use the masculine *kthīr* for all forms:

waqt ikthīr (m.) *qáhwa kthīr* (f.)
fulūs ikthīr (inan. pl.) *nās ikthīr* (an. pl.)

The following paragraph explains the initial vowel of forms like *ikthīr*.

18. Transition vowel

When three consonants form a block which is difficult to pronounce, a transition or relief vowel is introduced after the first of the consonants. This vowel is *i*, which is never stressed. Examine:

	'ákhadhu kthīr	(no block)
but:	*(nās kthīr)*	(block *s-k-th)* ⟶ *nās ikthīr*
	shánta ṣghīra	(no block)
but:	*shantāt iṣghīra*	(block *t-ṣ-gh*)
	ḥaḍrít-ha, ḥaḍrāt-hum	(no block)
but:	*ḥáḍirtu, ḥáḍirtak*	(block *ḍ-r-t*)
	shánta kbīra	(no block)
but:	*ash-shánta li-kbīra*	(block *l-k-b*)

This explains the apparently anomalous stress of words like *fáḍilkum* (Lesson 1) and *ḥáḍirtak/tik* (Lesson 2), and the alternative forms for e.g. *kthīr*, *ṣghīr* and *kbīr* given in the vocabulary.

When neighbouring consonants in the block are identical or compatible, we pronounce without the transition vowel:

ash-shánta ṣ-ṣghīra *kīs ṣghīr* *'akhádhkt táksī.*

19. ***júmal mithālīya* – Model sentences**

'akhádhna l-'asansáyr u nizílna'ila másbaḥ al-'utáyl.	We took the lift and went down to the hotel swimming-pool.
kamān baṭṭānīya fī ghúrftī, law samáḥt.	Another blanket in my room, please.
kayf máṭ9am al-'utáyl, 'akáltū fī?	How's the hotel restaurant, have you eaten in it?
rukkāb aṭ-ṭayyāra l-miṣrīya wíṣilū, walākin ba9d kam waqt táraku l-'utáyl.	The passengers of the Egyptian aircraft arrived, but after some time they left the hotel.
9ind al-istiqbāl sá'alū 'ísmī u 9unwānī fī 'amáyrka.	At Reception they asked my name and address in America.

20. ***at-tamārīn* – Exercises**

1. Make definite constructs:

e.g.: bāb, 'utáyl – bāb al-'utáyl

(a) shantāt, musāfir (b) sayyāra, mudīrna (c) miftāḥ, 'óuḍa, fu'ād

(d) jádwal, ṭayyārā́t (e) jawā́z, rā́kib

2. Make definite constructs with the noun *ṭā́lib*:
e.g.: 'ism – 'ism aṭ-ṭā́lib
(a) shánta (b) shantā́t (c) 'aghrā́ḍ
(d) tádhkara (e) ghúrfa

3. Make plural:
e.g.: muhándis – muhandisī́n
(a) mu9állim (b) sayyā́ra (c) mu9állima
(d) maṭā́r (e) musā́fir

4. Make plural:
e.g.: wíṣil. – wíṣilū.
(a) dákhalat. (b) ána nizílt. (c) shū 'amárti?
(d) 'int mā dafá9t. (e) aṭ-ṭayyā́ra ṭíli9at 9ala l-waqt.

5. Make singular:
e.g.: musāfirī́n – musā́fir
(a) mu9allimā́t (b) maṭārā́t (c) miṣrīyī́n
(d) muhandisī́n (e) 9árab

6. Make negative:
e.g.: tárak al-'utáyl al-youm. – mā tárak al-'utáyl al-youm.
(a) wajádt as-sayyā́ra. (b) dakhált al-ghúrfa? (c) fī́ rukkā́b ikthī́r.
(d) at-táksī wíṣil 'ílak. (e) al-musāfirī́n nízilū min aṭ-ṭayyā́ra.

7. Give the opposite:
e.g.: 'amā́m al-binā́ya – wára l-binā́ya
dakhált al-ghúrfa. – kharájt min al-ghúrfa.
(a) rikíbt at-táksī. (b) dā́khil al-júmruk (c) aṭ-ṭayyā́ra nízilat.
(d) fouq al-fársha (e) 'íla l-bálad

8. Add the adjective *'urúbbī,* making it agree:
e.g.: muhandisī́n – muhandisī́n 'urubbīyī́n
(a) sayyā́ra (b) sayyārā́t (c) 'íḥna
(d) rukkā́b (e) 'ínti

ad-dars ar-rābi9 – Lesson 4
fi l-balad – In Town

1. ***al-ḥiwār***

	9afwan	(also:) excuse me
	tánmiya	development
	simi9	to hear
	qarīb min	near to
	huna	here
Peter:	9afwan, wayn bank at-tánmiya?	Excuse me, where is the Development Bank?
	simi9t 'innu qarīb min huna.	I heard it was near here.
	shakhṣ	person
	shāri9	street
	maẓbūṭ	correct
	mish	not
	ba9īd 9an	far from
	thālith	third
	yamīn	right
	raqm	number
	tis9a	nine
shakhṣ fi sh-shāri9:	maẓbūṭ, mish ba9īd 9an huna. al-bank fi sh-shāri9 ath-thālith 9ala yamīnak. bināya kbīra, raqm tis9a.	That's correct, it's not far from here. The Bank's on the third street on your right. A big building, number nine.
	ba9dayn	then, afterwards
	9alayy	(here:) I have
	mou9id	appointment
	sifāra	embassy
	brīṭānī	British
Peter:	u ba9dayn 9alayy mou9id fi s-sifāra l-brīṭānīya.	Then I have an appointment at the British Embassy.
	hādhi	this, that
	hādha l-ḥayy	this quarter/part of town
	'aḥsan	better
ash-shakhṣ:	hādhi mish fī hādha l-ḥayy. 'aḥsan 'ilak bi t-taksī.	That's not in this part of town. For you it's better by taxi.
Peter:	shukran jazīlan.	Thank you very much.
ash-shakhṣ:	9afwan.	Don't mention it.
	sayyida	lady

	bouṣṭa	post office
	intáð̣ir, intáẓir	wait
	shwayy	a little
	'áyna9am	= *na9am*
Peter:	9afwan yā sayyidatī, fī́ bouṣṭa huna?	Excuse me, ma'am, is there a post office here?
as-sayyida:	bouṣṭa? intáð̣ir shwayy. 'ayna9am.	A post office? Wait a bit. Yes.
	'ishāra	signal, sign
	murūr	traffic
	mish kadha?	isn't that so?
	'imshī	walk (here:) go
	shimāl	left
	mitr	metre
	hunāk 'ishārat murūr, mish kadha? 'imshī 'ila shimālak 9ind al-'ishāra, wa l-bouṣṭa ba9d kam mitr, 9ala shimālak,	There's a traffic light over there, isn't there? Go to your left at the light, and the post office is after a few metres, on your left,
	sitta	six
	sab9a	seven
	mamnūn	grateful
	kthīr	(also:) very
	shī	thing
	mā́ fī shī	there's nothing.
	raqm sitta, sab9a, kadha.	number six, seven, something like that.
Peter:	mamnūn ikthīr	I'm very grateful.
as-sayyida:	9afwan. mā́ fī shī.	Don't mention it. It's nothing.

–

	9ala ra'sī	('on my head', here:) certainly
	ya9nī	it means, that is to say
	khamsa	five
	9ashra	ten
	daqāyiq	minutes
Peter:	'ila s-sifāra l-brīṭānīya, min faḍlak	To the British Embassy, please.
as-sawwāq:	9ala ra'sī.	Certainly
Peter:	ba9īd, ya9nī?	Is it far?
as-sawwāq:	la', khamsa, 9ashra daqāyiq.	No, five, ten minutes.
Peter:	ṭayyib.	Good.
as-sawwāq:	9afwan yā sīdī, ḥaḍirtak 'amayrkī?	Excuse me sir, are you

		American?
Peter:	la', 'inglīzī, min Cambridge, simi9t 9annu?	No, British, from Cambridge. Have you heard of it?
	ṭab9an	of course
	jāmi9a	university
	ma9rūf	famous
	fa	so, then
	daras	to study
	lugha	language
as-sawwāq:	ṭab9an, jāmi9a ma9rūfa. fa wayn darast al-lugha l-9arabīya?	Of course, a famous university. So where did you study the Arabic language?
	darast-ha	I studied it
	dimashq	Damascus
	sana	year
	wallāhi	Good Heavens
	9imilt-ha	you did it
	lahja	accent
	jamīl	beautiful
Peter:	darast-ha fī sūriya, fī dimashq. qabl kam sana.	I studied it in Syria, in Damascus. A few years ago.
as-sawwāq:	wallāhi, 9imilt-ha kwayyis jiddan. 9indak lahja jamīla.	Good Heavens, you did it very well. You have a good accent.
	laṭīf	kind (adjective)
	ṣaḥīḥ	true
Peter:	laṭīf jiddan.	Very kind (of you).
as-sawwāq:	ṣaḥīḥ ya9nī.	But it's true.

–

	hayāna	here we are
	tākhudh	you take
	dīnārayn	two dinars
	fakka	small change
	hayāna, hādhi hiya s-sifāra l-brīṭānīya.	Here we are, this is the British Embassy.
Peter:	kam tākhudh?	How much do I owe you?
as-sawwāq:	'ilak, dīnārayn.	For you, two dinars.
Peter:	hay khamsa. 9indak fakka?	Here are five. Have you got change?
	mā9alaysh	never mind, all right

as-sawwāq:	māˀ9alaysh, 9indī. tfaḍḍal. ma9 as-salāma.	That's all right, I've got (some). Here you are. Goodbye.
Peter:	shukran, 'alla yisallimak.	Thank you, goodbye.

2. ***9ibārāt***

mish kadha? Isn't that so?
mamnūn ikthīr, mamnūna kthīr, mamnūnīn ikthīr I'm/We're very grateful.
mā́ fī shī (stress on *mā́*) It's nothing.
9ala ra'sī ('on my head') Certainly (complying with a request). Note also, with the same meaning: *9ala 9aynī* 'on my eye'.
ṭab9an ('naturally') of course
ya9nī ('it means') that is to say. Also 'er ...' (looking for one's word).
wallāhi ('by God') Good Heavens. Expresses surprise or admiration.
kam tākhudh? How much do you charge ('take')?
mā9alaysh Never mind. Also a question, *mā9alaysh?* You don't mind?

3. ***mufradāt 'iḍāfīya***

***al-balad wa l-bināyāt wa l-ma'mūrīn* – Town, buildings, officials**

madkhal	entrance	*makhraj*	exit
maktab	office	*ra'īsī*	principal, main
maktaba	library, bookshop	*maḥallāt* (pl.)	department store
mustashfa	(masc.) hospital	*mafraq*	crossroad
dukkān	shop	*markaz*	centre
shurṭī	policeman	*ash-shurṭa, al-būlīs*	police force
mouqif baṣ	bus stop	*makhzan*	warehouse
sāḥa, maydān	square	*jisr*	bridge
masjid	mosque	*kanīsa*	church
timthāl	statue	*safīr*	ambassador
qunṣulīya	consulate	*qunṣul*	consul
wakāla	agency	*wakīl*	agent
wizāra	ministry	*wazīr*	minister
wizārat/wazīr:	Ministry/Minister of:		
aṣ-ṣinā9a	Industry	*al-9amal**	Labour
at-tijāra	Trade	*ad-difā9*	Defence
az-zirā9a	Agriculture	*at-tárbiya*	Education
aṣ-ṣiḥḥa	Health	*ad-dākhilīya***	Interior
*al-mālīya***	Finance	*al-khārijīya***	Foreign Affairs

* also, popularly, *wizārat/wazīr ash-shughl* (*shughl* 'work').
** abbreviated titles; in full, *wizārat/wazīr al-'umūr ad-dākhilīya/al-mālīya/ al-khārijīya* (*'umūr* 'affairs').

an-naḥū

4. Demonstratives

Here are the demonstrative adjectives or pronouns 'this, that, these, those':

	masculine	feminine	plural
this, these	*hādha*	*hādhi*	*hadhoul*
that, those	*hadhāk*	*hadhīk*	*hadhulāk*

The inanimate plural rule (1/5) applies here. The demonstrative adjective precedes its noun, which always has the article:

hādha l-maktab	this office	*hādhi s-sayyida*	this lady
hadhoul an-nās	these people	*hādhi sh-shantāt*	these cases

hadhāk (etc.) is used only when remoteness is emphasised; otherwise we use *hādha* (etc.) for both 'this/these' and 'that/those'.

When used as a pronoun (i.e. with no noun), the demonstrative has the appropriate gender and number of the inferred noun:

hādha ṭayyib. This is good.
hādhi ṭayyiba. This is/These are good. (of things)
hādhoul ṭayyibīn. These are good. (of people)

If the noun is unknown, the masculine is used:

shū hādha? What is this?

For 'this is ...' we restate with a pronoun. This is optional if the noun does not carry an article, but obligatory when it does:

hādha (huwa) kitāb/kitābī. This is a book/my book.
but: *hādha huwa l-kitāb.* This is the book.
since *hādha l-kitāb* ... means only 'this book ...', and is not a full sentence.

5. *hādha* in constructs

When a demonstrative adjective qualifies the attribute (i.e. the last noun) of a construct (3/4), it precedes that noun, interrupting the construct:

ṭarīq hādha l-balad *raqm hādhi s-sayyāra*

When it qualifies the theme (i.e. any earlier noun in the construct), it must follow the whole construct;

ṭarīq al-balad hādha/hādhi this road to town
raqm as-sayyāra hādha this car number

> Demonstrative rule: A demonstrative is the only word which may interrupt a construct.

6. Object pronouns

A direct object pronoun ('me, him' etc) takes the form of a suffix attached to the verb. These suffixes are identical to the possessive suffixes (2/8), except for 'me' which is *-nī*:

sa'alnī, sa'alak/sa'alik, sa'alu/sa'alha; sa'alna, sa'alkum, sa'alhum
he asked me, you, him (etc.)

When the verb form ends in a vowel, that vowel is stressed and the suffixes beginning with a vowel take the same form as with *fī*:

sa'alū́nī, sa'alū́k/sa'alū́ki, sa'alū́, sa'alū́ha; sa'alū́na, sa'alū́kum, sa'alū́hum
they asked me, you, him (etc.)

sa'altínī, sa'altí/sa'altíha	you asked me, him, her
sa'alná.	We asked him.
sa'altú?	Did you ask him?
sa'altíhum?	Did you ask them?

> Object pronoun rule: A vocalic verb-ending before a pronoun suffix is always long and stressed.

7. *'inn*: Indirect statements

A *direct statement* quotes another's words verbatim: 'He said: "I am ill".' An *indirect statement* paraphrases: 'He said that he was ill.'

The conjunction *'inn* 'that' is used to introduce indirect statements. A pronoun following *'inn* is expressed as a direct-object suffix attached to it. The second *n* is dropped before *-nī* and *-na*:

'innī, 'innak/'innik, 'innu/'innha; 'inna, 'innkum, 'innhum
that I, you, he, she; we, you, they ...

Indirect statement follows not only a verb of saying, but also a verb of perceiving. Further, in the Arabic indirect statement we retain the time-sequence or tense of the original statement. Compare the Arabic and English:

simi9t 'innu qarīb min huna.	I heard that it was ('is') near here.
9irifna 'innkum fi l-maktab.	We knew you were ('are') in the office.

We can omit the conjunction, as in English; we then use the subject (i.e. personal) pronoun:

simi9t, huwa qarīb min huna. *9irifna, 'intū fi l-maktab.*

The construction with *'inn* is considered more elegant.

> Indirect speech rule: In indirect speech the verb retains the tense of the original speaker.

8. *walākin*

The conjunction *walākin,* meaning 'but', can also take the appropriate object-pronoun suffix; its final *-n* doubles before a suffix beginning with a vowel:

walākinnī, walākinnak/walākinnik, walākinnu/walākinnu;
walākinna, walākinkum, walākinhum
but I, you, he, she; we, you, they ...

With *walākin,* the suffix is not obligatory as with *'inn*:

walākin(nī) mā 9irift ṭarīq al-balad.

9. *9ala*

9ala + pronoun suffix can mean 'to have as an obligation':

9alayna mou9id ma9 as-safīr.	*al-qunṣul, 9aláy shughl ikthīr al-youm.*
9alayk.	(It's) up to you (to do, to decide etc.)

Note also the shortened form *9a* + definite noun, meaning 'to':

9a dimashq	to Damascus	*9a l-bank*	to the bank

10. *hay*

hay + pronoun suffix takes the form *hayā́-*:

hayānī, hayāk/hayākī, hayā́/hayāha; hayāna, hayākum, hayāhum
here I am, here you are (etc.)

11. Numbers

Cardinal numbers (i.e. those denoting a quantity) from 0 to 10 are:

0	*ṣifr*		
1	m. *wā́ḥid*, f. *wā́ḥida*	2	m. *ithnáyn*, f. *thintáyn*
3	*thalā́tha*	4	*'árba9a*
5	*khámsa*	6	*sítta*
7	*sáb9a*	8	*thamā́niya*
9	*tís9a*	10	*9áshra*

Note:

- 0 is a noun, and cannot be used with a further noun.
- 1 follows its noun and agrees with it: *ghurfa wāḥida* *dīnār wāḥid*
- 2 has masculine and feminine forms, used mostly in counting, otherwise the quantity 'two' is better expressed with the dual of the noun; see below.
- 3 to 10 inclusive are invariable for gender; the counted noun follows them if indefinite:

  thalātha muhandisīn three engineers
  tis9a shantāt nine suitcases

  But if the noun is definite, the number behaves like an adjective:

  rukkābna l-'arba9a our four passengers
  al-bināyāt al-jamīla th-thamā́niya the eight beautiful buildings

12. Dual

The quantity 'two' is normally expressed with the *dual* form of the noun itself. All nouns, whether sound or not, form the dual with the stressed ending *-áyn* added to the singular, as follows:

- nouns ending in a consonant, add *-áyn*:
  safīráyn two ambassadors
- masculine nouns ending in *-ī* or *-a*, add *-yáyn*:
  ṣuḥufīyáyn two journalists *mustashfayáyn* two hospitals
- feminine nouns ending in *-a* (not *-ta/ṭa*), substitute *-táyn*:
  mu9allimtáyn two teachers *sayyārtáyn* two cars
- feminine nouns ending in *-ta/ṭa*, add *-táyn*:
  shantatáyn two suitcases

When adding a possessive suffix to a dual noun, drop the final *-n* and follow the pattern of *9ala* (2/8):

kitābáyya, kitābáyk/kitābáyki, kitābáy/kitābáyha;
kitābáyna, kitābáykum, kitābáyhum both my, your (etc.) books

Adjectives qualifying dual nouns of any kind are always in the *animate plural* form:

wazīrayn 'almānīyīn two German ministers
sayyārtayn 'almānīyīn two German cars

hadhoul al-kitābayn	these two/both these books

> Dual noun rule: An adjective (including a demonstrative) qualifying a dual noun is always in the animate plural form, even when the noun itself is inanimate.

13. *mish*

To negate any word or expression other than a verb, we use not *mā* but *mish* preceding the negated word or expression. We also use *mish* to negate the inferred verb 'to be' in present time:

al-bank mish ba9īd 9an huna.	The bank isn't far from here.
mish sitta, walākin sab9a.	Not six, but seven.
mish 'ana!	Not I/me!
mish kadha?	Isn't that so?

14. Adverbs

Many common adjectives can be used, in the m. sing. form, as adverbs (see 1/11). This is true of *kwayyis* and *kthīr*, among others:

shughlha kwayyis.	Her work is *good.* (adjective)
9imilat shughlha kwayyis.	She did her work *well.* (adverb)

The adverb *kthīr* 'very' may precede the modified word, breaking the qualifying word rule (1/11):

shughlha kwayyis ikthīr/kthīr kwayyis.

9imilat shughlha kwayyis ikthīr/kthīr kwayyis.

Some adverbs can be repeated to show intensity:

kthīr ikthīr	very much, lots and lots
shwayy ishwayy	little by little, gradually

15. *jumal mithālīya*

ba9d mou9idu ma9 as-safīr, kharaj min as-safāra u 'akhadh taksī 'ila wizārat al-khārijīya.	After his appointment with the ambassador, he left the embassy and took a taxi to the Ministry of Foreign Affairs.
fī sitta wizārāt u sifārtayn fī ḥayy al-balad hādha.	There are six ministries and two embassies in this part of town.
'imshī 9ala yamīnak 9ind al-'ishāra wa maktabna 9ala shimālak.	Go right at the lights and our office is on your left.
thamāniya rukkāb wiṣilū ba9d mā ṭili9at aṭ-ṭayyāra.	Eight passengers arrived after the aeroplane had taken off.
kharaj min al-jāmi9a, walākinnu mā wajad shughl khilāl waqt ṭawīl.	He came out of university but found no work for a long time.

16. ***at-tamārīn***

1. Add the right form of *hādha*:
e.g.: dukkān – hādha d-dukkān
(a) shurṭī (b) madkhal (c) wazīr al-9amal
(d) timthāl (e) sayyāra 'amayrkīya

2. Add the object pronoun suffix:
e.g.: 9irift (huwa) – 9iriftu
(a) 9irifna (huwa) (b) mā katabna (hiya) (c) simi9 ('ana)
(d) ṭalabū min ('int) (e) shū sa'altū (huwa)?

3. Make the sentence negative:
e.g.: wiṣilū – mā wiṣilū. huwa mabsūṭ – huwa mish mabsūṭ
(a) dakhalt al-bank. (b) hādha kthīr 9alayk. (c) fī 9indak fakka?
(d) katabu kwayyis. (e) shughlu kwayyis.

4. Make dual:
e.g.: tadkhkara – tadhkartayn; al-mu9allim – al-mu9allimayn
(a) sayyāra (b) sayyāra 'amayrkīya (c) al-balad
(d) ṣuḥufī (e) kitābu

5. Put the number with the noun:
e.g.: maḥall (3) – thalātha maḥallāt
(a) shanta (1) (b) muhandis (4) (c) rākib (2)
(d) shurṭī (6) (e) al-mustashfa (5)

ad-dars al-khāmis – Lesson 5
fi l-maktab – In the Office

1. ***al-ḥiwār***

(Peter calls at the Amman office to start his assignment.)

	9abdarraḥmān	Abdarrahman (name)
	'ashkurak	I thank you
	luṭfī	Lutfi (name)
	fannī	technical
9abdarraḥmān:	'ahlan yā sayyid Brown. tfaḍḍal.	Welcome, Mr Brown. Please come in.
Peter:	'ashkurak.	Thank you.
9abdarraḥmān:	'ana 9abdarraḥmān luṭfī, al-mudīr al-fannī. kayf al-ḥāl?	I'm Abdarrahman Lutfi, the Technical Manager. How are you?
Peter:	mabsūṭ jiddan, shukran. kayf ḥālak 'int?	Very well, thank you. How are you?
	al-ḥamdulilla	= *(al-)ḥamdilla*
	jawla	tour
	khallīnī	let me
	'ashraḥ	I explain
	tanẓīm	organisation
9abdarraḥmān:	al-ḥamdulilla. tfaḍḍal. yā sayyid Peter, qabl jawltak fi l-bināya, khallīnī 'ashraḥ lak tanẓīm u shughl ash-sharika,	Fine, thank you. Mr Brown, before your tour of the building, let me explain to you the organisation and work of the company,
	ḥatta	(also:) so that
	fikra	idea, thought
	ṣūra	picture, form, shape
	9āmm	general, public
	ḥatta tākhudh fikra 9an ash-sharika bi ṣūra 9āmma.	so that you get ('take') an idea of the company in general.
	tiẓhar	it appears
	kull	whole
Peter:	min al-kharij tiẓhar ash-sharika kbīra. kam shakhṣ fī́, fī kull ash-sharika?	From the outside the company looks big. How many people are there, in the whole company?
	mīya	hundred
	tis9īn	ninety

	qism	division, department
	khamst9ashr	fifteen
	9ishrīn	twenty
9abdarraḥmān:	mish ikthīr, mīya u tis9īn muwaẓẓaf. kam qism 9indu khamst9ashr, 9ishrīn shakhṣ bas.	Not many, 190 employees. Some departments have only fifteen or twenty people.
	mas'ūl 9an	responsible for
	takhṭīṭ	planning
	kama	as
	ta9raf	you know
	moujūd	present
	thalāthīn	thirty
	9idda	number
	mutakhaṣṣiṣ	specialising, specialist
	ḍarūrī	essential, vital
	walākin hādha l-qism mas'ūl 9an at-takhṭīṭ, kama ta9raf. 9indna moujūdīn thalāthīn muwaẓẓaf. 9iddit-hum mutakhaṣṣiṣīn fi t-takhṭīṭ al-fannī. hādha ḍarūrī 'ilna.	But this division's responsible for planning, as you know. We have thirty staff. A number of them are specialists in technical planning. That's essential for us.
	tudkhul	she enters
	maryam	Maryam (name)
	sikritayra	secretary
	ta9rafī	you know
	hilāl	Hilal (name)
(tudkhul maryam, sikritayrat al-mudīr.)		(Maryam, the manager's secretary, comes in.)
maryam:	'ismaḥ lī yā 9abdarraḥmān.	Excuse me, Abdarrahman.
9abdarraḥmān:	yā maryam, mā ta9rafi s-sayyid Peter Brown, mutakhaṣṣiṣ min mutakhaṣṣiṣīnna min Cambridge. yā Peter, sikritayrtī maryam hilāl.	Maryam, you don't know Mr Peter Brown, one of our specialists from Cambridge. Peter, my secretary Maryam Hilal.
	ma9rifa	knowledge, acquaintance
	furṣa	occasion, opportunity
	sa9īd	happy
maryam:	mabsūṭa bi ma9riftak, yā sayyid Peter. 'ahlan.	I'm pleased to meet you, Mr Brown. Welcome.

Peter:	furṣa sa9īda, yā sitt maryam. 'ahlan bīki.	Pleased to meet you also, Mrs Hilal.
	muhimm	important
	su'āl	question
	'aktub bi l-mākīna	I type, I'm typing ('writing with the machine')
	jawāb	reply
	risāla	letter
	ad-douḥa	Doha
9abdarraḥmān:	tfaḍḍalī yā maryam; fī shī muhimm?	Yes, Maryam, is there something important?
maryam:	su'āl iṣghīr, yā 9abdarraḥmān. 'aktub lak bi l-mākīna jawāb 'ila risālat al-wakīl fi d-douḥa.	A small question, Abdarrahman. I'm typing a reply to the agent's letter in Doha for you.
	maktūb	written
	mudda	period of time
	lāzim	necessary
	kalima	word
	ghalaṭ	mistake
	'uktubī	write
	walākin huna maktūb "li muddat shahr wāḥid". mish lāzim "shahrayn"?	But here it's written 'for a period of one month'. Shouldn't it be 'two months'?
9abdarraḥmān:	ṣaḥīḥ, yā maryam. kalimāt "shahr wāḥid" ghalaṭ. 'uktubī "shahrayn".	Correct, Maryam. The words 'one month' are a mistake. Write 'two months'.
	'aktubu	I('ll) write it
	tirja9	she returns
	mumtāz	excellent
	zouj	husband
	hassa	now
maryam:	shukran, 'aktubu kadha.	Thank you. I'll write it like that.
(tirja9 li maktabha.)		(She returns to her office.)
9abdarraḥmān:	sikritayra mumtāza, u laṭīfa jiddan. zoujha 9indna fī qism al-mālīya. u hassa, yā Peter, tfaḍḍal ma9ī.	An excellent secretary, and very pleasant. Her husband's with us in Finance Department. And now, Peter, please come with me.

2. *9ibārāt*

kayf al-ḥāl? How are you? (a less formal variant of *kayf ḥālak/ḥālik/ḥālkum?*) It is invariable for gender and number. Note also an even less formal variant *kayfak/kayfik/kayfkum?* which should be used only with close friends.
'akhadh fikra 9an to get an idea of.
bi ṣūra 9āmma in general.
mabsūṭ/mabsūṭa/mabsūṭīn bi ma9riftak/ma9riftik/ma9rifitkum. Pleased to meet you.
furṣa sa9īda ('a happy occasion') Pleased to meet you.
9imil jawla fī to make a tour of

3. *mufradāt 'iḍāfīya*

***al-'idāra l-9āmma wa l-khāṣṣa* – Public and private administration**

'idāra	administration	*qiṭā9*	sector
al-qiṭā9 l-9āmm	public sector	*barlamān*	parliament
waṭan	home country	*waṭanī*	national
dawla	state	*duwalī*	international
siyāsa	policy, politics	*siyāsī*	political
mas'ūl	official, person in charge	*mashghūl*	busy
rasmī	official (adjective)	*khāṣṣ*	special, private
al- qiṭā9 al-khāṣṣ	private sector	*mudīr 9āmm*	general manager
'intāj	production	*lajna*	committee
shu'ūn al-muwaẓẓafīn	personnel (matters)	*zamīl*	colleague
baḥth	discussion	*ijtimā9*	meeting
mīzānīya	budget	*nuskha*	copy
milaff	file	*barīd*	mail
waraqa	paper	*'āla kātiba, mākina*	typewriter
kambyutir	computer	*faks*	fax
barīd 'iliktrounī, 'īmayl	e-mail		

an-naḥū

4. Present tense of sound verbs

The Arabic present tense ('I do, I am doing'), often also called the *imperfect* tense, uses both personal prefixes and personal endings. Examine the present tense of *katab*:

('ana)	*'aktub*	*('iḥna)*	*nuktub*
('int)	*tuktub*	*('intū)*	*tuktubū*
('inti)	*tuktubī*		
(huwa)	*yuktub*	*(hum)*	*yuktubū*
(hiya)	*tuktub*		I, you, he, she (etc.) write(s)

The initial and middle (or first two) root letters come together throughout this tense, after the personal prefix. Examine now the present tense of three other verbs, *dafa9*, *9irif* and *nizil*:

'adfa9, tidfa9/tidfa9ī, yidfa9/tifa9; nidfa9, tidfa9ū, yidfa9ū
I, you, he (etc.) pay(s)
'a9raf, ta9raf/ta9rafī, ya9raf/ta9raf; na9raf, ta9rafū, ya9rafū

I, you, he (etc.) know(s)

'anzil, tinzil/tinzilī, yinzil/tinzil; ninzil, tinzilū, yinzilū

I, you, he (etc.) get(s) down

The vowels are different, except that the *'ana* person always has *a* as its first vowel. Almost all sound verbs follow one or other of these four patterns; we shall use *katab* as the model for them all.

We shall indicate new verbs with the basic forms of the past and present tenses, thus: *katab yuktub*. These are the *principal parts* of the verb.

Principal parts of other sound verbs encountered so far:

'amar yu'mur	to order	*daras yudrus*	to study
dakhal yudkhul	to enter	*kharaj yukhruj*	to go/come out
tarak yutruk	to leave	*shakar yushkur 9ala*	to thank for
ṭalab yuṭlub min	to ask (request)	*sa'al yis'al*	to ask (enquire)
samaḥ yismaḥ li	to permit	*sharaḥ yishraḥ*	to explain
ẓahar yiẓhar	to appear	*riji9 yirja9*	to return
rikib yirkab	to mount, get in	*ṭili9 yiṭla9*	to go/get up
simi9 yisma9	to hear	*fataḥ yiftaḥ*	to open
9imil yi9mal	to do/make		

5. Verbs with initial *hamza*

Two verbs with initial root letter *hamza* are irregular in the present, with *ā* instead of *[a']*:

'akhadh yākhudh:		*'akal yākul*:	
'ākhudh	*nākhudh*	*'ākul*	*nākul*
tākhudh	*tākhudhū*	*tākul*	*tākulū*
tākhudhī		*tākulī*	
yākhudh	*yākhudhū*	*yākul*	*yākulū*
tākhudh	I, you, he (etc.) take(s)	*tākul*	I, you, he (etc.) eat(s)

The combination *['a']* always becomes *'ā*. Thus the present tense of *'amar yu'mur* is:

'āmur, tu'mur/tu'murī, yu'mur/tu'mur; nu'mur, tu'murū, yu'murū

I, you, he (etc.) order(s)

We have not yet examined verbs with final root letter *hamza*, which are different.

6. Present tense of initial-*w* verbs

In the present tense of initial-*w* verbs the initial root letter *w* vocalises to (i.e. becomes a vowel) *ū* except in the *'ana* person, which also keeps the vowel of the personal prefix. Otherwise these verbs form their tenses like the sound verbs.

wiṣil yūṣal:		*wajad yūjid*:	
'awsal	*nūṣal*	*'awjid*	*nūjid*
tūṣal	*tūṣalū*	*tūjid*	*tūjidū*
tūṣalī		*tūjidī*	
yūṣal	*yūṣalū*	*yūjid*	*yūjidū*
tūṣal	I, you, he (etc.) arrive(s)	*tūjid*	I, you, he (etc.) find(s)

7. Negative of the present tense

Like the past tense, the present tense is negated by putting *mā* before the affirmative:

yudrusu l-9arabī. mā yudrusu l-9arabī. They (don't) study Arabic.

8. Use of the present tense

The present tense is used for all actions or situations occurring as they are reported, however expressed in English:

yūṣal al-youm. He arrives/is arriving today.
nirja9 li l-maktab. We're going back to the office.

It is also used for the near future:

'aktub al-jawāb al-youm. I'm writing/I'll write the answer today.

There is a separate future form, not consistently used, which we shall study later.

9. Imperative

The imperative or command form is derived from the present for all verbs. It exists only in the second persons *('int, 'inti, 'intū).*

For the affirmative imperative of sound verbs, substitute *' (hamza)* for the initial *t-* of the second persons, thus:

tuktub, tuktubī, tuktubū you write
→ *'uktub, 'uktubī, 'uktubū* write

so also, e.g.:

'udkhul, 'udkhulī, 'udkhulū enter
'inzil, 'inzilī, 'inzilū get down, get off

The imperative of initial-*w* verbs having the form *wiṣil yūṣal* or *wajad yūjid* is not used in spoken Arabic; another form is used, which we shall study later.

Three verbs with initial root letter *hamza* drop everything before the middle root letter to make their imperatives:

mur murī murū order *kul kulī kulū* eat
khudh khudhī khudhū take

The *negative* imperative of all verbs without exception is made by putting the negative particle *lā* before the appropriate second-person form of the present:

lā tuktub, lā tuktubī, lā tuktubū don't write

You may hear some speakers use *mā* here. *lā* is better.

10. Pronoun suffixes

Verbs in the present tense and the imperative take object-pronoun suffixes following the rules already learned:

ya9rafūna kwayyis. *mā tisma9hum?*
khudhu. *lā tuktubī*

11. *khallī-*

This verb, the structure of which we shall examine later, means 'let (me, him etc.)'. It is followed by the object pronoun (on the pattern of *fī*, see 2/8) and the present tense:

khallīnī, khallīk/khallīkī, khallī/khallīha; khallīna, khallīkum, khallīhum let me, you, him (etc.) ...

khallī yuktub al-jawāb. Let him write the reply.

khallī- is an imperative, with a negative formed regularly with *lā*:

lā tkhallīhum yisma9ūk. Don't let them/Let them not hear you.

khallī- and *lā tkhallī-* are both m. sing. and f. sing. The plural is *khallū-*, *lā tkhallū-*, addressing a group:

lā tkhallū yudkhul. Don't (pl.) let him (come) in.

12. Numbers 11–199

Cardinal numbers above 10 and below 200 are:

11	*'iḥd9ashr*	12	*ithn9ashr*
13	*thalatt9ashr*	14	*'arba9t9ashr*
15	*khamst9ashr*	16	*sitt9ashr*
17	*saba9t9ashr*	18	*thamant9ashr*
19	*tisa9t9ashr*	20	*9ishrīn*
21	*wāḥid(a) u 9ishrīn*	22	*ithnayn/thintayn u 9ishrīn*
30	*thalāthīn*	35	*khamsa u thalāthīn*
40	*'arba9īn*	50	*khamsīn*
60	*sittīn*	70	*sab9īn*
80	*thamānīn*	90	*tis9īn*
100	*mīya*	123	*mīya u thalātha u 9ishrīn*

In combinations of tens and units, the unit number comes first. All counting elements are connected with *u*.

When the expression is *indefinite*:

- if the last stated number is 1, or is higher than 10, the noun is singular:
  mīya u wāḥid muwaẓẓaf 101 employees
  mīya u sitta u thalāthīn muwaẓẓaf 136 employees
- if the last stated number is 3 to 10, the noun stands in the plural:
  mīya u khamsa muwaẓẓafīn 105 employees
- *mīya* immediately before a noun becomes *mīt*:
  mīt rākib 100 passengers

When the expression is *definite*, the number follows the noun, which is plural if the *entire number* is 3 or higher:

al-muwaẓẓafīn al-mīya u khamsīn the 155 employees
muwaẓẓafīn ash-sharika l-mīya u tis9īn the 190 company employees
muwaẓẓafīnhum as-sitta u sab9īn their 76 employees

13. *lī*

The form *lī, lak* (etc.) is used to imply 'on behalf of' or 'in the interest of', not necessarily expressed in English:

ta9raf lī maṭ9am kwayyis? Do you know (for my information) a good restaurant?

sa'alū lana l-mudīr. They asked the director for us/on our behalf.

14. Construct

Compound constructs exist, with more than one noun as either theme or attribute:

tanẓīm u shughl ash-sharika (two themes)
the organisation and work of the company

shughl al-qism 'aw ash-sharika (two attributes)
the work of the division or (of) the company

Do not confuse the compound construct with the 'string' construct (*miftāḥ ghurfat aṭ-ṭabīb*, 3/4).

We can express 'one of ...' as follows:

mutakhaṣṣiṣ min mutakhaṣṣiṣīnna one of our specialists ('a specialist from our specialists')

15. Interrogatives

Here are the main interrogative pronouns, adjectives and adverbs:

Pronouns	*mīn*	who	*shū*	what
	kam	how much/many	*li mīn*	whose
	'ayy wāḥid(a)	which one		
Adjectives	*kam*	how much/many	*'ayy*	which
	mīn	whose	*'ayy nou9 min*	what kind of
Adverbs	*kayf*	how	*laysh*	why
	mata	when	*wayn*	where

Some are already known to you. Note:

- The pronouns are all masculine singular, except for one feminine form *'ayy wāḥida*:
  mīn katab ar-risāla? Who wrote the letter?
- The adjectives *precede* their noun, with the exception of *mīn* 'whose', which forms a construct with its noun:
  'ayy kitāb? which book?
  (fī) maktab mīn? (in) whose office?
- Remember that after *kam* used as an adjective, the noun is always singular:
  kam shakhṣ? how many people?
- *'ayy* can be used non-interrogatively, meaning 'any':
  'ayy risāla any letter
  min 'ayy wāḥid minhum from any one of them
- Distinguish between the interrogative adverb *mata* 'when' and the non-interrogative conjunction *lamma* 'when':
  mata tarakt al-maktab? When did you leave the office?
  lamma tarakt al-maktab, riji9t li l-'utayl. When I left the office, I returned to the hotel.

16. Indirect questions

All the interrogatives can introduce indirect questions. The indirect speech rule (4/7) holds. Examine:

mā 9irift kayf yi9malu. I didn't know how he did ('does') it.
mā 9irift kayf 9imilu I didn't know how he had done ('did') it.

Indirect questions inviting the answer 'yes' or 'no' are introduced by *'idha* 'whether'. The indirect speech rule still applies:

sa'alt 'idha yūṣal al-youm.	I asked whether he was arriving today.
sa'alt 'idha wiṣil al-youm.	I asked whether he (had) arrived today.

17. Regional variations

In this lesson we deal with some pronunciation variations found in Egypt, the Levant, the Arabian Peninsula and North-west Africa.

q. In the Peninsula, *q* is pronounced as taught in this course. This is the pronunciation of the written language. In Egypt and the Levant, *q* is pronounced as ', i.e. like *hamza*, without deepened *ạ/ā̤*. Compare:

Peninsula, written language:	*ṭạrīq, qạbl, istiqbāl*
Egypt, Levant:	*ṭarī', 'abl, isti'bāl*

But the proper names *9irāq, dimashq* and *al-qāhira* 'Cairo' and their derivatives are pronounced with *q* everywhere.

j. In the Peninsula and North-west Africa, and in the written language, this consonant is pronounced *j*. In Egypt it has the sound *g*, i.e. that of hard English g (see Pronunciation, paragraph 3). In the Levant it is pronounced like s in English 'pleasure'. We can transcribe this consonant as *zh*. Examine:

Peninsula, written, NW Africa:	*jawāb, moujūd, 'intāj*
Egypt:	*gawāb, mougūd, 'intāg*
Levant:	*zhawāb, mouzhūd, 'intāzh*

dh, th. In Egypt and the Levant, these consonants are mostly pronounced as *d, t* or (less frequently) as *z, s* respectively. Note:

d, t:	*hāda* (etc.), *'akhad yākhud* (etc.), *itnayn/tintayn, talāta, tamā́niyi (= thamā́niya), itn9ashr, ktīr*
z, s:	*kaza, timsāl*

ḍ̄ and ***ẓ***. *ḍ̄* is the velarised counterpart of *dh*. In Egypt and the Levant, it is mostly pronounced *ẓ* (velarised *z*). This course gives *ẓ* where it is commoner. But in the Peninsula, and sometimes elsewhere, we hear the written pronunciation *ḍ̄*, in (e.g.) *muwaḍ̄ḍ̄af, ḍ̄ahar yiḍ̄har* (etc.), *maḍ̄būṭ, intáḍ̄ir*

18. *jumal mithālīya*

mudīr hādhi sh-sharika, mā 'a9rafu. 'int ta9rafu?	I don't know the director of this company. Do you?
li mīn hādhi n-nuskha? wajadt-ha fī milaffi l-9āmm.	Whose is this copy? I found it in my general file.
fi l-qism at-tijārī fī́ tis9at9ashr shakhṣ faqaṭ. – wallāhi, hādha mish ikthīr.	In the Commercial Division there are only nineteen people. – Good Heavens, that's not many.
bi ṣūra 9āmma, al-qiṭā9 al-khāṣṣ muhimm jiddan li l-waṭan.	In general, the private sector is very important for the country.
laysh mā katabt jawāb li risālat 'umūr al-khārijīya? – katabtu, mā wajadtu?	Why haven't you written a reply to Foreign Affairs' letter? – I've written it, haven't you found it?

19. *at-tamārīn*

1. Give the principal parts of the verb:
e.g.: katab – katab yuktub
(a) daras (b) wiṣil (c) 9irif
(d) shakar (e) 'akal

2. Give the affirmative imperative and negative imperative:
e.g.: sa'al yis'al – 'is'al, 'is'alī, 'is'alū; lā tis'al, lā tis'alī, lā tis'alū
(a) kharaj yukhruj (b) nizil yinzil (c) 'akhadh yākhudh
(d) samaḥ yismaḥ (e) katab yuktub

3. Make plural:
e.g.: yākhudh – yākhudhū
(a) 'aṭlub (b) lā tirkabī. (c) yushkur
(d) khallīnī 'anzil. (e) mā ta9raf?

4. Add the object-pronoun suffix:
e.g.: ta9raf (huwa) – ta9rafu
(a) mā yisma9ū ('iḥna) (b) ya9raf (hiya)
(c) khallīna nushkur(hum) (d) sa'alt ('int) (e) mā 'akalt (huwa)

5. Put the right form of *khallī-* before the verb:
e.g.: nis'alhum – khallīna nis'alhum
(a) yuṭlubū. (b) hiya tukhruj. (c) 'ajlis.
(d) yinzil huna. (e) nidfa9 'ujrat at-taksī.

6. Make an indirect question with *sa'alt*:
e.g.: ya9rafu l-9unwān. – sa'alt 'idha ya9rafu l-9unwān.
(a) laysh mā 'akhadht al-fulūs? (b) dafa9u l-ḥisāb.
(c) mata tūṣal as-sayyāra? (d) wayn al-mudīr?
(e) li mīn hādha l-milaff?

7. Put the number with the noun:
e.g.: sayyāra (16) – sitt9ashr sayyāra
as-sayyāra (6) – as-sayyārāt as-sitta
(a) shakhṣ (14) (b) musāfir (100) (c) al-musāfir (127)
(d) risāla (8) (e) muwaẓẓaf (30)

ad-dars as-sādis – Lesson 6
ziyāra 9ind al-'aṣdiqā' – A Visit to Friends

1. *al-ḥiwār*

(NB: In this dialogue one speaker uses the Egyptian form of spoken Arabic, examples of which are shown underlined in the vocabulary.)

	zār	he visited
	sābiq	former
	'ustādh	professor (title of respect used for any learned person)
	khalīl sulaymān	Khalil Suleiman (name)
	(khilāl 'iqāmtu fī 9ammān Peter zār mu9allimu s-sābiq li l-lugha l-9arabīya, al-'ustādh khalīl sulaymān.)	(During his stay in Amman Peter visited his former Arabic teacher Khalil Suleiman.)
	shuftak	I saw you
	zamān	time
	kunt	you were
	hal-ghayba	this absence
	jūwa	inside
	bilād	country
khalīl:	'ahlā-ā-ān yā Peter! mā shuftak min zamān! wayn kunt fī hal-ghayba? tfaḍḍal yā Peter, tfaḍḍal jūwa.	Welcome, Peter! I haven't seen you for ages! Where have you been all this time? Come in, Peter, come in please.
Peter:	'ahlan bīk yā 'ustādh. kayf ḥālak yā khalīl?	Same to you, professor. How are you, Khalil?
khalīl:	wallāhi, 'iḥna kwayyisīn. mā 9irift 'innak fi l-bilād.	Heavens, we're fine. I didn't know you were in the country.
	ṣār	it became
	shufnāk	we saw you
	ṣār lana waqt ṭawīl mā shufnāk.	It's a long time since we saw you ('It became for us a long time we didn't see you').
	'usbū9	week
	luṭfīya	Lutfiya (name)
	'inshalla	('if God wills') I hope
Peter:	'ayna9am, ṣār zamān ṭawīl. wiṣilt hādha l-'usbū9. u kayf luṭfīya? 'inshalla mabsūṭa?	Yes, it's been a long time. I arrived this week. And how is Lutfiya? Well, I hope?

ḍaḥak yiḍḥak	to laugh
ta9ālī	come
shūfī	look, see
zouja	wife
māshalla	('whatever God wishes') Good Heavens
kull shī	everything
tamām	perfection, perfect
mougūd	= *moujūd*

(khalīl yiḍḥak.) (Khalil laughs.)

khalīl:	hiya moujūda. yā luṭfīya, ta9ālī shūfī mīn.	She's here. Lutfiya, come and see who it is.

(tudkhul zoujtu luṭfīya.) (His wife Lutfiya comes in.)

luṭfīya:	māshalla, Peter! kayf al-ḥāl yā Peter?	Good Heavens, Peter! How are you, Peter?
Peter:	mabsūṭ jiddan, 'alla yisallimik yā luṭfīya. u 'inti?	I'm fine, thank you Lutfiya. And you?
luṭfīya:	kull shī tamām u 'int mougūd. u kayf Mary?	Everything's fine now you're here. And how's Mary?

tsallim 9alaykum	she sends her regards
ḥafaẓ yiḥfaẓ	to keep
'alla yiḥfaẓha	Good bless ('keep') her.
sallim 9alayha	give her my/our regards

Peter:	hiya kwayyisa, shukran. u tsallim 9alaykum.	She's well, thank you, and she sends her regards.
luṭfīya:	'alla yiḥfaẓha. sallim 9alayha.	God bless her. Give her our regards.

tis9at 'ashhur	nine months
bi9na	we sold
bayt	house
'igīna	= *'ijīna* we came
al-bayt da	= *hādha l-bayt*
ash-shām	Damascus; Syria
hina	= *huna*
min sha'n	for the sake of, because of

Peter:	kam waqt ṣār lakum fī 9ammān?	How long have you been in Amman?
luṭfīya:	tis9at 'ashhur bas. bi9na l-bayt da fī sh-shām u 'igīna li hina min sha'n	Only nine months. We sold that house in Damascus

	shughlna.	and came here because of our work.
	ruḥna	we went
	zurna	we visited
	9adad min	a number of
	'aṣdi'ā'	= *'aṣdiqā'* friends
	talāmīz	= *talāmīdh* pupils
	gāmi9a	= *jāmi9a*
	ṣayf	summer
	walākin ruḥna li sh-shām u zurna 9adad min 'aṣdi'ā'ī u talāmīzī fi l-gāmi9a khilāl aṣ-ṣayf.	But we went to Damascus and visited a number of my friends and pupils at the university during the summer.
	khabar	news
	shuft-hum	I saw them
	lissa	still; (+ negative:) not yet
	u shū l-khabar min talāmīz khalīl?	And what's the news of Khalil's pupils?
Peter:	mā shuft-hum min zamān, 'illa Liza. hiya lissa fi l-'umūr al-khārijīya.	I haven't seen them for a long time, apart from Liza. She's still with the Foreign Office.
	kānat	she was
	al-baḥrayn	Bahrain
	rāḥat	she went
	bayrūt	Beirut
	ka	as, in the capacity of
	mulḥaq	attaché
	thaqāfī	cultural
	kānat fi l-baḥrayn, u ba9dayn rāḥat 'ila bayrūt ka mulḥaq thaqāfī.	She was in Bahrain, then she went to Beirut as cultural attaché.
	'ahā́	ah!
	dāyiman	always
	tilmīdh	pupil
	shāṭir	clever
	mujtáhid (NB stress)	industrious
	u	(here:) while, when
	kān yudrus	he was studying
khalīl:	'ahā́, Liza. kānat tilmīdha mumtāza. walākin yā luṭfīya, Peter kān dāyiman tilmīdh shāṭir u mujtáhid kamān, u huwa kān yudrus 9indī.	Ah, Liza. She was an excellent pupil. But Lutfiya, Peter was always a clever and industrious pupil as

well, when he was studying with me.

wāḍiḥ	clear
nisī	he forgot
'abadan	ever; (+ negative:) never, not at all
ya9ṭīk al-9ā́fiya	('(God) give you health') well done!, keep it up!
'akhū́ī	my brother

	u min al-wāḍiḥ 'innu mā nisī 9arabīyitu 'abadan. ya9ṭīk al-9ā́fiya, yā 'akhū́ī.	And it's clear he hasn't forgotten his Arabic at all. Well done ('my brother').

'alla ya9fīk	('God restore you') thank you
9ala fikra	by the way, incidentally
9āwiz	wanting
'ahwi	= *qahwa*
shī	(also:) something
bārid	cold

Peter:	'alla ya9fīk yā 'ustādhī. laṭīf jiddan.	Thank you. You're most kind.
luṭfīya:	9ala fikra, yā Peter, shū 9āwiz, 'ahwi willa shī bārid?	By the way, Peter, what would you like, coffee or something cold?

2. *9ibārāt*

min zamān since a long time ago, for a long time now.

wayn kunt/kunti/kuntū fī hal-ghayba? ('Where were you in this absence?') Where have you been all this time?

'inshalla ('if God wills') I hope (so).

māshalla! Good Heavens! (expressing surprise or admiration).

yisallim/tsallim/yisallimū 9alayk/9alayha/9alaykum. He/she/they send(s) his/her/their regards.

sallim/sallimī/sallimū 9aláy/9alayha/9alayhum Give him/her/them my/our regards.

'alla yiḥfaẓu/yiḥfaẓha/yiḥfaẓhum ('God keep ...') God bless him/her/them. Used more frequently than its English counterpart.

'abadan ever, (+ negative) never, not at all. *'abadan!* Never!

ya9ṭīk/ya9ṭīkum al-9ā́fiya, ya9ṭīki l-9ā́fiya ('(God) give you health') Bravo; Well done. This is a greeting, with the response:

'alla ya9fīk/ya9fīki/ya9fīkum ('God restore you') Thank you.

9ala fikra by the way

3. ***mufradāt 'iḍāfīya. al-bayt wa l-9ayla*** **– House and Family**

shaqqa	apartment	*9imāra*	building, block
ṣāloun	living-room	*maṭbakh*	kitchen
gārāj	garage	*shubbāk*	window
sullam	staircase	*jinayna, bustān*	garden
fouq	(also:) upstairs	*taḥt*	(also:) downstairs
'ujra	(also:) rent	*ṣāḥib bayt*	landlord
'athāth	furniture	*kursī*	chair

ṭawla (Levant/Peninsula), *ṭarabayza* (Egypt/Sudan), *ṭābla* (NW Africa) table*

barrāda	refrigerator	*mukayyifa*	airconditioner
tádfiya	heating	*sakan yuskun*	to live (reside)
9ayla	family	*'oulād*	children
rajul	man	*mara*	woman
'ab	father	*'umm*	mother
walad	child, boy	*wālid*	parent
'ibn	son	*bint*	girl, daughter
'akh	brother	*'ukht*	sister

* *ṭawla* is from Italian, *ṭarabayza* from Greek, *ṭābla* from French.

an-naḥū

4. Past tense of hollow verbs

Hollow verbs are those whose middle root letter is one of the weak consonants *w* or *y*. In most forms of such verbs, the weak middle root letter vocalises, i.e. becomes a vowel. Examine the past tense of a typical hollow verb:

Root *sh w f*, first principal part *shāf* to see, look (at):

('ana)	*shuft*	*('iḥna)*	*shufna*
('int)	*shuft*	*('intū)*	*shuftū*
('inti)	*shufti*		
(huwa)	*shāf*	*(hum)*	*shāfū*
(hiya)	*shāf*	I, you, he, she (etc.) saw, looked (at)	

The personal endings are the same as for the sound verbs. Also, when the personal ending begins with a consonant, the middle root letter takes the form of its related short vowel: *w* becomes *u*. Elsewhere in the tense, the middle root letter becomes *ā*. Another example:

Root *r w ḥ*, first principal part *rāḥ* to go:

ruḥt, ruḥt/ruḥti, rāḥ/rāḥat; ruḥna, ruḥtū, rāḥū I, you, he (etc.) went

so also:

Root *k w n, kān*	to be	*q w l, qāl*	to say
z w r, zār	to visit	*q w m, qām*	to rise, get/stand up
s w q, sāq	to drive	*q w m, qām bi*	to undertake

Similarly, middle root letter *y* changes to *i* (the related short vowel) and *ā*, under the rule given earlier:

Root *ṣ y r*, first principal part *ṣār* to become:

ṣirt, ṣirt/ṣirti, ṣār/ṣārat; ṣirna, ṣirtū, ṣārū I, you, he (etc.) became

so also:

Root *b y 9, bā9*	to sell	*ṭ y r, ṭār*	to fly

j y b, jāb to bring *z y d, zād* to increase

Two important verbs with middle root letter *w* form their past tense as if this root letter were *y*:

Root *n w m,* first principal part *nām* to sleep:

nimt, nimt/nimti, nām/nāmat; nimna, nimtū, nāmū I, you, he (etc.) slept

Root *kh w f,* first principal part *khāf* or *khāf min* to fear:

khift, khift/khifti, khāf/khāfat; khifna, khiftū, khāfū I, you, he (etc.) feared

Hollow verb rule: In hollow verbs, the middle root letter, when vocalised, is short before a consonantal personal ending and long elsewhere.

5. Negative; Object pronoun

All these verbs form their negative past tense with *mā,* and take the object-pronoun suffixes, as do the sound verbs:

mā shuftu? Didn't you see him/it?

mā jābu. He didn't bring it.

6. *kān*

Unlike the concept 'to be' in present time, the past tense of *kān* is never omitted:

huwa moujūd, mish kadha? but: *kān moujūd, mish kadha?*

7. *kā́n fī*

The past form of *fī́* in its meaning 'there is, there are', and in its use with *9ind,* is expressed with *kā́n fī* 'there was, there were', negative *mā́ kān fī.* These expressions are normally invariable for gender and number. Note that the stress is on the first syllable of the whole expression in each case:

kā́n fī nās ikthīr fi l-maktaba. *mā́ kān fī 9indu waqt.*

The *fī* may be omitted from the affirmative *kān (fī) 9ind,* but not from the negative *mā́ kān fī 9ind.*

8. *ṣār li*

The past-tense form *ṣār* 'it became', with the preposition + pronoun suffix *lī, lak* (etc.), gives us an idiom indicating or enquiring how long a situation has been so for the person indicated:

kam waqt ṣār lak huna? How long have you been here?

ṣār lī shahrayn huna. I've been here for two months.

9. *ha-*

hādha (etc.) preceding a noun can be abbreviated to the invariable prefix *ha-*:

hādha l-balad ⟶ *hal-balad* *hādhi s-sayyāra* ⟶ *has-sayyāra*

hadhoul an-nās ⟶ *han-nās* *'ustādh hādha t-tilmīdh* ⟶ *ustādh hat-tilmīdh*

10. Circumstantial *u*

u can also mean 'while' (either in the sense 'when' or 'whereas') or 'now (that)', in some contexts. The *u* must be followed either by a personal pronoun or a negative *mā* or *mish* to give this meaning. We call such expressions *clauses of circumstance*:

kull shī tamām u 'int moujūd. Everything's fine now you're here.
kān mujtáhid u huwa (kān) ṭālib. He was hardworking when/while (he was) a student.
kunt 'ana fi l-baḥrayn u mā 'a9raf shū ṣār li l-'aṣdiqā'. I was in Bahrain, while/whereas I don't know what happened to my ('the') friends.

11. Broken plurals

We have already studied in 1/10 and 3/13 the regular or so-called sound plurals. Most nouns and many adjectives have an irregular or so-called broken plural, formed on a different pattern and without suffixes like the sound plurals. Some have more than one possibility. Here are the broken plurals of the most important nouns already learnt (singular/plural), grouped according to the plural pattern:

bank ***bunūk***	*'amr 'umūr*	*sha'n shu'ūn*	*bayt buyūt*
jisr jusūr	*baḥth buḥūth*	*ḍayf ḍuyūf*	
mudīr ***mudarā'***	*safīr sufarā'*	*wazīr wuzarā'*	*wakīl wukalā'*
zamīl zumalā'			
bāb ***'abwāb***	*ḥāl 'aḥwāl*	*shakhṣ 'ashkhāṣ*	*khabar 'akhbār*
shughl 'ashghāl	*waqt 'ouqāt*	*raqm 'arqām*	*qism 'aqsām*
fikra ***fikār***	*rajul rijāl*	*balad bilād*	
ghurfa ***ghuraf***	*'ouḍa 'uwaḍ*	*dawla duwal*	*furṣa furaṣ*
nuskha nusakh	*ṣūra ṣuwar*		
kitāb ***kutub***	*ṭarīq ṭuruq*		
maṭ9am ***maṭā9im***	*minshafa manāshif*	*madkhal madākhil*	*maktab makātib*
maktaba makātib	*makhraj makhārij*	*makhzan makhāzin*	*mou9id mawā9id*
shāri9 shawāri9	*daqīqa daqāyiq*	*tadhkara tadhākir*	
ṣandūq ***ṣanādīq***	*miftāḥ mafātīḥ*	*dīnār danānīr*	*'usbū9 'asābī9*
shubbāk shabābīk	*tilmīdh talāmīdh*	*bustān basātīn*	

and less common examples:

sayyid sāda	*'ustādh 'asātidha*	*ṣadīq 'aṣdiqā'*	*shahr 'ashhur*
su'āl 'as'ila	*bilād buldān*	*mara niswān* (from another root)	
ṭālib ṭullāb	*ṭabīb 'aṭibba*	*sana sinīn* (also sound:) *sanawāt*	

Before a plural beginning with *hamza*, the numbers from 3 to 9 add a final *-t*:

*thalātha**t** 'aṣdiqā'* three friends
*sitta**t** 'asābī9* six weeks
*thamāniya**t** 'ashhur* eight months

Learn also in this context the essential word *youm*, pl. *'ayyām* 'day':

*sab9a**t** 'ayyām* seven days

Here are important adjectives with broken plurals, some already known to you:

kthīr kthār *kbīr kbār*

ṣghīr ṣghār		*ṭawīl ṭiwāl*	
laṭīf luṭafā'		*shāṭir shuṭṭār*	
rkhīṣ rkhāṣ	cheap	*mnīḥ mnāḥ*	good
lazīz lizāz	pleasant	*qaṣīr qiṣār*	short
khafīf khifāf	light (in weight)	*ṣa9b ṣi9āb*	difficult
qadīm qudamā'	old (of things)	*faqīr fuqarā'*	poor
ghanī 'aghniyā'	rich	*9aẓīm 9uẓamā'*	huge, splendid
basīṭ busaṭā'	simple	*karīm kuramā'*	generous
naḍīf nuḍafā'	clean	*thaqīl thuqalā'*	heavy
marīḍ marḍa	sick	*jadīd judud*	new

Remember, with respect to the adjectives:

- *kthīr* is often used invariably (3/17),
- the inanimate plural rule (1/5) still holds,
- the adjective plurals shown above are used only with animate meaning, or with (animate or inanimate) dual nouns (Dual noun rule, 4/12).

Some adjectives have a broken *feminine*:

m. *'awwal*, f. *'ūla*, pl. (sound) *'awwalīn*	first
m. *'ākhar*, f. *'ukhra*, pl. (sound) *'ākharīn*	other

'awwal, and a broken plural *'awā'il*, are used as nouns with special meanings:

(fī) 'awwal as-sana	(at) the beginning of the year
(fī) 'awā'il as-sana	early in the year

Likewise *'ākhir* (NB not *'ākhar*) plural *'awākhir* 'last':

(fī) 'ākhir ash-shahr	(at) the end of the month
(fī) 'awākhir ash-shahr	late in the month

12. In addition to *'ākhar* and *'ākhir* shown above, the root *' kh r* provides a third important adjective. Do not confuse the three:

'ākhar, 'ukhra, 'ākharīn	other	(see above)
'ākhir, 'ākhira, 'āwākhir	last	(see above)
'akhīr, 'akhīra, 'akhīrīn	recent	

13. We shall show new nouns and adjectives having broken plurals thus: *qism 'aqsām*. Where no plural is shown, it is sound.

14. *'ab*, *'akh*, *'ukht*, *'umm*

These words merit special attention:

'ab 'ābā'	father	*'umm 'ummahāt*	mother
'ukht 'ikhwāt	sister	*'akh 'ikhwa*	brother(s) (in a family)
'akh 'ikhwān	brother/brethren (of a community)		

'ab and *'akh* add *-ū-* before the possessive suffixes, on the pattern of *fī*. Note the stress of *'abū́ī* and *'akhū́ī*:

'abū́ī, 'abūk/'abūki, 'abū́/'abūha; 'abūna, 'abūkum, 'abūhum my (etc.) father
'akhū́ī, 'akhūk/'akhūki, 'akhū́/'akhūha; 'akhūna, 'akhūkum, 'akhūhum my (etc.) brother

'akhūī also has the variant *'akhī*. The suffixed forms of *'akh-*, and also the expression *al-'akh* (with or without a name) are used as a cordial form of address or reference to a male colleague or friend:

tfaḍḍal, yā 'akhūī/'akhī. Please come in, old chap.
wiṣil al-'akh ḥasan. (Our friend) Hassan's arrived.

'ikhwān is commonly used to address or refer to a group of male associates; it can be used even in formal situations:

tfaḍḍalū, 'ikhwān. Help yourselves, friends/gentlemen/chaps.

Women use *'ukht 'ikhwāt* identically for women friends:

kayf ḥālik, yā 'ukhtī? How are you, dear?
al-'ikhwāt moujūdīn hassa. The girls are here now.

A Christian clergyman is addressed or referred to as *'abūna*.

'abū followed by the given name of the eldest son is a cordial way (used by men and women) of addressing or referring to a man:

'abū fu'ād 'Fuad's father'

Similarly, *'umm* (also pronounced *'imm* in this context) for a woman:

'umm/'imm ḥasan 'Hassan's mother'

If an Arab calls you *'akh* or *'ukht*, you have cause to feel flattered. You have been accepted as a friend.

15. Finally, *abū* is also used jocularly in construct, combined with a recognisable characteristic of a man:

'abū liḥya ('father of a beard') he/him with a beard
'abū 'aghlāṭ ('father of errors') the bungler

This picturesque idiom occurs in the opening lines of James Elroy Flecker's haunting drama of medieval Baghdad, 'Hassan' (1911). Our hero is unhappy in love, and is boring his friend Selim with the fact:

HASSAN *(rocking on his mat)*: Eywallah! Eywallah!
SELIM: Thirty-seven times have you made the same remark,
O father of repetition.

You should know this structure, but be wary of using it yourself.

16. Continuous past tense

The verb *kān* in the past tense, followed by another verb in the present, makes the *continuous past tense,* which can be used for a continuous or repeated action in the past:

... u huwa kān yudrus 9indī ... while he was studying with me
kān dāyiman yis'al ḥawlak. He always used to ask about you.

17. Use of adjectives

Most adjectives can be used as nouns, whether to indicate a person or persons, or an understood thing:

al-ghanī the rich man *al-9arab* The Arabs
al-muhimm 'innak moujūd. The important thing is that you're here.

'It is ... that ...' is often expressed with *min al-... 'inn ...*:

min al-wāḍiḥ 'innhum 'aghniyā' jiddan. It's clear (that) they're very rich.

18. Prepositions and conjunctions

Distinguish between prepositions and their related conjunctions. A preposition governs a noun or pronoun; a conjunction introduces a further clause (a clause is a group of words centred on a verb and its subject). A few examples:

preposition (+ noun/pronoun)		conjunction (+ clause)	
qabl	before	*qabl mā*	before
ba9d	after	*ba9d mā*	after
9ind	at the time of	*lamma*	when

wiṣilū qabl/ba9d al-ijtimā9.	They arrived before/after the meeting.
wiṣilū qabl mā/ba9d mā kharajt.	They arrived before/after I left.
shuft-ha 9ind wuṣūlha.	I saw her on her arrival.
shuft-ha lamma wiṣilat.	I saw her when she arrived.

19. Regional variations: Egypt and Sudan

We examine below two important characteristics of Egyptian and Sudanese speech.

da. The demonstrative *hādha* (etc.), used in the Levant and the Peninsula, is close to the standard written form. In Egypt and Sudan, another form is commoner:

da m., *di* f., *doul* pl.	this/these
dāk m., *dīk* f., *dulāk* pl.	that/those

When used as adjectives, they follow (NB) the qualified noun, which always has the article:

Levant/Peninsula	Egypt/Sudan	
hādha sh-shakhṣ	*ash-shakhṣ da*	this person
hadhīk ar-risāla	*ar-risāla di*	that letter
mudīr hādha l-bank / *mudīr al-bank hādha*	*mudīr al-bank da*	this bank manager/ the manager of this bank (see 4/5)

9āwiz. This word, meaning 'wanting', is used in Egypt and Sudan to express the verb 'to want'. It agrees with its subject, and can be followed by a direct object (noun or pronoun), or a present tense:

'ana 9āwiz jāwabu.	I want ('am wanting') his answer.
'int 9āwizu?	Do you want it?
hiya 9āwiza tuktub al-jawāb.	She wants to write the answer.

The past sequence 'wanted' is expressed with *kunt 9āwiz(a)* (etc.), with the same structures:

shū kānū 9āwizīn minnak?	What did they want from you?

In present time-sequence, this expression is negated with *mish*; in past sequence we negate the *kān* (etc.) with *mā* as usual:

'iḥna mish 9āwizīnu.	We don't want it.
mā kunna 9āwizīnu.	We didn't want it.

20. *jumal mithālīya*

ṣār lak kam waqt tudrus al-lugha — How long have you been

l-9arabīya?– ṣār lī kam shahr bas.	studying Arabic? – Only a few months.
jābū lana l-milaff ma9 'arqām 'intāj has-sana.	They brought us the file with this year's production figures.
kam nuskha lāzima? – 'i9mal 'arba9a nusakh, 'aḥsan.	How many copies are necessary? Make four copies, that's better.
muhandisīn ash-sharika zāru l-youm 9iddat ṭuruq wa jusur qadīma fi l-balad, ḥatta yākhudhū fikra bi-khuṣūṣ al-murūr 9alayha.	The company engineers today visited a number of old roads and bridges in the town, to get an idea of the traffic on them.
kayf 'ashraḥ lu r-risāla u huwa mā yifham al-9arabī?	How do I explain the letter to him, when he doesn't understand Arabic?

21. *at-tamārīn*

1. Give the first person singular and plural of the past tense:
e.g.: kān – kunt, kunna

(a) shāf (b) ṭār (c) sa'al
(d) nām

2. Put into the past continuous tense:
e.g.: darasti l-kitāb. – kunti tudrus al-kitāb.

(a) dakhalna l-bayt. (b) wiṣilū li l-balad. (c) yūṣalū 9indna.
(d) katabu l-jawāb. (e) sakan huna.

3. Put into the abbreviated form of *hādha* (etc.):
e.g.: hādhi s-sana – has-sana

(a) kutub hādha l-mu9allim (b) hadhoul aṭ-ṭullāb (c) fī hādha l-waqt
(d) 9ind hadhoul an-nās (e) hādha l-maktab

4. Give the plural:
e.g.: kitāb – kutub

(a) bayt (b) ṭarīq (c) zamīl
(d) mara (e) bint

5. Put into the plural:
e.g.: kitāb qadīm – kutub qadīma; musāfir 9arabī – musāfirīn 9arab

(a) ṭālib shāṭir u mujtáhid (b) makhzan ikbīr (c) nuskha wāḍiḥa
(d) shakhṣ laṭīf (e) ṣandūq thaqīl

6. Put into the past tense:
e.g.: fī́ 9indak fakka? – kā́n fī 9indak fakka?

(a) 9indna waqt ikthīr. (b) kam ṭālib fī́ huna?

(c) aṭ-ṭabīb 9ind al-marīḍ. (d) 'iḥna mish mabsūṭīn.
(e) huwa moujūd al-youm.

7. Put the number with the noun:
e.g.: ṭālib (3) – thalātha ṭullāb
(a) ṭālib (2) (b) 'ouḍa (12) (c) ṣūra (6)
(d) musāfir (4) (e) shakhṣ (1)

ad-dars as-sābi9 – Lesson 7
9ala t-tilifoun – On the Telephone

1. ***al-ḥiwār***

	tilifoun	telephone
	mahamma mahāmm	task, assignment
(Peter yi9mal mawā9id 9ala t-tilifoun ma9 9iddat 'ashkhāṣ min sha'n mahammtu.)		(Peter makes appointments by telephone with a number of people for the purpose of his assignment.)
	halóu	Hello (on the telephone)
	mitayn	two hundred
	sitt mīya	six hundred
	ṣawt 'aṣwāt	voice, noise
	madrasa madāris	school
	thānawī	secondary
Peter:	halóu, huna mitayn u thalātha u 'arba9īn, sitt mīya u sab9a u sab9īn?	Hello, is this 243677?
aṣ-ṣawt:	na9am, huna l-madrasa th-thānawīya l-fannīya. tfaḍḍal.	Yes, this is the secondary technical school. Can I help you?
	siyāda	Excellency (courtesy title)
	muta'assif	sorry
	hāshim	Hashim (name)
	ghāyib	absent
	musā9id	assistant
	khabar 'akhbār	(also:) message
Peter:	siyādat al-mudīr moujūd, law samaḥt?	Is the Director in, please?
aṣ-ṣawt:	muta'assif, ad-duktur hāshim ghāyib al-youm. 'ana musā9idu. fī khabar 'ilu?	I'm sorry, Dr Hashim is absent today. I'm his assistant. Is there a message for him?
	'ashūf	I see, I look
Peter:	'ana Peter Brown, muhandis min 'ingiltra, u lāzim 'ashūf siyādatu.	I am Peter Brown, an engineer from Britain, and, and I have to see the Director.
	9ala 9ilm bi	informed of, aware of
	'asaf	regret
	yiṣīr	it becomes (here:) it will do
al-musā9id:	na9am, sayyid Brown, 'ana 9ala 9ilm bi buḥūthkum. ma9 al-'asaf al-youm mā yiṣīr,	Yes, Mr Brown, I know about your discussions. Regrettably today won't do,

	yirūḥ	he goes
	mu'támar	conference
	'imkānīya	possibility
	tshūfu	you see him
	huwa yirūḥ 'ila mu'támar kull al-youm wa mā́ fī 'imkānīya tshūfu.	he's going to a conference all day, and there's no possibility of your seeing him.
	bukra	tomorrow
	yikūn	it will be
	mumkin	possible
	youm al-'aḥad	Sunday
	yishūfak	he sees you
	sā9a	hour, clock, watch
	nuṣṣ	half
	thulth	a third
	ra'ī 'ārā'	opinion
Peter:	u bukra, yikūn mumkin?	And tomorrow, will it be possible?
al-musā9id:	khallīnī 'ashūf, youm al-'aḥad, na9am, 'aṭlub minnu 'innu yishūfak fi s-sā9a tis9a u nuṣṣ, 9ashra 'illa thulth; shū ra'yak?	Let me see, Sunday, yes, I'll ask him to see you at half-past nine or twenty to ten; what do you think?
Peter:	fikra 9aẓīma. 'akūn hunāk fi s-sā9a tis9a u nuṣṣ. ma9 as-salāma.	Excellent idea. I'll be there at half-past nine. Goodbye.
	nshūfak	we see you
al-musā9id:	nshūfak bukra yā sayyid Brown. 'alla yisallimak.	We'll see you tomorrow, Mr Brown. Goodbye.

–

aṣ-ṣawt:	na9am.	Hello
	markaz marākiz	(here:) exchange
	mushkila mashākil	problem
	'aywa	yes
	numra numar	number
Peter:	'ismaḥ lī, huna l-markaz?	Excuse me, is that the exchange ('there')?
al-markaz:	na9am yā sīdī. fī́ mushkila?	Yes, sir. Is there a problem?
Peter:	'aywa. 9imilt numra, walākin mā́ fī ṣawt 'abadan.	Yes. I have dialled a number, but there's absolutely no sound.
	'arba9 mīya	four hundred
	yumkin	perhaps
	khaṭṭ khuṭūṭ	line
	kharbān	defective
al-markaz:	'ayy numra?	What number?
Peter:	'arba9 mīya u khamst9ashr, sitt mīya u wāḥid.	415601.

al-markaz:	daqīqa, 'ashūf. yumkin al-khaṭṭ kharbān.	One minute, I'll look. Perhaps the line's out of order.
Peter:	'akūn mamnūn jiddan.	I'll be very grateful.
	shūf	look
	yā sīdī	sir
	ghayr musta9mal	not used
al-markaz:	shūf yā sīdī, hādhi n-numra ghayr musta9mala. 'i9mal numra 'ukhra: 'arba9 mīya u khamst9ashr, sitt mīya u sab9īn.	Look, sir, this number is out of use. Dial another number: 415670.
Peter:	mumtāz. 'ashkurak jiddan.	Excellent. Thank you very much.
al-markaz:	9afwan.	Don't mention it.

2. *9ibārāt*

siyāda Excellency. Used either with a possessive suffix:

siyādatak/siyādatik/siyādātkum Your Excellency/Excellencies, *siyādatu/ siyādat-ha/siyādāt-hum* His/Her Excellency, Their Excellencies, or in construct with certain titles:

siyādat al-wazīr Your/His Excellency the Minister

siyādāt as-sufarā' Your/Their Excellencies the Ambassadors. It is used more frequently than its English counterpart.

9ala 9ilm bi informed of

shū ra'yak? (etc.) ('what's your opinion?') What do you think? This can also be followed by either a preposition + noun or pronoun:

shū ra'yak 9an/ḥawl/bi khuṣūṣ al-mushkila? or a verb in the present tense:

shū ra'yak ninzil li l-balad? What do you say we go down to town? The final *-ī* of *ra'ī* changes to *-y-* before a possessive suffix beginning with a vowel:

ra'yī, ra'yak/ra'yik, ra'yu

fī khabar 'ilu/'ilha/'ilhum? Is there a message for him/her/them?

3. *mufradāt 'iḍāfīya. at-tilifoun wa z-zaman* – Telephone and time

ḍarab yuḍrub tilifoun*	to telephone	*ittiṣāl*	(telephone) call
dalīl 'adilla	directory	*tilifounīyan*	by telephone
9āmil 9ummāl (tilifoun)	telephone operator (m.)		
9āmila(t) 9āmilāt (tilifoun)	telephone operator (f.)		
maqṭū9	cut off	*'ams*	yesterday
'awwal 'ams	the day before yesterday	*ba9d bukra*	the day after tomorrow
ṣubḥ 'aṣbāḥ	morning	*ẓuhr 'aẓhār*	noon, midday
ba9d aẓ-ẓuhr	afternoon	*nahār 'anhur*	daytime
layla layālī	night	*nuṣṣ layl*	midnight

ma9 murūr az-zaman/zamān with the passage of time

* (*ḍarab yuḍrub* to strike)

NB.: In some Arab countries the person being telephoned may answer simply with *mīn?* 'Who (is it)?', expecting the caller to identify him/herself first.

an-naḥū

4. Present tense of hollow verbs

In the present tense of hollow verbs the weak middle root letter vocalises. Since this tense has no consonantal endings, the vocalised root letter is always long *ū* or *ī*.

The prefixes and endings are the same as for sound verbs, except that the prefixes *t*- and *n*- have no vowel after them.

Verbs with middle root letter *w*:

Root *sh w f, shāf yishūf* to see, look (at):

'ashūf, tshūf/tshūfī, yishūf/tshūf; nshūf, tshūfū, yishūfū
I, you, he (etc.) look(s), see(s)

In some situations the personal prefixes *t*- and *n*- may need a transition vowel:

al-youm inshūf al-wazīr.

So also other middle-*w* verbs:

zār yizūr *qāl yiqūl* *rāḥ yirūḥ* *qām yiqūm (bi)*
sāq yisūq *kān yikūn*

The present tense of *kān yikūn* is used with future meaning:

'akūn mamnūn. I'll be grateful.
'int tkūn moujūd bukra? Will you be present tomorrow?

The two anomalous *w*-verbs have *-ā-* throughout the present:

Root *n w m, nām*:

'anām, tnām/tnāmī, yinām/tnām; nnām, tnāmū, yināmū
I, you, he (etc.) sleep(s)

Root *kh w f, khāf*:

'akhāf, tkhāf/tkhāfī, yikhāf/tkhāf; nkhāf, tkhāfū, yikhāfū
I, you, he (etc.) fear(s)

Verbs with middle root letter *y*:

Root *j y b, jāb* to bring:

'ajāb, tjāb/tjābī, yijāb/tjāb; njāb, tjābū, yijābū I, you, he (etc.) bring(s)

so also:

bā9 yibī9 *ṣār yiṣīr* *ṭār yiṭīr* *zād yizīd*

In the present tense all such verbs form their negatives, and take suffixes, in the usual manner: *tshūfū? ma njībha ma9na.*

5. Imperative of hollow verbs

To form the affirmative imperative of these verbs, drop the *t*- prefix of the present:

shūf/shūfī shūfū *jīb/jībī/jībū*

etc.; the negative imperative is formed regularly, by negating the appropriate person of the present tense with *lā*:

lā tqul/lā tqūlī/lā tqūlū etc.

6. *yiṣīr*

This word, used invariably, can mean 'it is acceptable':

bukra mā yiṣīr. Tomorrow won't do/Tomorrow's no good.
khamsa danānīr, yiṣīr? Five dinars, all right?

7. *yikūn*

The future of *fī́* is *yikū́n fī*; that of *mā́ fī* is *mā́ yikūn fī*. The verb is invariable, and the stress is on the first word of each expression:

yikū́n fī/ mā́ yikūn fī — there will/won't be
yikū́n fī/ mā́ yikūn fī nās ikthīr.

In the affirmative expression *yikū́n fī 9ind-* the *fī* is optional:

yikū́n (fī) 9indna mashākil ikthīr.

8. *mumkin, lāzim, yumkin*

These are important invariable verbal forms. They are all followed by the present tense, in the appropriate person. If the subject is expressed, it usually stays with the present-tense verb:

mumkin means 'may/might/can ...?' in questions and suggestions:

mumkin 'ashūf al-mudīr? — *mumkin itqūl lī mata fāḍī?*

The negative is formed with mish:

mish mumkin huwa yidfa9 al-ḥisāb? — Can't he pay the bill?

lāzim means 'must, have to':

lāzim 'ashūfu l-youm. — *lāzim yizūr as-safīr.*
lāzim huwa yishūf, mish 'ana. — *lāzim al-mudīr yirūḥ ma9hum.*

There are two negatives for *lāzim*. Note the difference in meaning:

mish lāzim nirja9. — We mustn't go back.
mish ḍarūrī nirja9. — We needn't go back.

yumkin expresses 'may/might' in statements of probability:

qālat lī 'inn yumkin mā trūḥ. — She told me that she might ('may') not go.

Following *mumkin, lāzim* and *yumkin*, the verb *yikūn* (etc.) has present (not future) meaning:

lāzim itkūnū moujūdīn bukra. — *mumkin al-mudarā' yikūnū hunāk?*

The past time of all three expressions is made with *kān* (negative *mā́ kān*), the future with *(mā́) yikūn*, all these forms being invariable here:

(mā) kān mumkin yudkhul? — Was('nt) he able to go in?
kān lāzim 'ashraḥ lu l-mushkila. — I had to explain the problem to him.
(mā) kān yumkin yikūn kadha. — It could(n't) be so.
(mā) yikūn lāzim inzūrhum. — We shall/sha'n't have to visit them.

9. *mumkin* or *lāzim* as adjectives

When *mumkin* or *lāzim* is used as an adjective ('possible, necessary'), it agrees with its noun or pronoun. The verb (if any) is not dependent upon it, and may be in any tense:

muta'assif, al-fikra mish mumkina. — *mish mumkin 'innu wiṣil 'ams.*
fī́ 9indak al-'aghrāḍ al-lāzima?

Finally, *yumkin* is also used as an adverb ('perhaps'). As with *mumkin*, the verb (if any) can be used in any tense in this context:

yumkin 9irif, yumkin la'. — Perhaps he knew, perhaps not.

10. Numbers above 199

The higher numbers are as follows:

200	*mitayn*	300	*thalāth mīya*
400	*'arba9 mīya*	500	*khams mīya*
600	*sitt mīya*	700	*sabi9 mīya*
800	*thamān mīya*	900	*tisi9 mīya*
1000	*'alf*	2000	*'alfayn*
1 million	*malyūn*	2 million	*malyūnayn*

Compounds are made following the rules already learned.

mīya, 'alf and *malyūn* are nouns. They have a dual and a plural:

mīya, mitayn, mīyāt   *'alf, 'alfayn, 'ālāf/'ulūf*

malyūn, malyūnayn, malāyīn

The duals are used for counting, with or without a noun, in a compound or not. The plurals are used to indicate indeterminate numbers; with a pronoun we use *min* + suffix; with a noun *min* + the article:

mīyāt, 'ālāf/'ulūf, malāyīn	hundreds, thousands, millions
mīyāt minhum/minha	hundreds of them
'ulūf min an-nās	thousands of people

mīya (*mīt* immediately before a noun) is singular after another number, including 3 to 9:

'arba9 mīya   *'arba9 mīt shakhṣ*

'arba9 mīya u thalāthīn shakhṣ

but *'ālāf* and *malāyīn* are used in the plural after 3 to 9, and in the singular otherwise:

khamsat 'ālāf (ṭālib)*	*khamsīn 'alf (ṭālib)*
'arba9a malāyīn (dīnār)	*arba9īn malyūn (dīnār)*

* Numbers 3 to 9 add *-t* before *hamza* (see 6/11). Further, the unit numbers do not lose their final *-a* before *malāyīn* as they do before *mīya* and *mīt.*

Telephone and similar long serial numbers are expressed differently in different Arab countries:

446762
- *'arba9a, 'arba9a, sitta, sab9a, sitta, ithnayn*
- *'arba9a u 'arba9īn, sab9a u sittīn, ithnayn u sittīn*
- *'arba9 mīya u sitta u 'arba9īn, sabi9 mīya u thnayn u sittīn*

11. Fractions and percentages

Fractions other than 'half' have the pattern of *thulth* 'third':

*nuṣṣ**	(one/a) half	*thulth*	(one) third
rub9	quarter	*khums*	fifth
suds	sixth	*sub9*	seventh
thumn	eighth	*tus9*	ninth
9ushr	tenth		

* Some speakers use the written form *niṣf*

wāḥid is not used, but the dual is:

an-niṣfayn	both halves	*thulthayn/khumsayn*	two thirds/fifths

The plurals are mostly formed on the model *'athlāth* 'thirds':

'anṣāf, 'athlāth, 'arbā9, 'akhmās, 'asdās, 'asbā9, 'athmān, 'atsā9, 'a9shār/9ushūr

halves, thirds, quarters, fifths, ...

These are the forms used without a numerator. Not all denominators are in frequent use; the commonest are:

(thalāthat) 'arbā9	(three) quarters
('arba9at) 'akhmās	(four) fifths
(sab9at) 'athmān	(seven) eighths
(tis9at) 'ash9ār	(nine) tenths

We can also express such fractions with the cardinal numbers and *min* or *9ala*:

khamsa min/9ala sab9a	five sevenths
'iḥd9ashr min/9ala 9ishrīn	eleven twentieths
wāḥid min/9ala thn9ashr	one twelfth
ithnayn min/9ala khamst9ashr	two fifteenths

For percentages we use *fi l-mīya* or *bi l-mīya*:

sittīn fi/bi l-mīya	sixty per cent

12. Time

Time on the hour is expressed with the number 1 to 12 (1 and 2 in the feminine), preceded, optionally, by *as-sā9a*:

(as-sā9a) wāḥida, thintayn, thalātha, 'arba9a, khamsa ... ithn9ashr

We do not use the dual of *sā9a* in this context.

Minutes in the first half-hour are expressed with *u* and *nuṣṣ/rub9/thulth* or a number of minutes; for minutes not in multiples of five add *daqīqa, daqīqtayn, daqāyiq* 'minute(s)':

(as-sā9a) sitta u nuṣṣ	half-past six
(as-sā9a) sab9a u rub9	a quarter past seven
(as-sā9a) tis9a u thulth	twenty past nine
9ashra u khamsa	five past ten
tis9a u 9ashra	ten past nine
'iḥd9ashr u daqīqtayn	two minutes past eleven
ithn9ashr u saba9t9ashr daqīqa	seventeen minutes past twelve

In the second half-hour we use *'illa* and the next hour:

'arba9a 'illa khamsa u 9ishrīn	twenty-five to four
'iḥd9ashr 'illa thulth	twenty to eleven
thalātha 'illa rub9	a quarter to three
khamsa 'illa daqīqtayn	two minutes to five

In the middle third of the hour, we can also refer to the half-hour:

(as-sā9a) tis9a u nuṣṣ u khamsa	twenty-five to ten
thalātha u nuṣṣ 'illa daqīqtayn	twenty-eight minutes past four
Note also: *kam as-sā9a?/as-sā9a kam?*	What time is it?
'At' is *fī*: *fī 'ayy sā9a?*	At what time?

13. Other time expressions

Distinguish between:

waqt 'ouqāt	time in general
zaman/zamān 'azmān	time in general, period of time
mudda mudad	period
fatra fatarāt	interval, period

marra	a time, occasion
youm 'ayyām	day (24 hours)
nahār, 'anhur	period of daylight, daytime
as-sā9a thintayn	two o'clock
sā9tayn	two hours

Note also an important noun *thāniya thawān* 'a second, seconds' and important adjectives:

jārī	current	*ḥāḍir*	present
māḍī	past	*muqbil, jāī*	next

jāī is invariable in this usage; the other adjectives agree with their noun. *jārī* and *māḍī* have f. and pl. forms like *fāḍī, fāḍiya, fāḍiyīn*:

as-sana l-jāī/l-muqbila — *al-fatra l-ḥāḍira/l-jāriya*
ash-shahrayn al-māḍiyīn

14. Days of the week

The days of the week are:

(youm) al-jum9a	Friday	*(youm) as-sabt*	Saturday
al-'aḥad	Sunday	*al-ithnayn*	Monday
ath-thalātha	Tuesday	*al-'arba9a*	Wednesday
al-khamīs	Thursday		

The word *youm* is often used, especially before those names most resembling the numbers.

15. Indirect commands and requests

Direct command or request is the imperative, studied in 5/9. Indirect command or request is expressed with *'inn* and the present tense:

'aṭlub minnu 'innu yishūfak.	I'll ask him to ('ask that he') see you.
ṭalabū minnī 'innī 'adkhul.	They asked me to come in.

The indirect speech rule (4/7) applies.

16. *ghayr*

This word is used as an invariable adjective meaning 'other, different'. It precedes the qualified noun when the latter is singular:

hādhī ghayr mushkila.	That's another/a different problem.

With a plural noun, it is usually followed by *min*, and the noun is defined. In this construction, *ghayr* can be regarded as a pronoun:

shuft hāshim u ghayr min az-zumalā'.	I saw Hashim and other colleagues ('others of the colleagues').
fī ghayr min 'aṣdiqā'ī moujūdīn?	Are there other friends of mine ('others of my friends') present?

When the noun is inferred, *ghayr* itself is usually made definite:

tuṭlub ikthīr min al-ghayr.	You're asking a lot of others ('the other').
mā fī ghayru.	There's nothing else/but this/other than this.
laysh tkhāf min ghayrak?	Why are you frightened of others?

ghayr is also used as a preposition, 'except (for), besides':

ghayr hādha, shū qālū lak?	What did they tell you besides this?

Note also *u ghayru/u ghayrha* 'and so on, etc.':

al-murūr, ya9nī sayyārāt, taksīāt u ghayru	traffic, that is to say cars, taxis and so on.

Finally, an important adverbial use of *ghayr*. It negates almost any adjective or other adverb, as an alternative to *mish*:

ghayr/mish mumkin	impossible
ghayr/mish musta9mal	unused, disused
ghayr 9arabī	non-Arab, un-Arab, non-Arabic

17. Regional variations: *u, a* → *i*

In Egypt and the Levant the short vowels *u* and *a* in the vicinity of *ī, i, ay* or *y* are frequently pronounced as *i*:

yimkin, 'imkānīyi, tiltayn (= thulthayn)

18. *jumal mithālīya*

'ana mish fāḍī bukra, walākin ba9d bukra yiṣīr.	I'm not free to morrow, but the day after tomorrow's all right.
shū ra'yak inqūl ba9d bukra, bayn as-sā9a 'iḥd9ashr u 'iḥd9ashr u thulth?	Supposing we say the day after tomorrow, between eleven o'clock and twenty past?
'uḍrub lī tilifoun lamma tūṣal li l-bayt.	Give me a ring when you get home.
fī 'awwā'il as-sana l-jāī mā́ yikūn fī maḥall 'ilhum. 'aḥsan 'ilhum 'innhum yūṣalū hassa.	Early next year there will be no room for them. It's better for them to arrive now.
kān lāzim yibī9u d-dukkān u yirūḥū 9a sh-shām. mā́ kān 'ilhum ghayr 'imkānīya.	They had to sell the shop and go to Damascus. There was no other possibility for them.
al-'oulād kānū yināmū u 'ana dakhalt.	The children were sleeping as I came in.

19. *at-tamārīn*

1. Give the principal parts of the verb:

e.g.: rāḥ – rāḥ yirūḥ

(a) shāf (b) ṭalab (c) nām
(d) ṭār (e) bā9

2. Put into the present tense:

e.g.: al-walad nām. – al-walad yinām.

(a) 'ana shuftu l-youm. (b) wayn rāḥ? (c) ṣirna 'aghniyā'.
(d) bā9ū bayt-hum fī bayrūt. (e) jibtu l-fulūs ma9kum?

3. Add *kān lāzim*, changing the verb where necessary:
e.g.: 'ana shuft-hum. – kān lāzim 'ashūfhum.
(a) ruḥna li l-balad. (b) 'ashūfu bukra. (c) zāru l-mudīr.
(d) jābu l-kutub? (e) ṭalabna minnu.

4. Give the affirmative and negative imperative:
e.g.: shāf – shūf, shūfī, shūfū; lā tshūf, lā tshūfī, lā tshūfū
(a) kān (b) khāf (c) kharaj
(d) qāl (e) jāb

5. Today is Saturday. Answer the questions:
e.g.: bukra yikūn 'ayy youm? – bukra yikūn youm al-'aḥad
(a) 'ams kān 'ayy youm? (b) ba9d bukra yikūn 'ayy youm?
(c) 9indak shughl al-youm? (d) 'awwal 'ams kān 'ayy youm?
(e) kam youm fī fi l-'usbū9?

6. Report the command or request, using *ṭalabt min ...*:
e.g.: rūḥū bukra. – ṭalabt minhum 'innhum yirūḥū bukra.
(a) shūfī kitābik. (b) jīb al-fulūs ma9ak. (c) rūḥ 9a l-madrasa.
(d) 'udkhulū 9indī. (e) 'irkabu t-taksī.

7. What time is it?
e.g.: 12.20 – as-sā9a 'iḥd9ashr u thulth
(a) 4.15 (b) 6.30 (c) 10.14
(d) 11.40 (e) 1.38 (two possibilities)

8. Read the number:
e.g.: 345 – thalāth mīya u khamsa u 'arba9īn
(a) 200 (b) 4,338 (c) 369½
(d) 4,500,000 (e) 772

9. Put the number with the noun:
e.g.: sana (3) – thalātha sanawāt/snīn
(a) youm (12) (b) 'usbū9 (2) (c) shahr (6)
(d) 'imkānīya (4) (e) thāniya (45)

ad-dars ath-thāmin – Lesson 8
at-ta9līm wa t-tadrīb – Teaching and Training

1. ***al-ḥikāya wa l-ḥiwār***

munāsib	suitable, appropriate
bada	he began
ma9had ma9āhid	institute
ta9līmī	educational
(ba9d mā 9imil Peter al-mawā9id al-munāsiba, bada jawltu fī 9iddat madāris wa ma9āhid ta9līmīya fi l-balad,	(After making the appropriate appointments, Peter began his tour of some schools and educational establishments in town,
yiḥkī	he talks
ta9āwun	cooperation
ta9līm	teaching, education
9ilmī	scientific
'aḥmad	Ahmad (name)
ḥatta yiḥkī ma9 al-mudarā' ḥawl at-ta9āwun 9ala t-ta9līm al-9ilmī wa l-fannī. fa 'awwal mou9id kān 9ind mudīr al-madrasa th-thānawīya l-fannīya, ad-duktur 'aḥmad hāshim.)	so as to talk to the directors about cooperation on scientific and technical education. His first appointment was with the Director of the Secondary Technical School, Dr Ahmad Hashim.)
'aẓunn	I suppose, I presume
ḥaka	he spoke, he talked
gharaḍ 'aghrāḍ min	purpose of
'aḥmad: 'ahlan yā sayyid Brown. 'ana 'aḥmad hāshim, mudīr al-madrasa.	Welcome, Mr Brown. I'm Ahmad Hashim, Director of the school.
Peter: furṣa sa9īda, yā 'ustādh 'aḥmad. 'aẓunn 'inn mudīrī ḥaka ma9ak bi khuṣūṣ al-gharaḍ min ziyārtī?	Very pleased to meet you, Dr Hashim. I presume my director has spoken to you about the purpose of my visit?
jalas yijlis	to sit
mas'ala masāyil	matter
'aḥibb	I like
'awwalan	firstly
(yijlisū.)	(They sit.)
'aḥmad: 'ayna9am, 'ana 9ala 9ilm bi l-mas'ala. 'aḥibb 'awwalan 'ashraḥ lak shughl al-madrasa.	Yes, I know about the matter. I would like first to explain to you the work of the school.
takhaṣṣuṣ	specialisation
mukhtálif	varied, various

	kullha	all of them
	ḥaql ḥuqūl	field
	'asāsī	basic
	9indna takhaṣṣuṣāt mukhtálifa, kullha fi l-ḥuqūl al-'asāsīya.	We have various specialisations, all of them in the basic fields.
	qarayt	I (have) read
	kull	all
	'asās 'usus	basis, foundation
	9ilm 9ulūm	science
Peter:	qarayt 'inn yudrusū 9indkum 'oulād u banāt kamān.	I read that boys and girls both study here.
'aḥmad:	ṭab9an. kull aṭ-ṭullāb wa ṭ-ṭālibāt yudrusū 'usus al-9ulūm.	Of course. All the students, boys and girls, study basic sciences ('the bases of science').
	bi ṣūra naẓarīya	theoretically
	qidir yiqdar	can, to be able
	al-'ān	now
	khiyāṭa	sewing, dressmaking
	ṭibākha	cookery
	bi-ṣūra naẓarīya, yiqdaru l-banāt yudrusū 'ayy takhaṣṣuṣ. ḥatta al-'ān yudrusū l-khiyāṭa wa ṭ-ṭibākha,	Theoretically, the girls can study any specialisation. Until now they have studied dressmaking and cookery,
	yījī	he comes
	ba9ḍ	some of
	yibdū	they begin
	kahraba	electricity
	mathalan	for example
	musta9idd	ready, prepared
	walākin lamma yīji l-youm wa ba9ḍ al-banāt yibdū yudrusu l-kahraba mathalan, 'ana musta9idd, wa l-ma9had musta9idd.	but when the day comes that some girls start studying electricity for example, I'm ready and the institute's ready.
	ẓannayt	I supposed/presumed
	waḍ9 'ouḍā9	situation, position
	mā huwa/hiya	what
	sharṭ shurūṭ	condition
	dukhūl	entry
Peter:	ẓannayt 'inna l-waḍ9 kadha. fa mā hiya shurūṭ ad-dukhūl fi l-ma9had?	I presumed that was the situation. So what are the conditions of entry to the institute?
	murashshaḥ	candidate
	illī	who, that, which (relative pronoun)

	raghba fī	wish for
	dirāsa	study
'aḥmad:	al-murashshaḥ illi 9indu raghba fi d-dirāsa huna,	The candidate who wants to study here,
	mutawassiṭ	middle, medium (adjective)
	shahāda	certificate
	yibda	he begins
	mamnū9	prohibited, forbidden
	lāzim yukhruj min al-madrasa l-mutawassiṭa ma9 ash-shahāda l-munāsiba. mā yiqdar yibda huna 'illa bi hādhi sh-shahāda. hādha mamnū9.	must come from the middle school with the appropriate certificate. He can't start here without this certificate. That's forbidden.
	9ādatan	usually
	'aktharīya	majority
	yibqū	they stay
	'imma ... 'aw	either ... or
	9ādatan mā́ fī mushkila. 'aktharīyat at-talāmīdh al-mutawassiṭīn, 9ind-hum shahāda. yibqū huna 'imma thalātha 'aw 'arba9a sanawāt.	Usually there's no problem; most middle-school pupils have a certificate. They stay here for either three or four years.
	ḥāla	case
	istithnā'ī	exceptional
	lājī	refugee
	'ajnabī ajānib	foreign
	fī ḥālāt istithnā'īya, ya9nī lājī 'aw 'ajnabī u kadha,	In exceptional cases, say a refugee or a foreigner or such,
	nḥuṭṭu	we put him, we place him
	ṣaff ṣufūf	class
	ḥatta	(also conjunction:) until
	tamm	it was/has been completed
	imtiḥān	(academic) examination
	taḥḍīrī	preparatory
	yumkin inḥuṭṭu fī ṣaff khāṣṣ ḥatta tamm imtiḥān taḥḍīrī.	we might put him into a special class until a preparatory examination has been completed.
	mafhūm	understood
	yihimmna	it is important for us
	9amalī	practical
Peter:	mafhūm. yihimmna kthīr at-ta9līm al-9amalī 'ayḍan.	I see. For us practical instruction is also very important.

ma9lūm	known, (here:) of course
mashghal mashāghil	workshop
hayk	so, therefore, thus
shirib yishrab	to drink
nafs-ha	herself

'aḥmad:	ma9lūm; ash-shughl fi l-mashghal ḍarūrī ya9nī. fa hayk, khallīna nzūr ba9dayn al-mashāghil ḥatta tākhudh fikra maẓbūṭa. walākin 'awwalan, tishrab qahwa, yā sayyid Peter? 9imilat-ha zoujtī nafs-ha.	Of course; work in the workshop is essential. So let's visit the workshops later so that you get an accurate impression. But first, will you have some coffee, Mr Brown? My wife made it herself.

2. *9ibārāt*

ḥatta l-'ān until now, up to now
al-gharaḍ min the purpose of

3. *mufradāt 'iḍāfīya. at-ta9līm wa t-tadrīb*

tárbiya	education, upbringing	*ibtidā'ī*	primary (school etc.)
tarbawī	educational	*tadrīb*	training
tadrīs	instruction	*mudarris*	instructor
'ijbārī	compulsory	*ikhtiyārī*	optional
thaqāfa	culture	*muthaqqaf*	educated, cultured
qirāya	reading	*kitāba*	writing
riyāḍīyāt	mathematics	*jabr*	algebra
ḥisāb	arithmetic	*handasa*	geometry, engineering
tārīkh tawārīkh	history, date	*jughrāfīya*	geography
kímiya	chemistry	*fíziya*	physics
fann funūn	art	*riyāḍa*	sport
liḥām	welding	*sibāka*	plumbing
tabrīd	refrigeration	*takyīf al-hawa*	air conditioning
nijāra	carpentry	*mikānīk*	mechanics
taqrīr taqārīr	report	*dibloum*	diploma
kullīya	faculty, college	*mutakharrij*	graduate
kaslān kasla	lazy	*jāhil juhhal*	ignorant

at-ta9līm al-'9ālī /al-jāmi9ī higher/university education
najaḥ yinjaḥ (fi mtiḥān) to pass (an examination)
rasab yursub (fi mtiḥān) to fail (an examination)
al-lugha l-9arabīya l-fuṣḥa; al-9arabīya l-fuṣḥa; al-faṣīḥ literary Arabic
al-lugha l-9arabīya d-dārija; al-9arabīya d-dārija; ad-dārij colloquial Arabic

an-naḥū

4. Past tense of doubled verbs

In doubled verbs the middle and final root letters are identical, e.g. *ḥaṭṭ* 'to put, to place'. These two root letters stay together in both tenses. Note the diphthong

-ay- inserted before the ending of the first two persons of the past tense:

Root *ḥ ṭ ṭ*, first principal part *ḥaṭṭ* to put, to place:

ḥaṭṭayt, ḥaṭṭayt/ḥaṭṭayti, ḥaṭṭ/ḥaṭṭat; ḥaṭṭayna, ḥaṭṭaytū, ḥaṭṭū
I, you, he (etc.) put, placed

so also:

ḥabb	to like, love	*ẓann*	to suppose
marr bi/9ala	to pass by	*madd*	to extend
ḥall	to solve	*tamm*	to be completed
ḥass	to feel	*dall*	to direct, indicate
shakk fī	to doubt	*hamm*	to be important
ð̣all/ẓall	to remain		

5. Present tense of doubled verbs

The present tense prefixes of doubled verbs are the same as for the hollow verbs (i.e. *t-* and *n-* have no vowel). The middle vowel of the verb varies with the verb: *ḥaṭṭ yiḥuṭṭ*:

'aḥuṭṭ, tḥuṭṭ/tḥuṭṭī, yiḥuṭṭ/tḥuṭṭ; nḥuṭṭ, tḥuṭṭū, yiḥuṭṭū
I, you (etc.) put(s), place(s)

so also:

ḥabb yiḥibb	*ẓann yiẓunn*	*marr yimurr bi/9ala*
madd yimudd	*ḥall yiḥill*	*tamm yitimm*
ḥass yiḥiss	*dall yidill*	*shakk yishukk fī*
hamm yihimm	*ð̣all yið̣all/ẓall yiẓall*	

6. Imperative of doubled verbs

The imperative of doubled verbs is formed under the same rules as for hollow verbs:

ḥuṭṭ/ḥuṭṭī/ḥuṭṭū; lā tḥuṭṭ/lā tḥuṭṭī/lā tḥuṭṭū

7. Past tense of final-weak verbs

Final-weak verbs have a weak (i.e. unstable) final root letter, *w*, *y* or *'*. In the past tense this final root letter takes the following forms:

- before consonantal personal endings *(-t, -ti, -na, -tū)*: *-ay-*
- in the third person masculine singular *(huwa)*: *-a*
- before the personal endings *-at* and *-ū*: it disappears

Apart from the third person m. sing. *(huwa)*, the personal endings are the same as for verbs with a sound final root letter.

Root *ḥ k y*, first principal part *ḥaka* to speak, to talk:

ḥakayt, ḥakayt/ḥakayti, ḥaka/ḥakat; ḥakayna, ḥakaytū, ḥakū
I, you (etc.) spoke, talked

so also:

Root *r j w, raja*	to request	*m sh y, masha*	to walk
r m y, rama	to throw	*j r y, jara*	to flow
*n w y, nawa**	to intend	*b d ', bada*	to begin
q r ', qara	to read		

* *nawa* has also a weak *middle* root letter, but this remains stable as *w*:

nawayt, nawayt/nawayti, nawa/nawat; nawayna, nawaytū, nawū

8. Present tense of final-weak verbs

Whereas in the past tense all three final weak root letters behave similarly, in the present tense each one has its own pattern. In the present tense each final root letter vocalises into a different vowel:

- final root letter *w* vocalises to *ū*
- final root letter *y* vocalises to *ī*
- final root letter **'** vocalises to *a*

and each is dropped before the vocalic personal endings *-ī* and *-ū*.

The prefixes are the same as for the sound verbs *('a-, ti-, ni-, yi-)*.

Final *w*; *raja yirjū*:

'arjū, tirjū/tirjī, yirjū/tirjū; nirjū, tirjū, yirjū I, you (etc.) request(s)

This is the only common final-*w* verb used in this form of spoken Arabic.

Final *y*; *ḥaka yiḥkī*:

'aḥkī, tiḥkī/tiḥkī, yiḥkī/tiḥkī; niḥkī, tiḥkū, yiḥkū I, you (etc.) speak(s)/talk(s)

so also:

masha yimshī *rama yirmī* *jara yijrī* *nawa yinwī* (*w* stable)

Final *hamza*; *bada yibda*:

'abda, tibda/tibdī, yibda/tibda; nibda, tibdū, yibdū I, you (etc.) begin(s)

so also: *qara yiqra*

9. Irregular final-weak verbs

Three final-weak verbs are irregular, two of them similarly:

Root *n s y, nisī yinsa* to forget; root *biqī yibqa* to remain:

Past: *nisīt, nisīt/nisīti, nisī/nisyat; nisīna, nisītū, nisū* I, you (etc.) forgot

biqīt, biqīt/biqīti, biqī/biqyat; biqīna, biqītū, biqū I, you (etc.) remained

Pres.: *'ansa, tinsa/tinsī, yinsa/tinsa; ninsa, tinsū, yinsū* I, you (etc.) forget(s)

'abqa, tibqa/tibqī, yibqa/tibqa; nibqa, tubqū, yibqū I, you (etc.) remain(s)

Root *' j y, 'aja yījī* to come:

Past: *'ijīt, 'ijīt/'ijīti, 'aja/'ajat; 'ijīna, 'ijītū, 'ajū* I, you (etc.) came

Pres.: *'ājī, tījī/tījī, yījī/tījī; nījī, tījū, yījū* I, you (etc.) come(s)

10. Imperative of final-weak verbs

The imperative of final-weak verbs is formed under the same rules as that of sound verbs:

'iḥkī/'iḥki/'iḥkū; lā tiḥkī/lā tiḥkī/lā tiḥkū

'insa/'insī/'insū; lā tinsa/lā tinsī/lā tinsū

The affirmative imperative of *'aja yījī* is not used. Use instead:

ta9āl/ta9ālī/ta9ālū (from another root) Come

The negative imperative is regular: *lā tījī/lā tījī/lā tījū* Don't come

Final-weak verb rule: In the tenses and imperative of final-weak verbs, the weak final root letter is dropped before the vocalic endings *–ī*, *-at* and *–ū*.

11. Negatives and pronoun suffixes

Both doubled and final-weak verbs are negated as usual: tenses with *mā*, imperative with *lā*. Suffixes are added as usual. For the final-weak verbs, the object pronoun rule (4/6) is especially important:

yiqrắ he reads it *lā tinsāhum* don't forget them

12. Auxiliary verbs

An auxiliary verb expresses the will, inclination or potential to carry out the action of another ('dependent') verb: 'He *wants* to know', 'I *can* go'. The English verbs italicised here are auxiliaries. Almost any Arabic verb whose meaning permits it can be used as an auxiliary. Examples are:

qidir yiqdar	can, to be able	*nawa yinwī*	to intend
bada yibda	to begin	*nisī yinsa*	to forget
ḥabb yiḥibb	to like	*khallī-*	let
najaḥ yinjaḥ	to succeed	*samaḥ yismaḥ li*	to permit

The auxiliary can be in any form, but the following dependent verb is always in the present tense, as after *mumkin, lāzim* and *yumkin*:

mā yiqdar yiḥkī 9arabī. He can't speak Arabic.
'anwī 'arūḥ ma9kum. I intend to go with you.
'aḥibb 'ākul huna. I like eating/to eat here.
lā tinsa tījī. Don't forget to come
khallīnī/'ismaḥ lī 'ashraḥ kayf. Let me/Permit me to explain how.
bada yimshī warāī. He began walking/to walk behind me.
mā qidirt/mā kunt 'aqdar 'ashūfu. I wasn't able to see him.
mā najaḥt ti9malu? Didn't you succeed in doing it?

The present tense of *kān yikūn* has present meaning after an auxiliary verb:

khallī́ yikūn kadha. Let it be so.

13. Adjective (relative) clauses

See 6/18 for the definition of a clause. Relative clauses are those which qualify an *antecedent*, i.e. a preceding noun or pronoun.

After a *definite* antecedent, we use the relative pronoun *illī* 'who, that, which':

at-tilmīdh illī yibda yudrus 9indna, lāzim yikūn 9indu ... The pupil who begins studying with us must have ...
at-tilmīdha llī katabat hādha ... the pupil who wrote that ...

In these examples *illī* is the subject of its verb. When *illī* is the direct or prepositional object of its verb (3/16), the verb or preposition carries the appropriate pronoun suffix:

al-kitāb illī qaraytu ... the book which I read (it) ...
wayn al-fulūs illī jibt-ha? Where's the money which you brought (it)?
al-bilād illī kānū yuskunū fī́ ... the country in which they were living/ which they were living in (it) ...
an-nās illī darast 9ind-hum al-9arabī ... the people with whom I studied Arabic/whom I studied Arabic with (them) ...

After an *indefinite* antecedent, *illī* is omitted:

Subject: *shakhṣ yiqūl hādha ...* a person who says that ...

Direct object: *kitāb qaraytu ...* a book which I (have) read ...
Prep. object: *bilād kānū yuskunū fī ...* a country which they lived in ...

In English we can often omit the relative pronoun at will: 'a/the person (whom) I met yesterday ...'. The Arabic rule is different, and is not optional.

Relative rule: The relative pronoun is omitted when the antecedent is indefinite.

14. Pronoun antecedent

In a relative sentence having a *pronoun* as antecedent, the same rules apply as shown above, except that the pronoun antecedents *huwa, hiya, hum* are omitted:

illī yiḥkī kadha ma ya9raf al-9arab. He who/Whoever talks like that doesn't know the Arabs.
shuftu llī 'aja? Did you see the person who came?
illī shuft-hum ... those (whom) I saw ...

15. Interrogatives

With the interrogative *'ayy* 'what, which' the pronoun suffix on the verb or preposition is optional:

'ayy kitāb tiqra/tiqrā? What book are you reading?
khilāl 'ayy fatra sakantū hunāk? For how long ('During what period') did you live there?

But better is *mā huwa/mā hiya* plus *illī*, with obligatory suffix:

mā huwa l-kitāb illī tiqrā? 'What is the book that you are reading?'
mā hiya l-fatra llī sakantū khilālha hunāk? 'What is the period during which you lived there?'

mā here is 'what', not a negative.

Note also *mīn illī*, often preferred to *mīn*:

mīn illī kān yiḥkī? Who ('is it who') was speaking?
mīn illī ḥaka ma9u 'ams? Who ('is it who') spoke to him yesterday?
mīn illī ḥakayt ma9u 'ams? Whom did you speak to ('Who is it that you spoke to') yesterday?

If you know French, you will recognise a close parallel for the first two examples:
Qui *est-ce qui* parlait? Qui *est-ce qui* lui a parlé hier?

16. *nafs*

The noun *nafs 'anfus* 'self' has three important uses:

- in the m. sing., in a definite construct: 'the same':
  nafs ash-shī the same thing *nafs an-nās* the same people
- reflexive or emphatic pronoun with suffix: '-self':
  9imilat-ha zoujtī nafs-ha. My wife made it herself.
  badū yishukkū fī 'anfus-hum. They began to doubt themselves.
- in its original meaning as a noun: 'self':
  i9timād 9ala n-nafs self-confidence

17. *ba9ḍ*

This word has three important uses:

- invariable reciprocal pronoun: 'each other':
  mashū 9an ba9ḍ They walked away from each other.
- reciprocal pronoun or noun: 'each other', repeated; first with a suffix, next with the article:
  mā 9irifū ba9ḍhum al-ba9ḍ. They didn't know each other.
- in a definite construct or with a possessive suffix: 'some (of)':
  ba9ḍ waqtak some of your time *ba9ḍ al-waqt* some of the time
  ba9ḍhum mā 'ajū 'abadan. Some of them did not come at all.

18. *kull*

Three important uses:

- as a definite noun: 'the whole':
  al-kull the whole (lot)
- before an indefinite singular noun: 'every, each':
  kull shī everything *kull wāḥid wāḥid bas!* Only one each!
- in a definite construct or with a possessive suffix: 'all (of)':
  kull al-'oulād all the children *kullu/kullha* all of it

19. *jamī9*

This is a synonym for *kull* 'all' in the plural only:

kull/jamī9 an-nās all the people *li l-jamī9* for all/everybody

20. Ordinal numbers

Ordinal numbers show a position in a sequence. The ordinal numbers 1st to 10th are as follows. All but the first two are derived on the model *thālith* 'third':

1st	*'awwal, 'ūla, 'awwalīn*	2nd	*thānī, thāniya, thāniyīn*
3rd	*thālith*	4th	*rābi9*
5th	*khāmis*	6th	*sādis*
7th	*sābi9*	8th	*thāmin*
9th	*tāsi9*	10th	*9āshir*

They are used in two ways:

- m. sing. form in indefinite construct with the qualified noun. The construct is, however, *definite* in meaning:
  rābi9 wāḥid the fourth one *thālith marra* the third time
- as an adjective, following and agreeing with the noun:
  as-sana l-'ūla the first year *ash-shahr as-sādis* the sixth month

thānī also means 'other':

thānī marra the other/another time; the second time
(fī) shī thānī? (Is there) anything else?

Note also *thānī youm* 'the next day'.

21. For ordinal numbers above 'tenth' we use the cardinal number following the noun, or after a noun such as *raqm*:

ad-dars (raqm) 'iḥd9ashr *al-youm al-9ishrīn*

22. *mithl*

Note the structure

mithl hādha sh-shakhṣ	a person like this/that; such a person
mithl hādhi l-buyūt	houses like this; such houses

Distinguish between:

preposition: *mithl*	like
conjunction: *mithl mā*	as
huwa mish mithlak.	He isn't like you
9imil mithl mā 9imilt 'ana.	He did as I did.

23. Activities, instruments, places

Some activities have typical patterns for profession, person, instrument and place:

Root		Profession, model *nijāra*		Person, model *najjār*	
n j r	carve:	*nijāra*	carpentry	*najjār*	carpenter
ṭ b kh	cook:	*ṭibākha*	cooking	*ṭabbākh*	cook
kh y ṭ	sew:	*khiyāṭa*	sewing	*khayyāṭ(a)*	tailor/dressmaker
s b k	smelt:	*sibāka*	smelting, plumbing	*sabbāk*	smelter, plumber
l ḥ m	weld:	*liḥām* (no final *-a*)	welding	*laḥḥām*	welder, butcher
n q sh	paint:	*niqāsha*	painting	*naqqāsh*	painter
		Instrument, models *miftāḥ mafātīḥ, minshafa manāshif*			
f t ḥ	open:	*miftāḥ mafātīḥ*		key	
n sh r	saw:	*minshār manāshīr*		saw	
s m r	nail:	*mismār masāmīr*		nail	
q y s	measure:	*miqyās maqāyīs*		measure(ment)	
n sh f	dry:	*minshafa manāshif*		towel	
		Place, models *maktab/maktaba makātib*			
k t b	write:	*maktab makātib*		office	
		maktaba makātib		library, bookshop	
ṭ b kh	cook:	*maṭbakh maṭābikh*		kitchen	
9 h d	know:	*ma9had ma9āhid*		institute	
sh gh l	work:	*mashghal mashāghil*		workshop	
9 m l	make:	*ma9mal ma9āmil*		workshop, laboratory	
ṭ 9 m	taste:	*maṭ9am maṭā9im*		restaurant	
d r s	study:	*madrasa madāris*		school	
ṣ n 9	fabricate:	*maṣna9 maṣāni9*		factory	
ḥ ṭ ṭ	put:	*maḥaṭṭa* (sound plural)		station	
ḥ k m	judge:	*maḥkama maḥākim*		law-court	
ṭ y r	fly:	*maṭār* (sound plural)		airport	
f r q	split:	*mafraq mafāriq*		crossroad	
n z l	reside:	*manzil manāzil*		residence	

24. Regional variations: Iraq, Gulf, North-west Africa

In Iraq and north-west Africa *q* is often pronounced *g*:

qal → *gāl* *qism* → *gism* *mafraq* → *mafrag*

An *a* or *ā* next to the *g* in such words may be velarised (see Pronunciation):
gạ̄l, mafrạg.

In Iraq and some parts of the Gulf, *k* next to a front or middle vowel *(i, ī, a, ā)* sounds in some words like ch in English 'church', a sound not represented in the Arabic alphabet. We can transcribe it *ch*:

kam ⟶ *cham* | *kayf ḥālik?* ⟶ *kayf ḥālich?*

Iraq and the Gulf have a special word for 'how', *shloun*:

shlounach/shlounich/shlounkum? = *kayfak/kayfik/kayfkum?*

Iraqis pronounce *ch* and *p* (the latter also as in English) for certain words borrowed from their Turkish and Persian neighbours:

chāī = shāī | *pouṣṭa = bouṣṭa*

25. ***jumal mithālīya***

at-ta9āwun ma9 mithl hal-'askhāṣ ghayr mumkin. mā yisma9ū 'abadan.	Cooperation with such people is impossible. They never listen.
mīn illī 'aja yiḥkī ma9kum?	Who (was it who) came to talk to you?
mīn illī 'ijīt tiḥkī ma9u?	Who did you come to talk to?
mā hiya l-fatra llī kānat tijrī khilālha l-buḥūth bayn al-ḥukūmtayn?	How long did the talks between the two governments go on ('flow')?
hiya mara muthaqqafa jiddan tiḥkī thalātha 'aw 'arba9a lughāt.	She is a very cultured woman who speaks three or four languages.
kānu l-mudarrisīn yiḥkū ma9 ba9ḍ bi khuṣūṣ tawārīkh al-imtiḥānāt.	The instructors were talking together about the examination dates.

26. ***at-tamārīn***

1. Give the principal parts of the verb:
e.g.: nawa – nawa yinwī

(a) bada (b) shakk (c) 'aja
(d) nisī (e) ẓann

2. Give the affirmative and negative imperative of the verb:
e.g.: ḥaka – 'iḥkī, 'iḥkī, 'iḥkū; lā tiḥkī, lā tiḥkī, lā tiḥkū

(a) dall (b) biqī (c) 'aja
(d) ḥaṭṭ (e) ḍaḥak

3. Put into the present tense:
e.g.: dallayna – ndill

(a) nisyat (b) marr (c) mā 'ajū
(d) shū nawaytū? (e) bada yiqra

4. Rephrase, using *qidir yiqdar* in the present tense:
e.g.: 'ana mā qarayt al-kitāb. – mā 'aqdar 'aqra l-kitāb.
(a) mashayna ḥatta l-mafraq. (b) 'int tiḥkī 9arabī?
(c) dallū lana ṭ-ṭarīq. (d) mā yibda l-youm. (e) 'asma9ak kwayyis.

5. Give the ordinal number, in the masculine and feminine:
e.g.: thalātha – thālith, thālitha
(a) ithnayn (b) wāḥid (c) thamāniya
(d) 'arba9a

6. Make the two sentences into one relative sentence:
e.g.: hay al-kitāb. 'akhadhtu minnu. – hay al-kitāb illī 'akhadhtu minnu.
hay kitāb. 'akhadhtu minnu. – hay kitāb'akhadhtu minnu.
(a) ta9raf al-mu9allim? katab hādha t-taqrīr.
(b) fī thānī su'āl. nisīt 'as'alu.
(c) 'ishraḥ lī l-mushkila. kuntū tiḥkū ḥawlha.
(d) wayn al-milaff? ḥaṭṭaytu 'amāmak yā 'akhūī.
(e) bā9ū bayt. sakanū fī min 9ishrīn sana.

ad-dars at-tāsi9 – Lesson 9
fi l-maṭ9am – In the Restaurant

1. ***al-ḥiwār***

(Dr Sharif has invited Peter out to dinner in a restautant.)

(9ala ṭarīq al-maṭ9am)		(On the way to the restaurant)
	twaṣṣilna	you take us
	'a9arrifak	I acquaint you with
Peter:	li wayn twaṣṣilna?	Where are you taking us?
fu'ād:	'a9arrifak 'aḥsan maṭ9am fi l-balad.	I'm going to introduce you to the best restaurant in town.
	jaddadū́	they renewed/ renovated it
	tamāman	completely
	jaddadū́ tamāman.	They have completely renovated it.

–

(fi l-maṭ9am)		(In the restaurant)
	zayy	like
	līsta	menu
fu'ād:	tfaḍḍal yā Peter, zayy baytak. hay al-līsta. shū tu'mur?	Here you are, Peter, make yourself at home. Here's the menu. What will you order?
	'afaḍḍil	I prefer
	mazza	maza (hors d'œuvres)
	dajāj	chicken
	musakhkhan	cooked in spices
	ruzz	rice
Peter:	'afaḍḍil 'abda bi l-mazza, u ba9dayn dajāj musakhkhan bi r-ruzz.	I prefer to begin with the maza,and then spiced chicken with rice.
fu'ād:	mumtāz. u shū tishrab yā Peter?	Excellent. And what are you drinking, Peter?
	bīra	beer
	rashīd	Rashid (name)
	gārsoun	waiter
	shouraba	soup
	banadūra	tomatoes
Peter:	bīra min faḍlak.	Beer, please
fu'ād:	yā rashīd ...	Rashid ...
(yīji l-gārsoun rashīd.)		(Rashid, the waiter, comes.)
rashīd:	na9am, yā duktur.	Yes, doctor.
fu'ād:	jīb lana min faḍlak wāḥid māzza u 'ilay shourabat banadūra, u ba9dayn	Please bring us one maza, and for me a tomato soup, and then

	ṣaḥn suḥūn	plate
	samak	fish
	maqlī	fried
	khuḍra	vegetables
	makhlūṭ	mixed
	min sha'n ḍayfī dajāj musakhkhan bi r-ruzz. 'ana 'ākhudh ṣaḥn samak maqlī bi khuḍra makhlūṭa.	for my guest spiced chicken with rice. I'll have a plate of fried fish with mixed vegetables.
	kās ku'ūs	(drinking) glass
	9araq	arrack
	ma9rūf	(here:) kindness
	ḥāḍir	ready, (here:) certainly
	9ala ṭūl	immediately
	u wāḥid bīra, fa 'ilayy, kās 9araq, 'i9mal ma9rūf.	And one beer, and for me a glass of arrack, if you would be so kind.
rashīd:	ḥāḍir. 9ala ṭūl.	Certainly. Right away.

–

Peter:	yā fu'ād, hal-maṭ9am mnīḥ jiddan.	Fuad, this restaurant is very good.
	'arkhaṣ	cheaper
	dhakar yudhkur	to mention
	lā 'aḥad	nobody
	yiqaddim	he offers, he serves
	'akl	food
	ḥilwiyāt	sweets, dessert
	fākiha fawākih	fruit
	tamr	dates
fu'ād:	ṣaḥīḥ. wa 'arkhaṣ min ghayru, kama dhakart lak. lā 'aḥad yiqaddim 'akl 'aḥsan. fa min sha'n al-ḥilwiyāt, shū tḥibb tu'mur? tḥibb fawākih?	Right. And it's cheaper than others, as I mentioned to you. And for dessert, what would you like to order? Would you like some fruit?
Peter:	'aḥibb at-tamr, min faḍlak.	I would like some dates, please.
fu'ād:	u qahwa ba9dayn?	And coffee afterwards?
	maẓbūṭa	(here:) Turkish coffee with medium sugar
	wala shī	nothing
	salāmtak	('your safety') no, thank you
	tuffāḥa	apple
Peter:	ma9lūm. 'afaḍḍilha maẓbūṭa, law samaḥt.	Of course. I prefer it medium sweet, please.
fu'ād:	shī thānī?	Anything else?

Peter:	wala shī, salāmtak.	Nothing, thank you.
fu'ād:	yā rashīd, 'i9mal ma9rūf u jīb lana tamr u tuffāḥa, u thnayn maẓbūṭa kamān.	Rashid, please bring us some dates and an apple, and also two medium sweet coffees.

–

(quddām 'utayl Peter) (in front of Peter's hotel)

	jārī, jāriya, jārīyīn	(also:) flowing
	quduman	ahead
fu'ād:	fa kayf shughlak, yā Peter? lissa jārī quduman?	So how's your work, Peter? Still moving ahead?
	ṣirt	(here:) I began
	ḥill ḥulūl	solution
	al-wāḥid	one (indef. pronoun)
	yijarrib	he tries
Peter:	bi ṣūra 9āmma, māshī kwayyis. ṣirt 'awjid kam mushkila, walākin nūjid ḥill 'ilha. lāzim al-wāḥid yijarrib.	In general, it's going well. I've begun to encounter a few problems, but we'll find a solution for them. One must try.
	ta9bān	tired
	'ashadd	stronger
	jadīdan	recently
	'idha	(here:) if
fu'ād:	walākin 'int mish ta9bān shwayy? fī ra'yī, kunt 'ashadd lamma shuftak jadīdan. 'uḍrub lī tilifoun 9ala ṭūl 'idha mish kwayyis. lā tinsa.	But aren't you a bit tired? I think you were stronger when I saw you recently. Ring me at once if you're not well. Don't forget.
	sharraftūna	('you honoured us') it was a great pleasure
	tsharrafna	('we were honoured') the pleasure's mine/ours
	qalbīyan	heartily, cordially
	tiṣbiḥ 9ala khayr	('awake in wellbeing') good night
	wa 'int bi khayr	('and you in wellbeing') good night
	sharraftūna yā Peter.	It was a great pleasure, Peter.
Peter:	tsharrafna yā fu'ād, wa 'ashkurak qalbīyan 9ala hal-masa. tiṣbiḥ 9ala khayr.	The pleasure's mine, Fuad, and thank you very much for this evening. Good night.
fu'ād:	wa 'int bi khayr, yā Peter.	Good night to you, Peter.

2. *9ibārāt*

zayy baytak/baytik/baytkum ('Like your house') Make yourself/yourselves at home.

'i9mal/'i9malī/'i9malū ma9rūf ('Do a kindness') Be so good as to ...

salāmtak/salāmtik/salāmitkum ('(I wish only) your safety') No, thank you. A polite way of refusing an offer.

jārī/jāriya quduman going ('flowing') ahead, proceeding

sharraftūna ('You honoured us') It was a great pleasure. Said by the host on parting, always in the plural. The guest's response is:

tsharrafna ('We were honoured') The pleasure's mine/ours. Also always plural.

tiṣbiḥ/tiṣbiḥī/tiṣbiḥū 9ala khayr ('Awake in wellbeing') Good night. Said by either the person leaving or the person staying. Response:

wa 'int/'inti/'intū bi khayr ('And you in wellbeing') Good night.

3. *mufradāt 'iḍāfīya. al-'akl wa l-mashrūbāt*

sufra sufar	dining table	*sikkīn sakākīn*	knife
shouka shuwak	fork	*mal9aqa malā9iq*	spoon
finjān fanājīn	cup	*khubz*	bread
miliḥ	salt	*filfil*	pepper
sukkar	sugar	*sukhn*	hot
zibda	butter	*jibna*	cheese
murabba	jam	*qinnīna qanānī*	bottle
nbīdh	wine	*9aṣīr*	juice
*ṃay**	water	*ṃay* ma9danī*	mineral water
thalj	ice	*būza/būẓa*	ice-cream
ḥalīb	milk	*maslūq*	boiled
laḥm	meat	*muḥammar*	roast(ed)
sāda	(invariable) plain	*ṭāza*	(invariable) fresh
ḥilu, f. *ḥilwa*	sweet	*mubahhar*	spicy
jou9ān, jou9a, jiyā9	hungry	*9aṭshān, 9aṭsha, 9iṭash*	thirsty

qahwa: *sāda* no sugar; *maẓbūṭ(a)* medium sweet; *ḥilwa* very sweet

* The word *ṃay (ṃạy)* has the only velarised *m* in spoken Arabic.

an-naḥū

4. Ordering food and drink

When ordering food and drink we use the masculine of 'one' and 'two'; we do not use the dual or plural of the noun:

wāḥid bīra *ithnayn qahwa* *thalātha shāī*

Also, with the exception of *ḥilwa*, the feminine adjective is little used:

'arba9a (qahwa) maẓbūṭ(a) four medium-sweet coffees

5. Collective nouns

Many living creatures, natural substances and artisanal products are designated with a singular collective noun, usually masc. with no plural, for the whole species or group:

samak	fish	*baqar*	cattle	*dajāj*	chickens
khayl	horses	*'ibil*	camels	*dhubāb*	flies
tuffāḥ	apples	*9inab*	grapes	*tīn*	figs

tamr	dates	*mouz*	bananas	*burtuqān*	oranges
bayḍ	eggs	*shajar*	trees	*ḥabb*	grains, seeds
ṭoub	bricks	*balāṭ*	tiles	*waraq*	foliage, paper

6. Most such words have a (fem.) unit noun with final *-a*, pl. sometimes sound, sometimes broken:

samaka 'asmāk	*baqara* cow
dajāja	*dhubāba dhubbān*
9inaba 'a9nāb	*tīna*
mouza	*tamra tumur*
tuffāḥa	*shajara*
burtuqāna	*bayḍa*

7. Some of the vegetables and fruits have an alternative unit noun formed with *ḥabba* (pl. *ḥubūb*) in construct. The plural of this form is little used:

ḥabbat tuffāḥ *ḥabbat 9inab/mouz/tin/tamr*

8. Two important animals have unit nouns different from their collectives:

ḥiṣān ḥuṣn	horse	*jamal jimāl*	camel

Otherwise, most mammals have only a unit noun:

kharūf khirāf	sheep	*kalb kilāb*	dog
bissa bisās	cat		
and note: *ḥayawān*	animal	*ḥashara*	insect
9aṣfūr 9aṣāfīr	bird		

9. Increased forms of verbs

The verbs studied so far are all in the so-called Form I or 'unincreased' form of the root. There exist also 'increased' forms, II to X, for all the verb classes. No root has all forms; some even lack Form I. Only existing forms may be used; do not derive your own. Form II is examined below.

10. Verbs of Form II

Verbs of Form II are built on the models:

- Verbs with sound final root letter: *ḥaḍḍar yiḥaḍḍir* to prepare
- Final-weak verbs: *rabba yirabbī* to educate, bring up

Note: The middle root letter doubles, and the vowels are invariable.

Form II verbs can take a direct object. Some have a causative meaning, i.e. they cause their object to perform the action of the verb. Personal endings and prefixes are as for Form I hollow verbs, except that the final-weak verb rule (8/10) applies to final-weak roots.

Sound final root letter (sound, initial-*w*, hollow, doubled classes):

Root *ḥ ḍ r*, Form II *ḥaḍḍar yiḥaḍḍir* to prepare:

Past: *ḥaḍḍart, ḥaḍḍart/ḥaḍḍarti, ḥaḍḍar/ḥaḍḍarat;*
ḥaḍḍarna, ḥaḍḍartū, ḥaḍḍarū I, you, he (etc.) prepared

Pres.: *'aḥaḍḍir, tḥaḍḍir/tḥaḍḍirī, yiḥaḍḍir/tḥaḍḍir;*
nḥaḍḍir, tḥaḍḍirū, yiḥaḍḍirū I, you, he (etc.) prepare(s)

so also many verbs, e.g.:

faḍḍal yifaḍḍil	to prefer	*9allam yi9allim**	to teach
nazzal yinazzil	to take down	*darras yidarris*	to instruct
qaddam yiqaddim	to offer/serve/present	*9arraf yi9arrif**	to acquaint
dhakkar yidhakkir bi	to remind	*ṣaddaq yiṣaddiq*	to believe
*kallaf yikallif**	to cost	*dabbar yidabbir*	to arrange
kassar yikassir	to shatter	*sharraf yisharrif*	to honour
jarrab yijarrib	to try	*ṣanna9 yiṣanni9*	to industrialise
khallaṣ yikhalliṣ	to finish	*sakkar yisakkir*	to shut
'akhkhar yi'akhkhir	to delay		
'aththar yi'aththir 9ala	to affect, have an effect on		
qarrar yiqarrir	to decide, to report	*jaddad yijaddid*	to renew, renovate

* Some of the verbs (e.g. those marked * above) take two direct objects:

t9allim al-'oulād al-ḥisāb.	She teaches the children arithmetic.
9arraft-hum al-mudīr.	I acquainted them with the director.
kallafnī fulūs ikthīr.	It cost me a lot of money.

In initial-*w* and hollow roots the weak root letter stabilises, i.e. keeps its consonantal form *w* or *y*:

waṣṣal yiwaṣṣil	to convey	*wazzaf yiwazzif*	to recruit
waqqaf yiwaqqif	to stop	*kawwan yikawwin*	to constitute
mawwal yimawwil	to finance	*zawwar yizawwir*	to show round
ṣawwar yiṣawwir	to depict, photograph		
ghayyar yighayyir	to change		

Final-weak

Root *r b w*, Form II *rabba yirabbī* to educate, bring up:

Past: *rabbayt, rabbayt/rabbayti, rabba/rabbat; rabbayna, rabbaytū, rabbū*
I, you, he (etc.) educated, brought up

Pres.: *'arabbī, trabbī/trabbī, yirabbī/trabbī; nrabbī, trabbū, yirabbū*
I, you, he (etc.) educate(s), bring(s) up

so also: *khalla yikhallī* to let, release *samma yisammī* to call, name

The final-weak verb rule (8/10) applies.

11. Imperative of Form II

The imperative of Form II is made in the same manner as for Form I hollow verbs:

jarrib/jarribi/jarribū	try	*khallī/khallī/khallū**	let, let go
lā tsakkir/lā tsakkirī/lā tsakkirū		don't shut	

* see 5/11 and 8/12.

12. *ṣār* as auxiliary verb

ṣār, in the past tense only, can mean 'to begin' as an auxiliary verb (see 8/12), mainly in involuntary or unwelcome situations:

ṣirt 'awjid mashākil.	I've begun to encounter problems.
ṣār yikassir al-'athāth.	He began breaking up the furniture.

13. Comparison of adjectives and adverbs

The comparative degree ('bigger') of simple (i.e. triliteral, basic form) adjectives and adverbs is made on the following models:

Root	Model	Comparative
Sound (three stable consonants)	*kbīr*	*'akbar*
Initial-*w*	*wāḍiḥ*	*'awḍaḥ*
Hollow (middle *w* or *y*)	*ṭawīl*	*'aṭwal*
Doubled (identical last two consonants)	*jadīd*	*'ajadd*
Final-weak (final *w* or *y*)	*qawī* strong	*'aqwa*

kbīr, 'akbar big(ger) *kthīr, 'akthar* much, more
ṣghīr, 'aṣghar small(er) *rkhīṣ, 'arkhaṣ* cheap(er), (more) cheaply
sarī9, 'asra9 fast(er) *qaṣīr, 'aqṣar* short(er)
wāsi9, 'awsa9 wide(r), (more) widely
wāḍiḥ, 'awḍaḥ clear(er), (more) clearly
ṭawīl, 'aṭwal long(er) *jadīd, 'ajadd* new(er)
qalīl, 'aqall little, less *khafīf, 'akhaff* light(er), (more) lightly
shadīd, 'ashadd (more) severe(ly), (more) vigorous(ly)
qawī 'aqwiyā', 'aqwa strong(er) *9ālī, 'a9la* high(er)

(*ṭayyib* forms a comparative *'aṭyab*, but *'aḥsan*, derived from a different root and learned in Lesson 4/1, is more often used for 'better'. *kwayyis* does not form a comparative.)

Comparative adjectives in this form are invariable for gender and number:

walad 'aqwa *bint 'aṣghar* *kutub 'arkhaṣ* *nās 'akbar*

For the comparatives of derived adjectives and adverbs (e.g. *nisba*, derivatives beginning with *mu-*), put *'akthar* after the adjective or adverb. The adjective agrees:

kitāb 'asāsī 'akthar a more basic book
nās muthaqqafīn 'akthar more cultured/educated people

Comparative adjectives, in whatever form, are always indefinite.

Decreasing comparison of all adjectives and adverbs is made with *'aqall*. The adjective agrees:

nās kuramā' 'aqall less generous people

'than' is *min* as a preposition (i.e. before a noun or pronoun) or *mimma* as a conjunction (i.e. before a clause, see 6/18):

huwa 'aqwa minnī. He is stronger than I/me.
'ana nisīt 'akthar mimma huwa ya9raf. I have forgotten more than he knows.

14. Superlative of adjectives

The superlative ('biggest') of adjectives is expressed by using the comparative in the same way as the ordinal numbers, i.e. either:

'akbar bayt the biggest house *'aṣghar walad* the smallest boy

or by making both noun and comparative adjective definite:

al-bayt al-'akbar
at-talāmīdh mujtahidīn al-'akthar/al-'aqall the most/least hardworking students

The latter is the only possibility with derived adjectives.

Note also: *'akbar al-'oulād* the biggest (one) of the children

A few important adjectives have a feminine superlative on the model *kbīr* → *kubra*, used whenever the adjective has to agree:

m. *'akbar*, f. *kubra* *'aṣghar, ṣughra* *'aḥsan, ḥusna*
'aṭwal, ṭūla *'a9la, 9ulya*

So: *'aṣghar bint* but: *al-bint aṣ-ṣughra*
ṣughra l-banāt *hiya ṣ-ṣughra fi ṣ-ṣaff*

The superlative of *adverbs* is studied in Lesson 11.

15. Equal comparison

Equal comparison ('as ... as') is expressed with *mithl*:

huwa ghanī mithlak. *huwa mish shāṭir mithilha.*

'as ... as possible' is expressed with the comparative, thus:

bi 'arkhaṣ mā yumkin as cheap(ly) as possible
bi 'asra9 mā yumkin as fast/soon as possible

Note also: *fī 'aqrab/'asra9 waqt mumkin* ('in the nearest/fastest time possible') as soon as possible

16. Indefinite pronouns

The indefinite pronouns are best summarised in tables. All are masc. singular. Examine:

Pronoun as subject of the verb

	some	any	none
animate	*al-wāḥid* one *fī́ 'aḥad* [1] someone	*'ayy wāḥid* anyone *'ayy shakhṣ* anyone	*mā́ fī shakhṣ* [1] no one *lā 'aḥad* [1] no one *mā́ fī 'aḥad* [1] no one
inan.	*fī́ shī* [1] something	*'ayy shī* anything	*mā́ fī shī* [1] nothing

Pronoun as object of the verb, or governed by a preposition

	some	any	none
animate	*al-wāḥid* one *shakhṣ* someone *'aḥad* someone	*'ayy wāḥid* anyone *'ayy shakhṣ* anyone	*'ayy wāḥid* [2] no one *'ayy shakhṣ* [2] no one *'aḥad* [2] no one
inan.	*shī* something	*'ayy shī* anything	*shī* [2] nothing

Note:

- Two of the words (*shakhṣ* and *shī*) used as pronouns are in fact singular nouns already known to us. *'aḥad* is a variant of *wāḥid*:

'ayy shakhṣ/'ayy wāḥid yiqdar yizawwirhum. Anyone can show them round.
waṣṣalt 'ayy shakhṣ/'ayy wāḥid li l-balad? Did you take anyone to town?
ta9raf shakhṣ yiqdar yidabbiru? Do you know someone who can fix it?
'akhadhū shī ma9hum. They took something with them.
dabbarū 'ayy shī? Did they arrange anything?
kán fī shī? Was there something?
lāzim al-wāḥid yijarrib. One must try.

- *Negation:* for the negative subject pronouns, it is the *pronoun* which is negated; for the object pronouns, it is the *verb*:
  lā 'aḥad yuqaddim mithl hādha l-'akl. No one ('There is no one who') serves food like this.
  mish lāzim yishukkū fī 'ayy shī. They must doubt nothing/mustn't doubt anything.
- The structures with *fí/má fī* are made past as shown in 6/7 and future as shown in 7/7. NB stress.
- The pronouns marked [1] are followed by an indefinite relative construction (see 8/13) with an *affirmative* verb. In other words, Arabic says 'There is no one who/nothing which does' rather than 'No one/nothing (does)'. Note also that, unlike *huwa, hiya* and *hum* (8/14), the indefinite pronouns shown above are not omitted when appearing as an antecedent:
  fí 'aḥad yuṭlub yiḥkī ma9ak. Someone ('There is someone who') is asking to talk to ('with') you.
  fí shī yihimmna kthīr fī hādhi l-mas'ala. Something ('There is something which') greatly interests us in this matter.
- The pronouns marked [2] are preceded by a negative verb. In other words, Arabic says 'not ... anything' rather than 'nothing'.
  mā shufna 'aḥad. We saw no one ('didn't see anyone').
  mā qarrarū shī. They decided nothing ('didn't decide anything').
  (mā) fī 9indna raghba fī shī thānī. We would like something/wouldn't like anything else.

17. Lastly, two shortened replies; *lā 'aḥad* 'nobody' and *wala shī* 'nothing':
mīn illī kunt tiḥkī ma9u? – lā 'aḥad. Who were you talking to? – Nobody.
kam kallafak? – wala shī. What did it cost you? – Nothing.

18. ***jumal mithālīya***

'aḥsan 'imkānīya, hiya 'inna njaddid al-maṣna9 kullu. The best possibility is that we renovate the whole factory.
ṣaddiqnī, yikallifak 'akthar bi kthīr kadha. Believe me, it costs you much more this way.
'afaḍḍil 'innak itwaṣṣilhum 'int, yā 'akhī. I prefer that you take them.
lāzim nu'mur kamān ṭoub; tibqa 9indna kam ṭouba bas. We need to order more bricks; we have only a few bricks left.

19. *at-tamārīn*

1. Give the principal parts of the verb:
e.g.: qarrar – qarrar yiqarrir
(a) faḍḍal (b) waqqaf (c) ḥabb
(d) rabba (e) ṣaddaq

2. Give the unit noun, with alternatives where possible:
e.g.: tamr – tamra, ḥabbat tamr
(a) baqar (b) tuffāḥ (c) balāṭ
(d) mouz (e) bayḍ

3. Give the comparative and superlative, m. sing., of each adjective:
e.g.: kbīr – 'akbar, al-'akbar
(a) ṭawīl (b) kwayyis (c) ḍarūrī
(d) rkhīṣ (e) muthaqqaf

4. Connect as one relative sentence:
e.g.: 'a9raf an-najjār. jaddadu. – 'a9raf an-najjār illī jaddadu.
(a) huwa mu9allim. dāyiman yishraḥ kwayyis.
(b) mā qidir yiwaqqif as-sayyāra. kān yisūqha.
(c) kān yisūq sayyāra. mā qidir yiwaqqifha.
(d) 9allamtu shī. mish lāzim yinsá 'abadan.
(e) qarrarū mas'ala. t-himmna kullna.

5. Re-express, putting the superlative adjective after the noun:
e.g.: 'akbar bināya – al-bināya l-kubra
'aḥsan ḥiṣān – al-ḥiṣān al-'aḥsan
(a) 'aṭwal kitāb (b) 'ajmal sayyāra (c) 'a9la shajara
(d) 'akram 'ab (e) 'akram 'umm

ad-dars al-9āshir – Lesson 10
mashrū9 jadīd – A New Project

1. ***al-ḥiwār***

(Peter is discussing a new project with Abdarrahman.)

	mudhakkira	memorandum
	mashrū9 mashārī9	project
9abdarraḥman:	ṭayyib yā Peter. qarayt mudhakkirtak, u khallīna nshūf mashrū9ak al-jadīd. tfaḍḍal.	Right, Peter. I've read your memo., so ('and') let's look at your new project. Go ahead.
	taḥsīn	improvement
	9alāqa	relation(ship)
	munaẓẓama	organisation (body)
	9āmil	working
Peter:	shukran. al-gharaḍ min hādha l-mashrū9 huwa taḥsīn 9alāqātna ma9 ghayr min al-munaẓẓamāt al-9āmila fi l-qiṭā9 al-khāṣṣ.	Thank you. The purpose of this project is the improvement of our relations with other organisations working in the private sector.
	ṣan9/ṣun9	manufacture, manufacturing
	taswīq	marketing
9abdarraḥman:	fi ṣ-ṣun9 bas, 'aw fi t-taswīq kamān?	In manufacturing only, or in marketing as well?
	wujha	direction, aspect
	tajmī9	collection
	ma9lūmāt (pl.)	information
	di9āya	advertising
Peter:	fī kull wujha, ya9nī fī tajmī9 al-ma9lūmāt, wa d-di9āya,	In every aspect, I mean in information gathering, advertising,
	khidma	service
	tawẓīf	recruitment
	wa l-khidmāt, wa t-tawẓīf u kadha.	services, recruitment and so on.
	shāmil	comprehensive
	bi l-'asas	basically
9abdarraḥman:	mashrū9 shāmil ya9nī. bi l-'asās gharaḍu mafhūm.	You mean a comprehensive project. Basically its purpose is clear ('understood').
	rāyiḥīn n'assis	we shall establish
	mukawwan min	composed of, consisting of
	mumaththil	representative

Peter:	rāyiḥīn n'assis lajna ṣghīra mukawwana min mumaththilīn al-qiṭā9	We shall establish a small committee consisting of representatives of the sector
	mandūb	delegate
	ghurfat tijāra	Chamber of Commerce
	tarwīj	promotion
	u mandūb ghurfat at-tijāra, tkūn mas'ūla 9an dirāsat u tarwīj al-mashrū9.	and a delegate from the Chamber of Commerce, which will be responsible for studying and promoting ('the study and promotion of') the project.
	tamwīl	financing
	kayfīya	mode, manner
	mu9ayyan	certain, definite
	'ījābī	positive
9abdarraḥman:	wa t-tamwīl?	And the financing?
Peter:	bi khuṣūṣ kayfīyat at-tamwīl lāzim inshūf taqrīr al-lajna. 'akthar mish mu9ayyan fī l-waqt al-ḥāḍir. 'inshalla yikūn taqrīrha 'ījābī.	As to the mode of financing, we'll have to see the committee's report. Nothing more is definite at present ('the present time'). Hopefully its report will be positive.
	ṣadar yuṣdur	be issued, appear
	shubāṭ	February
	ta9līmāt	(also:) instructions
9abdarraḥman:	mata yuṣdur?	When does it come out?
Peter:	fī 'awā'il shubāṭ.	In early February
9abdarraḥman:	waqt qaṣīr yā 'akhī.	(That's) a short time.
Peter:	ma9lūm. al-lajna lāzim itkūn 9ind-ha ta9līmāt wāḍiḥa jiddan.	Of course. The committee will have to have very clear instructions.

2. *9ibārāt*

bi l-'asās basically
ghurfat (at-)tijāra Chamber of Commerce
fī l-waqt al-ḥāḍir at present

3. *mufradāt 'iḍāfīya. al-'ijtimā9āt*

9ādī	ordinary	*ghayr 9ādī*	extraordinary
jadwal 'a9māl	agenda	*majāl al-baḥth*	terms of reference
ra'īs ru'asā'	chairman	*maḥḍar ijtimā9*	minutes
baḥath yibḥath	to discuss	*musawwada*	draft
wathīqa wathā'iq	document	*tawqī9*	signature
qarār	resolution	*táwṣiya*	recommendation

'aqallīya minority *taṣwīt* voting *ḥaḍar yuḥḍur* to attend

an-naḥū

4. Participles

Participles are verbal adjectives, e.g. 'writing, reading'. Arabic has two kinds of participles:

- active participles, describing or identifying the subject of the verb,
- passive participles, describing or identifying the object (direct or prepositional) of the verb.

Participles are formed regularly. Most have sound f. and pl. forms (but see paragraph 9 below).

5. Participles of Form I

Participles of Form I are made on the following models (the m. sing. is shown):

Verb class	Model verb	Active participle		Passive participle	
Sound (initial ') (middle ')	*katab* *'akal* *sa'al*	*kātib* *'ākil* *sāyil*	writing eating asking	*maktūb* *ma'kūl* *mas'ūl*	written eaten ('asked') responsible
Initial-*w*	*wajad*	*wājid*	finding	*moujūd*	('found') present
Hollow *(-w-)* *(-y-)*	*shāf* *bā9*	*shāyif* *bāyi9*	seeing selling	*mashūf* *mabī9*	seen sold
Doubled	*ḥaṭṭ*	*ḥāṭiṭ*	putting	*maḥṭūṭ*	put
Final-weak *(-w)* *(-y)* *(-')*	*raja* *ḥaka* *qara*	*rājī* *ḥākī* *qārī*	requesting speaking reading	*marjū* *maḥkī* *maqrū*	requested spoken read

Other examples, from verbs already known:

Class	Verb	Active participle		Passive participle	
Sound	*9irif*	*9ārif*	knowing	*ma9rūf*	known
	ṭalab	*ṭālib*	requesting	*maṭlūb*	requested
	'amar	*'āmir*	ordering	*ma'mūr*	ordered
Initial-*w*	*wiṣil*	*wāṣil*	arriving		
Hollow	*rāḥ*	*rāyiḥ*	going		
	khāf	*khāyif*	fearing	*makhūf*	feared
Doubled	*ḥass*	*ḥāsis*	sensing	*maḥsūs*	sensed, tangible
	shakk	*shākik*	doubting	*mashkūk fī*	doubted
Final-wk.*	*masha*	*māshī*	walking		
	bada	*bādī*	beginning	*mabdū*	begun
	jara	*jārī*	current ('flowing')		

As adjectives, the participles with a sound final root letter have a sound feminine and plural: *9ārif, 9ārifa, 9ārifīn; ma9rūf, ma9rūfa, ma9rūfīn.*

* Final-weak active participles follow the pattern of *fāḍī, fāḍiya, fāḍiyīn.*

6. Participles of Form II

The participles of all increased forms are made from the principal parts; the active participle from the second principal part and the passive participle from the first. Feminines and plurals are made as for Form I. Form II participles (m. sing.) are built as follows, for all classes:

- Active: replace the *yi-* prefix of the second principal part with *mu-,*
- Passive: prefix *mu-* to the first principal part.

ḥaḍḍar:	*muḥaḍḍir*	preparing	*muḥaḍḍar*	prepared
9allam:	*mu9allim*	teaching	*mu9allam*	taught
qaddam:	*muqaddim*	offering, presenting	*muqaddam*	offered, presented
kawwan:	*mukawwin*	constituting	*mukawwan*	constituted
rabba:	*murabbī*	educating	*murabba*	educated

7. Negation of participles

Since participles are adjectives, they are negated with *mish* or *ghayr,* not with *mā*:

mish/ghayr moujūd	not present
mish 9ārif	not knowing
mish/ghayr muḥaḍḍar	unprepared

8. Agreement of participles

An active participle agrees with the noun which it qualifies:

al-munaẓẓamāt al-9āmila fi l-qiṭā9 the organisations working in the sector

A passive participle qualifying a noun which is a direct object agrees with that noun:

at-taqārīr al-muqaddama 'ams	the reports presented yesterday
nās ma9rūfīn	well-known people

but a passive participle qualifying a noun which is a prepositional object is always made masculine singular; the gender and number of the noun are shown by a pronoun suffix attached to the preposition:

ma9lūmāt mashkūk fīha doubtful information ('information doubted about it')

al-buḥūth al-maqūm bīha	the discussions undertaken
al-maṭlūb minhum	those (of whom it is) requested

The final-weak participles have the following patterns for agreement:

m. s.:	active *murabbī*	passive *murabba*
an. pl.:	active *murabbiyīn*	passive *murabbayīn*
f.s./inan. pl.:	active *murábbiya*	passive *murabba*

9. Participles used as nouns

Like other adjectives, many participles serve as nouns, often with a special meaning; most active Form I active participles then have a broken plural:

I	*kātib kuttāb*	clerk (m.)	*kātiba*	clerk (f.)
	ṭālib ṭullāb	student (m.)	*ṭāliba*	student (f.)

	rākib rukkāb	passenger	*9āmil 9ummāl*	workman
	maktūb makātīb	letter	*9āmil 9awāmil*	factor
	ma9lūmāt (pl.)	information		
II	*mu9allim*	teacher (m.)	*mu9allima*	teacher (f.)
	mudarris	instructor	*muwaẓẓaf*	employee, clerk
	muqarrir	reporter	*murabbī*	educator

10. Verbal nouns

Verbal nouns denote the activity or result of the verb:

ma9rifa	knowledge	from:	*9irif ya9rif*	Form I
ta9līm	teaching	from:	*9allam yi9allim*	Form II

Form I verbal nouns are irregular; those of Forms II to X are derived regularly. Not every theoretically possible verbal noun is in use.

11. Verbal nouns of Form I

Many patterns exist for Form I verbal nouns. Some verbs have alternative patterns:

katab:	*kitāba*	writing
qara:	*qirāya*	reading
dakhal:	*dukhūl*	entry*
kharaj:	*khurūj*	exit*

* the action, not the place, which would be *madkhal* or *makhraj*.

ṭalab:	*ṭalab, maṭlab maṭālib*	request
daras:	*dirāsa*	study
najaḥ:	*najāḥ*	success
9irif:	*ma9rifa ma9ārif*	knowledge
baḥath:	*baḥth buḥūth*	discussion
dafa9:	*daf9 madfū9āt*	payment
riji9:	*rujū9*	return
nizil:	*nuzūl*	descent
sa'al:	*su'āl 'as'ila*	question
	mas'ala masāyil	matter
'amar:	*'amr 'awāmir*	order, command
	'amr 'umūr	matter, affair
'akhadh:	*'akhdh*	taking, acceptance
'akal:	*'akl*	food
wiṣil:	*wuṣūl*	arrival
bā9:	*bay9 buyū9*	sale
qāl:	*qawl 'aqwāl*	saying, utterance
kān:	*kawn*	existence
zād:	*ziyāda*	increase
qām bi:	*qiyām bi*	undertaking
khāf:	*khouf*	fear
nām:	*noum*	sleep
marr:	*murūr*	traffic
ḥall:	*ḥill ḥulūl*	solution

ḥaka:	*ḥikāya*	narrative
shakk:	*shakk shukūk*	doubt

12. Verbal nouns of Form II

Form II verbal nouns (shown here in the singular) are made on the following patterns:

Class	Model	Verbal Noun	
Sound	*ḥaḍḍar* *'akhkhar*	*taḥḍīr* *ta'khīr*	preparation delay
Initial-*w*	*waẓẓaf*	*tawẓīf*	recruitment
Hollow	*mawwal* *ghayyar*	*tamwīl* *taghyīr*	financing change
Doubled	*qarrar*	*taqrīr*	decision, report
Final-weak	*rabba*	*tárbiya*	education

Plurals are mostly sound, some broken. Some verbal nouns have alternative plurals with different meanings, e.g.:

taqrīr taqrīrāt decision *taqrīr taqārīr* report

More Form II verbal nouns:

darras:	*tadrīs*	instruction
kallaf:	*taklīf takālīf*	cost
9allam:	*ta9līm*	teaching; *ta9līmāt* instructions
qadam:	*taqdīm*	offer
sharraf:	*tashrīf*	honouring; *tashrīfāt* protocol
dabbar:	*tadbīr*	arrangement
	tadbīr tadābīr	measure, move
jarrab:	*tajrīb*	test
	tajriba tajārib	attempt, experiment
ṣanna9:	*taṣnī9*	industrialisation
waqqaf:	*tawqīf*	detention, parking
kawwan:	*takwīn*	formation
ṣawwar:	*taṣwīr*	depiction, photography
jaddad:	*tajdīd*	renewal, renovation

13. Use of verbal nouns

When a verbal noun has a direct object, the two terms are put into construct:

dirāsat al-lughāt	studying languages/the study of languages/language-study
tajmī9 ma9lūmāt	information-gathering

See 6/18. Often a preposition + verbal noun is used instead of a conjunction + verb. Compare

ḥatta yudrusu l-'arqām ('so that they study the figures')

with *li dirāsat al-'arqām* ('for the study of the figures')

– both best expressed in English as 'in order to study the figures'. So also:

khilāl taḥḍīr al-mizānīya	while preparing the budget ('during the preparation of the budget')
qabl baḥthha	before it is discussed ('before its discussion')

14. *rāyiḥ, rāḥ-*

rāyiḥ is the active participle of *rāḥ yirūḥ*. It can be used as an auxiliary (see 8/12) to form a future tense. The participle agrees with the subject of the verb:

rāyiḥ(a) 'aqaddim al-mīzānīya.	I'm (m./f.) going to present the budget.
rāyiḥīn inzawwirhum al-ma9had bukra.	We'll show them round the institute tomorrow.

We also use the short invariable form *rāḥ-* prefixed to the verb:

rāḥ'aqaddimha.	I'll present it.
rāḥinzawwirhum.	We'll show them round.

Like all participles, *rāyiḥ* (etc.) and *rāḥ-* are negated with *mish*:

mish rāḥ-/mish rāyiḥ 'addabiru.	I'm not going to arrange it.

This future tense is common in statements of intention.

15. Calendar

The months of the international (solar) calendar have two sets of names; one set is used in Asia, the other in Africa:

	Asia	**Africa**
Jan. Feb.	*kānūn (ath-)thānī, shubāṭ*	*yanāyir, fibrāyir*
Mar. Apr.	*'ādhār, nīsān*	*māris, 'abrīl*
May June	*'ayār, ḥazīrān*	*māyū, yūniyū*
July Aug.	*tammūz, 'āb*	*yūliyū, 'aghusṭus*
Sept. Oct.	*'aylūl, tishrīn (al-)'awwal*	*sibtambir, 'oktōbir*
Nov. Dec.	*tishrīn (ath)-thānī, kānūn (al-)'awwal*	*novimbir, disimbir*

For certain purposes the Muslim (lunar) calendar is in use. It is 354 or 355 days long, and dates from the flight of the Prophet Muhammad from Mecca to Medina in AD 622. The months, for reference, are:

1	*muḥarram*	2	*ṣafar*
3	*rabī9 al-'awwal*	4	*rabī9 ath-thānī*
5	*jumāda l-'ūla*	6	*jumāda l-'ukhra*
7	*rajab*	8	*sha9bān*
9	*ramaḍān*	10	*shawwāl*
11	*dhu l-qa9da*	12	*dhu l-ḥijja*

We use *'awwal* for the first, and cardinal numbers for other dates. 'On' is *fī*:

(fī) 'awwal/ 9ishrīn tammūz	(on) 1st/20th July
(fī) khamst9ashr muḥarram	(on) 15th Muharram

The year is expressed as follows:

(fī) sanat 'alf u tisi9 mīya u tis9a u sittīn (mīlādī)	(in) (AD) 1999
bayn santayn'alfayn u 'alfayn u tis9a	between 2000 and 2009
(fī) sanat 'alf u 'arba9 mīya u saba9t9ashr (hijrī)	(in) (AH) 1417

(AH = Anno Hegiræ, Year of the Flight)

Additional vocabulary for the calendar, including public holidays:

taqwīm taqāwīm	calendar	*moulūd an-nabī*	Prophet's Birthday
sana hijrīya	Muslim year, AH	*sana mīlādīya*	international year, AD
rabī9	spring	*kharīf*	autumn
shita	winter	*9īd 'a9yād*	festival, holiday
'ijāza	leave, holiday	*(9īd al-)milād*	Christmas

ra's as-sana New Year's Day (either calendar)
faṣl fuṣūl, mousim mawāsim season
al-9īd al-kabīr/9īd al-'aḍḥa* feast at the end of the pilgrimage
al-9īd aṣ-ṣaghīr/9īd al-fitr* feast at the end of fasting
*9īd al-fiṣiḥ/al-9īd al-kabīr** Easter
* *kabīr, ṣaghīr*: the written pronunciation is used.

16. *jumal mithālīya*

al-ma9had mukawwan min tis9a mudarrisīn u mitayn u sittīn tilmīdh.	The institute consists of nine instructors and 260 pupils.
takālīf ad-di9āya mish maktūba fī musawwadat al-mīzānīya l-'ūla.	Advertising costs are not shown ('written') in the first draft of the budget.
ma9rifat al-muḥāsabāt ḍarūrīya li fahm hādha t-taqrīr.	A knowledge of accounts is essential in order to understand this report.
rāyiḥīn yiqaddimū taqrīrhum fī 'awākhir 'ayyār 'aw 'awā'il ḥazīrān.	They will present their report in late May or early June.

17. *at-tamārīn*

1. Give the masculine singular of both participles of each verb:
e.g.: 9irif – 9ārif ma9rūf
(a) bā9 (b) jaddad (c) ṣaddaq
(d) katab (e) dabbar

2. Give the principal parts of the verb from which the participle is derived:
e.g.: mu9allim – 9allam yi9allim
(a) shāyif (b) muwaqqaf (c) maṭlūb
(d) mukawwan (e) muḥaḍḍir

3. Give the verbal noun:
e.g.: 9allam – ta9līm; fihim – fahm
(a) qara (b) rabba (c) ḥaḍḍar
(d) daras (e) 9irif

4. Give the principal parts of the verb from which the verbal noun is derived:
e.g.: ta9līm – 9allam yi9allim
(a) dirāsa (b) tadrīs (c) kawn
(d) takwīn (e) tadbīr

5. Make the participle fit the noun:
e.g.: al-lugha l-(maḥkī) – al-lugha l-maḥkīya
taghyīrāt (maqūm bi) – taghyīrāt maqūm bīha
(a) bi sabab al-'arqām al-(mashkūk fī)
(b) musawwadāt (muḥaḍḍar) 'ams
(c) al-'umūr al-(maktūb bi khuṣūṣ)
(d) min an-nās as-(sākin) huna
(e) li s-sikritayra l-(mas'ūl) 9an hādha sh-shughl

6 Give the date (international calendar) in both systems:
e.g.: 12/3/1996 – ithn9ashr māris/'ādhār, 'alf u tisi9 mīya u sitta u tis9īn
(a) 1/1/1998 (b) 15/6/2010 (c) 25/10/1880
(d) 11/8/1996 (e) 23/2/1978

ad-dars 'iḥd9āshr – Lesson 11
ziyārat maṣna9 – Visit to a Factory

1. *al-ḥikāya wa l-ḥiwār*

(NB: In this dialogue one speaker uses the Levantine form of spoken Arabic, examples of which are shown underlined in the vocabulary.)

tanfīdh	execution, fulfilment
kān yurīd	he wanted
yiqābil	he meets

(min sha'n tanfīdh mahammtu fī ḥaql at-tadrīb al-fannī Peter kān yurīd yiqābil kam mumaththil aṣ-ṣinā9a l-khafīfa.

(For the execution of his assignment in the field of technical training, Peter wanted to meet some representatives of light industry.

kānū nasharū	they had published
nashar yunshur	to publish
jarīda jarāyid	newspaper
maqāla	(press) article
ḍarūra	necessity

qabl wuṣūlu fi l-balad kānū nasharū fi l-jarīda maqāla ḥawl ḍarūrat han-nou9 min at-ta9āwun.

Before his arrival in the country they had published in the newspaper an article about the need for this sort of cooperation.

sā9adu	he helped him
'akhbaru bi	he informed him
lāqa	he found
yināsibhum	it suits them
ẓabṭ	accuracy, exactness

zamīlu 9abdarraḥmān sā9adu fī hādha l-gharaḍ. 'akhbaru bi 'innu lāqa khārij al-balad maṣna9 yināsibhum bi ẓ-ẓabṭ.)

His colleague Abdarrahman helped him in this aim. He told him that he had found, outside the town, a factory which exactly suited them.)

mushrif	supervisor
fāyiz ḥasanayn	Faiz Hassanein (name)

(fī qism al-'intāj li l-maṣna9. yiḥki l-mushrif fāyiz ḥasanayn.)

(In the factory's Production Division. The supervisor, Faiz Hassanein, is talking.)

'ism 'a'sām (underlined)	= *qism 'aqsām*
'intāzh (underlined)	= *'intāj*
'abl (underlined)	= *qabl*
warsha	workshop, shop floor

fāyiz: 'ahlan fī 'ism al-'intāzh, yā sayyid Peter. tfaḍḍal. 'abl mā

Welcome to Production Division, Mr Brown. Before we

	nzūr warshat al-'intāzh,	visit the production floor,
	<u>yimkin</u>	= *yumkin*
	<u>biddak</u>	you want
	iyyāha	her, it, them
	khāṣṣatan	especially
	<u>hāda</u>	= *hādha*
	yimkin fí 9indak 'as'ila biddak tis'alni yyāha, khāṣṣatan ḥawl hāda l-'ism?	perhaps you have some questions you wish to ask me, especially about this Division?
	<u>'iẓa</u>	= *'idha*
	<u>baẓharrib</u>	= *'ajarrib*
	<u>'aẓhāwibak</u>	= *'ajāwibak* I answer you
	'iza fí, bazharrib 'azhāwibak.	If there are, I'll try to answer you.
	qiṭ9a qiṭa9	part, component
	tintijū	you produce
Peter:	'ayy nou9 min al-qiṭa9 tintijū?	What kinds of parts do you produce?
	ḥadd ḥudūd	limit
	<u>bnintiẓh</u>	= *nintij* we produce
	<u>'iṭ9a 'iṭa9</u>	= *qiṭ9a qiṭa9*
	'unbūb 'anābīb	pipe, tube
	<u>blāstīkīyi</u>	= *blāstīkīya* plastic
	<u>shān</u>	= *sha'n*
	muwāṣalāt (pl.)	communications
	sūq 'aswāq (f.)	market
fāyiz:	shāyif, al-maṣna9 jadīd u lissa ṣghīr, li ḥadd al-'ān ibnintizh 'iṭa9 basiṭa bas, zayy 'anābīb u 'iṭa9 iblāstīkīyi min shān al-kahraba wa l-muwāṣalāt.	You see, the factory is new and still small; up to now we have produced only simple parts, like pipes and plastic components for electricity and communications.
Peter:	9āẓīm. hādha huwa l-ḥaql illī yihimmna qabl al-kull. fa kull 'intājkum min sha'n as-sūq ad-dākhilīya?	Splendid. This is the field which interests us above all. So all your production is for the internal market?
	istibdāl	substitution
	mustawrad	import (goods imported)
fāyiz:	tamāman. mā bnintizh 'illa min shān istibdāl al-mustawradāt.	Totally. We produce only for import substitution.
	law	if
	tawsī9	broadening, expansion
	wāfaqt 9ala	you agreed to
Peter:	wa 'aẓunn, yā sayyid fāyiz,	And I presume, Mr Hassanein,

	law kān fí furṣa li tamwīl tawsī9, fa 'int wāfaqt 9aláy?	if there were a chance of financing an expansion, you would agree to it?
	<u>*btis'al*</u>	= *tis'al*
	<u>*bi ṣūra rasmīyi*</u>	= *bi ṣūra rasmīya* officially
	<u>*la'ayna*</u>	= *laqayna* we found
	'iḍāfī	additional
	<u>*zhiddan*</u>	= *jiddan*
	<u>*mālīyi*</u>	= *mālīya*
	shakhṣīyan	personally
	fihim yifham	to understand
(fāyiz yiḍḥak.)		(Faiz laughs.)
fāyiz:	btis'al as-su'āl bi ṣūra rasmīyi? ma9lūm, law la'ayna tamwīl 'iḍāfī, fa kunt mabsūṭ zhiddan. walākin bi khuṣūs hāda, lāzim tiḥkī ma9 mudīrna li l-mālīyi shakhṣīyan. 'ana l-'intāzh bas, fāhim?	Are you asking officially? Of course, if we were to find additional financing, I would be very pleased. But on that, you must talk to our Finance Manager personally. I'm only Production, you understand?
	9ala kull ḥāl	in any case
	ḥatta u law	even if
	'a9ṭūna	they gave us
	<u>*mīzānīyi*</u>	= *mīzānīya*
	<u>*sū' 'aswā'*</u>	= *sūq 'aswāq*
	<u>*dākhilīyi*</u>	= *dākhilīya*
	9ala kull ḥāl, ḥatta u law 'a9ṭūna mīzānīyi 'awsa9, fa 'iḥna faḍḍalna tawsī9 min shān as-sū' ad-dākhilīyi. 'iza mā biddak tis'al ghayr su'āl, khallīna nshūf al-'ān al-warsha ...	In any case, even if they gave us a wider budget, we would favour expansion for the internal market. If you don't want to ask any other questions ('question'), let's look at the shop floor now ...

2. *9ibārāt*

li ḥadd al-'ān ('to the limit of now') up to now
9ala kull ḥāl in any case

3. *mufradāt 'iḍāfīya. aṣ-ṣinā9a wa l-iqtiṣād*

iqtiṣād	economy	*iqtiṣādī*	economic
ṣaddar yiṣaddir	to export	*ṣādirāt* (pl.)	exports
ra's māl	capital	*ḍarība ḍarāyib*	tax
istithmār	investment	*mādda mawādd*	material (noun)
mādda tijārīya	commodity	*si9r 'as9ār*	price
mādda 'awwalīya	raw material	*thaman 'athmān*	cost
ṣāḥib al-9amal, pl. *'aṣḥāb al-9amal*			employer

niqābat al-9ummāl	trade union
ṣana9 yiṣna9, verbal noun *ṣan9/ṣun9*	to manufacture
qiṭā9 al-khidmāt	services sector
rabiḥ yirbaḥ min, verbal noun *ribḥ 'arbāḥ*	to (make) profit from
khasir yikhsar, verbal noun *khasāra khasāyir*	to lose, make a loss

an-naḥū

4. Verbs of Form III

Verbs of Form III follow the pattern of Form II, except that instead of a doubled middle root letter they have long *-ā-* after the initial root letter, and their verbal nouns are different. To begin with, examine their principal parts. Models are:

- All classes except final-weak: *kātab yikātib* to write to, correspond with
- Final-weak: *lāqa yilāqī* to find, encounter

Most verbs of Form III have a direct object for the person affected. Compare two verbs with the same root:

Form I	*katab yuktub*	to write
Form III	*kātab yikātib*	to write to, correspond with

but there are some exceptions which add no special meaning.

Sound final radical (sound, initial-*w*, hollow; doubled do not occur):
Root *k t b, kātab yikātib* to write to:

Past: *kātabt, kātabt/kātabti, kātab/kātabat; kātabna, kātabtū, kātabū*
I (etc.) wrote to

Pres.:*'akātib, tkātib/tkātibī, yikātib/tkātib; nkātib, tkātibū, yikātibū*
I (etc.) write(s) to

so also:

sā9ad yisā9id	to help	*9āmal yi9āmil*	to treat
nāsab yināsib	to suit	*qābal yiqābil*	to meet
sāfar yisāfir	to travel	*qātal yiqātil*	to fight
ghādar yighādir	to leave	*wāfaq yiwāfiq 9ala*	to agree on/to
jāwab yijāwib	to reply to	*ḥāwal yiḥāwil*	to try
ḥāwar yiḥāwir	to dialogue with		

Final-weak: Root *l q y, lāqa yilāqī* to find, encounter:

Past: *lāqayt, lāqayt/lāqayti, lāqa/lāqat; lāqayna, lāqaytū, lāqū* I (etc.) found

Pres.:*'alāqī, tlāqī/tlāqī, yilāqī/tlāqī; nlāqī, tlāqū, yilāqū* I (etc.) find(s)

so also: *nāda yinādī* to call, to summon

The final-weak verb rule (8/10) applies.

5. Imperative of Form III

Follow the rules for Form II:

sā9id/sā9idī/sā9idū; lā tsā9id/lā tsā9idī/lā tsā9idū

6. Verbs of Form IV

Verbs of Form IV are made on the following models:

- Sound: *'arsal yursil* to send; *'antaj yintij* to produce
- Initial-*w*: *'awqaf yūqif* to stop
- Hollow: *'aḍāf yuḍīf* to add, to annex

- Doubled: *'ahamm yihimm* to concern, be important to
- Final-weak: *'ansha yunshī* to construct, create

The written forms of the present prefixes (*'u-, tu-, yu-, nu-*) are used in some verbs; in others the spoken forms *'a-, ti-, yi-, ni-*. Form IV is the only increased form to have this alternative vowelling, which is confined to the personal prefix. Most Form IV verbs have a direct object for the person affected, if they have a special meaning at all.

Sound: Root *r s l, 'arsal yursil* to send:

Past: *'arsalt, 'arsalt/'arsalti, 'arsal/'arsalat; 'arsalna, 'arsaltū, 'arsalū* I (etc.) sent

Pres.: *'ursil, tursil/tursilī, yursil/tursil; nursil, tursilū, yursilū* I (etc.) send(s)

so also:

'akhraj yukhrij	to publicise, expel	*'antaj yintij*	to produce
'az9aj yiz9ij	to disturb	*'a9jab yi9jib*	to please
'akhbar yukhbir bi	to inform	*'anjaz yinjiz*	to implement, accomplish

e.g.: *'akhbarna bi 'innu yījī.* He informed us that he was coming.
yi9jibnī kthīr. I like it ('It pleases me') a lot.

Initial-w: Root *w q f, 'awqaf yūqif* to stop:

Past: *'awqaft, 'awqaft/'awqafti, 'awqaf/'awqafat; 'awqafna, 'awqaftū, 'awqafū*

Pres.: *'ūqif, tūqif/tūqifī, yūqif/tūqif; nūqif, tūqifū, yūqifū*

so also:

'awjab yūjib 9ala to impose (e.g. a tax) on
'awshak yūshik 'inn to be on the point of (doing)
'awshak yūshik 9ala to be close to, almost to

e.g.: *'awshakt 'inn 'aqūl lak ...* I was on the point of telling you ...
'awshakū 9ala l-mughādara. They were close to departure.

Hollow: Root *ḍ y f, 'aḍāf yuḍīf* to add, to annex

Past; middle root letter *w* or *y* becomes *-a-* or *-ā-* (hollow verb rule, 6/4):
'aḍaft, 'aḍaft/'aḍafti, 'aḍāf/'aḍāfat; 'aḍafna, 'aḍaftū, 'aḍāfū

Present; middle root letter *w* or *y* becomes *-ī-* throughout the tense:
'uḍīf, tuḍīf/tuḍīfī, yuḍīf/tuḍīf; nuḍīf, tuḍīfū, yuḍīfū

so also:

'afād yufīd	to benefit	*'arād yurīd*	to want
'adhā9 yudhī9	to broadcast		

With *'arād yurīd* the continuous past is preferred to the past, which is little used:
'urīd 'asā9idak. I want to help you.
kunt 'urīd 'innak itsā9idnī. I wanted you to ('that you') help me.

Doubled: Root *h m m, 'ahamm yihimm* to concern, be important to:

Past; the identical root letters separate before a consonantal personal ending, and come together elsewhere:
'ahmamt, 'ahmamt/'ahmamti, 'ahamm/'ahammat;
'ahmamna, ahmamtū, 'ahammū

Present; identical to Form I *hamm yihimm*:
'ahimm, thimm/thimmī, yihimm/thimm; nhimm, thimmū, yihimmū

so also: *'aṣarr yiṣirr 9ala* to persist in, insist on

Final-weak: Root *n sh ', 'ansha yunshī* to construct, create:

Past; similar to Form I; the final-weak verb rule (8/10) applies:

'anshayt, 'anshayt/'anshayti, 'ansha/'anshat; 'anshayna, 'anshaytū, 'anshū

Pres.; the final-weak verb rule applies:

'unshī, tunshī/tunshī, yunshī/tunshī; nunshī, tunshū, yunshū

so also: root *l q y, 'alqa yulqī*: *'alqa khiṭāb* to deliver a speech

al-wazīr 'alqa khiṭāb ḥawl mashākilna l-iqtiṣādīya.

Root *9 ṭ w, 'a9ṭa ya9ṭī* to give to (irregular vowelling, see below)

This last verb is important. It takes two direct objects:

'a9ṭānī kitābu. (not *['a9ṭa lī ...]*) He gave me his book.

It has the syllable *a9ṭ* throughout (Pronunciation, paragraph 6):

Past: *'a9ṭayt, 'a9ṭayt/'a9ṭati, 'a9ṭa/'a9ṭat; 'a9ṭayna, 'a9ṭaytū, 'a9ṭū*

Pres.: *'a9ṭī, ta9ṭī/ta9ṭī, ya9ṭī/ta9ṭī; na9ṭī, ta9ṭū, ya9ṭū*

7. Imperative of Form IV

To make the imperative of Form IV, replace the *tu-, ti-, t-, ta-, tū-* of the present prefix as follows:

- *tu-, ti-, t-, ta-*: replace with *'a-*
  'akhrij/'akhrijī/'akhrijū *'a9ṭī/'a9ṭī/'a9ṭū*
- *tū-*: replace with *'aw-*
  'awqif/'awqifī/'awqifū

The negative imperative is regularly formed:

lā tiz9ij/lā tiz9ijī/lā tiz9ijū *lā ta9ṭī/lā ta9ṭī/lā ta9ṭū*
lā tūqif/lā tūqifī/lā tūqifū

8. Participles of Forms III and IV

Form III and IV participles are formed as follows:

- *Active,* Forms III and IV: replace the *yi-/yu-/ya-* prefix of the second principal part with *mu-*; replace *yū-* in Form IV with *mū-*.
- *Passive:* Form III (rare): prefix *mu-* to the first principal part.
  Form IV, all classes except initial-*w*: replace the *'a-* prefix of the first principal part with *mu-*.
  Form IV, initial-*w*: replace the first syllable *'aw-* of the first principal part with *mū-*.

			Active		Passive	
III	*kātab:*		*mukātib*	correspondent		
	sā9ad:		*musā9id*	assistant		
	nāsab:		*munāsib*	suitable		
	sāfar:		*musāfir*	traveller		
	qābal:		*muqābil*	opposite, remuneration		
	qātal:		*muqātil*	fighter		
		f.	*muqātila*	fighter aircraft		
	wāfaq:		*muwāfiq 9ala*	agreeing on/to	*muwāfaq 9ala*	agreed on/to
IV	*'arsal:*		*mursil*	sender	*mursal*	sent
	'az9aj:		*muz9ij*	annoying		
		pl.	*muz9ijāt*	discomforts		
	'a9jab:		*mu9jib*	admirable	*mu9jab*	admirer

'awjab:	*mūjib*	obligating	*mūjab*	obligatory
'ahamm:	*muhimm*	important		
'antaj:	*muntij*	productive		
'aṣarr:	*muṣirr*	persistent, resolute		
'afād:	*mufīd*	useful		
'adhā9:	*mudhī9*	announcer		
'aḍāf:			*muḍāf*	added
'a9ṭa:	*mu9ṭī*	donor	*mu9ṭa*	given,
			pl. *mu9ṭayāt*	data

9. Verbal nouns of Form III

Models for Form III verbal nouns:

- Sound, initial-*w*, hollow; *kātab*: *mukātaba* correspondence (rarer, see below) *qātal*: *qitāl* fight; *jāwab*: *jawāb* answer
- Final-weak; *lāqa*: *mulāqā́* encounter, pl. sound; adds -*t* before a suffix or when it is the theme of a construct (see below).

Most plurals are sound; a few are broken.

sā9ad:	*musā9ada*	help	*9āmal:*	*mu9āmala*	treatment
qābal:	*muqābala*	encounter	*qātal:*	*muqātala/qitāl*	fight
jāwab:	*jawāb 'ajwiba*	answer	*ḥāwal:*	*muḥawala*	attempt
ḥāwar:	*muḥāwara/ḥiwār*	dialogue			
lāqa:	*mulāqā́*	encounter (*mulāqātna* our encounter)			

10. Verbal nouns of Form IV

Models for Form IV verbal nouns:

- Sound; *'arsal*: *'irsāl* despatch
- Initial-*w*; *'awqaf*: *'īqāf* stoppage
- Doubled; *'aṣarr*: *'iṣrār* insistence, persistence
- Hollow; *'aḍāf*: *'iḍāfa* supplement (NB. final -*a*)
- Final-weak; *'ansha*: *'inshā'* creation, composition

Plurals, where they exist, are sound.

'az9aj:	*'iz9āj*	disturbance	*'antaj:*	*'intāj*	production
'akhraj:	*'ikhrāj*	expulsion	*'awjab:*	*'ījāb*	compulsion
'arād:	*'irāda*	wish	*'adhā9:*	*'idhā9a*	broadcasting
'a9ṭa:	*'i9ṭā'*	donation	*'alqa:*	*'ilqā'*	delivery (speech etc.)

11. Adjectives derived from verbal nouns

Many verbal nouns, especially those of the increased forms, produce *nisba* adjectives:

ta9līmī	instructional	*taḥḍīrī*	preparatory
tajrībī	experimental	*'ījābī*	positive
'irādī	intentional	*'iḍāfī*	additional, supplementary

12. We shall from now on introduce new verbs thus:

- Form I: *shakk yishukk* I *fī*, *shakk shukūk* to doubt (principal parts, preposition if any, verbal noun if useful);

- Forms II, III and V – X (once the increased form has been studied): *wāfaq* III *9ala* to agree on/to (first principal part, preposition if any);
- Form IV: *'arsal yursil* IV to send; *'aṣarr yiṣirr* IV *9ala* to insist on, to persist in (as for Forms II, III etc., but with both principal parts).

13. Pluperfect tense

kān followed by another verb, both in the appropriate person of the past tense, makes the pluperfect tense, which can be used to denote an action or state previous to another one expressed in the past tense:

kanū 'adhā9ū qabl mā 'aja. They had broadcast it before he came.

The pluperfect is not very common; the past tense is often preferred.

14. Conditional sentences

A conditional sentence states that something is true only if something else is true. We distinguish between real or possible conditions ('if it rains ...') and unreal or impossible conditions ('if I had known ...'):

Real conditions begin with *'idha* 'if'. Tenses can be as in English:

'akhbirnī, 'idha fī mushkila. Tell me, if there is a problem.
'idha huwa mish moujūd, (rāḥ-)'aḥkī ma9 musā9idu. If he isn't there, I'll talk to his assistant.

Or either verb, or both, can be in the past, with present meaning:

'idha mā kān moujūd, ḥakayt ma9 musā9idu.
'a9ṭī hādha 'idha 'aja. Give him this if he comes.

'Unless' is simply 'if ... not':

'idha mā sā9adtna ... Unless you/If you don't help us

We also know *'idha* meaning 'if' or 'whether' in indirect questions:

mā na9raf 'idha (yikūn) mumkin.

Unreal conditions begin with *law* 'if', with both verbs in one of the past tenses:

law kunt ghanī, sakant/kunt sākin fī bayt 'akbar. If I were rich I would live in a bigger house.

law lā is 'if not' (real/unreal); *law lā-* + pronoun suffix 'but for ...':

law lā, 'abqa fi l-bayt. If not, I'll stay at home.
law lā, mā laqaynā. If not, we wouldn't find it.
law lāk, mā najaḥna. But for you we wouldn't succeed.

'as if' is *ka 'inn*, which follows the indirect speech rule (4/7):

kān yiḥkī ka 'innu ya9rafhum. He spoke as if he knew them.

15. Concessive sentences

A concessive sentence states that something is true despite or irrespective of whether something else is true. Concessions ('although ...') begin with:

ḥatta u law	even if (unreal)	*ma9 'inn*	even though (real)
wayn mā	wherever	*mata mā*	whenever
mahma kān (etc.)/*mahma huwa/hiya*			whatever
mīn mā	whoever	*kayf mā*	however

so: *ḥatta u law qābaltu, mā kān yisā9idak.* Even if you meet him, he won't help you.

ma9 'innu ghanī yuskun fī bayt iṣghīr. Although he is rich he lives in a small house.

mahma kānat ash-shurūṭ/mahma hiya sh-shurūṭ, 'ana musta9idd. Whatever the conditions (might be/are), I'm ready.

16. All these conditions and concessions may be followed by *fa* 'then':

law 9irift (fa) 'akhbartak. If I knew (then) I would tell you.

mahma tqūl (fa) 'aṣaddiqak. Whatever you say, I believe you.

17. ***iyyā-***

A verb cannot take two pronoun suffixes. When a verb has two direct-object pronouns, we suffix one of them to the base-word *iyyā-*. Examine:

9arrafūni yyāhum. They introduced me to them.

'a9ṭīna yyāha. Give them to us.

al-'as'ila llī sa'alni yyāha the questions which he asked me

When the verb has one direct object and one object with *li*, we use *iyyā-* for the direct object:

lā tqūl lu yyá. Don't tell it to him.

We do not use *iyyā-* for the direct object when the other object has a preposition other than *li*:

'akhadhtu minnu. I took/got it from him.

katabu min sha'nhum. He wrote it for them.

18. Regional variations; Levant, Egypt

Present tense. In Levantine and Egyptian speech, the present tense of all verbs (including *yikūn* with its future meaning) has *b-* before the personal prefix. Initial *hamza* is dropped, and initial *y-* may be dropped, before the *b-* is added. A transition vowel is inserted where necessary:

bashrab, btishrab(ī), bishrab/byishrab *ba9ṭī, bya9ṭī, bna9ṭī*

bashūf, bitshūf, binshūf *bakūn, binkūn, bitkūnū*

But *b-* is omitted after an auxiliary or in an expression of time or purpose:

bnījī but: *khallīna nījī, rāyiḥīn nījī, mā bni'dar nījī*

byūṣal al-youm but: *lamma/ḥatta/'abl mā yūṣal al-youm*

***bid-*.** In the Levant and Egypt, the syllable *bid-* is used to form a quasi-verb meaning 'to want'. It takes (NB) the *possessive suffixes* to make its present tense, doubling the *d* before a vowel:

biddī, biddak/biddik, biddu/bid-ha; bidna, bidkum, bid-hum
I, you (etc.) want(s)

Its past tense is expressed with *kān biddī, kān biddak* (etc.), the *kān* being invariable. The negative of both tenses is formed with *mā*, not with *mish*:

(mā) biddak itsā9idnī? Don't/Do you want to help me?

kān bid-hum al-fulūs 9ala ṭūl. They wanted the money immédiately.

We use *iyyā-* to accommodate any pronoun direct object:

mā kān bidna yyá. We didn't want it.

19. Adverbs

Many adjectives in the m. sing. form can serve as adverbs: *kwayyis, maẓbūṭ*. Some other adverbs are formed by adding to the m. sing. of the adjective the ending *-an* (after *-ī, -yan)*:

jadīdan	recently	*qarīban*	soon
tamāman	completely	*rasmīyan*	officially
shadīdan	severely, vigorously	*youmī, youmīyan*	daily (adj./adverb)
sanawī, sanawīyan	annual(ly)	*shakhṣīyan*	personally

-an is also added to a few prepositions and nouns (after *-a, -tan*):

qablan	before(hand)	*ma9an*	together
ṣabāḥan	in the morning		
(*four*	boiling)	*fouran*	immediately
(*9āda*	habit)	*9ādatan*	usually
(*taqrīb*	approximation)	*taqrīban*	approximately
(*mathal 'amthāl*	example)	*mathalan*	for example
(*khāṣṣa*	particularity)	*khāṣṣatan*	especially
(*shakl 'ashkāl*	form)	(*mouḍū9 mawāḍī9*	subject)
	→ *shaklan wa mouḍū9an*	in form and substance	

We negate *-an* adverbs with *mish* or *ghayr*:

mish/ghayr rasmīyan unofficially

and we make their comparative either with the adjective or with *'akthar*:

'ashadd, shadīdan 'akthar more vigorously

20. Some adverbs are made with a preposition + noun. In some examples the noun is definite, in others indefinite:

(*suhūla*	ease)	*bi suhūla*	easily
(*ẓabṭ*	precision)	*bi ẓ-ẓabṭ*	precisely
(*sur9a*	speed)	*bi sur9a*	fast
(*shidda*	vigour, severity)	*bi-shidda*	vigorously, severely
(*tafṣīl tafāṣīl*	detail)	*bi t-tafṣīl*	in detail
(*ḥaqīqa ḥaqāyiq*	truth)	*fi l-ḥaqīqa*	in truth, indeed
(*shakk shukūk*	doubt)	*bi lā shakk*	doubtless, indubitably
		bi l-kād	almost; (+ negative) hardly

We make the comparative with *'akthar* after the noun, which is then indefinite:

bi suhūla 'akthar	more easily	*bi tafṣīl 'akthar*	in more detail

21. A third device used is *bi ṣūra* (*ṣura ṣuwar* 'form, image'):

bi ṣūra 9āmma	generally	*bi ṣūra naẓarīya*	theoretically
bi ṣura 9amalīya	in practice	*bi ṣūra wāḍiḥa*	clearly

Negation: *bi ṣura mish/ghayr wāḍiḥa* in an unclear manner

Comparison: *bi ṣura 'awḍaḥ* more clearly

bi ṣura 9āmma 'akthar more generally

22. The superlative adverb is best expressed with 'more ... than all':

hādha t-tilmīdh yiḥkī bi ṣura 'awḍaḥ min al-kull. This pupil speaks the most clearly ('more clearly than all').

23. Finally, note variants of adverbs given above:

min qarīb recently *9an qarīb, ba9d ishwayy* soon

24. Participial verb

The active participle is frequently used in place of a tense; it agrees adjectivally with its subject:

'ana rāyiḥ(a) I'm going. *shāyif/fāhim?* Do you see/understand?

hadhoul al-'ikhwān musāfirīn? Are these chaps travelling?

The participle implies mostly present, but sometimes recently past, time:

'ana sāmi9 9anha. I've heard of her/it/them.

ḥasan, mish shāyifu. Haven't seen Hassan.

When the subject is not stated, it is most commonly understood as first or third person in statements, and second or third person in questions:

musāfir(a) bukra. I'm/He's/She's travelling tomorrow.

musāfir(a) bukra? Are you/Is he/Is she travelling tomorrow?

mish bāqiyīn fi l-bayt. We/They aren't staying at home.

mish bāqiyīn fi l-bayt? Aren't you/they staying at home?

25. *'illa*

'illa with a negative verb means 'only':

mā 'adfa9 'illa bi dinār. I'll pay in dinars only.

26. *li*

This preposition permits us to make a compound similar to a construct, but with all its elements explicitly defined:

mudīrna li l-mālīya our Finance Manager

al-mudīr al-9āmm li l-maṣna9 the factory's General Manager

A construct, i.e. *mudīr al-maṣna9 al-9āmm*, is technically possible but it would break up the GM's title.

li can be put with a 'string' construct:

mushkilat tamwīl at-tadrīb al-fannī li sh-sharika the problem of financing the company's technical training

– and it removes the ambiguity of some constructs with an adjective:

mudīr al-bank as-sūrī (who or what is Syrian?)

but: *al-mudīr as-sūrī li l-bank/al-mudīr li l-bank as-sūrī*: no ambiguity.

27. jumal mithālīya

mumaththilīn al-9ummāl kānū yurīdū yiqābilū 'aṣḥāb al-9amal li buḥūth kānat it-himmhum kullhum.

The workers' representatives wanted to meet the employers for discussions which concerned all of them.

'aẓunn 'inn al-wazīr kān yiḥkī shakhṣīyan, u mā kān yinwī yulqī khiṭāb rasmī bi khuṣūṣ siyāsat al-ḥukūma l-iqtiṣādīya.

I presume the minister was speaking personally, and did not intend to make an official speech about the

	Government's economic policy.
nasharū fi l-jarāyid taqrīr maktūb fī 'inn 'arqām aṣ-ṣādirāt li rub9 as-sana 'a9la mimma kānat khilāl nafs al-mudda fi s-sana l-māḍiya.	They published in the newspaper a report which says ('in which is written') that the export figures for the quarter are higher than they were during the same period last year.
al-mas'ala ḍarūrīya; 'idha mā yiqdarū yākhudhu t-tadābīr al-munāsiba bi sur9a, khallīhum yiwāfiqū 9ala l-'aqall 9ala tadābīr taḥḍīrīya; law lā, fa nikhsar ḥatta 9ishrīn bi l-mīya min ar-ribḥ.	The matter is urgent; if they cannot take the appropriate measures quickly, let them agree at least on preparatory measures; if not, we shall lose up to twenty per cent of profits.

28. *at-tamārīn*

1. Answer the following questions on the narrative:
e.g.: fī 'ayy ḥaql kānat mahammat Peter?– kānat fī ḥaql at-tadrīb al-fannī.
(a) mīn illī Peter kān yurīd yiqābilu?
(b) mā huwa shughl fāyiz?
(c) shū kānū yintijū fi l-maṣna9?
(d) al-maṣna9 kān yintij min sha'n as-sūq ad-dākhilīya, willa l-'ajnabīya?
(e) mīn illī kān mas'ūl 9an as-siyāsa l-mālīya?

2. Give the principal parts and the verbal noun of each verb:
e.g.: sā9ad – sā9ad yisā9id, musā9ada
(a) 'adhā9 (b) jāwab (c) kharaj
(d) rabba

3. Give the principal parts of the verb of which this is a participle:
e.g.: munāsib – nāsab yināsib
(a) mukawwan (b) mursil (c) muwaẓẓaf
(d) mufīd (e) rākib

4. Re-express with a participial verb:
e.g.: 'int tifhām ar-risāla?– fāhim ar-risāla?
(a) 'ana mā 'asāfir bukra. (b) tshūfū? (c) mā 9irifna
(d) tījū ma9na?

5. Join the clauses as a conditional sentence:
e.g.: mā ta9raf. lāzim tis'al. – 'idha mā ta9raf, lāzim tis'al.
(a) 'ana 9iriftu. kunt 'aqūl lak iyyā.
(b) huwa muwāfiq. khallī yisā9idna.
(c) wiṣilū 'ams. 'ana shuft-hum.

(d) mish munāsib. 'akhbirnī.
(e) mā kān munāsib. kunt 'akhbartak.

6. Replace the noun objects with pronouns:
e.g.: 'a9ṭayt ṣadīqi l-fulūs. – 'a9ṭaytu yyāha.
(a) 'arsalna r-risāla li sh-sharika.
(b) qūl al-ḥikāya li-'aṣdiqā'ak.
(c) 9allam al-walad kitābat al-lugha l-9arabīya.
(d) kunt 'urīd 'as'al al-'ustādh nafs as-su'āl.
(e) 'uktub al-jawāb min sha'n al-mumaththilīn.

7. Put everything possible into the plural:
e.g.: 'ana simi9t at-taqrīr al-muwāfaq 9aláy.
– simi9na t-taqārīr al-muwāfaq 9alayha.
(a) mā dhakarat li l-khabar al-jadīd.
(b) musāfir hassa? 'ashūfak ba9dayn.
(c) fī tilmīdh yurīd yiqābilak.
(d) 'ana mish fāhim laysh 'int mā turīd tishraḥ li yyā́.
(e) hādhi hiya 'akbar mushkila llī lāzim 'aḥillha.

ad-dars 'ithn9āshr – Lesson 12
fi l-9iyāda – At the Surgery

1. *al-ḥikāya wa l-ḥiwār*

tarashshaḥ	he caught a cold
rashḥ	a cold
khoufan 9ala	fearing for
taqaddum	progress

(min youmayn Peter kān marīḍ. kān min al-wāḍiḥ 'innu tarashshaḥ rashḥ shadīd. fa khoufan 9ala taqaddum mahammtu,

(For two days Peter had been ill. It was clear that he had caught a severe cold. Fearing for the progress of his assignment,

tadhakkar	he remembered
talfan	he telephoned
'ashār yushīr IV *'ila*	to indicate, point out
layla hilāl	Leila Hilal (name)

tadhakkar mā qāl lu d-duktur fu'ād u talfan lu ṭālib musā9adatu. ad-duktur fu'ād kān khārij al-balad, walākin sikritayrtu 'ashārat 'ila ṭabība mumtāza, isimha layla hilāl.)

he remembered what Dr Sharif had said to him, and telephoned him asking for his help. Dr Sharif was out of town, but his secretary pointed out an excellent doctor called Layla Hilal.)

shū mālak?	what's wrong with you?
ḥarāra	heat, fever

duktur layla: shū mālak, yā sayyid Peter? 9indak ḥarāra? — What's wrong with you, Mr Brown? Do you have a fever?

Peter: mish 9ārif maẓbūṭ, yā duktur. — I don't know exactly, Doctor.

faḥaṣ yifḥaṣ I, *faḥṣ*	to examine (medically)
tfarjī	you show to
lisān 'alsina (m./f.)	tongue
'aḥmar, ḥamrā', ḥumr	red
ḥalq ḥulūq	throat

duktur layla: khallīnī 'afḥaṣak. mumkin itfarjīnī lisānak? ḥalqak 'aḥmar shadīd. — Let me examine you. Can you show me your tongue? Your throat's very red indeed.

daraja	degree
darajat ḥarāra	temperature
taba9	belonging to
li ḥusn al-ḥaẓẓ	fortunately
taraddadt	you hesitated

nshūf al-ḥarāra ... 'ayna9am, darajat al-ḥarāra taba9ak — We'll look at the temperature ... yes, your temperature's 39,

	tis9a u thalāthīn, mish qalīl. li ḥusn al-ḥaẓẓ mā taraddadt 'inn itshūfnī.	quite a lot. Fortunately you didn't hesitate in seeing me.
	barnāmaj barāmij	programme
	malān	full
Peter:	kayf 'a9mal, yā duktur? 9indī barnāmaj malān ...	What ('How') should I do, Doctor? I have a full programme...
	titbassam	she smiles
	lā budda min	there's no escaping
	majbūr	forced
	dār yidīr I *bāl-*	to take care, pay atttention
	tirtāḥ	you rest
	kāmil	complete, perfect
	mā físh	= *mā fī*
	9ilāj	treatment, cure
duktur layla:	(titbassam) 9ārifa, yā sayyid Peter, walākin lā budda min 'innak majbūr itdīr bālak. lāzim tirtāḥ 'usbū9 kāmil. law lā, mā físh 9ilāj.	(smiles) I know, Mr Brown, but there's no escaping it, you have to take care. You must rest for a whole week. If not, there's no cure.
	tadhkara tadhākir (ṭibbīya)	(here:) prescription
	dawā' 'ádwiya	medicine
	ṣaydalīya	pharmacy
	qurṣ 'aqrāṣ	tablet
	9adam	lack
	tanāwul	intake (food, drink)
	sāyil sawāyil	fluid, liquid
	khaṭir	dangerous
	'aktub lak tadhkara, khudh ad-dawā' min aṣ-ṣaydalīya, khudh qurṣ wāḥid thalātha marrāt bi l-youm, u lā tinsa tishrab mạy kthīr. 9adam tanāwul as-sawāyil khaṭir jiddan.	I'll write you a prescription; get the medicine from the pharmacy; take one tablet three times a day, and don't forget to drink a lot of water. Lack of fluid intake is very dangerous.
	taḥassant	you improved, got better
	taḥassun	improvement
	malmūs	tangible
	talfin	telephone
	'idha mā taḥassant taḥassun malmūs ba9d youmayn, talfin lī u 'ashūfak kamān marra.	If you haven't made a tangible improvement after two days, telephone me and I'll see you again.

	salāmtak	(here:) Get well.
Peter:	'ashkurik qalbīyan, yā duktur. 'ana kthīr mamnūn.	My sincere thanks, Doctor. I'm very grateful.
duktur layla:	9afwan yā sayyid Peter. salāmtak.	Glad to help, Mr Brown. Get well.
Peter:	'alla yisallimik, yā duktur.	Goodbye, Doctor.

2. *9ibārāt*

khoufan 9ala fearing for. *khāf yikhāf* I *9ala, khouf* to fear for. Note also *khoufan min* for fear of, fearing

shū mālī/mālak/mālik/mālu/mālha/mālna/mālkum/mālhum? What's wrong with me (etc.)?

mish qalīl ('not a little') quite a lot

li ḥusn al-ḥaẓẓ ('for good of fortune') by good fortune, fortunately. The opposite is *li sū' al-ḥaẓẓ* ('for ill of fortune') unfortunately.

lā budda min ('no escape from') There's no escaping ... This expression is followed by a noun, or by a clause beginning with *'inn*. Note also: *lā budda* It can't be helped.

dīr bālak/dīrī bālik/dīrū bālkum 9ala Take care about

salāmtak/salāmtik/salāmtu/salāmit-ha/salāmitkum/salāmit-hum ('your (etc.) safety') Get well. The response (as for all greetings with the root *s l m*) is *'alla yisallimak/yisallimik/yisallimu/yisallimha/yisallimkum/yisallimhum.*

3. *mufradāt 'iḍāfīya. al-jism wa ṣ-ṣiḥḥa* – Body and health

jism 'ajsām	body	*waja9 'oujā9*	pain
ra's ru'ūs	head	*'īd 'ayād* (f.)	hand, arm
ẓahr ẓuhūr, ḓahr ḓuhūr	back	*baṭn buṭūn*	stomach
ṣadr ṣudūr	chest	*qalb qulūb*	heart
sinn 'asnān	tooth	*9ayn 9uyūn* (f.)	eye
9iyāda	clinic, surgery	*9ālaj* III	to treat (medically)
dam	blood	*wazn 'ouzān*	weight
ṭibb	medicine (medical science)	*ṭibbī*	medical
ṣaḥīḥ ṣiḥāḥ	(also:) healthy (person)	*ḍa9īf ḍu9afā'*	weak
miriḍ yimraḍ I	to be/fall ill	*maraḍ 'amrāḍ*	sickness
faḥṣ ṭibbī	medical examination	*mumarriḍ(a)*	orderly, nurse
jarrāḥ	surgeon	*jirāḥī*	surgical
9amalīya	operation	*majrūḥ majārīḥ*	injured
'ibra 'ibar	needle, injection	*ḍarab yuḍrub* I *'ibra*	to inject

an-naḥū

4. Verbs of Form V

For Form V verbs we can use the following models:

- All classes except final-weak: *taqaddam yitqaddam* to advance, progress
- Final-weak: *tawalla yitwalla* to be put in charge

This increased form has three important characteristics:

- a prefix (*ta-* in the past tense and *t-* in the present),
- a doubled middle root letter
- (NB) the vowel *a* after the middle root letter in both tenses.

Written Arabic has the prefix *ta-* before both tenses, but in spoken Arabic it is usual to drop the *a* of this prefix in the present tense. In some expressions the *a* of the prefix is dropped in both tenses.

Most Form V verbs do not have a direct object; they often give the passive* or reflexive* meaning of Form II verbs.

* In a passive expression the subject does not *perform* the action, but *undergoes* it: 'The kitten is *being washed.*' In a reflexive expression, the action comes back to the subject: 'The kitten is *washing itself.*'

Examine:

9allam yi9allim II	to teach
ta9allam yit9allam V	(to be taught) to learn

Typical Form V tenses:

***All classes except final-weak*:**

Root *q d m, taqaddam yitqaddam* to advance, progress:

Past: *taqaddamt, taqaddamt/taqaddamti, taqaddam/taqaddamat; taqaddamna, taqaddamtū, taqaddamū* I (etc.) advanced, progressed

Pres.: *'atqaddam, titqaddam/titqaddamī, yitqaddam/titqaddam; nitqaddam, titqaddamū, yitqaddamū* I (etc.) advance(s), progress(es)

so also:

takallam yitkallam	to speak
tabassam yitbassam	to smile
tasharraf yitsharraf	to be honoured
tasallam yitsallam	to receive
tadhakkar yitdhakkar	to remember
tadakhkhal yitdakhkhal	to intervene
tarashshaḥ yitrashshaḥ	to catch a cold
taḥassan yitḥassan	to improve, get better
ta9arraf yit9arraf bi	to get acquainted with
ta9allaq yit9allaq bi	to depend on, pertain to
tamakkan yitmakkan min	to be capable of, to possess
ta'akhkhar yit'akhkhar	to be delayed
ta'assaf yit'assaf	to be sorry
takhaṣṣaṣ yitkhaṣṣaṣ fī	to specialise in
*taraddad yitraddad**	to hesitate

* *taraddad 'inn* when followed by a dependent verb:

taraddad 'inn yudkhul.	He hesitated to enter.

In initial-*w* and hollow verbs the weak root letter stabilises:

tawaqqaf yitwaqqaf 9ala	to depend on
tawassa9 yitwassa9	to expand
tawaqqa9 yitwaqqa9	to expect, await
*taṭawwar yiṭṭawwar***	to evolve

** present-tense prefix *t-* assimilates to *ṭ* of the root.

Final-weak: Root *w l y, tawalla yitwalla* to be (put) in charge:

Past: like Form II, but prefixed *ta-*:
tawallayt, tawallayt/tawallayti, tawalla/tawallat;
tawallayna, tawallaytū, tawallū I (etc.) was/were (put) in charge

Pres.: final root letter becomes *a* and the final-weak verb rule (8/10) applies:
'atwalla, titwalla/titwallī, yitwalla/titwalla; nitwalla, titwallū, yitwalllū
I (etc.) am/is/are (put) in charge

5. Verbs of Form VI

For Form VI we can use the following models:

- All classes except final-weak: *takātab yitkātab* to write to each other
- Final-weak: *talāqa yitlāqa* to come together, meet

Form VI is exactly like Form V, except for having long *ā* after the initial root letter instead of a doubled middle root letter. Form VI verbs often have a reciprocal meaning (= 'each other'); some of them correspond to Form III verbs:

kātab yikātib III	to write to, correspond with
takātab yitkātab VI	to write to each other, correspond

Examples of Form VI verbs:

All classes except final-weak:

Root *k t b, takātab yitkātab* to write to each other, correspond:

Past: *takātabt, takātabt/takātabti, takātab/takātabat;*
takātabna, takātabtū, takātabū

Pres.: *'atkātab, tkātab/tkātabī, yitkātab/titkātab; nitkātab, titkātabū, yitkātabū*

so also:

tabādal yitbādal	to exchange with each other
taẓāhar yitẓāhar	to demonstrate (politically)
tadākhal yitdākhal	to interfere
ta9āwan yit9āwan	to cooperate
tanāwab yitnāwab	to alternate
tanāwal yitnāwal	to reach for; to take (food, drink)

Final-weak: Root *l q y, talāqa yitlāqa* to come together, meet:

Past: *talāqayt, talāqayt/talāqayti, talāqa/talāqat; talāqayna, talāqaytū, talāqū*

Pres.: *'atlāqa, titlāqa/titlāqī, yitlāqa/titlāqa; nitlāqa, titlāqū, yitlāqū*

so also: *ta9āfa yit9āfa* to recover (in health)

6. Imperatives of Forms V and VI

For the imperatives of Forms V and VI, follow the rules for Form II:

Affirmative:	V *tkallam/tkallamī/tkallamū*
	VI *t9āwan/t9āwanī/t9āwanū*
Negative:	V *lā titraddad/lā titraddadī/lā titraddadū*
	VI *lā titdākhal/lā titdākhalī/lā titdākhalū*

7. Participles of Forms V and VI

For Form V and VI participles:

- *Active:* Replace the *yit-* prefixes of the second principal part with *muta-*, and (NB) change the *a* of the last syllable to *i* (for all classes except final-weak) or to *ī* (for final-weak verbs).

- *Passive* (rarer): Prefix *mu-* to the first principal part.

V *muta9allim*	educated; apprentice	*mutaqaddim*	foremost, advanced
muta9alliq bi	relevant/pertinent to	*mutakallim*	speaker
mutawaqqif 9ala	conditional/dependent on	*mutawaqqa9*	expected
muta'akhkhir	delayed, late	*muta'assif*	sorry
mutakhaṣṣiṣ	specialising, specialist	*mutawallī*	in charge
VI *mutaẓāhir*	demonstrator	*mutabādal*	mutual, reciprocal
mutanāwib	alternating	*mutanāwal*	available

8. Verbal nouns of Forms V and VI

To make the verbal nouns of Forms V and VI, replace the last *a* of the first principal part:

- in all classes except final-weak: with *-u-*.
- in final-weak verbs (rare): with *-ī*.

Examples (with some *nisba* derivatives):

V *taqaddum*	progress	*taqaddumī*	progressive
ta9arruf	acquaintance	*tadakhkhul*	intervention
tawassu9	expansion	*tawassu9ī*	expansionist
taraddud	hesitation	*takhaṣṣuṣ*	specialisation
taṭawwur	evolution	*taṭawwurī*	evolutionary
VI *tabādul*	exchange	*taẓāhur*	demonstration
ta9āwun	cooperation	*ta9āwunī*	cooperative
tadākhul	interference	*tanāwul*	intake (food/drink)

9. *mā* = what

mā is 'what' when introducing indirect questions and in the relative meaning 'that which'. In the indirect question we can instead use *shū*, except after a preposition, when *mā* is obligatory:

mish 9ārif mā/shū ṣār. but: *'ashār 'ila mā ṣār 'ams.*
tadhakkar mā qult lu (yyá) d-duktur. *tadhakkar mā 'ashart 'ilu 'ams.*

Note also *mimma* and *9amma* (for *[min mā, 9an mā]*), and the expression *mā yalī* 'what follows', 'the following':

'ashār 'ila mā yalī.	He pointed out the following.
mimma yalī, min al-wāḍiḥ 'inn ...	From what follows, it is clear that ...

'as follows' is *kama yalī.*

10. Absolute object

We often use as object of a verb a verbal noun having the same root as that verb. We call this structure the *absolute object*:

sa'alatnī su'āl.	She asked me a question.
taḥassant taḥassun malmūs.	You made ('improved') a tangible improvement.
jaddadū tajdīd mumtāz.	They have renovated it excellently.

The verbal noun may be of a different form from that of the verb:

tarashshaḥ (V) *rashḥ* (I) *shadīd.*	He caught a severe cold.

11. Special adjectives

Certain adjectives denoting common colours and some physical afflictions are based on the comparative-adjective pattern (see 9/13) in the masculine singular. They also have special forms for the feminine singular/inanimate plural, and the animate plural. Models are:

Root	Model			
	masc.	f. s./inan. pl.	an. pl	
Sound (3 consonants)	*'aḥmar*	*ḥamrā'*	*ḥumr*	red
Hollow (middle *w*)	*'aswad*	*sawdā'*	*sūd*	black
(middle *y*)	*'abyaḍ*	*bayḍā'*	*bīḍ*	white
Doubled (last letters)	*'ajashsh*	*jashshā'*	*jushsh*	hoarse
Final-wk. (*-w* or *-y*)	*'a9ma*	*'a9myā'*	*9umī*	blind

so also:

'azraq, zarqā', zurq	blue	*'akhḍar, khaḍrā', khuḍr*	green
'aṣfar, ṣafrā', ṣufr	yellow	*'a9raj, 9arjā', 9urj*	lame
'aṭrash, ṭarshā', ṭursh	deaf		

A few colours are *nisba* adjectives:

bunnī/binnī	brown	*ramādī*	grey

We make comparative and superlative of all these adjectives with *'akthar*, as with derived and *nisba* adjectives.

12. Quadriliteral verbs

A few verbs, some of them common, have quadriliteral roots, i.e. four root letters. We shall mark such verbs with Q.

Form IQ, examples:

tarjam yitarjim	to translate	*talfan yitalfin*	to telephone
barhan yibarhin 9ala	to prove	*zalzal yizalzil*	to shake
talfaz yitalfiz	to televise	*farja yifarjī**	to show to

* *farja* takes two direct objects: *farjú yyā́*. They showed it to him.

Form IQ tenses, imperatives and participles are similar to Form II triliteral. Thus, for *tarjam yitarjim* IQ:

Past: *tarjamt, tarjamt/tarjamti, tarjam/tarjamat; tarjamna, tarjamtū, tarjamū*
Pres.: *'atarjim, ttarjim/ttarjimī, yitarjim/ttarjim; ntarjim, ttarjimū, yitarjimū*
Imperatives: *tarjim/ī/ū* translate, *la ttarjim/ī/ū* don't translate
Participles: active *mutarjim* translator, passive *mutarjam* translated

Most Form IQ verbal nouns have one of the following patterns:

tarjama tarājim	translation	*burhān 9ala*	proof of
talfaza	television	*zilzāl*	shock, earthquake

Form IIQ, the only common increased form, resembles Form V triliteral throughout:

tazalzal yitazalzal	to quake	} NB: *ta-* in both tenses
tafalsaf yitafalsaf	to philosophise	

Imperative *tazalzal/ī/ū, lā tatazalzal/ī/ū*; active participle *mutazalzil* (no passive); verbal noun *tazalzul* quaking.
We shall show Form IQ verbs in the vocabulary in the same manner as Form I verbs (but without the second principal part, since this is regular in Form IQ); and Form IIQ verbs in the same manner as Form II verbs; see 11/12.

13. Circumstantial verbs

In 6/10 we studied the use of *u* in *circumstantial* expressions. Arabic has two other circumstantial structures expressing simultaneous actions. The first of these is with the active participle, agreeing with the subject of the main verb:

talfan lu ṭālib musā9adatu.	He telephoned asking for his help.
'ajū rākibīn (al-)khayl.	They came on horseback ('riding horses').

In some expressions, the written form of the singular participle, carrying the suffix *-an* (f. *-atan*) is used in spoken Arabic:

'aḍāf qāyilan 'inn ...	He went on to say ('He added, saying') ...
'aḍāfat qāyilatan ...	She went on to say ...

The second verbal structure puts the accompanying verb into the present tense, irrespective of the tense of the main verb:

talfan lu yuṭlub musā9adatu. *'ajū yirkabu l-khayl/yirkabū khayl.*

14. Age

A person's age is indicated with the noun *9umr 'a9mār* 'age', 'life':

9umru kam?	How old is he?	*9umrī thalāthīn.*	I'm thirty.

Note also:

9umrak/9umrik 'aṭwal.	I bow to your greater experience.

and the compound adjectives, not used when the age is stated:

kbīr as-sinn/kbīra s-sinn/kbār as-sinn	old
ṣghīr as-sinn/ṣghīra s-sinn/ṣghār as-sinn	young

15. *ḥusn, sū'; 9adam, 9adīm*

The nouns *ḥusn* 'good' and *sū* 'ill' form a number of constructs with special meaning:

ḥusn al-ḥaẓẓ	good luck	*sū' al-ḥaẓẓ*	bad luck
ḥusn al-ḥāl	good conditions	*sū' al-ḥāl*	poor conditions
ḥusn al-qaṣd	good will	*sū' al-qaṣd*	ill will
sū' al-mu9āmala	ill-treatment	*(li) sū' al-'idāra*	(by) mismanagement
li ḥusn al-ḥaẓẓ	fortunately	*li sū' al-ḥaẓẓ*	unfortunately

The noun *9adam* 'lack' can be used in construct with any definite verbal noun to make a negative concept, thus:

9adam at-tafāhum	misunderstanding
9adam at-ta9āwun	non-cooperation
waqqafu/'awqafu sh-shughl li 9adam at-tamwīl.	They stopped the work for lack of financing.

With a non-verbal noun, we interpose the verbal noun *wujūd* 'existence':

9adam wujūd al-mawādd al-'awwalīya	lack of raw materials

The corresponding compound adjective is formed with *9adīm* 'lacking':

9adīm at-ta9āwun uncooperative

16. *taba9*

The invariable word *taba9* is used in one of the following ways:

- as the theme of a definite construct qualifying a preceding noun:
  al-milaffāt taba9 al-9iyāda the files belonging to the clinic
- with a possessive suffix: 'mine', 'yours' (etc.):
  li mīn al-kutub? – (hiya) taba9ī Whose are the books? – (They're) mine.
- with a possessive suffix: 'my', 'your' (etc.) after a construct or other compound:
  darajat al-ḥarāra taba9u
  darajat ḥarartu } his temperature
  al-mudīr al-9āmm taba9hum
  al-mudīr al-9āmm lahum } their general manager

17. Regional variations: Negative *-sh/-shī*

In the Levant, Egypt and Sudan, a verb negated by *mā* and not already carrying an object-pronoun suffix is often given the suffix *-sh*:

mā kunnash 9ārifīn 'innak marīḍ. We didn't know you were ill.
mā kānsh moujūd. He wasn't there.

mā́ fī can also take *-sh*; it becomes *mā físh* (NB stress) or even simply *físh*:

mit'assif, (mā) físh 'imkānīyi. Sorry, there's no possibility..

In North-west Africa, *mā* before the verb or quasi-verb (even one carrying a pronoun suffix), with the suffix *-sh* or *-shī* after it, is the standard negative formula in speech:

mā 9indaksh/9indakshī fulūs? Have you no money?

18. *jumal mithālīya*

kayf ṣiḥḥat 9alī? – mimma simi9tu, yitḥassan ishwayy. 9imilū lu 9amalīya 'awwal 'ams, u 9indu waja9 'aqall, u yiẓhar 'innu yākul u yinām zayy al-9āda.
How's Ali? – From what I heard, he is improving gradually. They operated on him the day before yesterday, and he has less pain. It seems he is eating and sleeping normally.

al-mutaẓāhirīn taqaddamū ḥatta madkhal as-sūq, maḥall mā waqqafat-hum ash-shurṭa.
The demonstrators advanced as far as the market entrance, where the police stopped them.

qarrarat titkhaṣṣiṣ bi l-'amrāḍ ad-dākhilīya khoufan min 9adam wujūd 'imkānīyāt at-tawẓīf fī ḥaql aṭ-ṭibb al-9āmm.
She decided to specialise in internal diseases, fearing a lack of employment possibilities in the field of general medicine.

taraddadna taraddud ṭawīl qabl mā talfanna lak. fa nkhāf taṭawwurāt
We hesitated a long time before telephoning you. We

'akhṭar 'idha mā tadakhkhalt bi ṣūra 'ījābīya.	are afraid of more dangerous developments if you do not intervene in a positive manner.
law tamakkanna min jawāb 'ījābī, fa kān mumtāz; li sū' al-ḥaẓẓ al-ḥaqīqa ghayr shī.	If we were capable of a positive answer, that would be excellent. Unfortunately the reality is otherwise.
min al-mutawaqqa9 'inn al-lajna twāfiq 9ala tamwīl al-'iḍāfa llī ṭalabūha l-muwaẓẓafīn al-mutakhaṣṣiṣīn. lā budda 'inn ash-sharika majbūra 'inn tidfa9 al-'iḍāfa l-kāmila l-maṭlūba.	It is expected that the committee will agree on financing the increase which the specialised workers have requested. There is no getting away from it; the company is obliged to ('that it') pay the whole increase requested.

19. *at-tamārīn*

1. Give the principal parts of the verbs from which these words are derived:
e.g.: mutaẓāhirīn – taẓāhar yitẓāhar
(a) ḥikāya (b) takhaṣṣuṣāt (c) 'ījābī
(d) tadākhul (e) madkhal

2. Give the verbal noun of each verb:
e.g.: 'aḍāf – 'iḍāfa
(a) 'akhkhar (b) tawassa9 (c) tanāwal
(d) wiṣil (e) waẓẓaf

3. Give the affirmative and negative imperative, all forms:
e.g.: rāḥ – rūḥ, rūḥī, rūḥū'; lā trūḥ, lā trūḥī, lā trūḥū
(a) taqaddam (b) 'a9ṭa (c) 'aja
(d) ta9āwan (e) 'akal

4. Complete the sentence with the right form of *'aḥmar*:
e.g.: lisānu – lisānu 'aḥmar/ḥamrā'
(a) 9aynu (b) 9aynáy (c) al-kitāb
(d) al-kutub (e) as-sayyāra

5. Put into the present tense:
e.g.: tarjamu. – yitarjimu.
(a) talfanna lak al-youm. (b) farjānī kitāb jadīd.
(c) talfazū kull al-'akhbār. (d) taḥassan bi sur9a.
(e) mā tamakkanū min 'injāzu.

6. Collect together words of the same root:
e.g.: su'āl, sa'alū, mas'ūl, sāyil
mu9allima, 'imkānīya, ma9lūm, ma9rifa, yitmakkan, ma9lūmāt, n9arrifu, ta9allamat, yumkin, ta9līmī, ta9rīf, yi9allim, ma9rūfa, 9ulūm.
(a) mumkin ... (b) 9ilm ... (c) 9irif ...

7. Complete the sentence with the right pronoun:
e.g.: ... hiya shurūṭ ad-dukhūl? – mā hiya shurūt ad-dukhūl?
(a) ... illī kunt titkallam ma9u?
(b) ... mālak, yā 'akhūī?
(c) yitwaqqaf 9an ... turīd.
(d) nsīt kull ... qāl lana.
(e) mish 9ārif ... illī 9imilu.

ad-dars thalatt9ashr – Lesson 13
ziyārat al-qáriya – A Visit to the Village

1. ***al-ḥikāya wa l-ḥiwār***

iqtáraḥ	he suggested
sawa	together
qáriya qura	village
intáhaz al-furṣa	he seized the opportunity
ittáṣal bi	he contacted
mukhtār makhātīr	mayor (of a village)
(ba9d mā ta9āfa Peter, iqtáraḥ zamīlu 9abdarraḥmān 'innhum yizūrū sawa qáriyitu, u Peter intáhaz al-furṣa. fa 9abdarraḥmān ittáṣal bi l-mukhtār fī hādha sh-sha'n.)	(After Peter recovered, his colleague Abdarrahman suggested that they visit his village together. Peter seized the opportunity. So Abdarrahman contacted the mayor on this matter.)
'ashraf	Ashraf (name)
(9ind al-mukhtār 'abū 'ashraf fi l-qáriya)	(with Abu Ashraf, the mayor, in the village)
sharaf	honour
kaththar II	to increase (something)
khayr khuyūr	good (noun)
inqāl	it was said
'abū 'ashraf: 'ahlan wa sahlan, sayyid Peter. 'ilī sharaf ikbīr. kayf ḥālak?	Welcome, Mr Brown. It's a great honour for me. How are you?
Peter: 'ilna sh-sharaf, siyādat al-mukhtār. 'ana kthīr mabsūṭ, al-ḥamdulilla. fa kayf ḥaḍirtak? 'inshalla bi ṣiḥḥa?	The honour's mine, Mr Mayor. I'm very well, thank you. And how are you? In good health, I hope?
'abū 'ashraf: wallahi, sayyid Peter, mabsūṭ jiddan, yikaththir khayrak. walākin inqāl 'innak miriḍt?	Very well indeed, Mr Brown. God bless you. But it was said that you have been ill?
Peter: kunt ta9bān ishwayy, walākinnī kthīr 'aḥsan hassa, shukran.	I was a little tired, but I'm a lot better now, thank you.
mā 'ajmalha!	how beautiful it is!
manẓara manāẓir	view
nasama	person (in statistics)
'abū 'ashraf: al-ḥamdulilla. shū ra'yak 9an qariyitna, yā Peter?	Thank Heavens. What do you think of our village, Peter?
Peter: mā 'ajmalha! al-manẓara 9aẓīma min huna. kam nasama fī yuskunū fi l-qáriya?	How beautiful it is! The view is superb from here. How many people are there living in the village?

	9adad 'a9dād	number
	sākin sukkān	inhabitant
	izdād	it increased
'abū 'ashraf:	9adad as-sukkān izdād bi kthīr khilāl as-sanawāt al-māḍiya. qabl kam sana mā kān fí 'akthar min mitayn,	The population has greatly increased during the past years. Some years ago,there were no more than two hundred,
	iḥtallū	they occupied
	'isrā'īlī	Israeli
	ḍiffa ḍifāf	bank, shore, coast
	gharb	west
	intáqalū	they moved
	minṭaqa manāṭiq	region, area
	walākin lamma kānū ḥtallu l-'isrā'īlīyīn aḍ-ḍiffa l-gharbīya, intáqalū kthīr min an-nās li hal-manāṭiq. wa 'aktharīyat 'oulādhum lissa sākinīn huna.	But when the Israelis had occupied the West Bank, many people moved out to these areas. And most of their children still live here.
	ibtidā'	beginning
	i9támadū 9ala	they relied on
	ḥālhum	themselves
	9āsh yi9īsh I, *ma9īsha*	to live (be alive)
	kayf mā kān	somehow or other
	yishtághilū	they work
	fi l-ibtidā' i9támadū 9ala ḥālhum, kānū yi9īshū kayf mā kān, walākin hassa kthīr min ar-rijāl yirūḥū yishtághilū youmīyan fi l-balad,	In the beginning they relied on themselves, living somehow or other, but now many of the men go to work daily in town,
	zara9 yizra9 I, *zar9*	to farm, plant, cultivate
	'arḍ 'arāḍī (f.)	land
	yihtimmū fī	they look after
	ṭifl 'aṭfāl	child
	shābb shabāb	young man
	tazawwaj V *min*	to get married to
	u niswānhum yiẓallū huna, yizra9ū 'arḍhum, yihtimmū fī 'aṭfālhum. kthīr min ash-shabāb wa l-banāt tazawwajū min 'oulādna.	while their women stay here farming their land, looking after their children.Many of the young men and girls have married our children.
	yishtárikū	they participate
	ḥayā ḥayawāt	life
	'ahl 'ahālī	people
	'aḥad (m.), *'iḥda* (f.)	one (of)
	iftataḥna	we inaugurated

	masīḥī	Christian
Peter:	ya9nī yishtárikū fī ḥayāt al-qáriya tamāman?	So they participate fully in the life of the village?
'abū 'ashraf:	ṭab9an. 'ahilna, mīya bi l-mīya. u 'iḥdāhum mudīrat al-madrasa taba9na. qabl kam sana ftataḥna kanīsa ṣghīra, u kthīr min an-nās masīḥīyīn.	Of course. They're our people, a hundred per cent. One of them is the headmistress of our school. Some years ago we inaugurated a small church, as many of the people are Christian.
	ṭaqs	weather
	maṭar 'amṭār	rain
	rayy	irrigation
	9aqqad II	to complicate
	samad 'asmida	fertiliser
	nittákhidh	we take
	'ijrā'	measure
Peter:	9āẓīm. fa kayf kānat az-zirā9a has-sana, yā 'abū 'ashraf?	Excellent. And how was the farming this year, Abu Ashraf?
'abū 'ashraf:	mish baṭṭāl. fi l-ibtidā' kunt 'akhāf 9ala ṭ-ṭaqs, ya9nī kān al-maṭar basīṭ, wa r-rayy mu9aqqad. wa zdād ishwayy thaman al-ḥubūb wa s-samad. kunna majbūrīn nittákhidh 'ijrā'āt khāṣṣa.	Not bad. In the beginning I was afraid for the weather, that is to say, the rain was poor and the irrigation was complicated. And the price of seeds and fertiliser went up somewhat. We were forced to take special measures.
	intáhat	it ended
	murḍī, múrḍiya, murḍīyīn	satisfactory
	walākin nushkuralla ntáhat as-sana bi l-kull bi ṣūra múrḍiya.	But, thank Heavens, the year ended satisfactorily on the whole.
Peter:	al-ḥamdulilla.	Thank Heavens.
	baladīya	municipality; town/village hall
	'a9táqid	I believe
	shaykh shuyūkh	old man, elder
	yintáđirū, yintáẓirū	they wait for
	ijtáma9ū	they assembled, they congregated
	'ikrām	deference
'abū 'ashraf:	yā Peter, tfaḍḍal ma9ī li l-baladīya. 'a9táqid 'inn shuyūkh al-qáriya yintáđirūk, ijtáma9ū 'ikrāman 'ilak ...	Peter, come with me to the village hall. I believe the elders are waiting for you; they've gathered in your honour ...

2. *9ibārāt*

intáhaz al-furṣa. He seized the opportunity. See this verb below.
'ilna sh-sharaf. The honour is mine ('ours'). The plural is used, as with *sharraftūna/tsharrafna.*
yikaththir khayrak ('(God) increase your welfare') God bless you.
mā 'ajmalu/'ajmalha/'ajmalhum How beautiful he/she/it is/they are! This type of expression is studied below.
9adad as-sukkān ('the number of inhabitants') the population
kayf mā kān ('as it was') somehow; any way one (etc.) can/could
basīṭ busaṭā' ('simple') in poor supply (water, fuel etc.)
'ikrāman li in honour of. Adverbial form of *'ikrām,* verbal noun of *'akram yukrim* IV 'to treat with deference'.

3. *mufradāt 'iḍāfīya. al-jughrāfīya wa ṭ-ṭaqs* – Geography and weather

9ālam 9awālim; dunya (no pl.)	world	*qārra*	continent
'iqlīm 'aqālīm	region	*muḥīṭ*	ocean
baḥr 'abḥār	sea	*buḥayra*	lake
jabal jibāl	mountain	*sahil*	easy, (pl. *suhūl*) plain (noun)
wād widyān	valley	*nahr 'anhur*	river
ṣaḥra ṣaḥāra/ṣaḥrāwāt	desert	*wāḥa*	oasis
madīna mudun	city	*'ahl al-mudun*	townspeople
'ahl al-qura	country people	*fallāḥ*	peasant, farmer
khalīj khulūj	bay, gulf	*mīna mawānī*	port
jazīra juzur	island	*shibih jazīra*	peninsula
saḥāb (collective)	clouds	*saḥāba suḥub*	cloud
shams shumūs (f.)	sun	*qamar 'aqmār*	moon
sama samāwāt (m./f.)	sky	*shimāl*	north
janūb	south	*sharq*	east
shimāl sharqī/gharbī	NE/NW	*janūb sharqī/gharbī*	SE/SW
hawa 'áhwiya	air	*ḥārr*	hot
rīḥ riyāḥ (f.)	wind	*raml ramāl*	sand
9āṣifa 9awāṣif	storm	*9āṣifa ramlīya*	sandstorm
shita 'áshtiya; thalj thulūj	snow	*saqaṭ yusquṭ* I	to fall
maṭar yumṭur I	to rain	*thalaj yuthluj* I	to snow
yumṭur; as-sama tumṭur; yusquṭ al-maṭar			it's raining
yuthluj; as-sama tuthluj; yusquṭ ath-thalj			it's snowing
'āsiya	Asia	*'āsiyawī*	Asian
'afrīqiya	Africa	*'afrīqī*	African
al-khalīj al-9arabī	Arabian Gulf	*an-nīl*	Nile
al-furāt	Euphrates	*ad-dijla*	Tigris
al-baḥr al/'aḥmar	Red Sea		
al-muḥīṭ al-'aṭlasī/al-hādī/al-hindī		Atlantic/Pacific/Indian Ocean	
ash-sharq al-'adna/al-'awsaṭ/al-'aqṣa		Near/Middle/Far East	
al-jazīra/shibih al-jazīra l-9arabīya		Arabian Peninsula	
al-baḥr al-'abyaḍ al-mutawassiṭ		Mediterranean Sea	

an-naḥū

4. Verbs of Form VII

For verbs of Form VII we can use the following models:

- Sound: *insáḥab yinsáḥib* to withdraw, be withdrawn
- Hollow (rare): *inzār yinzār* to be visited
- Doubled: *inḍamm yinḍamm* to join, be annexed to
- Final-weak: *inláqa yinláqī* to be encountered

Initial-*w* verbs do not occur in Form VII.

Note also:

- the *i*- beginning the first principal part is a weak vowel,
- the first syllable of a Form VII verb is never stressed, despite the general rule.

We mark the stress wherever it is irregular.

Form VII often expresses the passive voice (see 12/4) of Form I:

I *saḥab yisḥab* to pull, withdraw (something)
VII *insáḥab yinsáḥib* to be withdrawn, withdraw (oneself), retreat (of an army)

Form VII verbs cannot take a direct object. Typical tenses:

Sound: Root *s ḥ b, insáḥab yinsáḥib* to withdraw, be withdrawn:

Past: *insaḥabt, insaḥabt/insaḥabti, insáḥab/insáḥabat;*
insaḥabna, insaḥabtū, insáḥabū

Pres.: *'ansáḥib, tinsáḥib/tinsáḥibī, yinsáḥib/tinsáḥib;*
ninsáḥib, tinsáḥibū, yinsáḥibū

so also:

inkátab yinkátib	to be written	*infáṣal yinfáṣil*	to be separated
infájar yinfájir	to explode	*inkásar yinkásir*	to be broken
inqásam yinqásim	to be divided	*inqálab yinqálib*	to be overthrown
in9áqad yin9áqid	to assemble, be convened		
*inbásaṭ yinbásiṭ**	to be pleased, enjoy oneself		

* In the past tense of this verb, the *t*- beginning any personal ending assimilates to the final root letter and becomes *ṭ*-:

inbassaṭṭ/inbassaṭṭi/inbassaṭṭū I was/you were pleased
but *inbásaṭat* (no assimilation) she was pleased

Hollow: the middle root letter becomes *a* or *ā*; the hollow verb rule (6/4) applies.

Root *z w r, inzār yinzār* to be visited:

Past: *inzart, inzart/inzarti, inzār/inzārat; inzarna, inzartū, inzārū*

Pres.: *'anzār, tinzār/tinzārī, yinzār/tinzār; ninzār, tinzārū, yinzārū*

so also: *inqāl yinqāl* to be said

Doubled: *a* after the initial root letter in both tenses; see also the rule given below:

Root *ḍ m m, inḍamm yinḍamm* to join, be annexed to:

Past: *inḍamamt, inḍamamt/inḍamamti, inḍamm/inḍammat;*
inḍamamna, inḍamamtū, inḍammū

Pres.: *'anḍamm, tinḍamm/tinḍammī, yinḍamm/tinḍamm;*
ninḍamm, tinḍammū, yinḍammū

so also:

in9add yin9add	to be counted	*inḥall yinḥall*	to be solved

Doubled verb rule: In all increased forms of doubled verbs except II and V, the identical root letters separate before a consonantal personal ending and fall together elsewhere.

Final-weak: Root *l q y, inláqa yinláqī* to be encountered:
Past: *inlaqayt, inlaqayt/inlaqayti, inláqa/inláqat; inlaqayna, inlaqaytū, inláqū*
Pres.; the final root letter becomes *ī* and the final-weak verb rule (8/10) applies:
'anláqī, tinláqī/tinláqī, yinláqī/tinláqī; ninláqī, tinláqū, yinláqū

5. Some Form VII verbs can be used to express '-able, -'ible':

ar-raml mā yin9add.	Sand is uncountable.
tis9a yinqásim bi thalātha.	Nine is divisible by ('in') three.

6. Verbs of Form VIII

For Form VIII we can use the following models:

- Sound: *iqtáraḥ yiqtáriḥ* to propose, suggest
- Initial-*w*: *ittáṣal yittáṣil bi/fī* to contact
- Hollow: *imtāz yimtāz* to be distinguished
- Doubled: *iḥtall yiḥtall* to occupy
- Final-weak: *ishtára yishtarī* (NB stress is regular in the present) to buy

Form VIII is derived like Form VII, but with *t* after the initial root letter instead of *n* before it. Further:

- the *i*- beginning the first principal part is a weak vowel, as with Form VII,
- the first syllable of a Form VIII verb is stressed only in the present tense of final-weak verbs with final root letter *w* or *y*. See under the final-weak verbs below.

Some Form VIII verbs give a figurative meaning to the root. Compare:

fataḥ yiftaḥ I	to open	*iftátaḥ yiftátiḥ* VIII	to inaugurate

But many add no special meaning.

Sound; Root *q r ḥ, iqtáraḥ yiqtáriḥ* to propose, suggest:
Past: *iqtaraḥt, iqtaraḥt/iqtaraḥti, iqtáraḥ/iqtáraḥat;*
iqtaraḥna, iqtaraḥtū, iqtáraḥū
Pres.: *'aqtáriḥ, tiqtáriḥ/tiqtáriḥī, yiqtáriḥ/tiqtáriḥ; niqtáriḥ, tiqtáriḥū, yiqtáriḥū*
so also:

ijtáma9 yijtámi9	to assemble, congregate		
iftákar yiftákir	to think	*iktáshaf yiktáshif*	to discover
i9táqad yi9táqid	to believe	*i9tábar yi9tábir*	to consider
iḥtáram yiḥtárim	to respect	*intákhab yintákhib*	to (s)elect
intaðar yintáðir, intáẓar yintáẓir	to wait for	*intáqal yintáqil*	to move away
ijtáhad yijtáhid	to exert oneself	*ishtághal yishtághil*	to work
ishtárak yishtárik fī	to participate in	*i9támad yi9támid 9ala*	to rely on
i'támar yi'támir	to deliberate	*iftátaḥ yiftátiḥ*	to inaugurate
iḥtámal yiḥtámil	to tolerate, be probable		
intáhaz yintáhiz	to seize (*(al-)furṣa* an opportunity/the opportunity)		

and many others.

'akhadh yākhudh I has an irregular Form VIII:

ittákhadh yittákhidh to take

Initial-w: initial *w* regularly assimilates to the *t* of Form VIII, giving principal parts beginning *itt-*, *yitt-*:

Root *w ṣ l, ittáṣal yittáṣil bi/fī* to contact:

Past: *ittaṣalt, ittaṣalt/ittaṣalti, ittáṣal/ittáṣalat; ittaṣalna, ittaṣaltū, ittáṣalū*

Pres.: *'attáṣil, tittáṣil/tittáṣilī, yittáṣil/tittáṣil; nittáṣil, tittáṣilū, yittáṣilū*

so also:

ittáḥad yittáḥid	to be united	*ittáfaq yittáfiq 9ala*	to agree on

Hollow:; the weak middle root letter appears as *a* or *ā*, and the hollow verb rule (6/4) applies.

Root *m y z, imtāz yimtāz* to be distinguished

Past: *imtazt, imtazt/imtazti, imtāz/imtāzat; imtazna, imtaztū, imtāzū*

Pres.: *'amtāz, timtāz/timtāzī, yimtāz/timtāz; nimtāz, timtāzū, yimtāzū*

so also:

iḥtāj yiḥtāj 'ila	to need	*irtāḥ yirtāḥ*	to rest

Doubled: The doubled verb rule shown in paragraph 4 above applies.

Root *ḥ l l, iḥtall yiḥtall* to occupy:

Past: *iḥtalalt, iḥtalalt/iḥtalalti, iḥtall/iḥtallat; iḥtalalna, iḥtalaltū, iḥtallū*

Pres.: *'aḥtall, tiḥtall/tiḥtallī, yiḥtall/tiḥtall; niḥtall, tiḥtallū, yiḥtallū*

so also:

imtadd yimtadd	to be extended
ihtamm yihtamm bi/fī	to be concerned by; to look after

Final-weak: Verbs with final root letter *w* or *y* are stressed in the present tense on the *prefix*. In all other circumstances the stress is on the root, as in the other classes.

Root *sh r y, ishtára yíshtarī* to buy:

Past: *ishtarayt, ishtarayt/ishtarayti, ishtára/ishtárat;*
ishtarayna, ishtaraytū, ishtárū

Pres.: *'áshtarī, tíshtarī/tíshtarī, yíshtarī/tíshtarī; níshtarī, tíshtarū, yíshtarū*

so also: root *n h w, intáha yíntahī* to end

but: root *b d ', ibtáda yibtádī* to begin, stressed on the root throughout.

7. The *t* of Form VIII is modified after certain initial root letters:

- after initial-root letter *ṭ, ḍ, ṣ, ẓ* or *ð̣* it becomes *ṭ*:
  iḍṭárab yiḍṭárib to clash *iṣṭána9 yiṣṭáni9* to manufacture
- after initial-root letter *d, dh* or *z* it becomes *d*:
  izdād yizdād to be increased

Note also *izdáwaj yizdáwaj* 'to be double'; irregular, with stable middle *w*.

8. Imperatives of Forms VII and VIII

Make imperatives for Forms VII and VIII as for Form II:

VII	*insáḥib/insáḥibī/insáḥibū*	*lā tinsáḥib/lā tinsáḥibī/lā tinsáḥibū*
VIII	*ibtádī/ibtádī/ibtádū*	*lā tibtádī/lā tibtádī/lā tibtádū*

9. Participles of Forms VII and VIII

Form VII and VIII participles are derived as usual. Form VII has no passive; its active participle usually has passive meaning:

- *Active*: replace the *yi-* prefix of the second principal part with *mu-*,
- *Passive* (VIII only): replace initial *i-* of the first principal part with *mu-*.

In all the participles, we keep the stress of the principal part, unless a stressed ending (e.g. a sound plural ending) is added:

VII	*munfáṣil*	separate(d)	*munfájir*	explosive
	munḥall	(being) solved		
VIII	*mu9táqad*	believed	*muḥtáram*	respected
	mushtárik	participant	*mushtárak*	joint, common
	mujtáhid	industrious	*mu9támad*	reliable; accredited
	mu'támar	conference	*muḥtámal*	bearable; probable
	muntákhib	elector	*muntákhab*	elected
	muttáḥid	united	*muḥtāj**	needy
	*mumtāz**	distinguished, excellent	*mumtadd**	extended
	*muḥtall**	occupying; occupied	*mubtádī*	beginner
	muḍṭárib	agitated	*muṣṭána9*	fabricated
	muzdáwij	double(d)		

* In the hollow and doubled classes the Form VIII active and passive partiples are the same.

10. Verbal nouns of Forms VII and VIII

The patterns for the verbal nouns of Forms VII and VIII are similar except that the only common Form VII verbal nouns are the sound and doubled ones. Models are given below. The stress is regular; plurals, if any, are sound:

Class	Form VII		Form VIII	
Sound	*insiḥāb*	withdrawal	*iqtirāḥ*	proposal
Initial-*w*		–	*ittiṣāl*	contact
Hollow		–	*imtiyāz*	distinction
Doubled	*inḍimām*	annexation	*iḥtilāl*	occupation
Final-weak		–	*ishtirā'*	purchase

Examples, some with *nisba* adjectives derived from them:

VII	*infiṣāl*	separation	*infiṣāli*	separatist
	infijār	explosion	*in9iqād*	convening
VIII	*ijtimā9*	meeting	*ijtimā9ī*	social
	i9tiqād	belief	*i9tibār*	consideration
	intiðār, intiẓār	wait, expectation	*iḥtirām*	respect
	ishtirāk	participation	*ishtirākī*	socialist
	intiqāl	transfer	*i9timād*	confidence; accreditation
	iḥtimāl	tolerance; probability	*ijtihād*	zeal
	intikhāb	election	*intikhābī*	electoral

iftitāḥ	inauguration	*iftitāḥī*	inaugural
ittikhādh	taking	*i'timār*	deliberation
ittiḥād	unity, union	*ittiḥādī*	federal
ihtimām	concern, attention	*imtidād*	extension
iḥtiyāj	need	*intihā'*	end
ibtidā'	beginning	*ibtidā'ī*	initial, primary
iḍṭirāb	commotion, riot	*izdiyād*	increase
iṣṭinā9	manufacture	*iṣṭinā9ī*	artificial

Note also:

i9timād 9ala	dependence on/confidence in
'awrāq al-i9timād	(diplomatic) credentials
'akhadh bi 9ayn al-i9tibār	to take into consideration
ibtidā'an min, i9tibāran min	starting from, with effect from

11. Abstract nouns

An important type of abstract noun (i.e. a noun denoting an idea) is derived by adding *-ya* (plural, if any, sound) to a *nisba* adjective:

ishtirākīya	socialism	*ta9āwunīya*	cooperativism
ittiḥādīya	federalism	*infiṣālīya*	separatism
tawassu9īya	expansionsim	*ra'smālīya*	capitalism
dīmuqrāṭīya	democracy	*diktātūrīya*	dictatorship

and note *ḥurrīya* 'freedom' (from *ḥurr 'aḥrār* 'free').

12. Exclamations

We can form an exclamation with *mā* 'what' followed by the comparative form of a simple adjective (i.e. not a participle and not *nisba*), with a possessive suffix:

mā 'ajmalu/'ajmalha!	How beautiful it is!
mā 'akramak/ik/kum	How kind you are.

13. *kayf mā kān* (etc.)

Note these invariable expressions:

kayf mā kān	somehow or other, any way one (etc.) can/could		
wayn mā kān	somewhere or other	*mīn mā kān*	anyone at all
mata mā kān	at some/any time	*mahma kān*	anything at all

Those with pronouns are found mostly as direct or prepositional objects:

is'al mīn mā kān. *huwa mabsūṭ bi mahma kān*

14. Reflexive *ḥāl-*

ḥāl, invariable but with a possessive suffix, can be used like *nafs 'anfus* (see 8/16) to express the reflexive pronoun '-self/-selves':

saḥab ḥālu u riji9 li l-qáriya.	He took ('dragged') himself off and returned to the village.
ṣārū yishukkū fī 'anfus-hum/ḥālhum.	They began to doubt themselves.
ni9támid 9ala 'anfusna/ḥālna.	We rely on ourselves.
(kānat i)kthīr shāyifa ḥālha.	She is/was very conceited.

In this last idiom we use only a participial verb, not a tense.

15. Passive voice

It is incorrect to express the *agent* ('by whom') of a passive expression in Arabic. However, many Arab journalists use *min qibal* 'on the part of' for 'by', imitating European style. Use this idiom yourself very sparingly, if at all:

al-mustashfa nfátaḥ min qibal al-wazīr.
al-fatra mumaddada min qibal ash-sharika.

16. *shibih*

This noun, meaning 'resemblance', forms compound adjectives or nouns meaning 'semi-', 'quasi-' etc.

har-risālāt ash-shibih rasmīya	these semi-official letters
'ijrā'āt shibih ḥukūmīya	quasi-governmental measures

With a noun, *shibih* forms a construct:

shibih al- jazīra l-9arabīya	the Arabian peninsula
shibih al-qārra l-hindīya	the Indian subcontinent

17. Diminutives

Diminutive nouns are derivatives denoting something smaller than the original. Most Arabic diminutives are made on one of three models:

kitāb → *kutayyib*	booklet	*baḥr* → *buḥayra*	lake
{ *bāb* → *buwayb*	small door		
{ *kalb* → *kulayb*	puppy		

18. *jumal mithālīya*

'a9táqid 'inn 'aḥsan shī 'inna nintáðir ḥatta yittáṣil bīna ba9d al-ijtimā9.	I think the best thing for us is to wait for him to contact us after the meeting.
'akhāf 'inn yikūn 9adam at-tafāhum bayn al-mushtarikayn fī hādha l-mu'támar.	I fear there will be mutual misunderstanding between both participants at this conference.
khilāl al-mu'támar aṣ-ṣuḥufī taba9u l-wazīr 'akhbarna bi qtiráḥ al-ḥukūma l-jadīd bi khuṣūṣ mushkilitna r-ra'īsīya, u hiya l-insiḥāb min al-'arāḍi l-muḥtalla.	During his press conference the minister informed us of the Government's new proposal concerning our main problem, namely the withdrawal from the occupied territories.
hādha t-tafṣīl muhimm, walākin min al-muḥtámal 'innhum mā yākhudhū́ bi 9ayn al-i9tibār. lāzim 'iḥna nudhkuru marra thā́niya ḥatta mā yinsū́.	This detail is important, but it is likely that they will not take it into consideration. We must mention it again ourselves so that they don't forget it.
'akhbarnī bu ṣūra shibih rasmīya bi 'inn yikūn al-intiðār ṭawīl li 9adam al-muwāfaqa bayn al-mumaththilayn ar-ra'īsīyīn.	He informed me semi-officially that the wait will be a long one because of disagreement between the two chief representatives.

19. ***at-tamārīn***

1. Give the principal parts and the verbal noun of each verb:
e.g.: insáḥab – insáḥab yinsáḥib, insiḥāb
(a) sā9ad (b) kān (c) ittákhadh
(d) 'ansha (e) waẓẓaf

2. Put into the present tense:
e.g.: intakhabú l-youm. – yintákhibu l-youm.
(a) ṭab9an ishtarakna fi l-mu'támar.
(b) inqāl 'innu marīḍ.
(c) ash-shurṭa ḥtallat al-bināya.
(d) iktashaft shī jadīd?
(e) tawassa9at 'imkānīyat at-ta9āwun baynna u baynhum.

3. Use a tense instead of the participle:
e.g.: shāyifu 'ams? – shuftu 'ams?
(a) wāṣilīn fi l-layl, 'aftákir.
(b) mish 9ārifīn laysh.
(c) huwa kthīr muḥtāj 'ila musā9adatna.
(d) mīn sākin huna?
(e) fāhimnī yā 'akhūī?

4. Give the active participle of the verb:
e.g.: taqaddam – mutaqaddim
(a) infáṣal (b) 'arsal (c) masha
(d) iḥtāj (e) ittáḥad

5. Make one conditional sentence from the two sentences:
e.g.: kunna 9ārifīn. 'akhbarnāk min qabl.
– law kunna 9ārifīn, 'akhbarnāk min qabl.
(a) huwa mish moujūd. 'attáṣil bi zamīlu.
(b) mā ndīr bālna. yikūn fí nfijār shadīd.
(c) kān yidīr bālu. má kān fī mithl hādha l-infijār.
(d) kānat al-'as9ār 'aqall. qidirna níshtarī 'akthar.

6. Make feminine everything possible:
e.g.: huwa tilmīdh mumtāz yishtághil kwayyis.
– hiya tilmīdha mumtāza tishtághil kwayyis.
(a) 'abú rajul laṭīf wa kbīr as-sinn.
(b) aṭ-ṭabīb kān yiḥāwil yisā9id al-marīḍ.
(c) ta9raf al-mu9allimīn al-judud?
(d) ittáṣal fīnī 'ams.
(e) laysh mā tiḥtárimu ḥtirām 'akthar?

7. Fill the blank with the appropriate verbal noun, of the form indicated, from the list:
ta9āwun, kitāba, muḥāwala, tanẓīm, fahm, ishtirāk, intikhāb
e.g.: (VIII) az-zumalā' fī hādhi (III) ḍarūrī.
– ishtirāk az-zumalā' fī hādhi l-muḥāwala ḍarūrī.
(a) 9adam (VI) bayn az-zamīlayn huwa l-mushkila r-ra'īsīya.
(b) huwa yifhamnī (I) kāmil.
(c) mish qādir 'aqra (I) 9ala hal-warqa.
(d) ba9d (VIII) al-ishtirākīyīn inbásaṭu kthīr.
(e) 'ana mas'ūl 9an (II) hādha l-qism li sh-sharika.

6. Collect together words of the same root:
e.g.: tafāhum, muwaẓẓaf, tawẓīf, fahm
– tafāhum, fahm; muwaẓẓaf, tawẓīf
mutakallimīn, mafātīḥ, 'abwāb, buwayb, infátaḥat, kalima, iftitāḥ, mumtadd, yin9add, bawwāb, 9adad, yiftaḥ
(a) bāb ... (b) fataḥ ... (c) 9idda ...
(d) madd ... (e) takallum ...

ad-dars 'arba9t9ashr – Lesson 14
fi s-sūq – In the Market

1. *al-ḥikāya wa l-ḥiwār*

	yistafīd min	he benefits from
	li 'annu	because
	ḥaraka	movement
	yistaghrib min	he is astonished at
	biḍā9a baḍāyi9	merchandise
	nawwa9 II	to assort, to vary
(li ḥadd al-'ān Peter mā qidir yistafīd min ziyārat as-sūq li 'annu kān 9indu shughl ikthīr. dāyiman inbásaṭ ikthīr min al-ḥaraka wa l-ḥayā wa l-'aṣwāt, fi s-sūq. kān dāyiman yistaghrib min al-baḍāyi9 al-munawwa9a l-muqaddama hunāk.)		(Up to now Peter had not been able to have the benefit of a visit to the market because he had had a lot of work. He always greatly enjoyed the movement, the life and the noises in the market. He was always astonished at the varied goods offered there.)
	qammāsh	draper, cloth merchant
	ḥusayn	Hussein (name)
(fi s-sūq; 9ind al-qammāsh ḥusayn)		(in the market; at Hussein the cloth merchant's)
	fattash II *9an*	to look for
ḥusayn:	'ahlan yā sidī. tfaḍḍal. tfattish 9an shī mu9ayyan?	Welcome, sir. Are you looking for something in particular?
	fustān fasātīn	(woman's) dress
	ṣayfī	summer (adjective)
	loun 'alwān	colour
	qmāsh 'aqmisha	cloth
	qābil li l-ghasīl	washable
	wāṭi'	low
Peter:	na9am, 'aḥibb 'ashūf shī min sha'n fustān ṣayfī 'ila zoujti.	Yes, I would like to see something for a summer dress for my wife.
ḥusayn:	tfaḍḍal huna. hay kull al-'alwān, qmāsh qawī u khafīf li ṣ-ṣayf, u qābil li l-ghasīl tamāman. 'a9ṭīk iyyā́ 9ala 'awṭa' 'as9ār.	Come this way. Here we have all the colours, strong and light cloth for the summer, and completely washable. I'll give it to you at the lowest prices.
Peter:	hādha ṭayyib. kam yikallif?	This is good. How much does it cost?
ḥusayn:	'a9ṭīk iyyā́ li kam mā turīd.	I'll give it to you for however much you want.
	'ākhir kalima	('the last word') your final price
	fāṣal III	to bargain

	jins 'ajnās	sort, kind, quality
	thābit	firm, stable
	ghālī, ghāliya, ghāliyīn	expensive
	nista9mil	we use
	khāṭ yikhīṭ I, *khayṭ*	to sew
Peter:	la', qūl lī 'ākhir kalima, u mā 'urīd 'afāṣil ma9ak.	No, tell me your final price, I don't want to bargain with you.
ḥusayn:	wallāhi, tis9a danānīr bi l-mitr. jinsu mumtāz, mustawrad min al-yābān, wa l-'alwān thābita mīya fi l-mīya.	Well, nine dinars a metre. It's of excellent quality, imported from Japan, colours 100 per cent fast.
Peter:	ghālī shwayy, walākin yi9jibnī kthīr. li fustān ṣayfī, kam lāzim nista9mil? zoujti tkhīṭu nafs-ha.	It's a bit expensive, but I like it a lot. For a summer dress, how much must we use? My wife will sew it herself.
	santimitr	centimetre
	9arḍ 9urūḍ	width
	kaffa II	to suffice
	qaṣṣ yiquṣṣ I	to cut
ḥusayn:	mīya u khamst9ashr santimitr bi l-9arḍ, yikaffī mitrayn u nuṣṣ. 'a9ṭīk iyyā li thnayn u 9ishrīn dīnār, muwāfiq?	115 cm wide, two and a half metres will be enough. I'll give it to you for twenty-two dinars, agreed?
Peter:	kthīr kwayyis. quṣṣ lī mitrayn u nuṣṣ.	Very good. Cut me two and a half metres.
ḥusayn:	tikram	Certainly
	ikhṭār VIII	to choose, select
	mabrūk!	Congratulations!
	bārak III *fī*	to bless
	'amān	safety, safekeeping
	hay al-iqmāsh. ikhṭart ikwayyis, yā sīdī. mabrūk!	Here's the cloth. You chose well, sir. Congratulations!
Peter:	'alla yibārik fīk. tfaḍḍal.	Thank you.
ḥusayn:	u hay al-fakka. mamnūn jiddan. fī 'amān 'illā.	And here's the change. Thank you very much. Goodbye.
Peter:	fī 'amān al-karīm.	Goodbye.

2. *9ibārāt*

'ākhir kalima ('the last word') your best/last price

tis9a danānīr bi l-mitr nine dinars a metre

mīya u khamst9ashr santimitr bi l-9arḍ 115 cm wide ('in width')

mabrūk ('blessed') Congratulations! A greeting; the response is: *'alla yibārik fīk/fīki/fīkum* ('God bless you') Thank you.

fī 'amān 'illā ('in the safety of God') Goodbye. A greeting; the response is: *fī 'amān al-karīm* ('in the safety of the Generous One') Goodbye.

3. ***mufradāt 'iḍāfīya. al-mushtarayāt wa l-malābis*** **– Shopping, clothes**

shakl 'ashkāl	(also:) pattern	*ṭūl 'aṭwāl*	length, height
wazan yūzin I	to weigh	*qās yiqīs* I	to measure
zabūn zabāyin	customer	*... bi kam?*	how much is ...?
zawwad II	to supply	*kammīya*	quantity
tawaffar V	to be plentiful	*nāqiṣ nuqqaṣ*	in short supply
khaffaf II	to reduce	*badhla*	suit
grām	gram	*kīlou*	kilogram
banṭaloun	trousers	*labas yilbis* I	to wear
qamīṣ qumṣān	shirt	*jakayt*	jacket, coat
kundura kanādir	shoe	*kalsa*	sock
blūza	blouse	*gravāt*	necktie
tannūra tanānīr	skirt	*burnayṭa barānīṭ*	hat
malābis taḥtānīya	underclothes	*ghassal* II	to wash
ghasīl	washing, laundry	*kawa yikwī* I, *kawī*	to iron
shatawī	winter (adjective)	*naððaf* II *9ala n-nāshif*	to dry-clean

an-naḥū

4. Verbs of Form IX

Form IX is a rare and unimportant increased form. It is included here so that the list of forms is complete. You may prefer, at least provisionally, to omit this paragraph, or to use it solely for reference.

Form IX has only verbs denoting colours or physical defects. It has only sound and hollow classes, both with stable root letters throughout. Form IX behaves somewhat like a Form VIII doubled verb, but without the *-t-* after the first root letter.

Model root *ḥ m r*, *iḥmarr yiḥmarr* to go red, to blush:

Past: *iḥmarart, iḥmarart/iḥmararti, iḥmarr/iḥmarrat;*
iḥmararna, iḥmarartū, iḥmarrū I (etc.) went red, blushed

The initial *i-* of the first principal part (hence also of the past tense) is a weak vowel.

Pres.: *'aḥmarr, tiḥmarr/yiḥmarrī, yiḥmarr/tiḥmarr;*
niḥmarr, tiḥmarrū, yiḥmarrū I go red, blush (etc.)

so also:

iṣfarr yiṣfarr	to go yellow	*izraqq yizraqq*	to go blue
ikhḍarr yikhḍarr	to go green	*iswadd yiswadd*	to go black
ibyaḍḍ yibyaḍḍ	to blanch, go white	*i9wajj yi9wajj*	to become bent

Imperatives: *iḥmarr* (etc.), *lā tiḥmarr* (etc.)

Active participle: *muḥmarr* **Verbal noun**: *iḥmirār*

Form IX cannot have a direct object and has no passive participle.

5. Verbs of Form X

Form X has many useful verbs, made on the following models:

- Sound: *ista9mal yista9mil* to use
- Initial-*w*: *istawrad yistawrad* to import
- Hollow: *istarāḥ yistarīḥ* to rest

- Doubled: *istaḥaqq yistaḥiqq* to deserve
- Final-weak: *istathna yistathnī* to except

Some students find that Form X is most easily formed by reference to the structure of Form IV (11/6-8, 10). Take the pattern of the appropriate verb class in Form IV and change it as follows to give Form X:

- Principal parts:
  IV *'a-, yu-/yi-* → X *ista-, yista-* respectively
  IV *'aw-, yū-* → X *istaw-, yistaw-* respectively
- Imperative (see paragraph 6 below):
  IV *'a-, 'aw-* → X *ista-, istaw-* respectively
  IV *lā tu-, lā ti-, lā t-, lā ta* → X *lā tista-*
  IV *lā tū-* → X *lā tistaw-*
- Participles (see paragraph 7 below):
  IV *mu-, mū-* → X *musta-, mustaw-* respectively
- Verbal noun (see paragraph 8 below):
  IV *'i-, 'ī-* → X *isti-, istī-* respectively

One essential difference, however, between Forms IV and X is that while the first principal part of IV begins with *hamza*, that of Form X begins with weak *i-*.
Form X has two main additional meanings:

- causative, or seeking to achieve the result implied in the root:
  ista9mal yista9mil to use (to put something to work)
  ista'dhan yista'dhin to ask permission
- ascribing a quality to a thing or person:
  istaḥsan yistaḥsin to consider (a person/thing) good

Many have a person or thing as direct object.
Sound: Root *9 m l, ista9mal yista9mil* to use:
Past: *ista9malt, ista9malt/ista9malti, ista9mal/ista9malat;*
ista9malna, ista9maltū, ista9malū
Pres.: *'asta9mil, tista9mil/tista9milī, yista9mil/tista9mil;*
nista9mil, tista9milū, yista9milū
so also:

ikstakhdam yistakhdim	to employ
istaghraq yistaghriq	to last
istaḥḍar yistaḥḍir	to summon
istaqbal yistaqbil	to receive
istankar yistankir	to reject
istathmar yistathmir	to invest
istaḥsan yistaḥsin	to consider good
ista9lam yista9lim 9an	to enquire of
istaghrab yistaghrib min	to be astonished at
istaghfar yistaghfir min	to apologise for
istakbar yistakbir	to consider great; to be arrogant
istafham yistafhim 9an	to enquire about
istabdal yistabdil	to exchange, substitute
ista'dhan yista'dhin	to ask permission
ista'naf yista'nif	to resume

ista'jar yista'jir to rent (as tenant)

and many others.

Initial-w: Root *w r d, istawrad yistawrid* to import:

Past: *istawradt, istawradt/istawradti, istawrad/istawradat;*
istawradna, istawradtū, istawradū

Pres.: *'astawrid, tistawrid/tistawridī, yistawrid/tistawrid;*
nistawrid, tistawridū, yistawridū

so also:

istawṣaf yistawṣif to consult (a doctor)
istawṭan yistawṭin to settle (in a place)

Hollow: The hollow verb rule (6/4) applies.

Root *r w ḥ, istarāḥ yistarīḥ* to rest:

Past: *istaraḥt, istaraḥt/istaraḥti, istarāḥ/istarāḥat; istaraḥna, istaraḥtū, istarāḥū*

Pres.: *'astarīḥ, tistarīḥ/tistarīḥī, yistarīḥ/tistarīḥ; nistarīḥ, tistarīḥū, yistarīḥū*

so also:

istafād yistafīd min to benefit from *istashār yistashīr* to consult
istajāb yistajīb to grant a request

The last cited root *(j w b)* has a variant with stable middle root letter:

istajwab yistajwib to interrogate

Doubled: The doubled verb rule (13/4) applies.

Root *ḥ q q, istaḥaqq yistaḥiqq* to deserve:

Past: *istaḥqaqt, istaḥqaqt/istaḥqaqti, istaḥaqq/istaḥaqqat;*
istaḥqaqna, istaḥqaqtū, istaḥaqqū

Pres.: *'astaḥiqq, tistaḥiqq/tistaḥiqqī, yistaḥiqq/tistaḥiqq;*
nistaḥiqq, tistaḥiqqū, yistaḥiqqū

so also:

istaqall yistaqill to be independent; to consider small
ista9add yista9idd to be ready
istamarr yistamirr fī/9ala to continue with
istamarr yistajwibnī He continued to interrogate me.

Final-weak: Root *th n y, istathna yistathnī* to except:

Past: *istathnayt, istathnayt/istathnayti, istathna/istathnat;*
istathnayna, istathnaytū, istathnū

Pres.; *'astathnī, tistathnī/tistathnī, yistathnī/tistathnī;*
nistathnī, tistathnū, yistathnū

so also: *istaghna yistaghnī 9an* to do without

One important Form X final-weak verb is anomalous, with doubled middle root letter and final *-a* in the present tense:

istanna yistanna to wait for

6. Imperative of Form X

Derive Form X imperatives as for Forms VII and VIII, or by comparison with Form IV (para. 5 above):

ista9mil/ista9milī/ista9milū *lā tistarīḥ/lā tistarīḥī/lā tistarīḥū*

7. Participles of Form X

Derive Form X participles as for Forms VII and VIII:

- Active: replace the initial *yi-* of the second principal part with *mu-*,
- Passive: replace the initial *i-* of the first principal part with *mu-*,

– or derive by comparison with Form IV (para. 5 above).

musta9mil	user	*musta9mal*	used
mustakhdim	employer	*mustakhdam*	employed
mustaḥsan	approved	*mustankar*	objectionable
mustaqbil	(radio, TV) receiver	*mustaqbal*	future (adj./noun)
mustathmir	beneficiary	*musta'jir*	tenant
mustawrid	importer	*mustawrad*	imported
mustawṣaf	clinic	*mustawṭin*	native
mustarīḥ	restful	*mustarāḥ*	lavatory
mustashār	counsellor	*mustajīb 'ila*	responsive to
mustaḥiqq	deserving	*mustaqill*	independent
musta9idd 'ila	ready for	*mustamirr*	continuous
mustathna	excepted		

8. Verbal nouns of Form X

Models for verbal nouns (plurals are sound):

- Sound: *isti9māl* use, utilisation
- Initial-*w*: *istīrād* import(ation)
- Hollow: *istirāḥa* rest
- Doubled: *istiḥqāq* merit
- Final-weak: *istithnā'* exception

– or derive by comparison with Form IV (para. 5 above).

You will also notice that the sound, doubled and final-weak verbal noun patterns are similar to those of Forms VII and VIII.

Other examples:

istikhdām	employment	*istiqbāl*	reception
istithmār	investment	*istibdāl*	substitution
istighrāb	astonishment	*istinkār*	rejection
isti'jār	tenancy	*isti'nāf*	resumption
istijwāb	interrogation	*istiqlāl*	independence
istimrār	continuation	*isti9dād*	readiness

9. *li 'ann-*

When *li 'ann-* 'because' is followed by a pronoun, that pronoun is suffixed to it. When no pronoun follows it, it becomes *li 'annu*:

'astaḥiqq al-'iḍāfa li 'annī shtaghalt daraja 'ūla I deserve the increase because I have worked well ('first class').

ruht wara ṭ-ṭabīb li 'annu 'ummī kānat marīḍa. I went for ('after') the doctor because my mother was ill.

10. -able (etc.)

The sound adjective *qābil li*, followed by a definite verbal noun, expresses the meaning of English '-able, -ible' (etc.). It is negated with *ghayr*:

qābil li t-tajdīd	renewable	*qābila li l-ghasīl*	washable
ghayr qābil li l-ihtimām	unremarkable		
qābil li t-tamdīd	extensible (*maddad* II to extend)		

11. *jumal mithālīya*

'aja li l-maktab lābis badhla ṣayfīya, bi haṭ-ṭaqs!	He came to the office wearing a summer suit, in this weather!
illī yi9āmil an-nās bi haṣ-ṣūra mā yistaḥiqq iḥtirām al-ghayr.	Whoever treats people in this manner does not deserve the respect of others.
al-isti9māl al-maẓbūṭ li l-lugha d-dārija l-muthaqqafa huwa 'ishārat shakhṣ yifham 'usus al-lugha l-9arabīya.	The correct use of the educated spoken language is the mark of a person who understands the essentials of Arabic.
mish lāzim nistaghnī 9an ta9āwanu fi l-mustaqbal; hay ghalaṭna fi l-ibtidā'.	We shouldn't forgo his cooperation in the future; that was our mistake in the beginning.
duwal al-9ālam al-mustaqilla wa t-taqaddumīya kullha tistankir mithl hādha l-'ijrā'.	All the independent and progressive nations of the world will reject such a measure.

12. *at-tamārīn*

1. Give the active and passive participles, m. sing., of each verb:
e.g.: istaqbal – mustaqbil, mustaqbal

(a) fihim	(b) istawrad	(c) iḥtāj
(d) 'arsal	(e) istarāḥ	

2. Give the verbal noun of each verb in Ex. 1:
e.g.: istaqbal – istiqbāl

3. Give the first person singular, and the third person plural, of the past tense of each verb:
e.g.: istashār – istashart, istashārū

(a) istaghna	(b) inḥall	(c) nisī
(d) istajwab	(e) istaḥaqq	

4. Rephrase each sentence, beginning it with *mish lāzim*:
e.g.: 'ana staghnayt 9an musā9adatu. – mish lāzim 'astaghnī 9an musā9adatu.
(a) istashārū mutakhaṣṣiṣ fī hal-mouḍū9.
(b) ista9malat 'ibāra mish kwayyisa,
(c) huwa dāyiman musta9idd yit9āwan.
(d) istannaytnī khārij al-bayt.
(e) jaddadu 9ala ṭūl.

5. Put into the present tense:
e.g.: ista9malnā. – nista9milu.
(a) inqāl 'innu marīḍ.
(b) inḥallat al-mushkila.
(c) istabdalt shī fi l-mākīna?
(d) nisū u mā dafa9u l-ḥisāb.

6. Collect together words of the same root:
e.g.: jawāb, qabl, yijāwibū, istiqbāl, muqbila
– jawāb, yijāwibū; qabl, istiqbāl, muqbila
yi9malū, istithnā'īya, 9ulūm, isti9māl, 9ilmī, thānawīya, ma9lūm, mu9āmala, nista9lim, ithnayn
(a) thintayn ... (b) ta9līm ... (c) 9imil ...

ad-dars khamst9ashr – Lesson 15
al-'akhbār – The News

1. *al-'akhbār*

NB: This text introduces the written language read on television and the radio. Written forms are *underlined* in the vocabulary.

nashra	bulletin, publication
rā́diyo	radio
'awjaz yūjiz IV	to summarise
mūjaz	summary
naba' 'anbā'	information, (pl.) news
yawm	= *youm*
thānī 9ashar	twelfth
(khallīna nisma9 qiṭ9a qaṣīra min nashrat al-'akhbār 9ala r-rā́diyo.)	(Let us hear a short piece of the news bulletin on the radio.)
sayyidātī wa sādatī, 'ilaykum al-'ān mūjaz al-'anbā' li hādha l-yawm ath-thānī 9ashar min tishrīn al-'awwal.	Ladies and gentlemen, we bring you now a news summary for today, the twelfth of October.
salām	peace
'a9lan yi9lin IV	to announce
9aqad ya9qid I, *9aqd*	to tie; to hold (a conference etc.)
9aqadahu	= *9aqadu*
9āṣima 9awāṣim	capital (city)
bi khuṣūṣ al-mu'támar li s-salām fi sh-sharq al-'awsaṭ 'a9lan wazīr al-khārijīya 'ams fī mu'támar ṣuḥufī 9aqadahu bi l-9āṣima,	Concerning the peace conference in the Middle East, the Foreign Minister announced yesterday at a press conference which he held in the capital,
'anna	= *'inn*
fāwaḍ III	to negotiate
bayna	= *bayn*
jānib jawānib	side
lā	= *mā* (negative)
yata9allaq	= *yit9allaq*
'a9lan 'anna sti'nāf al-mufāwaḍāt bayna l-jānibayn lā yata9allaq bi l-mushtarikayn faqaṭ,	that the resumption of negotiations between both sides depends not only on the two participants,
bal	but, but rather
mawqif min	= *mouqif min* attitude towards
'isrā'īl	Israel
bal yata9allaq 'ayḍan bi mawqif ad-duwal al-gharbīya min siyāsat	but also on the attitude of the western countries towards the

'isrā'īl.	policy of Israel.
hādha, wa	furthermore
9abbar II *9an*	to express
'amal bi 'āmal bi	hope (noun) for
'aḥabb yiḥibb IV	= *ḥabb yiḥibb* I
sa tata9āwan	= *rāḥtit9āwan*
hādhihi	= *hādhi*
hādha, wa 9abbar al-wazīr 9an al-'amal bi 'anna jamī9 ad-duwal al-muḥibba li s-salām sa tata9āwan fī hādhihi l-mas'ala.	Furthermore, the minister expressed the hope that all peace-loving nations would cooperate in this matter.
'ukkid	it was confirmed
maṣdar maṣādir	source
sa tabda'	= *rāḥtibda*
fa 'ukkid min maṣdar qābil li l-i9timād 'anna l-mufāwaḍāt sa tabda' marra 'ukhra fī 'awākhir al-'usbū9 'inshalla.	It was confirmed from a reliable source that the negotiations will hopefully restart towards the end of the week.
mā zāl lā yazāl	not to stop, to continue
muḥāwalātiha	= *muḥāwalāt-ha*
min 'ajl	for (the sake of)
allátī	= *illī*
lā yumkin	= *mā yumkin*
'an	= *'inn*
tubālagh	it is exaggerated
'ahammīya	importance
'ahammīyatuha	= *'ahammīyit-ha* their importance
kullihi	= *kullu*
wa mā zālat al-ḥukūma muḥāwalātiha min 'ajl isti'nāf hādhihi l-mufāwaḍāt allátī lā yumkin 'an tubālagh 'ahammīyatuha li salām al-9ālam kullihi.	The government is continuing its attempts to get these negotiations resumed, whose importance for the peace of the whole world cannot be overstated.
'afād yufīd IV *bi*	(here:) to inform
warad yūrid I	to come in, arrive
ḥadath yaḥduth I	to happen, take place
khilāla l-yawmayn al-māḍiyayn	= *khilal al-youmayn al-māḍīyīn*
tufīd al-'anbā' al-wārida min 'afrīqiya l-janūbīya 'anna l-iḍṭirābāt allátī ḥadathat khilāla l-yawmayn al-māḍiyayn	It is reported from South Africa that the riots which took place over the last two days
qad	(not translated – see paragraph 11 below)
sabbab II	to cause

khasā'ir	= *khasāyir* (here:) damage
balagh yiblagh I	to amount to
tablagh	= *tiblagh*
qad sabbabat khasā'ir tablagh 'akthar min malyūn doulār.	caused damage amounting to over a million dollars.
fī khilāl	in the course of
ḥāditha ḥawādith	event
qutil	he was killed
9indama	= *lamma*
'aṭlaq yiṭlaq IV *an-nār*	to open fire
ḥashd ḥushūd	crowd
wa fī khilāl hādhihi l-ḥawādith qutil ithn9ashr shakhṣ 9indama 'aṭlaq an-nār al-būlīs 9ala l-ḥashd.	In the course of these events, twelve people were killed when the police opened fire on the crowd.

2. *9ibārāt musta9mala fi l-'idhā9a*

'ilaykum al-'ān (We bring) to you now. An ellipsis used in broadcasting.
hādha, wa ... Furthermore ... *hādha* refers to the previous passage.
dawla/duwal muḥibba li s-salām peace-loving nation(s) ('states')
maṣdar qābil/maṣādir qābila li l-i9timād reliable source(s)
tufīd al-'anbā' bi ('the news benefits (us) with') It is reported ...

3. *mufradāt 'iḍāfīya. as-siyāsa wa l-9alāqāt ad-duwalīya*
– Politics and international relations

(hay'at) al-'umam al-muttáḥida	United Nations (Organisation)
al-wilāyāt al-muttáḥida (l-'amrīkīya/li 'amayrka)	United States (of America)
al-ittiḥād al-'urubbī	European Union
as-sūq al-'urubbīya l-mushtáraka	Common Market
jāmi9at ad-duwal al-9arabīya	League of Arab States
al-bank ad-duwalī	World Bank
ṣandūq an-naqd ad-duwalī	International Monetary Fund
al-ittiḥād as-sufiyātī/as-sufiyayti (s-sābiq)	(the former) Soviet Union
aṣ-ṣīn ash-sha9bī	People's Republic of China
al-9ālam ath-thālith	third world
dawla nấmiya	developing country
dawla ṣinā9īya	industrialised country
dawla kubra	superpower
maṣlaḥa maṣāliḥ	(legal/political) interest
rū́siya	Russia
sulṭa	authority
ḥukm dhātī	autonomy
hay'a	corps, body, group
mandūb	(also:) commissioner
9uḍw 'a9ḍā'	member

ḥizb 'azḥāb	(political) party
mu9āraḍa	opposition
majlis majālis	council
malik mulūk	king
mamlaka mamālik	kingdom
'amīr 'umarā'	prince, emir
'imāra	principality, emirate
dustūr dasātīr	constitution
jumhūrīya	republic
jumhūrī	republican
ra'īs (al-jumhūrīya)	President (of the Republic)
ra'īs al-wuzarā'	Prime Minister
majlis al-wuzarā'	cabinet (of ministers)
nāyib nuwwāb	deputy, member of lower house of Parliament
shaykh shuyūkh	(also:) senator
'amīn 9āmm	secretary-general
majlis an-nuwwāb/ash-shuyūkh	lower/upper house of Parliament
nāṭiq(a) bi lisān	spokesman/-woman
qaḍīya qaḍāya	cause, case
ittifāq	(spoken) agreement
ittifāqīya	(written) agreement, treaty
thawra	revolution
inqilāb	coup d'état
ḥarb ḥurūb (f.)	war
'irhāb	terrorism
shuyū9ī	communist
ṣahyūnī	Zionist
tamyīz 9unṣurī	racial discrimination
9unṣurīya	racism, racialism

an-naḥū

4. Broadcasting

Broadcast news is read in written Arabic. We study in paragraphs 5 to 12 below those elements of written usage which will help you to follow the news.

5. Passive

See 12/4. Written Arabic has passive tenses as well as active tenses. For the news, we need to be able to recognise only the third persons singular and plural (animate and inanimate). The passive tenses differ from the active tenses only in their vowels. In general, the passive pattern is *u-i* for the past tense and *u-a* for the present tense, with variations for weak (initial-*w*, hollow, final-weak) and for doubled root letters. Examples (meaning 'he/it was/is ...', m. sing.):

I	*fuhim yufham*	understood	*'ukhidh yu'khadh*	taken
	wujid yūjad	found	*sīq yusāq*	driven
	mudd yumadd	extended	*rúmiya yurma*	thrown
II	*9ullim yu9allam*	taught	*súmmiya yusamma*	named

III	*kūtib yukātab*	written to	*wūfiq yuwāfaq*	agree
	ḥūwil yuḥāwal	attempted	*nūdiya yunāda*	summoned
IV	*'ursil yursal*	sent	*'urīd yurād*	wanted
	'unshi' yunsha'	constructed		
V	*tudhukkir yutadhakkar*	remembered	*turuddid yutaraddad**	hesitated
VI	*tubūdil yutabādal*	exchanged	*tunūwil yutanāwal*	consumed
VIII	*u9túbir yu9tábar*	considered	*uttúkhidh yuttákhadh*	taken
	*uḥtīj yuḥtāj**	needed	*uḥtull yuḥtall*	occupied
	ushtúriya yushtára	bought		
	(NB: Present-tense stress also irregular in this verb)			
X	*ustukhdim yustakhdam*	employed	*ustufīd yustafād**	benefited
	ustuqill yustaqall	considered small	*ustúthniya yustathna*	excepted

* For verbs which take no direct object, the meaning is impersonal: *turuddid* 'there was hesitation', *yuḥtāj 'ila* 'there is need of'. The impersonal passive always stands in the masc. sing. form.

6. Two common and easy impersonal expressions with passive meaning can be constructed using an active verb plus a definite verbal noun.

tamm/tammat I in the past tense, 'it was completed' plus a definite verbal noun (which may be one in construct) gives a completed passive meaning in past time:

tamm baḥth al-mouḍū9. — The matter was/has been discussed.
tammat dirāsat al-mouḍū9. — The matter was/has been studied.

jara yijrī I (*jara yajrī* in written pronunciation) 'to flow', in the past or present tense, plus a definite verbal noun (which may be one in construct) gives a passive meaning relating to an ongoing action or situation, past or present as appropriate:

tijrī/tajrī mufāwaḍat aṭ-ṭalab. — The demand is being negotiated.
jarat dirāsat al-mawḍū9/al-mouḍū9 mudda ṭawīla. — The matter was (being) studied at length.

The verbal noun can also be from a verb with no direct object:

tamm al-wuṣūl 'ila l-ittifāq 9ala l-'as9ār. Agreement was reached on prices.

Do not interpret the opening verb too literally in this construction.

7. Written verb prefixes and endings, active voice.

In the written active voice the present-tense personal prefixes of all forms, I to X, and the prefix of Forms V, VI and IIQ in both tenses, all have a vowel (i.e. they form a syllable). This vowel is *u* for the present-tense prefixes of Forms II, III, IV and IQ; and *a* everywhere else, thus:

Personal prefixes, present tense	Forms II, III, IV, IQ:	*'u-, tu-, yu-, nu-*
	Forms I, V-X, IIQ:	*'a-, ta-, ya-, na-*
Prefix of Forms V, VI and IIQ (both tenses):		*ta-*

In addition, verb forms with a sound final root letter often have a further short vowel. This vowel is usually dropped in pronunciation when the verb carries no object-pronoun suffix; but when there is such a suffix, the vowel is retained. The vowel is always *-a-* or *-u-*:

katab	he wrote	but:	*katabahu*	he wrote it

nursil we send but: *nursiluha* we send it

Do not let the presence of this vowel (or the unfamiliar form of the pronoun suffix) confuse you.

8. Diphthongs

The pronunciation of the written language has *aw* for spoken *ou*: *yawm* (for *youm*).

9. Written sentence structure

In written Arabic the verb often precedes its subject; this structure is called a *verbal sentence*. In such a sentence, when the subject is a noun, the verb is always in the singular, even if the subject is plural:

'a9lan al-wazīr/al-wuzarā' 'anna ... *dakhalat al-mu9allimāt aṣ-ṣaff.*

When the subject precedes the verb, the sentence is known as a *nominal sentence*, and the verb agrees normally with its subject. A nominal sentence may begin with the conjunction *'inna*, which adds no meaning. If the subject is a pronoun, it is suffixed to *'inna*:

al wazīr ('inna l-wazīr) 'a9lan 'anna ... *('innahum) qālu l-yawm ...*
al-ḥikāya ('inna l-ḥikāya) ṭawīla.

10. Negative

In written Arabic, the negative of the present tense is formed with *lā*. *mā* is used only for the past tense:

lā yata9allaq bi d-duwal an-nāmiya faqaṭ.
mā ta9allaq bi waḍ9 ad-duwal an-nāmiya.

But note the use of *lā* with the past tense to express a negative wish (in both written and spoken Arabic):

lā samaḥ 'alla God/Heaven forbid.

11. *qad*

The verbal particle *qad* may be used to reinforce a past tense in written Arabic. It adds no other meaning:

al-iḍṭirābāt (qad) 'antajat khasā'ir tablagh ...

12. Written future

Written Arabic does not use *rāyiḥ/rāḥ*. The written future has the particle *sawfa* or *sa* before the present tense:

sawfa/sa tastaghriq az-ziyāra yawmayn. The visit will last two days.

13. *mā zāl*

Note the Form I hollow verb *zāl yazāl* 'to cease', following the pattern of *nām yinām* but with *-a-* in the present prefixes:

Past: *zilt, zilt/zilti, zāl/zālat; zilna, ziltū, zālū*
Pres.: *'azāl, tazāl/tazālī, yazāl/tazāl; nazāl, tazālū, yazālū*

Its main use is in the negative, as an auxiliary meaning 'to continue'. The written negative particle is always used, even in unscripted speech:

lā yazālū muḥāwalāt-hum li sti'nāf al-mu'támar. ('They are continuing their efforts for the resumption of the conference.')
They are still trying to get the conference resumed.
lā yazāl yuṭlub musā9adatak. He is still asking for your help.
mā zilna nistafīd min ta9āwanu. We continued to benefit from his cooperation.
mā zālū yuskunū fī bayrūt. The are/were still living in Beirut.

14. Verb forms

The ten forms of the triliteral verb merit recapitulation. Here are the models again (first principal part, sound class only), with comments:

Form, model		Meaning, use	Frequency
I	*katab*	basic; with or without direct object	very high
II	*ḥaḍḍar*	causative or intensive of I; with direct object	high
III	*kātab*	= I but with person direct object	high
IV	*'arsal*	causative of I, with direct object	high
V	*taqaddam*	passive or reflexive of I, II; mostly with no direct object	very high
VI	*takātab*	reciprocal of I, II or III; mostly with no direct object	high
VII	*insáḥab*	passive of I; no direct object	middle
VIII	*iqtáraḥ*	no additional meaning; direct object	very high
IX	*iḥmarr*	colours, physical defects; no direct object	very low
X	*ista9mal*	seeking or causing action or state of I; ascribing a quality to something/someone; with or without direct object	very high

15. *jumal mithālīya*

waṣal (= wiṣil) al-yawm ṣabāḥan fī dimashq min al-qāhira wazīr al-khārijīya l-miṣrī, 9ala ziyāra rasmīya tastaghriq yawmayn. wa 'ukhbirna min maṣdar ḥukūmī bi 'anna gharaḍ hādhihi z-ziyāra yata9allaq bi qaḍīyat al-lāji'īn (= al-lājīyīn) fi l-minṭaqa.

This morning, the Egyptian Foreign Minister arrived in Damascus from Cairo on an official visit lasting two days. It has been learned from a government source that the purpose of this visit has to do with the question of refugees in the region.

tuhimmuna (= t-himmna) mas'alat al-'irhāb al-9ālami htimāman kabīran, wa taḥtāj 'ila ta9āwun jamī9 ad-duwal al-muḥibba li s-salām.

The question of world terrorism concerns us greatly, and needs the cooperation of all peace-loving countries.

lā yūjad ḥall dā'im (= ḥill dāyim) li l-mashākil fi sh-sharq al-'awsaṭ 'illa bi

No lasting solution of the problems in the Middle East

ḥall qaḍīyat al-filasṭinīyīn.	will be found without a solution to the case of the Palestinians.
'inn al-9alāqāt bayna d-duwal an-nā́miya wa d-duwal aṣ-ṣinā9īya hiya l-mushkila l-markazīya llátī 'amāmana (= 'amāmna).	Relations between the developing countries and the industrialised countries are the central problem facing ('before') us.
kayfa (= kayf) yumkin 'an nufāwiḍ mithla (= mithl) hādhihi l-ittifāqīya wa mā zilna nabḥath siyāsatana (= siyāsitna) d-dākhilīya?	How is it possible for us to negotiate this sort of convention while we are still discussing our internal policy?

16. ***at-tamārīn***

1. Give the active voice, in spoken Arabic, of each passive verb:
e.g.: 'ursil – 'arsal

(a) yusta9mal	(b) ustu9milat	(c) yūjad
(d) uḥtīj 'ila	(e) yustaghna 9an	

2. Re-express in spoken form:
e.g.: 'inna l-wazīr 9abbar 9an fikratihi fi l-mu'támar.
– al-wazīr 9abbar 9an fikritu fi l-mu'támar.
(a) qāl as-sufarā' 'inna l-mushkila mu9aqqada.
(b) kutibat risāla tuhimmuna jamī9ana.
(c) mā hiya l-mas'ala llátī dhakaraha?
(d) sa 'aktub al-jawāb al-'ān.

3. For each of these verbal derivatives, give the principal parts and the form (I-X) of the original verb:
e.g.: isti9māl – ista9mal yista9mil X

(a) qawlna	(b) muntakhibīn	(c) 'inshā'u
(d) tárbiyitu	(e) tafāhum	

4. Complete the sentence with the right preposition:
e.g.: kull shī yitwaqqaf ...hum. – kull shī yitwaqqaf 9alayhum.
(a) mā najaḥū, 'aftákir, ... 9adam at-taḥḍīr.
(b) mā́ fī 9indu 'ayy i9timād ... nafsu.
(c) at-tafāhum ...ī u ...ak ḍarūrī.
(d) shū tiftákir ... hādha?

Part II

Written Arabic

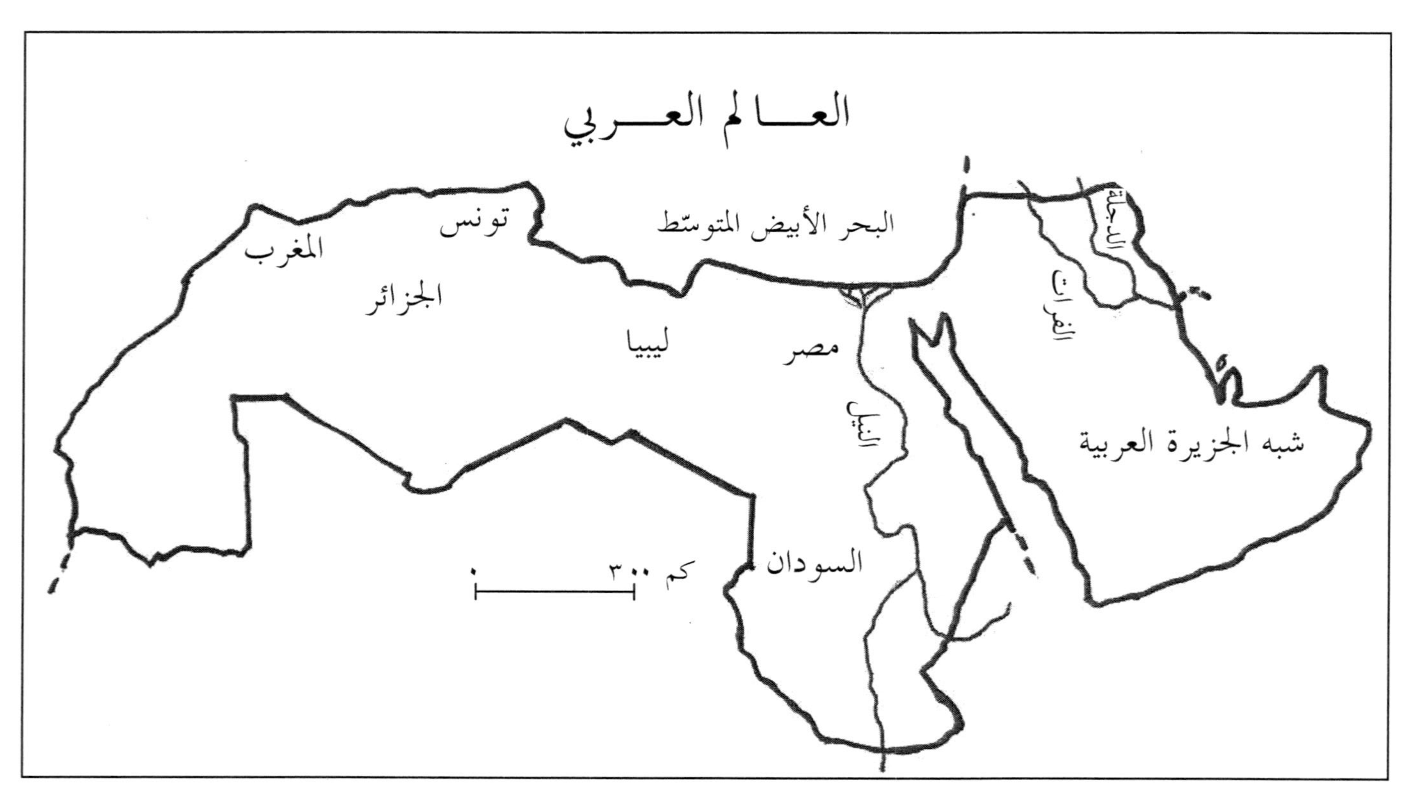
العالم العربي
البحر الأبيض المتوسّط
تونس
المغرب
الجزائر
ليبيا
مصر
النيل
الفرات
الدجلة
شبه الجزيرة العربية
السودان
٣٠٠ كم
٠

الدرس السادس عشر
ad-dars as-sādis 9ashar – Lesson 16
القراءة والكتابة
al-qirā'a wa l-kitāba – Reading and Writing

1. Certain important principles first:

- Arabic writing runs from right to left ←←.
- Many letters ('joined letters') are joined to the letter following them in the same word. Most such letters have different forms for different positions in the word. A few letters ('disjoined letters') are never joined to the left, i.e. to a following letter. They have only one form.
- Short vowels are normally not written. There is a means of marking them, but it is rarely used.

2. We use the following terms to refer to the different forms of a joined letter:

- 'initial' form, i.e. either beginning a word, or after a letter not joined to its left,
- 'medial' form, i.e. joined on both sides,
- 'final' form, i.e. ending the word and joined to the preceding letter,
- 'isolated' form, i.e. standing alone; for all but a few letters this is identical to the final form.

3.

ا	***a, 'a*** ***u, 'u*** ***i, 'i***

This letter, called *'alif*, is disjoined, i.e. it is not joined to the following letter. It rests on the line of writing. When isolated or initial it is written downwards, thus: ا . Write a whole line, starting at the right of the page: ↓

ا ا ا ا ا ا ا ا ا ا ا ا ا ا ا ا ا ا ا ا

Beginning a word, *'alif* indicates any weak short vowel, or *hamza* plus a short vowel.

4.

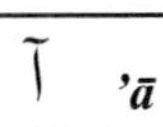

hamza plus long vowel *ā* beginning a word is expressed with the combination called *'alif madda*. *'alif madda* is disjoined, like *'alif*. Write a line: ←↓

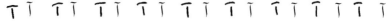

5.

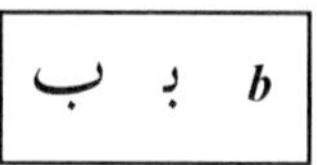

The consonant *b* is expressed with the letter *bā'*, which is a joined letter (i.e. joined to the following letter in the same word). It has a short initial/medial form ﺑ and a full isolated/final form ب . *bā'* rests on the line of writing. Write: ←

b ﺑ ﺑ ﺑ ﺑ ﺑ ﺑ ﺑ ﺑ ب ب ببب ب ب ب ب ب ب

We can now write the words *'ab* and *'āb*:

'ab اب اب اب اب اب اب اب *'āb* آب آب آب آب آب آب آب

6. Medial *'alif* almost always expresses *ā*. Final *'alif* also in theory expresses *ā*, but in practice final *ā* is almost always pronounced short: *a* (see Pronunciation, paragraph 2).

Whereas initial or isolated *'alif* is written downwards, medial or final *'alif* is struck upwards from its junction with the preceding letter. Now write:

bāb باب باب باب باب باب باب باب باب

7. Always *write* your words; do not trace or draw them. Avoid retouching a badly written word at this stage; rewrite it rather.

8.

ت	ﺗ	*t*
ث	ﺛ	*th*

The joined letters *tā'* and *thā'* (sounds *t* and *th*) are written in a manner identical to *bā'* except for their dots. *bā'*, *tā'* and *thā'* are 'toothed' letters; the initial/medial form ﺑ without its dot(s) is a 'tooth'. The forms given above are as in print. In handwriting, two dots are often written like a hyphen (-) and three like a circumflex accent (^). Write:

t ﺗ ﺗ ﺗ ﺗ ﺗ ﺗ ﺗ ﺗ ت ت ت ت ت ت ت ت ت ت

th ﺛ ﺛ ﺛ ﺛ ﺛ ﺛ ﺛ ﺛ ث ث ث ث ث ث ث ث ث ث

We can now write *thābit* (long *ā* written, short *i* not written):

ثابت ثابت ثابت ثابت ثابت ثابت *thābit*

9.

ن ﻧ *n*

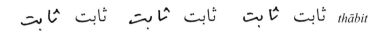

The sound *n* is written with the joined letter *nūn*. Initial/medial *nūn* ﻧ is a toothed letter, normally resting on the line of writing; isolated/final *nūn* ن is deeper than *bā'* etc., and when joined it swoops below the line of writing and up again. In rapid handwriting, the dot of isolated/final ن often becomes a small hook:

print ن handwriting ن

Write both isolated/final forms:

n ن ن ن ن ن ن ن ن ن ن ن ن

We can now write a few other words. Wherever the written pronunciation or the choice of word differs from the spoken, we show the latter in angular quotation marks ‹ ›. Read and write:

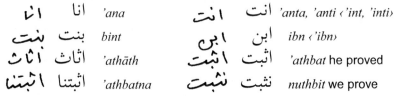

انت	انت	*'anta, 'anti ‹'int, 'inti›*	انا	انا	*'ana*
ابن	ابن	*ibn ‹'ibn›*	بنت	بنت	*bint*
اثبت	اثبت	*'athbat* he proved	اثاث	اثاث	*'athāth*
نثبت	نثبت	*nuthbit* we prove	اثبتنا	اثبتنا	*'athbatna*

The initial *'alif* written in some of these words is not itself a short vowel; it provides a 'seat' for the unwritten short vowel. Words beginning with a vowel of any kind, or with *hamza*, must begin with *'alif* in writing. Initial *hamza* can be added (we learn it below), but it is usually left unwritten.

10.

ﻳ	***y, ī, ay***
ي	***y, ī, ay***
اﻳ	***'ī, 'ay***

The joined letter called *yā'* represents:

- beginning the word (short form, ﻳ): the consonant *y*,
- in the middle of the word (short form, ﻳ): the consonant *y*, the long vowel *ī* or the diphthong *ay*,
- at the end of the word (full form, ي): *ī* or *ay*,
- after *'alif* اﻳ at the beginning of a word: *'ī* or *'ay*.

The short form is a toothed letter. The full form swoops below the line of writing and up again. Write:

ي ي ي ي ي ي ي ي يي يي يي يي

In the combination of initial tooth + full-form *yā'* ي the tooth stands above the *yā'*, the junction becomes an acute angle, and the ي loses its first bend. Write:

ني ني *nī* بي بي *bī* تي تي *tī*

Read and write:

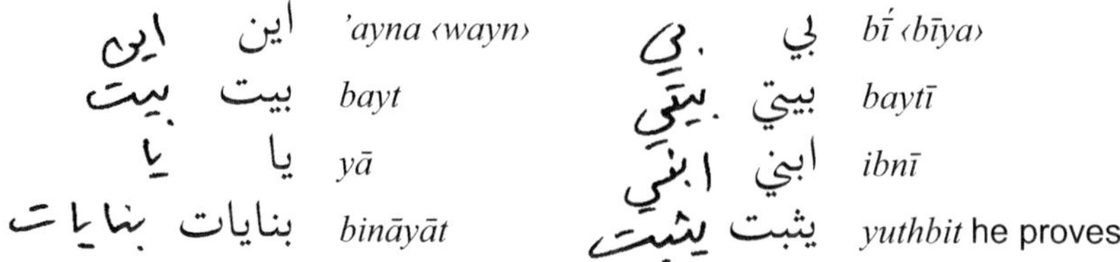

بي *bī ‹bīya›*
اين *'ayna ‹wayn›*
بيتي *baytī*
بيت *bayt*
ابني *ibnī*
يا *yā*
يثبت *yuthbit* he proves
بنايات *bināyāt*

11.

ا ل ل

The sound *l* is expressed with the joined letter *lām*. This letter has the same height as *'alif*. Its short form rests on the line, while its full form swoops slightly below.

Despite first appearances, *lām* is never confused with *'alif* because one is joined and the other is not. Write:

ا ل ل ل ل ل ل ل ل ل ل ل ل ل ل ل ل ل

Read and write:

البيت	*al-bayt*	البنت	*al-bint*
ثلث	*thulth*	ثالث	*thālith*
بال	*bāl*	لي	*lī*
لبنان	*lubnān*	اليابان	*al-yābān*

12. The article is always written with *lām*, no matter how pronounced. Read and write:

الثالث	*ath-thālith*	النيل	*an-nīl*

13. The combination *lām-'alif* is written in special ways both in print and in handwriting. When writing by hand, detach the *'alif* and strike it downwards, either vertically to the foot of the *lām* or diagonally towards its angle. Examine the forms:

- when not joined to the previous letter:
  printed لا handwritten لا لا
- when joined to the previous letter:
  printed ـلا handwritten ـلا ـلا

Read and write:

لا لا *lā* ثلاثين ثلاثين *thalāthīn*

The combination [لا] is never found in correctly written Arabic.

14.

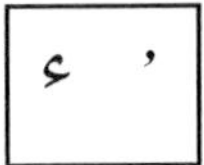

hamza has only one form, and it is never joined to anything. Write:

Beginning a word it is written above or below *’alif*, so:

أ	*’a, ’u*
إ	*’i*

However, it is usually left unwritten at the beginning of a word. *hamza* is never written together with آ *’alif madda.*

15. When a word beginning with *hamza* receives a prefix, the *hamza* ceases to be initial, and must therefore be written. Read and write:

الأثاث الأثاث *al-’athāth* الإبل الإبل *al-’ibil*

16. Note how certain sound plural and dual endings are written:

ات ات *-āt* ين ين *-īn, -ayn*

يات يات *-yāt, -iyāt,- īyāt*

Read and write:

بنات بنات *banāt* لبنانيات لبنانيات *lubnānīyāt*

بنايات بنايات *bināyāt* بيتين بيتين *baytayn*

Do not attempt yet to write the f. sing./inan. pl. endings *-iya, -īya*. These endings have a different spelling, which we study later.

17. Words consisting of one letter are always written as one with the next word, the spelling of which is usually unchanged, except that any unwritten *hamza* must now be added (paragraph 15 above). Initial *'alif* of the second word, or its article, is retained. Read and write:

بأنابيب	*bi-'anābīb*	بالبيت	*bi l-bayt*
بالأثاث	*bi l-'athāth*	بابني	*bí bnī*
بأثاثنا	*bi-'athāthina ‹'athāthna›*		
ببيتي	*bi baytī*	بالإبل	*bi l-'ibil*
		بالبيت الثالث	*bi l-bayt ath-thālith*

Similarly, *'alif madda* keeps its *madda* after the article and after an attached one-letter word. Read and write:

الآن *al-'ān*

18. After *li*, exceptionally, the article (but not the word) loses its *'alif*. This is the only such exception. Read and write:

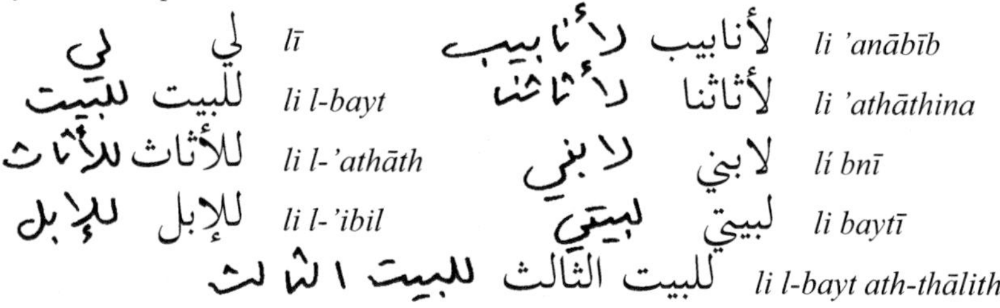

لي	*lī*	لأنابيب	*li 'anābīb*
للبيت	*li l-bayt*	لأثاثنا	*li 'athāthina*
للأثاث	*li l-'athāth*	لابني	*lí bnī*
للإبل	*li l-'ibil*	لبيتي	*li baytī*
		للبيت الثالث	*li l-bayt ath-thālith*

19. Two successive identical consonants with an intervening vowel are both written. But doubled consonants (i.e. two successive identical consonants with *no* intervening vowel) are written single. Read and write:

ان	*'anna ‹'inn›*	اني	*'annī ‹innī›*
لأن	*li 'anna ‹li 'ann›*	لأني	*li 'annī*
بأن	*bi 'anna ‹bi 'inn›*	بن	*bunn* coffee
بني	*bunnī*	تل تلال	*tall tilāl* hill

Three important exceptions:

- initial *lām* is retained after the article:

  اللبن *al-laban* milk (written), yoghurt (spoken)

- two letters *yā'* for *yi, yay, īyī, īyay*:

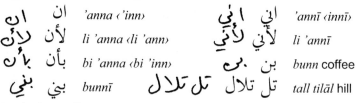

  لبنانيين *lubnānīyīn/-īyayn*

  ليبيين *lībīyīn/-īyayn* يابنيين *yābānīyīn/-īyayn*

- no more than two identical consecutive letters are written, even if logic demands more: للبن *li l-laban.*

20.

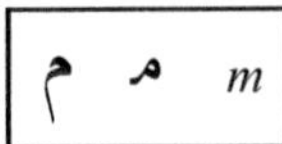

The sound *m* is expressed with the joined letter *mīm*. The bead of this letter rests on the line of writing; the tail of the full form extends straight down.

The initial and isolated forms of *mīm* are written either anticlockwise or clockwise; the medial and final forms are best written anticlockwise. Write:

In other words, when joined to the preceding letter, mīm is best approached from the top. This gives special combinations in handwriting, and sometimes in better print. Examine:

tooth + *m*

middle tooth* + *m*

lm

mm

* i.e. a tooth preceded by any joined letter.

Read and write:

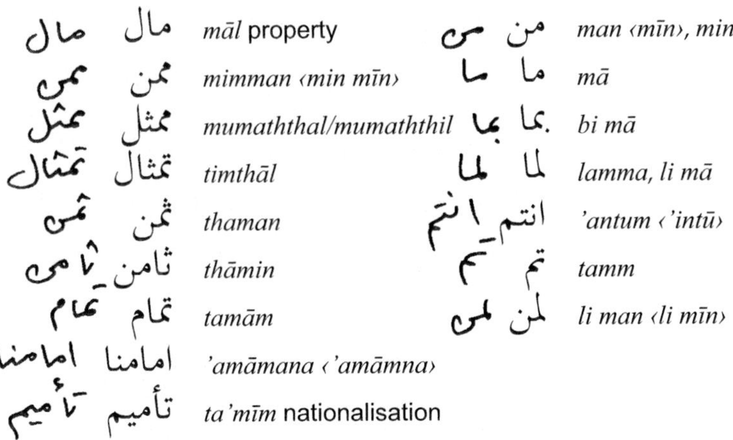

مال	*māl* property	من	*man ‹mīn›, min*
ممن	*mimman ‹min mīn›*	ما	*mā*
ممثل	*mumaththal/mumaththil*	بما	*bi mā*
تمثال	*timthāl*	لما	*lamma, li mā*
ثمن	*thaman*	انتم	*'antum ‹'intū›*
ثامن	*thāmin*	تم	*tamm*
تمام	*tamām*	لمن	*li man ‹li mīn›*
امامنا	*'amāmana ‹'amāmna›*		
تأميم	*ta'mīm* nationalisation		

21.

و	***w, ū, aw***
او	***'ū, 'aw***

The disjoined letter *wāw* represents:

- beginning the word: the consonant *w*,

- in the middle or at the end of the word: the consonant *w*, the long vowel *ū* or the diphthong *aw ‹ou›*,
- after *'alif* at the beginning of a word: او *'ū* or *'aw ‹ou›*.

wāw has only one form. Its ring lies on the line of writing, and its tail curves below. Write:

و و و و و و و و و و و و و و

Read and write:

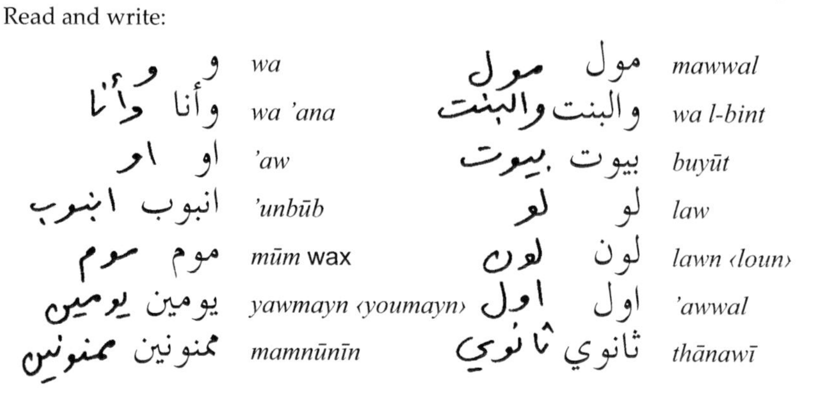

و و	*wa*		مول مول	*mawwal*
وأنا وأنا	*wa 'ana*		والبنت والبنت	*wa l-bint*
او او	*'aw*		بيوت بيوت	*buyūt*
انبوب انبوب	*'unbūb*		لو لو	*law*
موم موم	*mūm* wax		لون لون	*lawn ‹loun›*
يومين يومين	*yawmayn ‹youmayn›*		اول اول	*'awwal*
ممنونين ممنونين	*mamnūnīn*		ثانوي ثانوي	*thānawī*

22.

ه	ـه	ـهـ	ـﮩـ	هـ	*h*

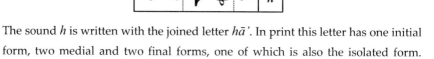

The sound *h* is written with the joined letter *hā'*. In print this letter has one initial form, two medial and two final forms, one of which is also the isolated form. They are used as follows:

- initial form: هـ . This form is also used instead of the isolated form to head a list in e.g. an index or directory.
- medial form: ـﮩـ or ـهـ . The form ـﮩـ is the commoner of the two in print; in handwriting only ـهـ is used.
- final form ـه ; isolated form ه. The form ـه is very commonly written as ـہ . All forms lie on the line of writing, with the exception of the lower parts of ـﮩـ and ـهـ .

  Write:

  هـ هـ هـ هـ هـ هـ هـ هـ هـ هـ

  ـهـ ـهـ ـهـ ـهـ ـهـ ـهـ ـهـ ـهـ ـهـ ـهـ

  ـه ـه ـه ـه ـه ـه ـه ـه ـه ـه

  ـہ ـہ ـہ ـہ ـہ ـہ ـہ ـہ ـہ ـہ

  ه ه ه ه ه ه ه ه ه ه

Read and write:

هو	*huwa*	هنا	*huna*
هم	*hum*	هي	*hiya*
مهما	*mahma*	مهم	*muhimm*
هام	*hāmm* important	اهم	*’ahamm*
يهم	*yuhimm* ‹*yihimm* IV›	به	*bihi* ‹*bī́*›
بنته	*bintuhu* ‹*bintu*›	له	*lahu* ‹*lu*›
ابنه	*ibnuhu* ‹*’ibnu*›	لهم\لهم	*lahum*
بينه	*baynahu* ‹*baynu*›	بها\بها	*biha*
بينهم	*baynahum* ‹*baynhum*›	لها\لها	*laha*
اليهم	*’ilayhim* ‹*’ilayhum*›	اليها	*’ilayha*
اليه	*’ilayhi* ‹*iláy*›	اهتمام	*ihtimām*

23. Note the special spelling of *allāh* ‹*’alla/’allāh*›: الله *allāh.*

24. A variant of final *hā’*, joined or isolated, also expresses the feminine and inanimate plural word-ending *-a*. In this usage the letter is written with the dots of *tā’*, and the resulting hybrid letter ة or ـة is called *tā’ marbūṭa* “bound *tā’*”. In handwriting the two dots are usually omitted for the sound *a*, and restored when the ending is *t* in construct. Read and write:

تامة	*tāmma* complete	ثلاثة	*thalātha*
ثابتة	*thābita*	الثالثة	*ath-thālitha*
آلة	*’āla* machine	آلة الأب	*’ālat al-’ab*
		مهمة	*muhimma, mahamma*
		مهمة الابن	*mahammat al-ibn*
		مهمة ابني الهامة	*mahammat ibni l-hāmma*

tā’ marbūṭa occurs only finally. Before a possessive suffix or a dual ending we write the *t* of such words with ت *tā’*. The *a* before the *t* is kept in written pronunciation. Read and write:

آلتنا	*’ālatuna* ‹*’ālitna*›	آلتي	*’ālatī*
		مهمته	*mahammatuhu* ‹*mahammtu*›
		مهمتين	*mahammatayn* ‹*mahammtayn*›

Like *–īyāt* (paragraph 16 above), *-ī́ya* and *–iya* have one *yā’*:

مالية	*mālīya*	ثانوية	*thānawīya*

ثانية *thāniya* النامية *an-nāmiya*

25. التمارين ***at-tamārīn***

1. Read aloud:

e.g.: ابني ibnī

(a) بيت (b) ثانوية (c) مهم
(d) الأثاث (e) لأني

2. Join the letters to make a word or expression. Read it aloud:

e.g.: ل ب ن ا ن → لبنان lubnān

(a) ا ه ت م ا م (b) ا ل ت ل ا ل (c) م م ث ل ي ن
(d) آ ل ا ت ي (e) ب ا ل ل ب ن

3. Write:

e.g.: al-bayt البيت

(a) bintī (b) al-mālīya (c) li l-bayt
(d) mahammatī (e) an-nīl

4. Write *hamza* wherever it is possible:

e.g.: لاني ← لأني

(a) ابن (b) آلات (c) بالنيل
(d) اثبتت (e) للابن

5. Write *hamza* wherever it is essential:

e.g.: لاني ← لأني

(a) ان (b) بان (c) اثبتنا
(d) الثالث (e) امامي

6. Prefix ب and ل in turn to each word:

e.g.: اللبن ← باللبن، للبن

(a) ابني (b) التمثال (c) اللبناني
(d) اللون (e) اول

7. Write in the plural:

e.g.: بنت ← بنات

(a) ممنون (b) البيت (c) الأم
(d) المهمة (e) انبوب

الدرس السابع عشر
ad-dars as-sābi9 9ashar – Lesson 17
القراءة والكتابة
al-qirā'a wa l-kitāba – Reading and Writing

1.

شـ ش	sh

سـ س	s

The joined letters *sīn* and *shīn* express the sounds *s* and *sh* respectively. The two letters are written identically except for the dots. The letter rests essentially on the line, the extra curve of the full form swooping below and up again, like *nūn*. The two points are usually 'ironed out' in handwriting into a long shallow curve: initial form medial form final form isolated form

The points may be restored for extra clarity. Write each form:

s سـ سـ

sh شـ شـ

Read and write:

سنة	*sana*	سنوات	*sanawāt*
السنة	*as-sana*	تسلم	*tasallam*
اسم	*ism ‹'ism›*	باسمي	*bísmī*
اساس	*'asās*	اسس	*'usus*
شمال	*shimāl*	الشام	*ash-shām*
شاب	*shābb*	الشاب	*ash-shābb*

السنة الشمسية *as-sana sh-shamsīya*

2.

ز	z

ر	r

The sounds *r* and *z* are expressed with the disjoined letters *rā'* and *zayy* respectively. The letters extend below the line. Write:

r ر z ز

In handwriting, a middle tooth, i.e. one joined to a preceding letter, may assume a special form when followed by *rā'/zayy,* as it does before *mīm* (16/20). Compare handwritten and printed forms:

teeth + *r/z*	سر
l + tooth + *r/z*	لىر
m + tooth + *r/z*	مىر
s + tooth + *r/z*	سسر

Read and write:

مرور	*murūr*	سرور	*surūr* pleasure
مرة	*marra*	مسرور	*masrūr* pleased
مستمر	*mustamirr*	اشارة	*'ishāra*
استمرار	*istimrār*	نار	*nār*
ليرة	*līra*	امتار	*'amtār*
رمل	*raml*	مرسل	*mursil/mursal*
رسالة	*risāla*	اشتريت	*ishtarayt*
التربية	*at-tárbiya*	زار	*zār*
زيارة	*ziyāra*	لازم	*lāzim*
زميل	*zamīl*	وزير	*wazīr*
تمييز	*tamyīz*	زمن	*zaman ‹zamān›*

3.

ضـ ض *ḍ*	صـ ص *ṣ*

ṣ and *ḍ* are written respectively with the joined letters *ṣad* and *ḍād*, identical but for the dot over the loop. The short form has a tooth-like element after the loop; it is always present and should not be omitted. Write:

ṣ صـ صـ ص ص

ḍ ضـ ضـ ض ض

The quasi-tooth behaves like a middle tooth as described in paragraph 2 above, when followed by *rā'/zayy* or *mīm*. Read and write:

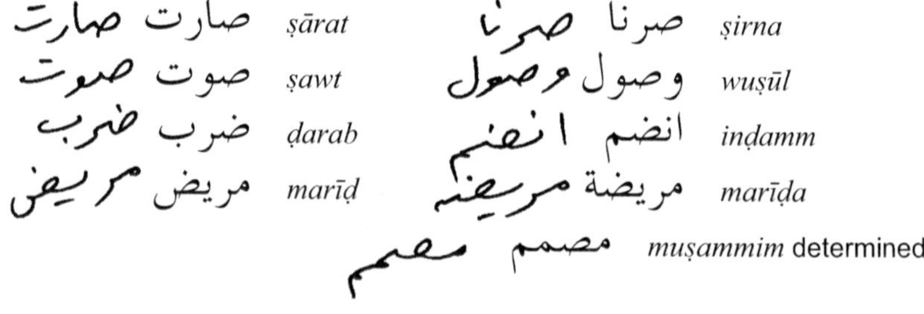

صارت	*ṣārat*	صرنا	*ṣirna*
صوت	*ṣawt*	وصول	*wuṣūl*
ضرب	*ḍarab*	انضم	*inḍamm*
مريض	*marīḍ*	مريضة	*marīḍa*
		مصمم	*muṣammim* determined

4. *hamza*

See 16/14. The writing of *hamza* is somewhat complex. It can be written in four ways:

- above or below *'alif*: أ إ
- above *wāw*: ؤ
- above *yā'* without its dots: ئ ى
- alone: ء

Within this framework, hamza is written in its logical place in the word. Details are given below.

Initial *hamza*. We studied the writing of *hamza* as initial sound in 16/14.

5. Medial *hamza*

hamza as neither initial nor final sound is written:

ئيـ ئي	-'ī-
يئـ	-ī'-/-ay'-

ؤو ئو*	-'ū-

أ	-a'-/-'a-
ؤ	-u'-/-'u-
ئـ	-i'-/-'i-

* The form ئو is less common.

Read and write:

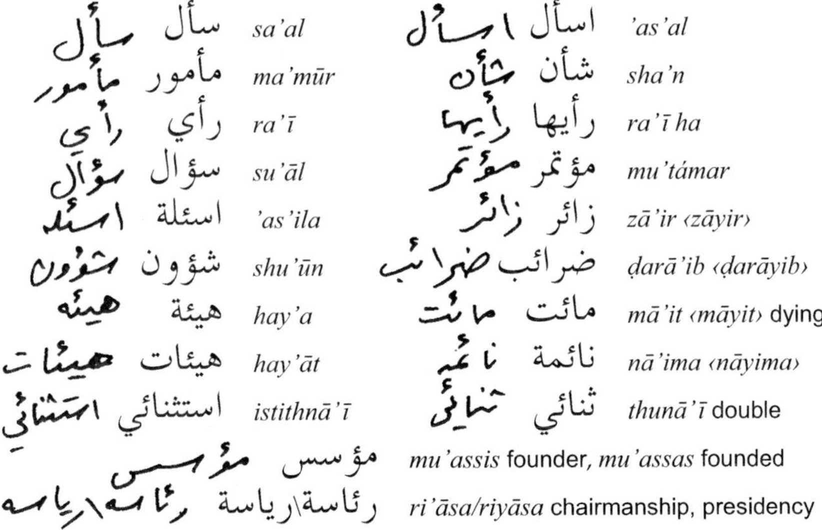

سأل sa'al
اسأل 'as'al
مأمور ma'mūr
شأن sha'n
رأي ra'ī
رأيها ra'ī ha
سؤال su'āl
مؤتمر mu'támar
اسئلة 'as'ila
زائر zā'ir ‹zāyir›
شؤون shu'ūn
ضرائب ḍarā'ib ‹ḍarāyib›
هيئة hay'a
مائت mā'it ‹māyit› dying
هيئات hay'āt
نائمة nā'ima ‹nāyima›
استثنائي istithnā'ī
ثنائي thunā'ī double
مؤسس mu'assis founder, mu'assas founded
رئاسة\رياسة ri'āsa/riyāsa chairmanship, presidency

Remember that *hamza* never appears with *madda* (16/14). The glottal stop is already present in *madda*: الآن *al-'ān*.

6. Final *hamza*

hamza ending the word is written:

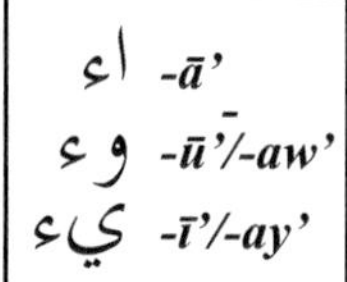

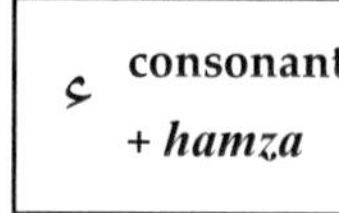

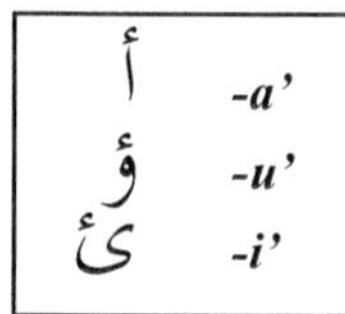

Read and write:

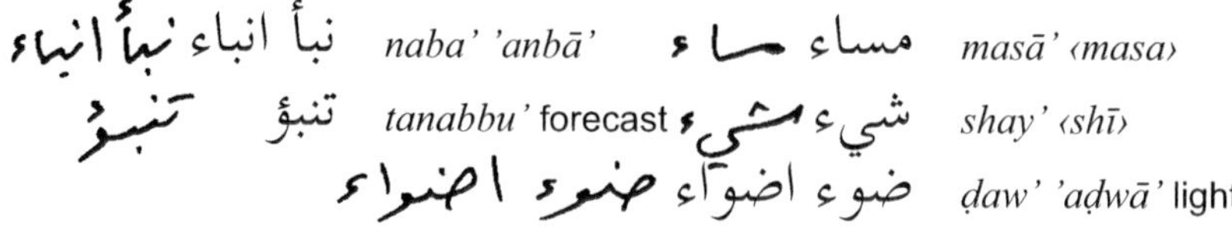

نبأ انباء *naba' 'anbā'* مساء *masā'* ‹*masa*›

تنبؤ *tanabbu'* forecast شيء *shay'* ‹*shī*›

ضوء اضواء *ḍaw' 'aḍwā'* light

7. Initial *hamza* may be omitted in writing. Medial and final *hamza* are always written.

8.

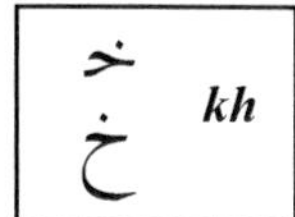

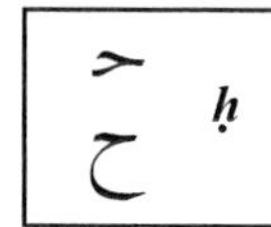

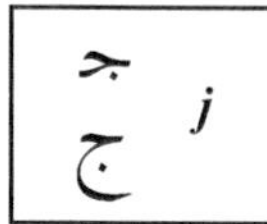

The sounds *j*, *ḥ* and *kh* are expressed respectively with the joined letters *jīm*, *ḥā'* and *khā'*, which are identical but for the dot. The short form and the head of the full form rest on the line; the full form has a 'reverse' downward swoop. Write:

جـ *j*

حـ *ḥ*

خـ *kh*

In handwriting, and in better print, medial/final *jīm* etc. are joined to the preceding letter from the left-hand corner, i.e. from the beginning of the outline. In typescript, and sometimes in print, they are joined at or near the right-hand corner. Compare (*jīm* only):

tooth/teeth + *j* سج سجـ

lj, mj مج مجـ

sj, jj جج جـجـ

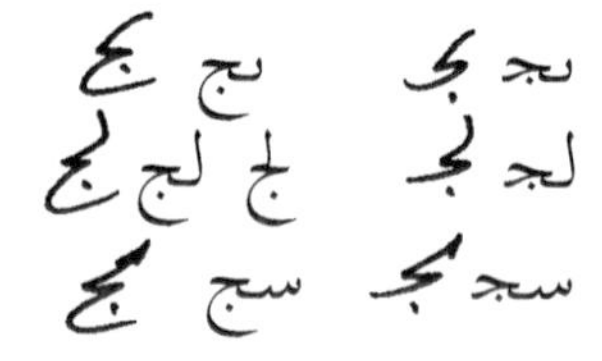

Read and write:

نتيجة نتائج *natīja natā'ij* result

جملة جمل *jumla jumal* sentence

جزء اجزاء *juz' 'ajzā'* part

مجنون مجانين *majnūn majānīn* mad

جميل	*jamīl*	انتج	*'antaj*
مجبور	*majbūr*	لجنة	*lajna*
حج	*ḥajj* pilgrimage	زوج	*zawj ‹zouj›*
زوجة	*zawja ‹zouja›*	انجز	*'anjaz*
الجواب	*al-jawāb*	اجوبة	*'ajwiba*
جواز	*jawāz*	اجنبي	*'ajnabī*
مستأجر	*musta'jir*	لاجئ	*lāji' ‹lājī›*
اجراء	*'ijrā'*	اجراءات	*'ijrā'āt*
احتياج	*iḥtiyāj*	حول	*ḥawla ‹ḥawl›*
محبوب	*maḥbūb*	حرارة	*ḥarāra*
بحث	*baḥth*	صباح	*ṣabāḥ*
صحيح	*ṣaḥīḥ*	محترم	*muḥtáram*
صحة	*ṣiḥḥa*	محتمل	*muḥtámal*
الريح	*ar-rīḥ*	استراحة	*istirāḥa*
الأخ	*al-'akh*	الأخت	*al-'ukht*
خرج	*kharaj*	خارج	*khārij*
اخضر	*'akhḍar*	يخبر	*yukhbir*
خاصة	*khāṣṣa*	تخصص	*takhaṣṣuṣ*
الخليج	*al-khalīj*	انتخاب	*intikhāb*

9.

ذ *dh* د *d*

The disjoined letters *dāl* and *dhāl*, identical but for the dot, express the sounds *d* and *dh* respectively. These letters rest on the line. Write:

ذ ذ ذ ذ ذ ذ *dh* د د د د د د *d*

Do not confuse *dāl/dhāl* and *rā'/zayy*. *rā'/zayy* is struck downwards, and is joined to the preceding letter at its head. *dāl/dhāl* strikes down and left, and is joined to the preceding letter at its middle or corner. Further, the special handwritten joining of *rā'/zayy* after a middle tooth (paragraph 2 above) does not apply to *dāl/dhāl*. Compare (*rā'* and *dāl* only):

r	ر ر	*d*	د د
teeth + *r*	سر سر	teeth + *d*	سد سد
mr	مر مر	*md*	مد مد
sr	سر سر	*sd*	سد سد

Read and write:

مد	مد	*madd*	دخل	دخل	*dakhal*
مدخل	مدخل	*madkhal*	اداره	ادارة	*'idāra*
شديد	شديد	*shadīd*	جديد	جديد	*jadīd*
ميدان	ميدان	*maydān*	مدد	مدد	*maddad*
ازدوج	ازدوج	*izdáwaj*	بدأ	بدأ	*bada' ‹bada›*
يريد	يريد	*yurīd*	بدون	بدون	*bidūni ‹bidūn›*
ابتداء	ابتداء	*ibtidā'*	ابتدائي	ابتدائي	*ibtidā'ī*
استاذ	استاذ	*'ustādh*	اساتذه	اساتذة	*'asātidha*
تلميذ	تلميذ	*tilmīdh*	تلاميذ	تلاميذ	*talāmīdh*
اتخذ	اتخذ	*ittákhadh*	منذ	منذ	*mundhu ‹mundh›*
اذا	اذا	*'idha*	اخذت	اخذت	*'akhadht/'akhadhat*

Note two important but irregularly written words with this last letter:

هذا *hādha* هذه *hādhihi ‹hādhi›*

in which long *ā* in the first syllable is not written with *'alif.*

10.

ظ *ð/ẓ*	ط *ṭ*

The sounds *ṭ* and *ð/ẓ* are written written respectively with the letters *ṭā'* and *ðā'* (also called *ẓā'*), which are identical but for the dot. Although these are joined letters, they have only one form, resting on the line. *ṭā'* and *ẓā'* do not have the quasi-tooth after the loop which we find with *ṣād/ḍād* (paragraph 3 above). Write the loop first, clockwise, then the upright:

ظ ظ ظ ظ ظ ظ ظ *ð/ẓ* ط ط ط ط ط ط ط *ṭ*

Read and write:

طار	طار	*ṭār*	طائره	طائرة	*ṭā'ira ‹ṭayyāra›*
حطط	حطط	*ḥaṭṭat*	مطار	مطار	*maṭār*
الشرطه	الشرطة	*ash-shurṭa*	وطني	وطني	*waṭanī*
طلبنا	طلبنا	*ṭalabna*	خطاب	خطاب	*khiṭāb*

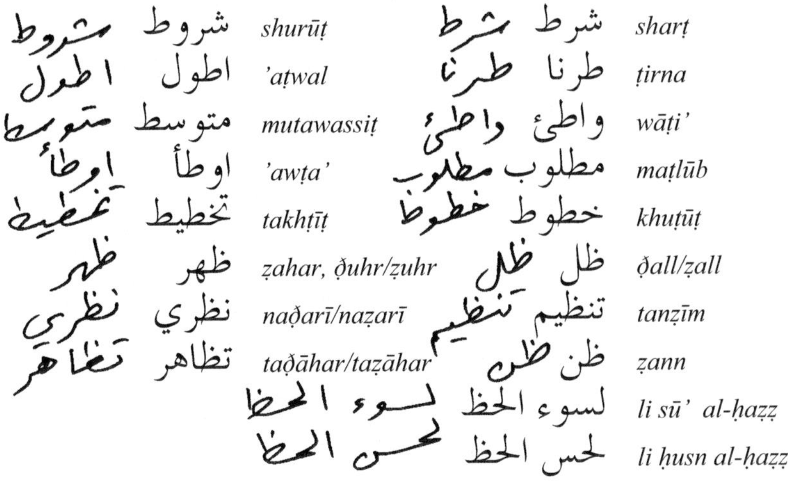

شروط	*shurūṭ*	شرط	*sharṭ*
اطول	*'aṭwal*	طرنا	*ṭirna*
متوسط	*mutawassiṭ*	واطئ	*wāṭi'*
اوطأ	*'awṭa'*	مطلوب	*maṭlūb*
تخطيط	*takhṭīṭ*	خطوط	*khuṭūṭ*
ظهر	*ẓahar, ðuhr/ẓuhr*	ظل	*ðall/ẓall*
نظري	*naðarī/naẓarī*	تنظيم	*tanẓīm*
تظاهر	*taðāhar/taẓāhar*	ظن	*ẓann*
		لسوء الحظ	*li sū' al-ḥaẓẓ*
		لحسن الحظ	*li ḥusn al-ḥaẓẓ*

See the chapter on Pronunciation, paragraph 5. The choice of *ð* or *ẓ* varies between speakers and between styles. Many favour *ð* in written pronunciation.

11. In the root *ḍ b ṭ*, the letter ض *ḍād* is pronounced, anomalously, like ظ *ð/ẓ* in both spoken and written Arabic. Note:

مضبوط	*maẓbūṭ*	بالضبط	*bi ð-ðabṭ/bi ẓ-ẓabṭ*
ضابط ضباط	*ðābiṭ/ẓābiṭ ðubbāṭ/ẓubbāṭ* officer		

12. التمارين

1. Read aloud:

e.g.: لا ينتظر lā yantáðir

(a) الزميل (b) وصول (c) الشرطة
(d) الانتخابات (e) تداخل

2. Write as one word. Read it aloud:

e.g.: مـ سـ ر و ر يـ ن → مسرورين masrūrīn

(a) ا ل ل ا ز م ة (b) م ل ا ب س (c) م ت ظ ا ه ر ي ن
(d) خ ر ج ن ا (e) ا ل ن ظ ر ي

3. Write *hamza* wherever it is essential:

e.g.: لاني ← لأني

(a) بالابن (b) اجزا (c) مسوول
(d) بالطايرة (e) اللاجى

4. Write:

e.g.: marīḍa مريضة

(a) tamwīl (b) marratayn (c) bi l-'amrāḍ

(d) an-natīja l-'ījābīya (e) al-mustawradāt muhimma.

5. Write the verbal noun of each verb. Read your answer aloud:

e.g.: tamwīl تمويل ← مول

(a) سأل (b) اتخذ (c) طلب

(d) احترم (e) استأجر

الدرس الثامن عشر

ad-dars ath-thāmin 9ashar – Lesson 18

القراءة والكتابة

al-qirā'a wa l-kitāba – Reading and Writing

1.

ع	ـع	ـعـ	عـ	*9*
غ	ـغ	ـغـ	غـ	***gh***

The sounds *9* and *gh* are written with the joined letters *9ayn* and *ghayn*. Each has four forms: one initial, one medial, one joined-final and one isolated. The short form, and the head of the full form, rest on the line; the full form has a 'reverse' swoop downwards. In the medial and joined-final forms, the bead is formed clockwise ↻, and the letter is joined from below. Write:

9 عـ عـ عـ عـ عـ عـ ـعـ ـعـ ـعـ ـعـ ـعـ ـعـ

9 ع ع ع ع ع ع ـع ـع ـع ـع ـع ـع

gh غـ غـ غـ غـ غـ غـ ـغـ ـغـ ـغـ ـغـ ـغـ ـغـ

gh غ غ غ غ غ غ ـغ ـغ ـغ ـغ ـغ ـغ

You will note that the head of these letters is 'open' when no joined letter precedes, and 'closed' after a joined letter. Read and write:

'a9ṭayt	اعطيت	اعطيت	*9an*	عن	عن
'idhā9a	اذاعة	اذاعه	*9arḍ*	عرض	عرض
9āmm	عام	عام	*9ashara ‹9ashra›*	عشرة	عشره
na9am	نعم	نعم	*ta9āwun*	تعاون	تعاون
rub9 sā9a	ربع ساعة	ربع ساعه	*rābi9a*	رابعة	رابعه
ṣa9b	صعب	صعب	*ba9d*	بعد	بعد
ijtimā9	اجتماع	اجتماع	*ṭabī9ī*	طبيعي	طبيعي
'usbū9ayn	اسبوعين	اسبوعين	*'usbū9*	اسبوع	اسبوع
ijtimā9āt	اجتماعات	اجتماعات	*'asābī9*	اسابيع	اسابيع
gharbī	غربي	غربى	*mu9allimīn*	معلمين	معلمين
'aghrāḍ	اغراض	اغراض	*gharaḍ*	غرض	غرض
mashghūl	مشغول	مشغول	*ishtághal*	اشتغل	اشتغل

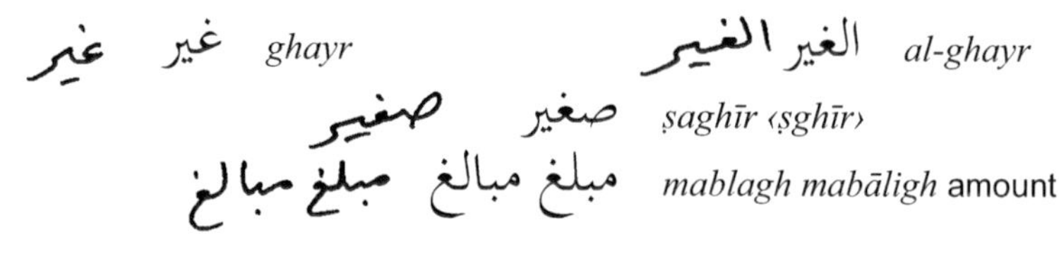

غير *ghayr* الغير *al-ghayr*
صغير *ṣaghīr* ‹*ṣghīr*›
مبلغ مبالغ *mablagh mabāligh* amount

2.

ى	*-a (-ā)*

Final *ā* (almost always pronounced short, see Pronunciation, paragraph 2, and Lesson 16/6) has an alternative spelling; it is written with an undotted *yā'* in some words. This letter is called *'alif maqṣūra* "abbreviated *'alif* ". It expresses -*a* in the following types of word:

- final root letter of a final-weak verb: رمى *rama* اعطى *'a9ṭa*
- feminine superlative adjective: الأعلى *al-'a9la* الصغرى *aṣ-ṣughra*
  الأولى *al-'ūla* الأخرى *al-'ukhra*
- a few broken plurals: مرضى *marḍa*
- a few anomalous nouns, which we examine in Lesson 24 (see the word *mustashfa* 'hospital' below);
- a few other words: على *9ala* الى *'ila*
  حتى *ḥatta* احدى *'iḥda*

In the three commonest monosyllables regularly pronounced with final long *ā*, the vowel is spelt with *'alif*:

لا *lā* ما *mā* يا *yā*

3. *'alif maqṣūra* can occur only finally. When an ending is added, *'alif maqṣūra* is replaced by the phonetically appropriate letter (or an unwritten short vowel). Read and write:

مشت *mashat* انتهت *intáhat*
اشتريت *ishtarayt* احدانا *'iḥdāna* one (f.) of us

After ي *yā'*, *'alif maqṣūra* must be replaced by *'alif*:

العليا *al-9ulya*

Outside language books, isolated *yā'* often appears without its dots: ى. In this book we shall maintain ي for *yā'*, and show ى only for *'alif maqṣūra*.

4.

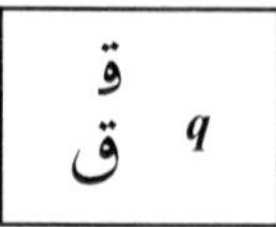

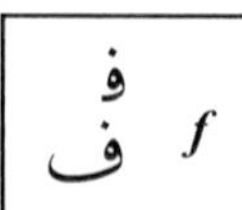

The sounds *f* and *q* are written with the joined letters *fā'* and *qāf* respectively. Final/isolated *qāf* swoops like *nūn*; final/isolated *fā'* is shallow like *bā'*, resting on the line. All forms are dotted on the ring. Write each form:

f فـ فـ ـفـ ـفـ ـفـ ـفـ ـف ـف ف ف ف ف

q قـ قـ ـقـ ـقـ ـقـ ـقـ ـق ـق ق ق ق ق

Read and write:

فاضين	*fāḍīn ‹ fāḍīyīn›*	فعل	*fi9l action*
نفس	*nafs*	اضافية	*'iḍāfīya*
الضفة	*aḍ-ḍiffa*	ضيف	*ḍayf*
افاد	*'afād*	افتتح	*iftátaḥ*
مفتش	*mufattish* inspector	في	*fī*
لطيف	*laṭīf*	فيه	*fīhi‹ fī›*
موظف	*muwaẓẓaf*	مشرف	*mushrif*
يبقى	*yabqa ‹yibqa›*	فهو	*fa huwa*
قلنا	*qulna*	افريقيا	*'afrī́qiya*
استقبال	*istiqbāl*	قالت	*qālat*
الحق	*al-ḥaqq* right (noun)	اقامة	*'iqāma*
فقط	*faqaṭ*	اقترحت	*iqtaraḥt*
قوي	*qawīy ‹qawī›*	العراق	*al-9irāq*
بقي	*báqiya ‹biqi›*	اقوى	*'aqwa*
موقف من	*mawqif ‹mouqif› min*		
المستشفى	*al-mustashfa*		
فمن المفهوم	*fa min al-mafhūm*		
دقيقة دقائق	*daqīqa daqā'iq ‹daqāyiq›*		
من المتوقع	*min al-mutawaqqa9*		
صحيفة صحف	*ṣaḥīfa ṣuḥuf* newspaper		

5.

ـك	ك	كـ	*k*

The sound *k* is written with the joined letter *kāf*. This letter always rests on the line, and is tall like *lām*. Its handwritten shape is different from its printed shape.

In handwriting, the letter is upright, and the 'headstroke' of the short form is written last. Examine:

initial/medial *k*

final/isolated k

The final form ك is often replaced by ك . ك is not used in handwriting.

In fast handwriting, the flourish of the final/isolated form ك is often written as an extension of the curve of the base, similarly to the dot of *nūn*. Write:

k

There are special handwritten forms for *kāf-'alif, kāf-lām* and *kāf-lām-'alif.* The loop is written clockwise, being approached from below if the combination is joined to the preceding letter. Write:

kā

kl

kl

klā

Read and write:

كيف	*kayfa ‹kayf›*	اكلنا	*'akalna*
كل	*kull*	ضحك	*ḍaḥik ‹ḍaḥak›*
كلا	*kila* both	كتابة	*kitāba*
دكان	*dukkān*	امكانية	*'imkānīya*
كبيرة	*kabīra*	الكبرى	*al-kubra*
ممكن	*mumkin*	كنت	*kunt*
كانت	*kānat*	الشك	*ash-shakk*
بكم	*bi kam*	للكل	*li l-kull*
كلمة	*kalima*	هناك	*hunāka‹ hunāk›*

اوشك على *'awshak 9ala*

الله يبارك فيكم *allāh yubārik fīkum*

المشكوك فيه *al-mashkūk fīhi‹ fī›*

6. Arabic transcription

There are no Arabic letters allocated in standard fashion to the sounds *g* or *v* occurring in foreign words. The letters ج *jīm,* غ *ghayn* and ك *kāf* are variously used in words of foreign origin with *g*, and the form ڤ ڨ is often used for *v*: ڤيزا *vīza* غرام\جرام *grām*

In transcribing into Arabic, some texts show ا *'alif* for both long and short a, و *wāw* for both long and short o or u, and ي *yā'* for both long and short e or i. This is especially the case with proper names, but the usage varies. Examine:

هامبورج	*hamburg*	بروكسل	*bruksil* Brussels
لندن	*landan* London	واشنطن	*wāshinṭun* Washington

Foreign proper names beginning with two consonants are often given a transition vowel marked with ا *'alif*: استكهولم *istok-holm* Stockholm

You may also encounter, in foreign words, the Ottoman and Persian letters پ پ *p* and چ چ *ch*, the latter sometimes also used to transliterate the sound *g*. Remember that in Egypt ج is pronounced *g* even when read from text.

7. The alphabet

We have now learned the whole alphabet. Here are the letters (isolated form), with names, in their alphabetical order:

ا	*'alif*
ب ت ث	*bā' tā' thā'*
ج ح خ	*jīm ḥā' khā'*
د ذ ر ز	*dāl dhāl rā' zay*
س ش	*sīn shīn*
ص ض ط ظ	*ṣād ḍāḍ ṭā' ðā'/ẓā'*
ع غ ف ق	*9ayn ghayn fā' qāf*
ك ل م ن	*kāf lām mīm nūn*
ه و ي	*hā' wāw yā'*

In dictionaries, *hamza* is placed with *'alif*, *wāw* or *yā'* as appropriate; *tā' marbuṭa* with *hā'*, and *'alif maqṣūra* with *yā'*. See 16/22 for ھ as the isolated form of *hā'* in an alphabetical list, and paragraph 3 above for the alternative forms of isolated *yā'*.

8. Pointing

There exist also various orthographic signs, only rarely used, indicating short vowels, doubled consonants etc. Most people read more easily without them. A word or text carrying these signs is said to be 'pointed'. Pointing can be full or partial, as needed.

9. Short vowels

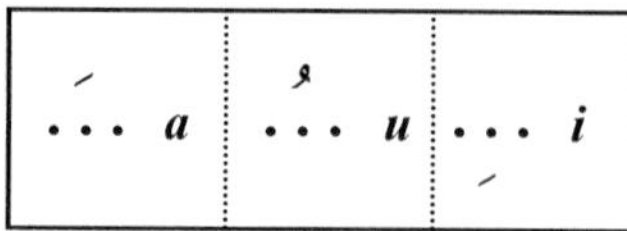

These marks are written above (for *a* and *u*) or below (for *i*) the letter or *hamza* preceding them. Thus:

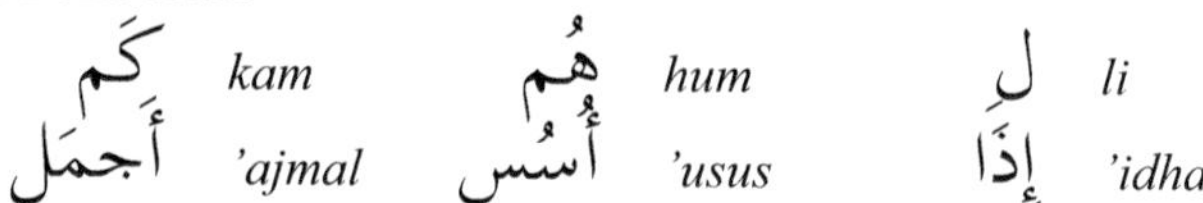

These signs are called *fatḥa (a)*, *ḍamma (u)* and *kasra (i)*.

10. Long vowels and diphthongs

The three short-vowel signs shown above may also be used to show the corresponding long vowel *(ā, ū, ī)* when written immediately before *'alif, wāw* or *yā'*; *fatḥa* written immediately before *wāw* or *yā'* can be used to show the diphthong *aw* and *ay* respectively:

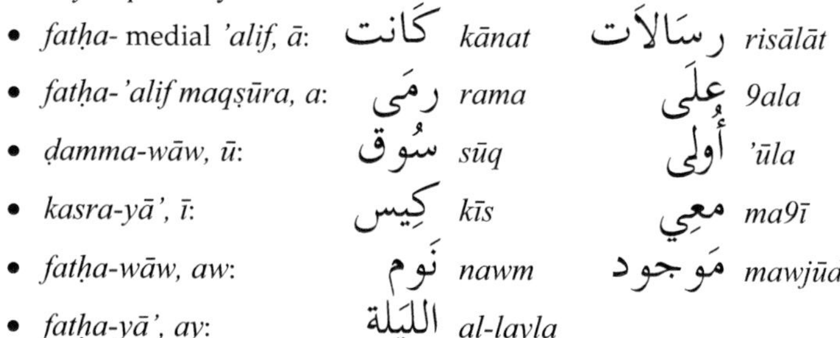

- *fatḥa*- medial *'alif, ā*: كَانت *kānat* رسَالَات *risālāt*
- *fatḥa-'alif maqṣūra, a*: رمَى *rama* عُلَى *9ala*
- *ḍamma-wāw, ū*: سُوق *sūq* أُولى *'ūla*
- *kasra-yā', ī*: كِيس *kīs* معِي *ma9ī*
- *fatḥa-wāw, aw*: نَوم *nawm* مَوجود *mawjūd*
- *fatḥa-yā', ay*: اللَيلة *al-layla*

These can be used in partial pointing to avoid ambiguity:

- *kasra-fatḥa*: active/passive participles; m. dual/sound plural:

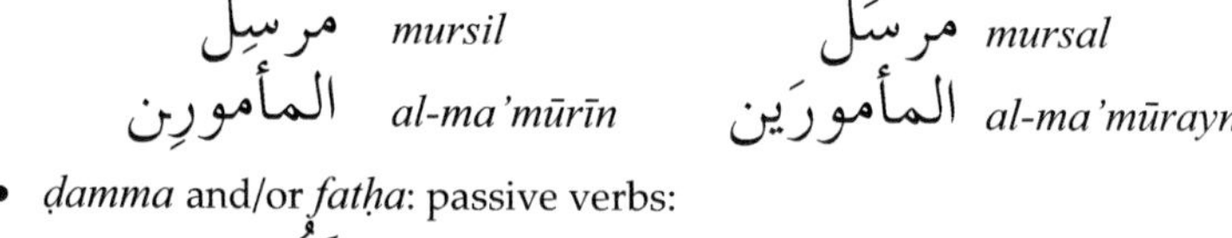

- *ḍamma* and/or *fatḥa*: passive verbs:

كُتبت *kutibat* يوجَد *yūjad*

11.

ً ا *-an*	ً ة *-atan*

The noun-, adjective- and adverb-ending *-an* is written with a doubled *fatḥa* called *fatḥa tanwīn* (*tanwīn* is translated as 'nunation' in English). When added to a m. ending, *fatḥa tanwīn* is followed by *'alif*; when added to the ending *-a* it is put over the *tā' marbuṭa*. Read and write:

جدًا *jiddan* — اولاً *'awwalan*

رسميًا *rasmīyan* — مثلاً *mathalan*

خاصةً *khāṣṣatan* — عادةً *9ādatan*

شديدًا *shadīdan* — غدًا *ghadan ‹bukra›*

شكلاً وموضوعًا *shaklan wa mawḍū9an*

كتب طالبًا *katab ṭāliban ‹ṭālib›*

سأل سؤالاً صعبًا *sa'al su'ālan ṣa9ban ‹su'āl ṣa9b›*.

fatḥa tanwīn is used in partial pointing only for clarity. We shall meet it later over *'alif maqṣūra*, and other examples of *tanwīn*, with the other short vowels.

12. Small *'alif*

In a few words medial *-ā-* is unwritten; we can point it with a small *'alif*-like sign above the preceding consonant:

هٰذا *hādha* — ذٰلك *dhālika ‹hadhāk›*

ولٰكن *walākin*

Small *'alif* is shown only in full pointing.

13. *sukūn, hamzat al-waṣl, waṣla, hamzat al-qaṭ9*

A small ring ◌ْ, called sukūn, above a letter indicates that the letter has no following vowel. This sign is also used to point a diphthong:

اسْمي *ismī* — قلْب *qalb* — يَوْمَيْن *yawmayn*

In the grammar of written Arabic, an initial weak vowel is said to have *hamzat al-waṣl* ('the *hamza* of connection'). This term can be misleading, for no glottal stop is pronounced. When the weak initial vowel is dropped after a preceding vowel in the same phrase, you may sometimes see the weak vowel pointed with *waṣla*, a sign resembling the loop of *ṣād*, written over the *'alif*, thus:

بٱسمي *bi smī* — في ٱلحقيقة *fi l-ḥaqīqa*

Both *sukūn* and *waṣla* are found only in full pointing.

hamza indicating a glottal stop is called *hamzat al-qaṭ9* ('the *hamza* of severance'). This is the one which we have been studying. Outside this present paragraph, the term *hamza* in this book always means *hamzat al-qaṭ9*.

14. *shadda*

A doubled consonant (including that of an assimilated article) may be pointed with the sign ـّـ called *shadda*, above the letter:

معلّم *mu9allim* تقدّم *taqaddum* الرّمل *ar-raml*

shadda is sometimes used in partial pointing for clarity. Examine:

ذكر *dhakar* ذكّر *dhakkar*

علم *9ilm* علّم *9allam*

15. Short vowels with *shadda*

When combined with *shadda*, *kasra* is pointed either above the letter but below the *shadda*, or below the letter. The other two short vowels lie above the *shadda*:

معلِّم\معلّمِ *mu9allim* معلَّم *mu9allam* تقدُّم *taqaddum*

16. Of the non-alphabetical letters and signs, the following are mandatory, both in handwriting and in print:

- final and medial *hamza*,
- *madda*,
- the dots on *ṭā' marbūṭa* in the theme of a construct.

The following are often omitted:

- initial *hamza* (print and handwriting),
- *fatḥa tanwīn* after *'alif* and after *ṭā' marbūṭa* (print and handwriting),
- the dots on *ṭā' marbūṭa* other than in the theme of a construct (in handwriting).

The following can be useful in partial pointing:

- initial *hamza* (especially Form IV),
- *fatḥa, ḍamma* and *kasra* (participles, passive, dual),
- *shadda* (Forms II and V).

All other non-alphabetical letters and signs are found only in full pointing and not in everyday print or handwriting.

17. التمارين

1. Read aloud:

e.g.: هو تعافى تمامًا. huwa ta9āfa tamāman.

(a) غرفة فاضية (b) البنت الصغرى (c) بعيد عن القرية

(d) اذا كان هنا (e) شكروني قلبيًا.

2. Add the missing last letter, which is *'alif, 'alif maqṣūra* or *ṭā' marbūṭa*. Read the word or expression:

e.g.: al-kubra الكبرى ← الكبر...

(a) بالمستشف... (b) الأساتذ...

(c) هذ... هو الصديق

(d) مشـ... (e) اجوبـ... ايجابيـ...

3. Put the verb into the *huwa* form. Read aloud both the original verb form and your answer:

e.g.: ishtarayt, ishtára اشترى ← اشتريت

(a) استثنينا (b) استغنيت (c) اعطيت

(d) ربّيت (e) مشينا

4. Write the adverb which is derived from the word given. Read both the word given and your adverb:

e.g.: shadīd, shadīdan شديدًا ← شديد

(a) جديد (b) عادة (c) مثل

(d) خاصة (e) رسمي

5. Write:

e.g.: at-ta9āwun ḍarūrī. التعاون ضروري.

(a) al-lugha l-9arabīya ṣa9ba.

(b) fī hādha l-balad

(c) kunna masrūrīn jiddan, shukran.

(d) dafa9at 'aqall mimma dafa9na l-yawm.

(e) al-'anbā' al-wārida min baghdād

6. Point partially, with initial *hamza*, with *shadda*, and with *fatḥa tanwīn*. Then read aloud:

e.g.: *'aghrāḍ hāmma jiddan* أغراض هامّة جدًّا ← اغراض هامة جدا

(a) اسم الصديق (b) تتكلم سريعا. (c) اكبر مني

(d) التدخل اشد مما كان قبلا.

(e) هو موظف في الجمرك.

الدرس التاسع عشر
ad-dars at-tāsi9 9ashar – Lesson 19
التأمين at-ta'mīn – Insurance

1. جمل مثالية

(a)

تأمين	*ta'mīn*	insurance
مؤمّن	*mu'ammin*	insurer
مؤمّن عليه	*mu'amman 9alayhi ‹9aláy›*	insured

في حقل التأمين الاعتماد المتبادل بين المؤمّن والمؤمّن عليه ضروري.

fī ḥaql at-ta'mīn al-i9timād al-mutabādal bayna l-mu'ammin wa l-mu'amman 9alayhi ḍarūrī.

In the insurance field, mutual confidence between the insurer and the insured is essential.

(b)

مدير الهندسة	*mudīr al-handasa*	Chief Engineer
تقويه	*táqwiya*	reinforcement
امن	*'amn*	safety, security
صهريج صهاريج	*ṣahrīj ṣahārīj*	tank (container)
تخزين	*takhzīn*	storage
قسط اقساط	*qisṭ 'aqsāṭ*	premium, instalment

مدير الهندسة على علم بالاقتراحات الجديدة لتقوية الأمن في صهاريج التخزين من اجل تخفيف قسطنا السنوي.

mudīr al-handasa 9ala 9ilm bi l-iqtirāḥāt al-jadīda li táqwiyat al-'amn fī ṣahārīj at-takhzīn min 'ajl takhfīf qisṭina s-sanawī.

The Chief Engineer knows about the new proposals to increase ('reinforce') the safety of the storage tanks with a view to reducing our annual premium.

(c)

شركته	*sharikatihi*	‹*sharikatu*›
فشل	*fashal*	failure
مفاضاتنا	*mufāwaḍātina*	‹*mufāwaḍātna*›
تعويض	*ta9wīḍ*	compensation
موقّت، مؤقّت	*muwaqqat, mu'aqqat*	provisional, temporary
بوليصة بواليص	*būlīṣa bawālīṣ*	(insurance) policy
بواليصته	*būlīṣatihi*	‹*būlīṣatu*›

وضع شركته صعب بعد فشل مفاوضاتنا في غرفة التجارة من اجل التعويض الموقّت تحت شروط بوليصته الشاملة.

waḍ9 sharikatihi ṣab9 ba9da fashal mufāwaḍātina fī ghurfat at-tijāra min 'ajl at-ta9wīḍ al-muwaqqat taḥt shurūṭ būlīṣatihi

His company's situation is difficult after the failure of our negotiations in the Chamber of Commerce for

sh-shāmila.		provisional compensation under the terms of his comprehensive policy.

(d)	مقبول	*maqbūl*	acceptable
	ملحق	*mulḥaq*	(also:) annex(ed)
	به	*bihi*	‹bī›
	جدول جداول	*jadwal jadāwil*	(also:) table (of data)
	رسم رسوم	*rasm rusūm*	drawing

إن التقرير حول الخسارة مقبول ولكن في الوثيقة الملحقة به كثير من الجداول والرسوم المعقّدة.

'inna t-taqrīr ḥawla l-khasāra maqbūl walākin fi l-wathīqa l-mulḥaqa bihi kathīr min al-jadāwil wa r-rusūm al-mu9aqqada.	The damage report is acceptable, but in the document attached to it there are many complicated tables and drawings.

(e)	حسب	*ḥasaba*	according to
	مؤرّخ	*mu'arrakh*	dated
	حريقة حرائق	*ḥarīqa ḥarā'iq*	fire
	نوبة نوب	*nawba nuwab*	shift, turn

حسب الرسالتين المؤرّختين امس المسؤل عن الحريقة هو مشرف نوبة الليل.

ḥasaba r-risālatayn al-mu'arrakhatayn 'ams al-mas'ūl 9an al-ḥarīqa huwa mushrif nawbat al-layl.	According to the two letters dated yesterday, the person responsible for the fire is the night shift supervisor.

2. مفردات إضافية — التأمين

عقد عقود	*9aqd 9uqūd*	contract	ضمان	*ḍamān*	guarantee
سمسار سماسير	*simsār samāsīr*	broker	سرقة	*sariqa*	theft
وقاية	*wiqāya*	protection	انتهاء	*intihā'*	expiry
طرف ثالث	*ṭaraf thālith*	third party	طلب	*ṭalab*	claim
مخاطرة	*mukhāṭara*	risk			

المساهمة (في الأرباح)	*al-musāhama (fi l-'arbāḥ)*	participation (in profits)
كارثة كوارث (طبيعية)	*kāritha kawārith (ṭabī9īya)*	(natural) disaster
الضمان الاجتماعي	*aḍ-ḍamān al-ijtimā9ī*	social security

النحو

3. In studying written Arabic, we shall note only those points which are useful and which are different from spoken Arabic. Everything learned in Part I is valid for written Arabic, unless indicated otherwise. Conversely, any written form or structure may be included in everyday speech; the degree of 'elevation' bestowed by its use will vary with choice and context.

4. Full pronunciation and short pronunciation

In written Arabic the nouns, adjectives, verbs and numbers have a greater battery of inflexions or endings than in spoken Arabic. Many of these inflexions are not written with letters of the alphabet, but are visible only when the text is pointed. In very formal scripted speech, the inflexions are all pronounced. We can call this 'full' pronunciation.

But at the end of a phrase in formal speech, and in all positions in normal use, the inflexions are pronounced only when a suffix is added to the word; otherwise they are dropped. We can call this 'short' pronunciation. You should use short pronunciation , which is simpler and commoner. It also gives us forms much more like the spoken language which we have studied in Part I.

Short pronunciation rule: In short pronunciation, grammatical inflexions not written with an alphabetical letter are, with very few exceptions, pronounced only when followed by a suffix.

We study first nouns and adjectives.

5. Case

In written Arabic, nouns and adjectives are declined, i.e. they have cases, three in number:

- Nominative ('nom.') for the subject of the verb or implied verb,
- Accusative ('acc.') for the direct object or complement of a verb; also for the subject in certain contexts;
- Genitive ('gen.') for all elements of a construct except the first; or after a preposition.

6. Definite nouns

When a definite noun has the possessive suffix ي *-ī* 'my', or has no suffix, the noun has a form identical to its spoken form, if we allow for the fact that in written pronunciation *tā' marbūṭa* is pronounced *-at* before a suffix (see 16/24):

العقد	*al-9aqd*	عقدي	*9aqdī*
الوثيقة	*al-wathīqa*	وثيقتي	*wathīqatī*

But when a possessive suffix other than ي *-ī* is added, we first add a case-ending: *-u* for the nom., *-a* for the acc., *-i* for the gen. The rules for stress still hold. The endings are shown ***bold*** in these examples:

	العقد هنا.	*al-9aqd huna.*
but:	عقدنا هنا.	*9aqd**u**na huna.*
	يعرف عقدي.	*ya9rif ‹ya9raf› 9aqdī.*
but:	يعرف عقدكم.	*ya9rif 9aqd**a**kum.*
	في البوليصة	*fi l-būlīṣa*
but:	في بوليصتنا	*fī būlīṣat**i**na*

The same rules apply with a broken plural:

	الوثائق هنا.	*al-wathā'iq huna.*
but:	وثائقنا هنا.	*wathā'iq**u**na huna.*
	يعرف وثائقكم.	*ya9rif wathā'iq**a**kum.*
	من وثائقكم	*min wathā'iq**i**kum*
	الأساتذة	*al-'asātidha*
	اساتذتي	*'asātidhatī*
but:	من اساتذتها	*min 'asātidhat**i**ha ‹'asātidhat-ha›*

Full pronunciation has these endings all the time except at the end of a phrase; in short pronunciation we pronounce them, irrespective of the position of the word, only when they are 'trapped' between the noun and the suffix.

Definite adjectives follow the noun pattern in full pronunciation; but since adjectives never take suffixes, their short pronunciation is the same as in spoken Arabic.

7. Indefinite nouns and adjectives

Indefinite words occur only without a possessive suffix, since this suffix would make them definite. But we need to know one ending which is sounded even in short pronunciation. It is the indefinite accusative ending *-an* (*-tan* after final *-a*, *-yan* after final ي *-ī*). It is pointed with *fatḥa tanwīn* (18/11, 16). Pronounce it in the following situations, which constitute an exception to the short pronunciation rule:

- in the singular participle of a circumstantial expression (12/13):

كتب طالبًا مساعدتنا.	*katab ṭāliban musā9adatana.*
كتبت طالبةً مساعدتنا.	*katabat ṭālibatan musā9adatana.*

- in adverbial forms:

جدًّا *jiddan* عادةً *9ādatan* كثيرًا *kathīran*

- in the absolute object:

سأل سؤالاً فنّيًا. *sa'al su'ālan fannīyan.*
يعرف معرفةً تامّةً. *ya9rif ma9rifatan tāmmatan.*

- whenever else it is written with *'alif*:

أخذ كتابًا\كتبًا. *'akhadh kitāban/kutuban.*

From the examples you can see that these rules apply equally to singular and to broken plural nouns and adjectives.

(For the record only, there exist also the indefinite nominative ending *-un*, pointed *ḍamma tanwīn* ٌ or ٌ ; and the indefinite genitive *-in*, pointed *kasra tanwīn* ٍ . In short pronunciation, these are heard only in a few set phrases which we can learn as vocabulary.)

8. Sound feminine plural nouns and adjectives

Definite nouns carrying the sound feminine plural ending ات *-āt* are subject to the same rules as the singular and broken plural nouns and adjectives covered by paragraph 6 above, with the exception that the ending for both the accusative and genitive is *-i*; *[-a]* does not occur:

الرسالات *ar-risālāt* رسالاتي *risālātī*

but: رسالاتنا هنا. *risālāt**u**na huna.*
كتبت رسالاتها. *katabat risālāt**i**ha.*
حسب رسالاتها *ḥasaba risālāt**i**ha*

In written Arabic, animate f. pl. nouns must have a f. pl. adjective, which is always sound:

(ال)معلّمات (ال)مصريات *(al-)mu9allimāt (al-)miṣrīyāt ‹miṣrīyīn›*

(For the record, indefinite endings *-un* [nom.], *-in* [acc./gen.] also occur with sound feminine plurals, but are never heard in short pronunciation; we can ignore them.)

9. Dual and sound masculine plural nouns and adjectives

Dual (m. and f.) and sound masculine plural nouns and adjectives have endings which are the same for definite and indefinite forms:

- nominative ان *-ān* (dual; ة becomes ت as usual) and ون *-ūn* (m. pl.):

(ال)معلّمان (ال)حاضران *(al-)mu9allimān (al-)ḥāḍirān*
(ال)معلّمتان (ال)حاضرتان *(al-)mu9allimatān (al-)ḥāḍiratān*
(ال)معلّمون (ال)حاضرون *(al-)mu9allimūn (al-)ḥāḍirūn*

- accusative and genitive ين *-ayn* (dual) and ين *-īn* (m. pl), as in spoken Arabic:

من الكتابين *min al-kitābayn* للمأمورين *li l-ma'mūrīn*
مهمّة المعلّمتين *muhammat al-mu9allimatayn*

(For the record, the full forms are *-āni/-ayni* and *-ūna/īna*.)

The final ن *-n* is dropped before a possessive suffix and when the word is the theme of a construct:

مكتباها *maktabāha* في مكتبيها *fī maktabayha*
مسؤولو قسمي *mas'ūlū qismī* من ممثّليكم *min mumaththilīkum*

The long vowel rule (2/10) holds as usual before an article, and the original stress is maintained:

ممثّلو الشركة *mumaththilú sh-sharika*
مع ممثّلي الشركة *ma9a mumaththilí sh-sharika*

Note however:

- the dual diphthong *-ay* (like all diphthongs) is never shortened:

مديري الشركة *mudiray ash-sharika*

- *-ūn* + *-ī* becomes *-īya*: معلّميّ *mu9allimīya* my teachers

10. Agreement of adjectives

Note paragraph 8 above for animate f. pl. adjectives. The inanimate plural rule (1/5) applies throughout written Arabic also. But the dual noun rule (4/12) does not apply; an adjective qualifying a dual noun must also be dual in written Arabic:

صحفيان لبنانيان *ṣuḥufīyān lubnānīyān ‹lubnānīyīn›*
في رسالتين رسميتين *fī risālatayn rasmīyatayn ‹rasmīyīn›*

11. A few nouns and adjectives (e.g. types *muḥāmī, fāḍī, mustashfa*) decline differently. We study them later.

12. *tā' marbūṭa*

Where a noun ending in ة *tā' marbūṭa* is followed by an adjective carrying the article, some speakers use full pronunciation even when the rest of the sentence is spoken with short pronunciation. This exception to the short pronunciation rule is not obligatory:

السنة الماضية *as-sanatu l-māḍiya* or *as-sana l-māḍiya*
في السنة المقبلة *fī s-sanati l-muqbila* or *fī s-sana l-muqbila*

This practice usually covers only the noun, not the adjective.

13. Possessive suffixes

The possessive suffixes ي *-ī,* ها *-ha,* نا *-na,* كم *-kum* and هم *-hum* are the same as in the spoken language. The other written possessive suffixes are:

ك *-ka ‹-ak›* ك *-ki ‹-ik›* ه *-hu ‹-u›*

and the third-person dual, not found in spoken Arabic: هما *-huma* of them both (m./f.).

(There are other persons, the 2nd and 3rd persons animate f. pl., used for an exclusively female group; and the 2nd person dual. But these occur so rarely, even in writing, that they need not concern us here. If you need them, they can be found in 26/13.)

14. We have seen that certain noun endings are modified before certain suffixes. There is one more change to note: after ي *-ī/-ay* or the case-ending *-i,* the suffixes *-hu, -huma, -hum* become *-hi, -hima, -him*:

عند مهندسيه *9inda muhandisīhi/muhandisayhi*
في مكتبه\مكتبهما *fī maktabihi/maktabihima*
جواب على رسالتيهم الأخيرتين *jawāb 9ala risālatayhim al-'akhīratayn*
a reply to their last two letters

15. Prepositions

Written prepositions are the same as those of the spoken form, except that they mostly add *-a* (unwritten, can be pointed), e.g.:

بعد *ba9da* قبل *qabla*
but not: من *min* عن *9an*

Further, داخل *dākhil(a)* and خارج *khārij(a)* are often pronounced short when they have no suffix, even in formal reading.

Learn also: لدى *lada* 'in the presence of', عبر *9abra* 'through, beyond', and the spelling of جنب *jamba.*

All prepositions except إلاّ *'illa* 'except' (see below) govern the genitive case.

داخل\خارج مصنعنا *dākhil(a)/khārij(a) maṣna9ina*
بعد\قبل المؤتمر *ba9da/qabla l-mu'támar*
حسب\ضد عقده *ḥasaba/ḍidda 9aqdihi*
خلال\منذ اسبوعين *khilāla/mundhu 'usbū9ayn*
عند\بين المهندسين *9inda/bayna l-muhandisīn*

The noun governed by إلاّ *'illa* goes into the case dictated by the noun's own function in the sentence when the sentence is negative:

ما حضر إلاّ المهندسون. *mā ḥaḍar 'illa l-muhandisūn.* (nom.)

Only the engineers ('None but the engineers') attended.

but into the *accusative*, irrespective of its own grammatical function, when the sentence is affirmative:

كلّهم حاضرون إلاّ المهندسين. *kulluhum ḥāḍirūn 'illa l-muhandisīn.*

(acc.) All of them are present except the engineers.

16. Pronoun suffixes on prepositions

The pronoun suffixes used after prepositions are identical to the possessive siffixes, with some modifications:

- A short vowel at the end of a preposition is dropped when ي *-ī* is suffixed; for other suffixes the vowel is retained:

معي	*ma9ī*	بي	*bī ‹bīnī›*
معك	*ma9aka*	بكم	*bikum*

- من *min* and عن *9an* before ي *ī* become منّي *minnī* and عنّي *9annī*, as in spoken Arabic (but: منه *minhu ‹minnu›*, عنك *9anka, 9anki ‹9annak, 9annik›*.
- لدى *lada* follows the pattern of على *9ala*:

عليّ	*9alayya*	لديّ	*ladayya*
علينا	*9alayna*	لديها	*ladayha*

- After ي *-ī/-ay* and the preposition ب *bi*, the suffixes *-hu, -huma, -hum* become *-hi, -hima, -him*:

فيه	*fīhi ‹fī́›*	فيهما	*fīhima*
به	*bihi ‹bī́›*	بهم	*bihim*
عليه	*9alayhi ‹9aláy›*	عليهم	*9alayhim*
لديه	*ladayhi*	لديهم	*ladayhim*

17 **التمارين**

NB.: From this point forwards, all noun and adjective expressions in the exercises should be read as *nominative case* unless the grammar or spelling requires otherwise.

1. Read aloud:

e.g.: ما هو طلب المؤمّن عليه؟ mā huwa ṭalab al-mu'amman 9alayhi?

(a) مأمور من مأموري القسم المالية (b) شركتان كبيرتان

(c) الشركة مسؤولة عن دفع القسط. (d) متخصّص في التأمين
(e) في مدرسة ابتدائية

2. Write:

e.g.: fī ḥālat al-kāritha ṭ-ṭabī9īya في حالة الكارثة الطيعية

(a) ma9a mufattisháy l-jumruk ar-ra'īsīyayn

(b) ma9a mufattishí l-jumruk ar-ra'īsīyīn

(c) intihā' al-9aqd

(d) fi s-sanati l-muqbila

(e) fi l-būlīṣatayn ash-shāmilatayn

3. Add the possessive suffix indicated. Read your answer aloud:

e.g.: taqrīruhu huna. تقريره هنا. ← تقرير (هو) هنا.

fī taqrīrihi في تقريره ← في تقرير (هو) .

(a) وثيقة (انا) (b) زملاء (انا)
(c) تخفيف قسط (هو) (d) شروط مقبولة (هي)
(e) حسب بوليصة (هو)

4. Add the pronoun suffix indicated. Read your answer aloud:

e.g.: 9alayhim عليهم ← على (هم)

(a) عند (هم) (b) خلال (هي)
(c) مع (انا) (d) بين (هما)
(e) لدى (انا)

5. Write in the plural:

e.g.: المفتّشون الرئسيون ← المفتّش الرئسي

(a) الوكيل المسؤول (b) اجتماع هامّ
(c) ممثّل مصري (d) البوليصة المعقّدة
(e) وكالة اجنبية

6. Write in the singular:

e.g.: زميل جديد ← زملاء جدد

(a) المخاطرات الأجنبية (b) الممثّلون
(c) زميلات جديدات (d) الوثائق الملحقة
(e) العقود المؤرّخة امس

الدرس العشرون
ad-dars al- 9ishrūn – Lesson 20
النقل والمواصلات an-naql wa-l-muwāṣalāt
Transport and Communications

1. جمل مثالية

(a)

شحن	*shaḥn*	load
بواسطة	*bi-wāsiṭat*	by means of
نظرًا ل	*naðaran li*	in view of
حجم حجوم	*ḥajm ḥujūm*	volume, bulk

سنرسل الشحن بواسطة الطريق نظرًا لحجمه الكبير.

sa nursil ash-shaḥn bi wāsiṭat aṭ-ṭarīq naẓaran li ḥajmihi l-kabīr. — We shall send the load by road in view of its great volume.

(b)

تصل	*taṣil*	‹*tūṣil*›
سفينة سفن	*safīna sufun*	ship
اللاذقية	*al-lādhiqīya*	Latakia
يستغرق	*yastaghriq*	‹*yistaghriq*›
تفتيش	*taftīsh*	inspection
على الأقلّ	*9ala l-'aqall*	at least
حصول على	*ḥuṣūl 'ala*	access to

تصل السفينة اليوم إلى اللاذقية وسيستغرق تفتيش الجمرك يومين على الأقلّ والحصول على البضائع قبل يوم الخميس غير ممكن.

taṣil as-safīna l-yawm 'ila l-lādhiqīya wa sa tastaghriq taftīsh al-jumruk yawmayn 9ala l-'aqall wa l-ḥuṣūl 9ala l-baḍā'i9 qabla yawm al-khamīs ghayr mumkin. — The ship will reach Latakia today, and customs inspection will take at least two days. Access to the goods is impossible before Thursday.

(c)

ناقلة	*nāqila*	freighter, tanker
ضخم ضخام	*ḍakhm ḍikhām*	huge
ناقلة ضخمة	*nāqila ḍakhma*	supertanker
نقل	*naql*	transport
بترول	*bitroul*	oil (petroleum)
أحدث	*'aḥdatha* IV	to bring about
مستودع	*mustawda9*	container

كما غيّر إنشاء الناقلات الضخمة نقل البترول قد أحدث أيضًا استعمال المستودعات تغييرًا كاملاً في قطاع نقل البضائع.

kama ghayyar 'inshā' an-nāqilāt — Just as the creation of supertankers

aḍ-ḍakhma naql al-bitroul qad 'aḥdath 'ayḍan isti9māl al-mustawda9āt taghyīran kāmilan fī qiṭā9 naql al-baḍā'i9.	has changed the transport of oil, so the use of containers has wrought a complete change in the goods transport sector.

(d)	رابطة روابط	*rābiṭa rawābiṭ*	link
	قمر صناعي	*qamar ṣinā9ī*	satellite
	سلك أسلاك	*silk 'aslāk*	wire
	لاسلكي	*lāsilkī*	wireless, radio (adj.)

منذ إنشاء رابطة بواسطة قمر صناعي زادت مواصلاتنا اللاسلكية زيادةً ملموسةً.

mundh 'inshā' rābiṭa bi wāsiṭat qamar ṣinā9ī zādat muwāṣalātuna l-lāsilkīya ziyādatan malmūsatan.	Since the creation of a satellite link, our radio communications have increased appreciably.

(e)	سكّة سكك حديدية	*sikka* (pl. *sikak*) *ḥadīdīya*	railway
	حدود	*ḥudūd* (pl.)	frontier
	تكلّفنا	*tukallifuna*	‹*tkallifna*›

عدم وجود سكّة حديدية بين المنطقة الصناعية والحدود هو مشكلة كبيرة علينا تكلّفنا كثيرًا.

9adam wujūd sikka ḥadīdīya bayna l-minṭaqa ṣ-ṣinā9īya wa l-ḥudūd huwa mushkila kabīra 9alayna tukallifuna kathīran.	The absence of a railway between the industrial area and the frontier is a great problem to us, costing us much.

2. مفردات إضافية ـ النقل والمواصلات

قطار قطر	*qiṭār quṭur*	train	مربوط	*marbūṭ*	linked
باخرة بواخر	*bākhira bawākhir*	ship	جوّي	*jawwī*	air (adj.)
شبكة شباك	*shabaka shibāk*	network	برّي	*barrī*	land (adj.)
طنّ أطنان	*ṭunn 'aṭnān*	ton(ne)	بحري	*baḥrī*	sea (adj.)
خطّ جوّي	*khaṭṭ jawwī*	airline	وجّه	*wajjaha* II	to send
متر مكعّب	*mitr muka99ab*	cubic metre	على متن	*9ala matn*	on board
بوليصة شحن	*būlīṣat shaḥn*	bill of lading, air waybill			

النحو

3. Subject pronouns

The pronouns أنا *'ana*, هو *huwa*, هي *hiya* and هم *hum* are the same in writing as in spoken Arabic. The other pronouns are:

1st person pl.: نحن *naḥnu* ‹*'iḥna*›

2nd persons: أنت *'anta* ‹*'int*›, *'anti* ‹*'inti*› أنتم *'antum* ‹*'intū*› and one which is found only in writing:

3rd person dual ('both of them'): هما *huma* (m. and f., animate/inanimate)

The 2nd and 3rd person pl. forms given above are in fact m. pl.; throughout written Arabic, these forms apply to groups of male persons or mixed company. There exist other pronouns (2nd person m./f. dual, 2nd and 3rd persons f. pl.) too rare, even in writing, to concern us. These are explained in 26/13 for reference.

4. Principal parts of verbs

Principal parts are usually quoted in full pronunciation. For verbs with a sound final root letter, these parts have *-a* and *-u* respectively after that letter, thus:

Sound	كتب يكتب	*kataba yaktubu*	‹*katab yuktub*›
Hamzated (i.e. one root letter is ء *hamza**)	أخذ يأخذ سأل يسأل قرأ يقرأ	*'akhadha ya'khudhu* *sa'ala yas'alu* *qara'a yaqra'u*	‹*'akhadh yākhudh*› ‹*sa'al yis'al*› ‹*qara yiqra*›
Initial-*w*	وصل يصل	*waṣala yaṣilu*	‹*wiṣil yūṣal*›
Hollow	قال يقول باع يبيع نام ينام	*qāla yaqūlu* *bā9a yabī9u* *nāma yanāmu*	‹*qāl yiqūl*› ‹*bā9 yibī9*› ‹*nām yinām*›
Doubled	ظلّ يظلّ	*ḍ̣alla yaḍ̣allu*	‹*ḍ̣all yiḍ̣all*›
Quadriliteral	ترجم يترجم	*tarjama yutarjimu*	‹*tarjam yitarjim*›

(This is Form I/IQ; the rule applies equally to Forms II – X and IIQ.)

* In written Arabic, sound verbs with one root letter *hamza* (initial, medial or final) form their own class; see paragraph 5 below.

The root vowels of the written Form I verb are sometimes different from the vowel used in spoken Arabic:

وصل يصل *waṣala yaṣilu* ‹*wiṣil yūṣal*›
عرف يعرف *9arafa ya9rifu* ‹*9irif ya9raf*›

Good dictionaries (see paragraph 12 below) show these vowels.

In short pronunciation (i.e. when the verb is used in a sentence), the final *-a* and *-u* are retained only when a pronoun suffix is added; otherwise these final vowels are dropped. They are printed ^{superscript} in the tenses shown below.

In introducing new verbs of Form IV we shall no longer include the second principal part, since its prefix is regular *(yu-)* in written Arabic.

5. Tenses of verbs with a sound final radical

Typical tenses of such verbs:

Past:

Root كتب, يكتب كتب *kataba yaktubu* I ‹*katab yuktub*›:

كتبت	*katabt*^{u}	كتبنا	*katabna*
كتبت	*katabt*^{a}	كتبتم	*katabtum*
كتبت	*katabti*		
كتب	*katab*^{a}	كتبوا	*katabū*
كتبت	*katabat*		

3rd person dual: m. كتبا *katabā*, f. كتبتا *katabatā*, final *'alif* pronounced long.

Present:

Root كتب, يكتب كتب *kataba yaktubu* I ‹*katab yuktub*›:

أكتب	*'aktub*^{u}	نكتب	*naktub*^{u}
تكتب	*taktub*^{u}	تكتبون	*taktubūna*
تكتبين	*taktubīna*		
يكتب	*yaktub*^{u}	يكتبون	*yaktubūna*
تكتب	*taktub*^{u}		

3rd person dual: m. يكتبان *yaktubāni*, f. تكتبان *taktubāni*

Root رسل, يرسل أرسل *'arsala yursilu* IV ‹ *'arsal yursil* ›:

أرسل	*'ursil*^{u}	نرسل	*nursil*^{u}
ترسل	*tursil*^{u}	ترسلون	*tursilūna*
ترسلين	*tursilīna*		
يرسل	*yursil*^{u}	يرسلون	*yursilūna*
ترسل	*tursil*^{u}		

3rd person dual: m. يرسلان *yursilāni*, f. ترسلان *tursilāni*

Several things to bear in mind:

- See 15/7 for the choice of vowel (*a* or *u*) in the present prefix, and in the prefix of Forms V, VI and IIQ.
- In the present tense, the final *-i* of the هي form and of the dual forms, and the final *-a* of the endings *-īna* and *-ūna*, are retained, exceptionally, even in short pronunciation.
- The final *-u* or *-a* elsewhere are in short pronunciation kept only before a suffix.

- The final *'alif* of وا *-ū* (past tense, هم form) is silent.
- Hamzated verbs:
  - verbs with final-radical *hamza*, final-weak in spoken Arabic, follow the sound pattern in written Arabic:
    قرأت *qara't*[u] (etc.), not *‹qarayt›* (etc.) in the past.
  - أخذ يأخذ *'akhadha ya'khudhu* I and أكل يأكل *'akala ya'kulu* I are regular in written Arabic (not *[yākhudh, yākul]* etc.).
  - *[hamza-'alif-hamza]* is always written آ *'alif-madda*; this means that we write آخذ *'ākhudh*, آكل *'ākul*.
- Initial-*w* and doubled verbs do not fully conform; see below.

6. Initial-*w* verbs

The written initial-*w* verbs follow the sound pattern, except that in Form I the initial root letter و *w* is dropped in the present tense:

Root وصل, وصل يصل *waṣala yaṣilu* I *‹wiṣil yūṣal›*:

أصل	*'aṣil*[u]	نصل	*naṣil*[u]
تصل	*taṣil*[u]	تصلون	*taṣilūna*
تصلين	*taṣilīna*		
يصل	*yaṣil*[u]	يصلون	*yaṣilūna*
تصل	*taṣil*[u]		

3rd person dual: m. يصلان *yaṣilāni*, f. تصلان *taṣilāni*

So also:

وجد يجد	*wajada yajidu* I to find
ورث يرث	*waratha yarithu* I to inherit
وقف يقف	*waqafa yaqifu* I to stop

Written Arabic also has a few rare verbs with initial root letter ي *yā'*.

7. Doubled verbs

In written Arabic, the doubled verb rule (13/4) applies also to the past tense of Form I:

Root دلّ, دلّ يدلّ *dalla yadullu* I *‹dall yidill›*:

دللت	*dalalt*[u]	دللنا	*dalalna*
دللت	*dalalt*[a]	دللتم	*dalatum*
دللت	*dalalti*		
دلّ	*dall*[a]	دلّوا	*dallū*
دلّت	*dallat*		

3rd person dual: m. دلّا *dallā*, f. دلّتا *dallatā*

(The -*ay*- of the spoken form is taken from the final-weak verbs.)

8. Increased forms

For the increased forms of all these verbs, use as base the models already known to you, bearing in mind the comments made above concerning the short final vowel before a suffix, and the vowel of the present prefix and of the prefix of Forms V, VI and IIQ.

9. Participles and verbal nouns

Form the participles and verbal nouns of these verbs on the models known to you, except that:

- root letter *hamza* does not 'soften' into -*y*- as it sometimes does in spoken Arabic:

  سائل *sā'il* not ‹*sāyil*› (active participle Form I)

  قراءة *qirā'a* not ‹*qirāya*› (verbal noun Form I)
- the active participle of Form I of hollow verbs also has *hamza* in the middle, not -*y*-: قائل *qā'il* not ‹*qāyil*›
- the active participle of Form I of doubled verbs follows the model حاطّ *ḥāṭṭ*:

  Root شكّ → شاكّ *shākk* (not ‹*shākik*›).

In addition, remember that the participles and verbal nouns have a case-ending before a suffix (Lesson 19).

10. Imperative

The written imperative is rarely met outside literature and advertisement; it mostly resembles the spoken form. Examples:

- تفضّل\تفضّلي\تفضّلوا *tafaḍḍal/tafaḍḍalī/tafaḍḍalū* V (NB silent final *'alif* in the plural)
- انظر\انظري\انظروا *unẓur/unẓurī/unẓurū* 'see ...' (in text references), from نظر ينظر *naḍ̄ara yanḍ̄uru* I; see paragraph 11 below.
- قف *qif* 'Stop', (seen on traffic signs). This is the m. sing. imperative of وقف يقف *waqafa yaqifu* I. See paragraph 6 above, and also 5/9.

In written Arabic, only Form IV has *hamza* beginning its imperative; the imperatives of Forms I (NB), VII, VIII, IX and X have a weak vowel.

Compare أرسل *'arsil* IV send

with افتح *iftaḥ* I open انظر *unḍ̄ur* I see (quoted above)

11. Use of certain verbs

Certain spoken-Arabic verbs are not used in writing, and vice versa. A few important differences:

- The written form of *‹qidir yiqdar›* I is little used as a written auxiliary; we use instead a Form X hollow verb which we learn later.
- For *‹rāḥ yirūḥ›* write ذهب يذهب *dhahaba yadhhabu* I.
- Do not write *‹shāf yishūf›*; write نظر ينظر *naðara yanðuru* I for 'to see' and نظر ينظر إلى *naðara yanðuru* I *'ila* for 'to look at'. We shall learn later a second, more common verb for 'to see'.

12. Use of the dictionary

Arabic dictionaries are of two kinds:

- The most recent dictionaries list entries alphabetically by words in both parts, as in European-language dictionaries. These later dictionaries present no special difficulty. A good word-based dictionary is the *Arabic Dictionary* (Arabic-English, English-Arabic) of N. Awde and K. Smith, pub. Bennett and Bloom.
- Traditional dictionaries, in the part translating from Arabic, list all words based on triliteral and quadriliteral roots alphabetically *by the root* and not by the word. Thus معلّم *mu9allim,* تعليم *ta9līm* and استعلم *ista9lama* are all listed under علم , before علن and its derivatives. Words not based on such roots are listed alphabetically among them. Remember that *'alif* is not a root letter; weak root letters are always either و or ي. Root-letter *hamza* is listed under *'alif, wāw* or *yā'*, depending on its vowel. The most prestigious root-based Arabic-English dictionary is Hans Wehr's *Dictionary of Modern Written Arabic,* pub. Otto Harrassowitz, also Spoken Language Services Inc.

13. التمارين

1. Read aloud:

e.g.: يصل بعد يومين. yaṣil ba9da yawmayn.

(a) تسلّمت رسالتكم.
(b) المواصلات اللاسلكية
(c) قد قرأنا التقرير.
(d) على متن طائرة اليوم
(e) أرسلناه بالبريد الجوّي.

2. Write:

e.g.: qara'na shurūṭ ad-daf9 al-maktūba fī 9aqdihim.

قرأنا شروط اللدفع المكتوبة في عقدهم.

(a) wajjahū lī risāla ṭawīla maktūb fīha jadwal 'as9ārihim.

(b) al-ḥukūma taqūm bi tamdīd shabakat aṭ-ṭuruq ath-thānawīya.

(c) 'irsāl al-baḍā'i9 bi l-ḥajm yukallifuna 'aqall mimma yukallif bi l-wazn.

(d) takūn būlīṣat ash-shaḥn 9ala matn bākhirat 'KOBI MARU' min Yokohāma.

(e) al-wizāra tanshur jadāwil aṣ-ṣādirāt 9ādatan fi l-jarīdatayn ar-rasmīyatayn.

3. Put into the plural:

e.g.: دخل ← دخلوا

(a) أُنظُر (b) زار (c) آخذ
(d) تقول (e) دلّ

4. Put into the present tense:

e.g.: تكلّمنا ← نتكلّم

(a) بعنا (b) ارسلوا (c) حطّطتم
(d) (انا) استجوبت (e) صرنا

5. Put into the past tense:

e.g.: يدخلون ← دخلوا

(a) يصلون (b) آخذ (c) يوجب على
(d) نشكّ في (e) نستبدل

6. Give the principal parts, participles (m. sing.) and verbal noun:

e.g.: دبّر ← دبّر يدبّر، مدبِّر مدبَّر، تدبير

(a) ابتدأ (b) ارسل (c) كان
(d) استورد (e) سأل

7. Give the root under which each word is found in a dictionary based on roots:

e.g.: قالوا ← قول

(a) استفاد (b) انظر (c) مددتم
(d) يرث (e) يخاف (f) استيراد
(g) المسؤول (h) ازدياد (j) اتخذنا
(k) اتفقنا

الدرس الحادي والعشرون
ad-dars al-ḥādī wa l-9ishrūn – Lesson 21
ادارة شؤون الموظّفين ’idārat shu’ūn al-muwaðða fīn
Personnel Management

1. جمل مثالية

(a)

متأكّد من	*muta'akkid min*	convinced of, sure of
ظرف ظروف	*ðarf ðurūf*	condition, circumstance
سالم	*sālim*	sound (adjective)
أيّد	*'ayyada* II	to support
تأييد	*ta'yīd*	support
تأييدًا ل	*ta'yīdan li*	in support of

اننا متأكّدون من ان قسم شؤون الموظّفين يقوم بخدمة مهمّة جدًّا وهي انشاء ظروف سالمة تأييدًا للإنتاج.

’innana muta’akkidūn min ’anna qism shu’ūn al-muwaðða fīn yaqūm bi khidma muhimma jiddan u hiya ’inshā’ ðurūf sālima ta’yīdan li l-’intāj.

We are convinced that Personnel Department performs an important service, i.e. the creation of sound conditions in support of production.

(b)

صغير صغار	*ṣaghīr ṣighār*	(also) junior

ستقوم الشركة بتوظيف عدد اضافي من العمّال والموظّفين الصغار خلال الشهرين المقبلين.

sa taqūm ash-sharika bi tawðīf 9adad ’iḍāfī min al-9ummāl wa l-muwaðða fīn aṣ-ṣighār khilāl ash-shahrayn al-muqbilayn.

The company will recruit an additional number of workmen and junior staff during the next two months.

(c)

أضرب	*'aḍraba* IV	to strike (from work)
إضراب	*'iḍrāb*	strike
سبب أسباب	*sabab 'asbāb*	cause
خلاف	*khilāf*	dispute
كبار	*kibār*	(in def. construct) senior, leading
مجلس إدارة	*majlis 'idāra*	board of directors

الإضراب في قسم الإنتاج صار سببًا لخلاف شديد بين كبار ممثّلي النقابة ومجلس الإدارة للشركة.

al-’iḍrāb fī qism al-’intāj ṣār sababan li khilāf shadīd bayna kibār mumaththilí n-niqāba wa majlis al-’idāra li sh-sharika.

The strike in Production Department became the cause of a serious dispute between the leading union representatives and the company’s board of directors.

(d)	قانون قوانين	*qānūn qawānīn*	law
	طبّق	*ṭabbaqa* II	to apply
	تطبيق	*taṭbīq*	application
	إجراءات	*'ijrā'āt*	(pl., also:) procedure
	تسوية	*táswiya*	settlement (of problem etc.)
	شكوه شكوات	*shakwa shakawāt*	complaint
	سجّل	*sajjala* II	to register
	تسجيل	*tasjīl*	registration

حسب قانون العمل عند العمّال حقّ تطبيق الإجراءات الموافق عليها لتسوية الشكوات بعد تسجيل شكوتهم.

ḥasaba qānūn al-9amal 9inda l-9ummāl ḥaqq taṭbīq al-'ijrā'āt al-muwāfaq 9alayha li táswiyat ash-shakawāt ba9da tasjīl shakwatihim.	According to the Labour Law, workers have the right to apply ('of application of') the agreed procedure for settling complaints after registration of their complaint.

(e)	رقّى	*raqqa* II	to promote
	ترقية	*tárqiya*	promotion
	مرتفع	*murtáfi9*	high
	استقال	*istaqāla** X	to resign
	استقالة	*istiqāla*	resignation

* from root قيل.

عدم وجود امكانيات الترقية في الأقسام الفنّية هو سبب العدد المرتفع للاستقالات عند كبار الموظّفين في السنة الماضية.

9adam wujūd 'imkānīyāt at-tárqiya fi l-'aqsām al-fannīya huwa sabab al-9adad al-murtáfi9 li l-istiqālāt 9inda kibār al-muwaððafīn fi s-sana l-māḍiya.	The lack of promotion possibilities in the technical departments is the cause of the high number of resignations among senior staff last year.

2. مفردات إضافية – إدارة شؤون الموظّفين

وظيفة وظائف	*waðīfa waðā'if*	job	مؤهّل	*mu'ahhal*	qualified
مهنة مهن	*mihna mihan*	profession	درجة	*daraja*	grade
راتب رواتب	*rātib rawātib*	salary	اجر اجور	*'ajr 'ujūr*	wages
عزل يعزل	*9azala ya9zilu* I	to dismiss	عزل	*9azl*	dismissal

شغل اضافي	*shughl 'iḍāfī*	overtime work
جدول رواتب	*jadwal rawātib*	pay scale
مؤهّلات	*mu'ahhilāt*	qualifications
بدل ابدال	*badal 'abdāl*	allowance

النحو

3. Object Pronouns

The object-pronoun suffixes added to verbs are identical to the pronoun suffixes added to prepositions, except for ني *-nī* 'me'. The verb gets full pronunciation before a suffix. Further, two endings of the past tense and the imperative are modified before a suffix:

- تُمْ (2nd person, m. pl. past) adds و *-ū-*:
  وجّهتموها *wajjahtumūha*   ساعدتمونا *sā9adtumūna*
- *-ū* (3rd person m. pl. past, and imperative) drops its silent *'alif*:
  عزلوه *9azalūhu*   انظروها *unđurūha*

4. Complements

Most verbs denoting 'being' or 'becoming' have a complement (see 2/6; it is also known as a *predicate*). The complement is either a noun or an adjective. Important verbs taking a complement include:

كان يكون *kāna yakūnu* I to be
صار يصير *ṣāra yaṣīru* I to become
ظلّ يظلّ *đalla yađallu* I to remain
دام يدوم *dāma yadūmu* I to persist, still to be
ما زال لا يزال *mā zāla lā yazālu* I still to be
ما عاد لا يعود *mā 9āda lā ya9ūdu* I to be no longer

The noun or adjective complement stands in the *accusative* case, and is normally indefinite (see 19/7):

كان مريضًا. *kān marīḍan.* He was ill.
صرنا مرشّحين. *ṣirna murashshaḥīn.* We became candidates.
صار وضع العمّال واضحًا نتيجةً لتطبيق القانون الجديد.
ṣār waḍ9 al-9ummāl wāḍiḥan natījatan li taṭbīq al-qānūn al-jadīd. The workers' situation became clear as a result of the application of the new law.

Complements also occur in definite form, but these are rarer:

كان هو المدير\مديرنا. *kān huwa l-mudīr/mudīrana.*
He was the director/our director.

Complement rule: The complement of a verb stands in the accusative case.

For our requirements (short pronunciation, no pointing), this rule matters to us only when the complement has a m. indefinite acc. sing. ending (اً *-an*), a dual ending (ين *-ayn*), a sound m. pl. ending (ين *-īn*), or a possessive suffix (19/6). The complement rule applies only after a verb; in a verbless sentence of the type

انا مبسوط *'ana mabsūṭ* (1/6) the complement stands in the nominative. Compare:

العامل غائب. *al-9āmil ghā'ib.* The workman is absent.
العامل كان غائبًا. *al-9āmil kān ghā'iban.* The workman was absent.

In 19/9 we learned that the dual and sound pl. endings ين *-ayn/-īn* drop their final ن *-n* from the theme of a construct:

صارا موظفي الشركة. *ṣārā muwaððafay ash-sharika.*
صاروا موظفي الشركة. *ṣārū muwaððafī sh-sharika.*

The theme of a construct cannot have a *tanwīn* ending:

صار مديرًا. *ṣār mudīran.*
but: صار مديربنك. *ṣār mudīr bank.*
صارت سكرتيرةً. *ṣārat sikritayra.*
but: صارت سكرتيرة وزير. *ṣārat sikritayrat wazīr.*

5. Negatives

Verbs are negated with لا *lā* in the present tense and ما *mā* in the past:

ما دفعنا البدل. *mā dafa9na l-badal.*
لا ندفع البدل. *lā nadfa9 al-badal.*

We shall learn later a more common and stylish negative for verbs with past meaning.

The negative ‹*mish*› is not used in written Arabic. For the negative of 'to be' in present time, the hollow verb ليس *laysa* I 'not to be' is used. This verb is past tense in form but present in meaning. It is always pronounced with full final vowels:

لست	*lastu*	لسنا	*lasna*
لست	*lasta*	لستم	*lastum*
لست	*lasti*		
ليس	*laysa*	ليسوا	*laysū*
ليست	*laysat*		I, you, he (etc.) am/is/are not

3rd person dual: m. ليسا *laysā*, f. ليستا *laysat*

This verb takes a complement, which goes into the accusative case:

ليس مريضًا. *laysa mariḍan.* He is not ill.
ليسوا غائبين. *laysū ghā'ibīn.* They are not absent.

The other use of ‹*mish*›, i.e. to negate adjectives and adverbs, is covered by غير *ghayr*; the negated word is put into the *genitive*:

زملاؤنا غير حاضرين. *zumalā'una ghayr ḥāḍirīn.*

وصلت لنا رسالة غير رسمية. *waṣalat lana risāla ghayr rasmīya.*

6. Interrogatives

The commonest interrogatives are:

Pronouns:	من *man ‹mīn›*	ماذا\ما *mādha/mā ‹shū›*
	لمن *li man ‹li mīn›*	كم *kam*
Adjectives:	كم *kam*	ايّ *'ayy*
	من *man ‹mīn›*	
Adverbs:	كيف *kayfa ‹kayf›*	أين *'ayna ‹wayn›*
	متى *mata*	لماذا\لما *li mādha/li mā ‹laysh›*

Use them as you do their spoken equivalents (see 5/15), but note:

- after كم *kam* the noun stands in the *indefinite accusative* singular:

  كم مرشّحًا حاضرون؟ *kam murashshaḥan ḥāḍirūn?*

  kam is not used in written-language *statements* (see 2/9).
- أيّ *'ayy* has also non-interrogative-meaning, 'any':

  أيّ واحد منهم *'ayy wāḥid minhum* any (one) of them

  أيّ *'ayy* has an optional f. sing. form أيّة *'ayya*, not consistently used.

  Do not confuse أيّ *'ayy* 'which/any' with أي *'ay* meaning 'i.e.':

  أمس، أي يوم الأحد *'ams, 'ay yawm al-'aḥad* yesterday, i.e. Sunday

7. Sentence structure: statements

Arabic sentences expressing a statement can be either 'nominal' or 'verbal'.

8. Nominal sentences

See 15/9. A nominal sentence is one which follows the English pattern, with subject before verb:

رسالتكم وصلت أمس. *risālatukum waṣalat 'ams.*

هي وصلت أمس. *hiya waṣalat 'ams.*

Sentences in which the verb is implied count as nominal sentences:

المرشّحون هنا. *al-murashshaḥūn huna.*

A nominal statement may also be introduced by a conjunction. Some of these, based on the conjunctions أنّ *'anna* or إنّ *'inna*, behave in a special manner. The most important such conjunctions are:

أنّ	*'anna* that	إنّ	*'inna* (see below)
لأنّ	*li 'anna* because	(و)لكنّ	*(wa)lākinna* but

كأنّ *ka 'anna* as if, as though

Note:

- إنّ *'inna* adds no meaning to the sentence; it merely announces that a nominal statement follows.
- With أنّ *'anna* and كأنّ *ka 'anna* the indirect speech rule (4/7) applies.

The subject of the clause introduced by one of these conjunctions is always in the *accusative* case; if a pronoun, it is suffixed:

إنّ المندوبين وصلوا أمس. *'inna l-mandūbīn waṣalū 'ams.*
إنّهم وصلوا أمس. *'innahum waṣalū 'ams.*

Nominal sentence rule: In a sentence beginning with *'inna* or *'anna* or one of their derivatives, the subject stands in the accusative case.

Any complement follows its own rule, i.e. it remains nominative if the sentence has no verb, but becomes accusative if it follows a verb of being or becoming (paragraph 4 above):

ولكنّ المهندسين حاضرون. *walākinna l-muhandisīn ḥāḍirūn.*
ولكنّهم حاضرون. *walākinnahum ḥāḍirūn.*
لأنّ المندوبين غائبون. *li 'anna l-mandūbīn ghā'ibūn.*
لأنّ المندوبين كانوا غائبين. *li 'anna l-mandūbīn kānū ghā'ibīn.*

9. The conjunctions إنّ *'inna* and أنّ *'anna* and their derivatives have alternative forms when ني *-nī* and نا *-na* are suffixed:

انّني	*'innanī/'annanī*	or	انّي	*'innī/'annī*
انّنا	*'innana/'annana*	or	انّا	*'inna/'anna*

10. Verbal sentences

In a verbal sentence making a statement the verb comes earlier than the subject. The verb is always a stated (i.e. not implied) verb. In such sentences, when the subject is a noun, the verb is always singular, even if the subject is dual or plural (see 15/9). Since noun subjects are always 3rd person, this rule affects only verbs in the 3rd persons:

وصل المرشّحون أمس. *waṣal al-murashshaḥūn 'ams.*
أعلن المدراء أن ... *'a9lan al-mudarā' 'anna ...*

When the subject is an implied pronoun, the verb has its usual ending, including dual or plural if appropriate:

استقلنا\استقالا\ استقالوا أمس. *istaqalna/istaqālā/istaqālū 'ams.*

An inanimate plural verb counts as singular:

وصلت الرسالات امس. *waṣalat ar-risālāt 'ams.*

When the verb consists of more than one element (e.g. in the continuous past or the pluperfect tenses), only the first element precedes the subject in a verbal sentence. The other elements follow the subject and have full agreement with it:

كان العمّال يضربون\أضربوا. *kān al-9ummāl yuḍribūna/'aḍrabū.*

The workmen were striking/had struck.

Similarly, when a subject has two verbs, only one can precede the subject. The other must follow the subject, with full agreement:

دخل العمّال وبدأوا العمل. *dakhal al-9ummāl wa bada'u l-9amal.*

Verbal sentence rule: When the verb has a noun subject and precedes it, the verb stands in the singular even when the subject is dual or plural.

11. Future

The written equivalent of *‹rāyiḥ/rāḥ›* is the particle سوف *sawfa* or س *sa* immediately preceding the present tense (see 15/12):

سوف نقوم\سنقوم بتطبيق جدول الرواتب الجديد قريبًا.

sawfa/sa naqūm bi taṭbīq jadwal ar-rawātib al-jadīd qarīban.

We can form a negative future with سوف لا *sawfa lā*:

سوف لا يضربون. *sawfa lā yuḍribūna.*

But this is not very common. We shall study later a commoner negative future.

12. قال يقول *qāla yaqūlu*

The verb قال يقول *qāla yaqūlu* I is unique in that its conjunction for indirect speech is إنّ *'inna*, not أنّ *'anna* as for other verbs of speech:

أعلنوا أنّهم موافقون. *'a9lanū 'annahum muwāfiqūn.*

but: قالوا إنّهم موافقون. *qālū 'innahum muwāfiqūn.*

13. Sentence structure: questions

In written Arabic, questions are introduced by an interrogative word. Questions inviting an answer other than 'yes' or 'no' are introduced by the appropriate interrogative word, usually a pronoun or adverb such as in paragraph 6 above.

Questions inviting the answer 'yes' or 'no' must be introduced by one of the following interrogative particles:

هل *hal* (for affirmative questions only)

أ *'a* (for affirmative or negative questions)

دفعت الأجور. *dafa9t al-'ujūr.*

هل دفعت الأجور؟ *hal dafa9t al-'ujūr?*
أما دفعتها؟ *'a mā dafa9taha?*

أ *'a*, being a one-letter word, is written as one with the following word. Its initial *hamza* is almost always written, for clarity.

We introduce indirect questions either by one of the interrogatives listed in Paragraph 6 above, or (for 'yes/no' questions) by هل *hal* or ما إذا *mā 'idha*:

لا نعرف هل\ما إذا تصل قريبًا. *lā na9rif hal/mā 'idha taṣil qarīban.*

The indirect speech rule (4/7) applies.

14. *'iyyā-*

The written equivalent of the particle *iyyā-* (see 11/17) is إيّا... *'iyyā-* (NB: It has initial *hamza*, not a weak vowel). It is used in written Arabic when there are two direct-object pronouns:

سألونا إيّاه بعد المؤتمر. *sa'alūna 'iyyāhu ba9da l-mu'támar.*
They asked us (about) it after the conference.

but not otherwise; the rule given in 11/17 does not apply. Compare written and spoken forms:

شرحه لنا. *sharaḥahu lana. ‹sharaḥ lana yyā́.›*

This particle is far less common in written than in spoken Arabic.

15. **التمارين**

1. Read aloud:

e.g.: هل كتبت الوزارة جوابًا ايجابيًا؟

hal katabat al-wizāra jawāban 'ījābīyan?

(a) ان حل المشكلة يظهر لنا غير ممكن.
(b) دمنا متأكدين من ضرورة التدخل.
(c) هل تريد الإدارة استئناف المفاضات؟
(d) انّنا مسرورون جدًّا باقتراحكم حول مقابل الشغل الإضافي.
(e) أما تسلمت التقرير؟ اننا ارسلناه قبل اسبوعين.

2. Write:

e.g.: li mādha lā tuwāfiq an-niqāba 9ala qtirāḥina bi khuṣūṣ at-ta9wīḍ?

لماذا لا توافق النقابة على اقتراحنا بخصوص التعويض؟

(a) mā ra'yuka ḥawl jadwal al-'abdāl al-jā́riya?

(b) hal naðartum jadwal ar-rawātib li s-sanati l-muqbila?

(c) 'inna sh-sharika lā turīd taṭbīq hādhihi l-'arqām al-jadīda.

(d) sa yastaghriq al-'iḍrāb waqtan qaṣīran faqaṭ li 9adam ta'yīd an-niqābatayn.

(e) 'innana na9tábir ṭalab al-9ummāl ghayr maqbūl.

3 Repeat the sentences of Ex. 2 in spoken Arabic:

e.g.: li mādha lā tuwāfiq an-niqāba 9ala qtirāḥina bi khuṣūṣ at-ta9wīḍ?

– ‹laysh an-niqāba mā twāfiq 9ala qtirāḥna bi khuṣūṣ at-ta9wīḍ?›

4. Make negative:

e.g.: هو حاضر. ← ليس حاضرًا.

(a) استقبلته. (b) يستقبله. (c) يتمكن منه.

(d) زميله مريض. (e) يهمنا كثيرًا.

5. Make a question based on the underlined word or expression:

e.g.: زاروا المصنع امس. ← متى زاروا المصنع؟

(a) قمتم بإرسال الجواب. (b) نظرنا التظاهر.

(c) هو غائب لأنه مريض. (d) باعه لزميله.

(d) كانوا مأمورين في قسم المالية.

6. Recast the sentence, beginning with the verb:

e.g.: المدراء اجتمعوا امس. ← اجتمع المدراء امس.

(a) الممثّلون ذهبوا الى المؤتمر.

(b) المفتّشون قرأوا الوثيقة بالتفصيل.

(c) ممثّلو الشركة قالوا ان الاتفاقية مقبولة.

(d) الوزير يفهم تمامًا ان الوضع معقد.

(e) المتظاهرون خرجوا من المصنع ودخلوا الشارع الرئيسي.

7. Repeat the sentences of Ex. 6, beginning each one with ان :

e.g.: المدراء اجتمعوا امس. ← ان المدراء اجتمعوا امس.

الدرس الثاني والعشرون
ad-dars ath-thānī wa l-9ishrūn – Lesson 22
البترول al-bitroul – Petroleum

1. جمل مثالية

(a)

استكشف	*istakshafa* X	to explore
استكشاف	*istikshāf*	exploration
حفر يحفر حفر	*ḥafara yaḥfiru* I, *ḥafr*	to drill
بئر آبار	*bi'r 'ābār* (f.)	well
بعد ابعاد	*bu9d 'ab9ād*	distance
كيلومتر، كم	*kīlumitr*	kilometre, km
ساحل سواحل	*sāḥil sawāḥil*	shore, coast

تم استكشاف هذا الحقل قبل عشرين سنة وحفرنا اول بئر تجريبية على بعد ثمانية كيلومترات من الساحل بعد سنتين.

tamm istikshāf hādha l-ḥaql qabla 9ishrīn sana wa ḥafarna 'awwal bi'r tajrībīya 9ala bu9d thamāniya kīlumitrāt min as-sāḥil ba9da sanatayn.

This field was explored twenty years ago, and we drilled the first test well at a distance of eight km from the coast two years later ('after two years').

(b)

نفط	*nafṭ*	oil
نفط خام	*nafṭ khām*	crude oil
ضغط	*ḍaghṭ*	pressure
ضخّ يضخّ	*ḍakhkha yaḍukhkhu* I	to pump
طلمبة	*ṭulumba*	pump

يمر النفط الخام تحت ضغط طبيعي الى محطة الإنتاج بواسطة انابيب ثابتة فمن المحطة نضخّه بطلمبات حتى الناقلة.

yamurr an-nafṭ taḥt ḍaghṭ ṭabī9ī 'ila maḥaṭṭat al-'intāj bi wāsiṭat 'anābīb thābita fa min al-maḥaṭṭa naḍukhkhuhu bi ṭulumbāt ḥatta n-nāqila.

The crude oil travels ('passes') to the production station under natural pressure through fixed pipes, and ('so') from the station we pump it ('with pumps') to the tanker.

(c)

جهاز اجهزة	*jihāz 'ajhiza*	installation, plant, rig
كرّر	*karrara* II	to refine
تكرير	*takrīr*	refining
جزّأ	*jazza'a* II	to separate
زيت زيوت	*zayt zuyūt*	oil
زيت خام	*zayt khām*	crude oil
كسر كسور	*kasr kusūr*	fraction

زفت	*zift*	bitumen, tar
شحّم	*shaḥḥama* II	to lubricate
تشحيم	*tashḥīm*	lubrication
ديزل	*dīzil*	diesel
بنزين	*binzīn*	petrol, gasolene
كيروسين	*kirusīn*	kerosene, paraffin
غاز	*ghāz*	gas

في جهاز التكرير يجزّئون الزيت الخام الى كسوره الثقيلة كالزفت والموم والزيوت التشحيم وإلى كسوره الخفيفة كالديزل والبنزين والكيروسين والغاز.

fī jihāz at-takrīr yujazzi'ūna z-zayt al-khām 'ila kusūrihi th-thaqīla ka z-zift wa l-mūm wa zuyūt at-tashḥīm, wa 'ila kusūrihi l-khafīfa ka d-dīzil wa l-binzīn wa l-kirusīn wa l-ghāz.

In the refinery they separate the crude into its heavy fractions such as bitumen, wax and lubricating oils, and light fractions such as diesel, gasolene, kerosene and gas.

(d)

منتوج	*mantūj*	product
بتروكيميائيات	*bitrukīmiyā'īyāt*	petrochemicals

في نفس الوقت تنفصل المنتوجات الكيميائية للاستعمال في الصناعة. فمع مرور الزمن صار انتاج البتروكيميائيات اهم بكثير مما كان سابقًا لاقتصاد صناعة النفط.

fī nafs al-waqt tanfaṣil al-matūjāt al-kīmīyā'īya li l-isti9māl fī ṣ-ṣinā9a. fa ma9a murūr az-zaman ṣār 'intāj al-bitrukīmīyā'īyāt 'ahamm bi kathīr mimma kān sābiqan li qtiṣād ṣinā9at an-nafṭ.

At the same time, the chemical products for use in industry are separated. With the passage of time, the production of petrochemicals has become much more important than previously for the economy of the oil industry.

2. مفردات اضافية – البترول

جهاز حفر	*jihāz ḥafr*	drilling rig	حفّار	*ḥaffār*	driller
طين	*ṭīn*	mud	زلزالي	*zilzālī*	seismic
برميل براميل	*barmīl barāmīl*	barrel	قوة	*qūwa*	power, strength
احتياطي	*iḥtiyāṭī*	reserve	قطّر	*qaṭṭara* II	to distil
سوّق	*sawwaqa* II	to market	استهلك	*istahlaka* X	to consume

النحو

3. Demonstratives

In the written demonstrative adjectives and pronouns, only the dual forms vary for case (two forms for three cases):

	Singular		Plural
this/these	m. هذا *hādha*	f. هذه *hādhihi*	m./f. هؤلاء *hā'ulā'i*
that/those	m. ذلك *dhālika*	f. تلك *tilka*	m./f. أولئك *'ūlā'ika*

Dual			
these two/ both these	nom.	m. هذان *hādhāni*	f. هاتان *hātāni*
	acc./gen.	m. هذين *hādhayni*	f. هاتين *hātayni*
those two/ both those	nom.	m. ذانك *dhānika*	f. تانك *tānika*
	acc./gen.	m. ذينك *dhaynika*	f. تينك *taynika*

The written demonstrative is used exactly in the same way as its spoken counterpart. The unwritten long *ā* can be pointed with small *'alif*:

ذٰلك *dhālika* هٰؤلاء *hā'ulā'i*

'ūlā'ika has an alternative spelling: أولائك.

4. Subjunctive

The *subjunctive* tense (in full terminology, the subjunctive mood of the present tense) is used for certain common structures. To form the subjunctive, take the present tense and:

- change the full-form ending *-u* to *-a* (pronounced in short pronunciation only before a suffix):

  اكتب *'aktub*[a], تكتب *taktub*[a], يكتب *yaktub*[a] (etc.)

- drop the final syllables نَ *-na* (2nd person f. sing.m, 2nd/3rd persons pl.) and نِ *-ni* (dual):

  تكتبي *taktubī*; تكتبوا *taktubū*, يكتبوا *yaktubū*;
  يكتبا *yaktubā*, تكتبا *taktubā*

These rules are valid for all verbs, Forms I-X, IQ and IIQ, with a sound final root letter. Note especially the silent *'alif* of وا *-ū* which is not written before a suffix.

Negative future. The particle لن *lan* 'will not' is followed by a subjunctive verb. This is commonly used as a negative of س\سوف . Examine:

سوف يبدأون الإنتاج. *sawfa yabda'ūna l-'intāj.* } They will (not)
but: لن يبدأوا الإنتاج. *lan yabda'u l-'intāj.* } start production.

Clauses of purpose. Clauses expressing purpose are mostly introduced by the one of the conjunctions (many of them synonyms, as you see):

أنْ *'an* so that, to لئلاّ *li 'allā́ (= li 'an lā)* so that... not

ل *li,* لأنْ *li 'an,* كي *kay,* لكي *li kay,* حتّى *ḥatta* so that

Do not confuse أنْ *'an* with أنّ *'anna* (21/8). أنْ does not take a pronoun suffix.

The verb expressing the purpose stands in the subjunctive in written Arabic:

ارسلنا التقرير لكي ينظروا النتائج. *'arsalna t-taqrīr li kay yanđuru n-natā'ij.* We sent the report for them to ('so that they should') see the results.

اوفقنا الطلمبات لئلا يزيد الضغط. *'awfaqna ṭ-ṭulumbāt li 'allā yazīd aḍ-ḍaghṭ.* We stopped the pumps so that the pressure would not increase.

Indirect command and request. See 7/15. The conjunctions أنْ *'an* 'that' and ألاّ *'allā́* 'that ... not' (NB stress) introduce indirect command and request, expressed in written Arabic with the subjunctive:

طلبنا منهم ان\\الا يبدأوا الحفر. *ṭalabna minhum 'an/'allā́ yabda'u l-ḥafr.* We asked them (not) to start ('that they should (not) start') the drilling.

The clause following any of these purpose or indirect-command conjunctions has verbal-sentence structure (21/10):

استعملنا طلمبات إضافية لكي يستأنف الحفارون الإنتاج.

ista9malna ṭulumbāt 'iḍāfīya li kay yasta'nif al-ḥaffārūn al-'intāj.

We used extra pumps so that the drillers might resume production.

5. Auxiliary verbs

Many written verbs when used as auxiliaries are followed by أنْ *'an* plus the dependent verb in the subjunctive. Important auxiliaries of this type include:

- some used personally (i.e. with a 1st-, 2nd- or 3rd-person subject):

استطاع يستطيع	*istaṭā9a yastaṭī9u* X	‹*qidir yiqdar* I›
(كان) يريد	*(kān) yurīd* IV	‹*(kān) yurīd* IV›
حاول يحاول	*ḥāwala yuḥāwilu* III	‹*jarrab* II, *ḥāwal* III›
فضّل يفضّل	*faḍḍala yufaḍḍilu* II	‹*faḍḍal* II›
سمح يسمح ل	*samaḥa yasmaḥu* I *li*	‹*samaḥ yismaḥ* I *li*›

- some used impersonally (see below), the three commonest being:

(كان) يجب	*(kān) yajib*	‹*(kān) lāzim*›
(كان) يجوز	*(kān) yajūz*	‹*(kān) mumkin*›
(كان) يمكن	*(kān) yumkin*	‹*(kān) yumkin*›

The clause following أنْ *'an* has verbal-sentence structure.

حاولوا ان يستبدلوا الطلمبة. *ḥāwalū 'an yastabdilu ṭ-ṭulumba.*

لا نستطيع ان نزيد الإنتاج. *lā nastaṭī9 'an nazīd al-'intāj.*

ما سمحوا له انْ يوقفها. *mā samaḥū lahu 'an yūqifaha.*

For كان يريد *kān yurīd,* the continuous past is preferred to the past:

كنا نريد ان نساعدكم. *kunna nurīd 'an nusā9idakum.*

يجب *yajib,* يجوز *yajūz* and يمكن *yumkin* are always third person m. sing. They have two uses; either in an impersonal structure:

يجب\يجوز\يمكن ان ترسله. *yajib/yajūz/yumkin 'an tursilahu.*

You must/may/might send it. ('It is obligatory/permitted/likely that ...')

or the person affected can be expressed as the object, thus:

يجب على *yajib 9ala* يجوز ل *yajūz li*

يمكن *yumkin* + direct object

يجب علينا\يجوز لنا\يمكننا ان نؤيده. *yajib 9alayna/yajūz lana/yumkinuna 'an nu'ayyidahu.* We must/may/might support him.

كان يجب (علينا) ان نستقبله. *kān yajib (9alayna) 'an nastaqbilahu.*

We had to/were obliged to receive him.

6. In each case, an alternative structure is often used to replace the conjunction + verb with a verbal noun for the desired/preferred/obliged/permitted/likely etc. action. This verbal noun is always definite.

Examine and compare (V = conjunction + verb; N = verbal noun):

V: ما استطاعوا ان يتصلوا به. *mā staṭā9ū 'an yattáṣilū bihi.*

They could not ('that they') contact him.

N: ما استطاعوا الاتصال به. *mā staṭā9u l-ittiṣāl bihi.*

They could not contact ('were not capable of contact with') him.

V: كان يجب ان نتخذ اجراءات ضرورية. *kān yajib 'an nittákhidh 'ijrā'āt ḍarūrīya.* We had to ('It was obligatory that we') take urgent measures.

N: كان يجب علينا اتخاذ اجراءات ضرورية. *kān yajib 9alayna ttikhādh 'ijrā'āt ḍarūrīya.* It was necessary for us to take urgent measures ('The taking of urgent measures was ...').

7. When the auxiliary verb itself is situated in a verbal sentence, it also follows the verbal sentence rule shown in 21/10; this is important when the auxiliary is used in a compound tense:

كان المهندسون يريدون ان يبدأوا الحفر.

kān al-muhandisūn yūrīdūna 'an yabda'u l-ḥafr.

8. Comparison of adjectives

See 9/13, 14. All the rules for using the model *'akbar* (etc.) for the comparative of simple adjectives are valid also for written Arabic.

The feminine superlatives ending in *-a* are written with *'alif maqṣūra*, except for العليا (see 18/2, 3):

آسيا الصغرى *'āsiya ṣ-ṣughra* Asia Minor

The comparative of derived adjectives is different from the spoken construction. In written Arabic we use the comparative اكثر *'akthar* or اشدّ *'ashadd*; not following the adjective, but *preceding the corresponding noun* (verbal noun if the adjective is a participle), in the indefinite accusative, thus:

هذا اكثر ضرورةً. *hādha 'akthar ḍarūratan* ('greater in necessity') ‹*ḍarūrī 'akthar*›.

هو اكثر اجتهادًا. *huwa 'akthar ijtihādan* ‹*mujtáhid 'akthar*›.

Here *tanwīn* is an adverbial form, and is therefore pronounced.

9. Comparison of adverbs

For adverbs compounded with a noun, we form the comparative by putting اكثر *'akthar* after the noun, which must be indefinite:

بسهولة، بسهولة اكثر *bi suhūla, bi suhūla 'akthar*

easily ('with ease'), more easily ('with more ease')

بالضبط، بضبط اكثر *bi ḍ-ḍabṭ*, bi ḍabṭ 'akthar*

precisely, more precisely ('with precision/more precision')

*see 17/11

For common adverbs ending *-an*, the comparative is the same as that of the adjective from which it is derived: كثيرًا\\اكثر *kathīran/'akthar*, قليلاً\\اقلّ *qalīlan/'aqall*, شديدًا\\اشدّ *shadīdan/'ashadd*. With less common adverbs of this type it is often better to use the device shown above:

سريعًا، بسرعة اكثر *sarī9an, bi sur9a 'akthar* fast, faster ('with more speed')

or بصورة *bi ṣūra* with the appropriate comparative adjective:

بصورة اسرع *bi ṣūra 'asra9* faster ('in a faster manner')

For the superlative, we must rephrase: 'with more ... than all':

حللنا هذه المشكلة بسهولة اكثر من الكل.

ḥalalna hādhihi l-mushkila bi suhūla 'akthar min al-kull.

10. قد *qad*

In Lesson 15 we learned the use of قد *qad* with the past tense. لقد *laqad* is a synonym of قد *qad* in this usage:

(ل)قد تمت المفاوضات امس. *(la)qad tammat al-mufāwaḍāt 'ams.*

قد *qad* (not *laqad*) with the present tense means 'perhaps':

قد يحل المشكلة بتأييدكم. *qad yaḥull al-mushkila bi ta'yīdikum.*

11. التمارين

NB.: During this lesson we have progressively shown less pointing with *shadda* and *fatḥa tanwīn*. From this paragraph onwards, this pointing will be further reduced.

1. Read aloud:

e.g.: تنتج الشركة منتوجات بترولية مختلفة.

tuntij ash-sharika mantūjāt bitroulīya mukhtálifa.

(a) ظننا انه من الضروري ان يستمر البحث.

(b) اهتممت بدراسة الوثيقة اهتماما كاملاً.

(c) يقوم قسم الهندسة بدراسة الأرقام.

(d) هل تستطيع الشركة تجديد تنظيم اقسامها؟

(e) يخبرنا ممثلي شركة التسويق بأنها لن توظف اي ممثل اضافي خلال الصيف.

2. Write:

e.g.: lā yastaṭī9 al-muhandisūn 'an yabda'u l-9amalīyāt az-zilzālīya qabla ntihā' al-'amṭār.

لا يستطيع المهنسون ان يبدأوا العمليات الزلزالية قبل انتهاء الأمطار.

(a) yajūz li sh-sharika sti9māl jihāz ḥafr thālith fī ḥālat iktishāf iḥtiyāṭīyāt 'iḍāfīya fi l-qiṭā9 al-janūbī.

(b) 'inna t-taswīq lā tajrī bi suhūla taḥt tilka ð̣-ð̣urūf al-fannīya.

(c) yumkin 'an yastaghriq al-ḥafr at-tajrībī waqtan ṭawīlan.

(d) laqad ḥāwalat al-buldān al-muntija li n-nafṭ takhfīf 'intājiha.

(e) yajūz lana 'an nastahlik 'akthar mimma stahlaknāhu fi s-sanati l-māḍiya.

3. Recast the sentence, beginning with the expression given in parentheses:

e.g.: (يجوز) يصل اليوم. ← يجوز ان يصل اليوم.

(a) (يجوز) يكتبون الجواب هذا الأسبوع.

(b) (لا يستطيع) يقول لي المبلغ.

(c) (تريد) الوكالة تقوم باستبدال ممثلها بالكويت.

(d) (نفضل) لا نتعاون في هذا الأمر.

(e) (يمكننا) هل نتكلم مع السلطات بخصوص الموضوع؟

4. Make plural:

e.g.: كان رئيس القسم يدرس الموضوع وقتا طويلا.

← كان رؤساء الأقسام يدرسون المواضيع وقتا طويلا.

(a) انني مشغول جدا صباحا.

(b) لا يمكنك ان تجد مشكلة في مثل هذه المسألة.

(c) ما كان مستعدا ان يدفع المبلغ.

(d) لا يزال الحفر التجريبي غير منتج.

(e) ان الجانبين يحاولان ان يتعاونا.

5. Recast the sentence, using a conjunction + verb:

e.g.: يجب عليه تغيير سياسته. ← يجب عليه ان يغير سياسته.

(a) يطلبون منا تعاوننا.

(b) لماذا لا يريد الاستفادة من هذه الفرصة؟

(c) تفضل الشركة تطبيق اجراءات اخرى.

(d) ماذا فهمت من قوله؟

(e) يجب عليك تعبير عن رأيك.

6. Put the correct form of هذا (etc.) and ذلك (etc.) with each noun or noun expression:

e.g.: سيارة ← هذه السيارة، تلك السيارة

(a) سيارتان (b) اشخاص (c) مدير البنك

(d) مدرس (e) وقت

الدرس الثالث والعشرون
ad-dars ath-thālith wa l-9ishrūn – Lesson 23
من الصحف min aṣ-ṣuḥuf
From the Newspapers

NB.: In the reading passage of this lesson we meet a typeface used in the press.

1. للقراءة

(a) منظّمة الصحّة العالمية *munaðḍamat aṣ-ṣiḥḥa l-9ālamīya* World Health Organisation, WHO

قادمًا من *qādiman min* arriving from

الإمارات (العربية) المتحّدة *al-'imārāt (al-9arabīya) al-muttáḥida* United Arab Emirates

شقيق شقائق *shaqīq shaqā'iq* sister-(state etc.)

وصل الى بيروت مساء امس المدير الإقليمي لمنظمة الصحة العالمية لشرق البحر الأبيض المتوسط قادماً من دولة الإمارات المتحدة الشقيقة. وغرض الزيارة يتعلق بالجولة التي يقوم بها المدير في المنطقة لتفتيش مشاريع المنظمة.

waṣal 'ila bayrūt masā' 'ams al-mudīr al-'iqlīmī li munaðḍamat aṣ-ṣiḥḥa l-9ālamīya li sharq al-baḥr -'abyaḍ al-mutawassiṭ qādiman min dawlat al-'imārāt al-muttáḥida sh-shaqīqa. wa gharaḍ az-ziyāra yata9allaq bi l-jawla llátī yaqūm biha l-mudīr fi l-minṭaqa li taftīsh mashārī9 al-munaðḍama.

The Regional Director, Eastern Mediterranean, of the World Health Organisation arrived yesterday morning in Beirut from the ('sister state of the') United (Arab) Emirates. The purpose of the visit has to do with the inspection tour of the organisation's projects which the director is making in the region.

(b) توجّه الى *tawajjaha* V *'ila* to make/head for

متوجّهًا الى *mutawajjihan 'ila* (heading) for

طرابلس *ṭrāblus* Tripoli

وفد وفود *wafd wufūd* delegation, mission

وزاري *wizārī* ministerial

الّذي *alládhī* ‹illī›

منظّمة الدول المصدّرة للنفط (اوبيك) *munaðḍamat ad-duwal al-muṣaddira li n-nafṭ ('oubek)* Organisation of Petroleum Exporting Countries (OPEC)

نفى ينفي *nafa yanfī* I to deny, to repudiate

نفي *nafy* denial, repudiation

ادّعى	*iddá9a* VIII	to allege, to claim
ادّعاء	*iddi9ā'*	allegation, claim

غادر العاصمة امس متوجهاً الى طرابلس تحت رياسة وزير شؤون البترول وفد البحرين الى اجتماعات المؤتمر الوزاري الذي ستعقده منظمة الدول المصدرة للنفط (اوبيك) في العاصمة الليبية غداً. وقال الوزير الى ممثلي الصحافة الوطنية والدولية قبل المغادرة انه ينفي نفياً شديداً الادعاء ان قضية تخفيف الإنتاج تكون اهم موضوع البحوث.

ghādar al-9āṣima 'ams mutawajjihan 'ila ṭrāblus taḥt riyāsat wazīr shu'ūn al-bitroul wafd al-baḥrayn 'ila jtimā9āt al-mu'támar al-wizāri lládhī sa ta9qiduhu munaḍḍamat ad-duwal al-muṣaddira li n-nafṭ ('oubek) fī l-9āṣima l-lībīya ghadan. wa qāl al-wazīr 'ila mumaththilí ṣ-ṣaḥāfa l-waṭanīya wa d-duwalīya qabla l-mughādara 'innahu yanfī nafyan shadīdan al-iddi9ā' 'anna qaḍīyat takhfīf al-'intāj takūn 'ahamm mawḍū9 al-buḥūth.

Led by ('Under the leadership of') the Minister of Petroleum Affairs, the Bahrain delegation left the capital yesterday for Tripoli for the meetings of the ministerial conference to be held by the Organisation of Petroleum Exporting Countries (OPEC) in the Libyan capital tomorrow. Before departure, the minister told representatives of the national and international press that he strongly denied the allegation that the question of reducing production will be the main topic of discussion ('the discussions').

(c)

ابو ظبي	*'abū ḍabī*	Abu Dhabi
سعادة	*sa9āda*	= سيادة *siyāda*
المقرّرة عقده	*al-muqarrara 9aqduhu*	which it has been decided to hold ('the holding of which has been decided')
مقرّ مقارّ	*maqarr maqārr*	headquarters
امانة	*'amāna*	secretariat
قاد يقود	*qāda yaqūdu* I	to lead, to head
نيابةً عن	*niyābatan 9an*	deputising for

غادر ابو ظبي صباح امس سعادة وزير المواصلات والنقل على رأس وفد دولة الإمارات للاجتماعات السنوية لمجلس الاقتصادي العربي المقررة عقدها بمقر الأمانة العامة لجامعة الدول العربية بعد غداً. ويقود الوفد وزير المواصلات والنقل نيابةً عن سعادة وزير الاقتصاد والتجارة.

ghādar 'abū ḍabī ṣabāḥ 'ams sa9ādat

His Excellency the Minister of

wazīr al-muwāṣalāt wa n-naql 9ala ra's wafd dawlat al-'imārāt li l-ijtimā9āt as-sanawīya li l-majlis al-iqtiṣādi l-9arabī l-muqarrara 9aqduha bi maqarr al-'amāna l-9āmma li jāmi9at ad-duwal al-9arabīya ba9da ghadan. wa yaqūd al-wafd wazīr al-muwāṣala wa n-naql niyābatan 9an sa9ādat wazīr al-iqtiṣād wa t-tijāra.

Communications and Transport left Abu Dhabi yesterday morning heading the Emirates' delegation to the annual meeting of the Arab Economic Council which it has been decided to hold at the head-quarters of the General Secretariat of the League of Arab States the day after tomorrow. In leading the deputation the Minister is deputising for H. E. the Minister of Economy and Trade.

(d)

جرى يجري	*jara yajrī* I	*‹jara yijrī›*
امريكي	*'amrīkī*	*‹'amayrkī›*
بدّل	*baddala* II	to exchange
تبديل	*tabdīl*	exchange
طوّر	*ṭawwara* II	to develop
تطوير	*taṭwīr*	development
مورد موارد	*mawrid mawārid*	resource
طاقة	*ṭāqa*	energy
اتمّ	*'atamma* IV	to conclude/complete

تجري بين الولايات المتحدة الأمريكية واليابان منذ شهر بحوث من اجل عقد اتفاقية لتبديل المعلومات الفنية المتعلقة بتطوير موارد جديدة للطاقة ومن المحتمل ان تتم الحكومتان مفاوضة الموضوع في وقت قريب.

tajrī bayna l-wilāyāt al-muttáḥida l-'amrīkīya wa l-yābān mundhu shahr buḥūth min 'ajl 9aqd ittifāqīya li tabdīl al-ma9lūmāt al-fannīya l-muta9alliqa bi taṭwīr mawārid jadīda li ṭ-ṭāqa wa min al-muḥtámal 'an tutimm al-ḥukūmatān mufāwaḍat al-mawḍū9 fi waqt qarīb.

Talks have been going on ('flowing') for a month between the United States of America and Japan with a view to concluding an agreement for the exchange of technical information concerning the development of new energy resources. It is likely that both governments will conclude negotiation on ('of') the matter soon.

النحو

2. Relative pronoun

The written equivalent of *‹illī›* is الّذي *alládhī*, which agrees in gender and number with its antecedent, but varies for case only in the dual:

	Masculine		Feminine	
Sing., all cases	الّذي	alládhī	الّتي	allátī
Dual, nom.	اللذان	alladhāni	اللتان	allatāni
acc./gen.	اللذين	alladhayni	اللتين	allatayni
Pl., all cases	الّذين	alladhīna	اللواتي	allawātī

The double لل *lām* written in the dual and in the feminine plural is pronounced like the لّ *lām-shadda* elsewhere.

الذي *alládhī* (etc.) is used exactly as is ‹*illī*› in spoken Arabic:

هذه هي الوثيقة التي قرأت عنوانه فيها.

hādhihi hiya l-wathīqa llátī qara't 9unwānahu fīha.

هذا تقرير لا استطيع ان اعتمد عليه. *hādha taqrīr lā 'astaṭī9 'an 'a9támid 9alayhi.*

من الدي مسؤول عن هذا؟ *man alládhī mas'ūl 9an hādha?*

ما هي الأرقام التي تشك فيها؟ *mā hiya l-'arqām allátī tashukk fīha?*

When the antecedent is the whole preceding clause, we provide an all-purpose antecedent , الأمر *al-'amr*:

مرض المدير الأمر الذي عقد مفاوضاتنا.

mariḍ al-mudīr, al-'amr alládhī 9aqqad mufāwaḍātina.

3. Final-weak verbs

Look again at Lesson 8 to identify these verbs. Whereas in spoken Arabic this sub-class includes also verbs with final root letter *hamza*, in written Arabic it does not (see 20/5). The final root letter of all written final-weak verbs is و *wāw* or ي *yā'*.

4. The two tenses of final-weak verbs have, in the first and second persons sing. and pl., the usual endings (i. e. those of the sound verbs, as in spoken Arabic). Short pronunciation operates with these endings as usual. The only likely difficulty is the pronunciation and spelling of the final root letter.

5. Form I of final-weak verbs

In 8/7, we have instructions concerning the form of the final root letter in the past tense. For the written final-weak verbs, read those instructions as follows:

Past:

- for *‹ay›* (1st and 2nd persons sing. and pl.):
  in final-*wāw* و verbs: ـَوْ *-aw-*; in final-*yā'* ي verbs: ـَيْ *-ay-*
- for *‹-a›* (3rd person m. sing.): ى \ ا *-a*
- before personal endings ت *-at* and وا *-ū*, the root letter disappears as in spoken Arabic (final-weak verb rule, 8/10). It disappears also before the feminine dual ending تا *-atā*.

(For verbs of the type نسي *násiya* [*‹nisī›*, 8/9], read the three indents mentioned as ـِي *-ī*, ي *-iya* and – ['root letter disappears'] respectively.)

For the present tense, substitute the form of the final root letter given in 8/8 as follows:

Present:

- final-*wāw* و verbs: و *-ū*
- final-*yā'* ي verbs: ي *-ī*
- final-*yā'* ي verbs like نسي ينسى *násiya yansa* I: ى *-a*

These are dropped before the personal endings ين *-īna*, ون *-ūna*.

6. The written language pronounces *ay* and *aw* for *ī* and *ū* respectively in many positions; but *ī* and *ū* are used and accepted by almost all educated speakers even if not always strictly correct.

7. Important final-weak verbs in Form I, in both tenses (full written pronunciation, for the record):

Final root letter و ***wāw***:

رجا يرجو *raja yarjū* to request
دعا يدعو *da9a yad9ū* to summon
عفا يعفو ل *9afa ya9fū li* to excuse

Past:	عفوت	*9afawt*^{u}	عفونا	*9afawna*
	عفوت	*9afawt*^{a}	عفوتم	*9afawtum*
	عفوت	*9afawti*		
	عفا	*9afa*	عفوا	*9afaw*
	عفت	*9afat*		

3rd person dual: m. عفوا *9afawā*, f. عفتا *9afatā*

Present:	اعفو	*'a9fū*	نعفو	*na9fū*
	تعفو	*ta9fū*	تعفون	*ta9fūna*
	تعفين	*ta9fīna*		
	يعفو	*ya9fū*	يعفون	*ya9fūna*

تعفو *ta9fū*

3rd person dual: m. يعفوان *ya9fuwāni*, f. تعفوان *ta9fuwāni*

***Final root letter* ي *yā'*:**

رمى يرمي *rama yarmī* to throw
جرى يجري *jara yajrī* to flow
نفى ينفي *nafa yanfīi* to deny, repudiate
حكى يحكي *ḥaka yaḥkī* to narrate*
مشى يمشي *masha yamshī* to walk

* NB meaning. The written verb 'to speak' is تكلّم *takallama* V.

Past:	مشيت	*mashayt*[u]	مشينا	*mashayna*
	مشيت	*mashayt*[a]	مشيتم	*mashaytum*
	مشيت	*mashayti*		
	مشى	*masha*	مشوا	*mashaw*
	مشت	*mashat*		

3rd person dual: m. مشيا *mashayā*, f. مشتا *mashatā*

Present:	امشي	*'amshī*	نمشي	*namshī*
	تمشي	*tamshī*	تمشون	*tamshūna*
	تمشين	*tamshīna*		
	يمشي	*yamshī*	يمشون	*yamshūna*
	تمشي	*tamshī*		

3rd person dual: m. يمشيان *yamshiyāni*, f. تمشيان *tamshiyāni*

***Final root letter* ي , pattern نسي *násiya*:**

نسي ينسى *násiya yansa* to forget
بقي يبقى *báqiya yabqa*** to remain
رضي يرضى ب *ráḍiya yarḍa bi* to approve of, be satisfied with
لقي يلقى *láqiya yalqa* to meet

** This verb can have an accusative complement: بقي فقيرا. *báqiya faqīran.*

Past:	نسيت	*nasīt*[u]	نسينا	*nasīna*
	نسيت	*nasīt*[a]	نسيتم	*nasītum*
	نسيت	*nasīti*		
	نسي	*násiya*	نسوا	*nasū*
	نسيت	*násiyat*		

3rd person dual: m. نسيا *násiyā*, f. نسيتا *násiyatā*

Present:	انسى	*'ansa*	ننسى	*nansa*
	تنسى	*tansa*	تنسون	*tansawna*

تنسين	*tansayna*		
ينسى	*yansa*	ينسون	*yansawna*
تنسى	*tansa*		

3rd person dual: m. ينسيان *yansayāni*, f. تنسيان *tansayāni*

Final root letter ي, with *-a* in both principal parts:

سعى يسعى الى *sa9a yas9a 'ila* to strive for

Past:	سعيت	*sa9aytu*	سعينا	*sa9ayna*
	سعيت	*sa9ayta*	سعيتم	*sa9aytum*
	سعيت	*sa9ayti*		
	سعى	*sa9a*	سعوا	*sa9aw*
	سعت	*sa9at*		

3rd person dual: m. سعيا *sa9ayā*, f. سعتا *sa9atā*

Present:	اسعى	*'as9a*	نسعى	*nas9a*
	تسعى	*tas9a*	تسعون	*tas9awna*
	تسعين	*tas9ayna*		
	يسعى	*yas9a*	يسعون	*yas9awna*
	تسعى	*tas9a*		

3rd person dual: m. يسعيان *yas9ayāni*, f. تسعيان *tas9ayāni*

8. Certain spelling rules apply, for final *-a* in Form I:

- When final root letter و *wāw* changes to *a*, it is always spelt with ا *'alif*. See رجا *raja* etc. in paragraph 7 above.
- When final root letter ي *yā* changes to *a*, it is spelt with ى *'alif maqṣūra* when no suffix follows, but with ا *'alif* before a suffix (since *'alif maqṣūra* occurs only finally):

نفى *nafa* he denied but: نفاه *nafāhu* he denied it

9. Increased forms

The principal parts of the increased forms have only the endings ى *-a* or ي *-ī*, the vocalised final root letter following the final-weak verb rule (8/10):

II	ربّى يربّي	*rabba yurabbī*
III	نادى ينادي	*nāda yunādī*
IV	أعطى يعطي	*'a9ṭa yu9ṭī*
V	تلقّى يتلقّى	*talaqqa yatalaqqa* ro acquire, to receive
VI	تعافى يتعافى	*ta9āfa yata9āfa*
VII	انقضى ينقضي	*inqáḍa yanqáḍī* to be finished
VIII	اشترى يشتري	*ishtára yashtárī* (NB stress in present)

	ادّعى يدّعي	*iddá9a yaddá9ī* to allege
X	استثنى يستثني	*istathna yastathnī*

The special stress of Forms VII and VIII, studied in Lesson 13, applies in written Arabic too, except that the written present tense of VIII also has the irregular stress.

The ى *'alif maqṣūra* of all increased forms, irrespective of the original final root letter, changes to ا *'alif* when a suffix is added.

10. Participles of final-weak verbs, Form I

The masculine active participle of final-weak Form I is anomalous:

Root رمى يرمي ، رمي *rama yarmī* I:

m. sing. indefinite:	رامٍ	*rāmin*
m. sing. definite:	الرامي	*ar-rāmī*
m. pl.:	(ال)رامون\ين	*(ar-)rāmūn/īn*
f. sing.:	(ال)رامية	*(ar-)rắmiya*
f. pl.:	(ال)راميات	*(ar-)rāmiyāt*

These are the nom. forms (with also the gen. of the masc. pl.). The other forms, including the dual, are too rare to concern us.

It is to this group that participles like the following belong:

فاضٍ (الفاضي)	*fāḍin (al-fāḍī)*
ماضٍ (الماضي)	*māḍin (al-māḍī)*
ماشٍ (الماشي)	*māshin (al-māshī)*
جارٍ (الجاري)	*jārin (al-jārī)*

The Form I passive participle has the patterns *marjūw* for final-*wāw* verbs and *mansīy* for final-*ya'* verbs. Otherwise it is regular:

Root رجو:	مرجوّ	*marjūw* requested
Root نسي:	منسيّ	*mansīy* forgotten
Root نفي:	منفيّ	*manfīy* denied, repudiated

It is common to ignore the ending of the indefinite form in pronunciation and to pronounce the definite form ending throughout.

11. Participles of final-weak verbs: increased forms

In Forms II-X, the active participle has the same endings as in Form I:

Root أرضى ، رضي IV to satisfy:

m. sing. indef.:	مرضٍ	*murḍin*
m. sing. def.:	المرضي	*al-murḍī*
f. sing.:	(ال)مرضية	*(al-)múrḍiya*

In the passive participle, the indefinite m. sing. has *fatḥa tanwīn*:

Root استثنى, ثني X:

m. sing. indef.: مستثنًى *mustathnan*

m. sing. def.: المستثنى *al-mustathna*

Root ربّى, ربو II:

m. pl.: مربّون\ين *murabbūn/īn*

f. sing.: مربّاة *murabbā*

f. pl.: مربّات *murabbāt*

The comment made at the end of paragraph 10 above applies here.

12. Verbal nouns of final-weak verbs

The spoken Arabic models for the verbal nouns are all valid for written Arabic, except Forms V and VI, whose verbal noun has the same endings as the masculine singular active participle:

تلقّى يتلقّى *talaqqa yatalaqqa* V to acquire:

تلقٍّ (التلقّي) *talaqqin (at-talaqqī)* acquisition

تلاقى يتلاقى *talāqa yatalāqa* VI to encounter:

تلاقٍ (التلاقي) *talāqin (at-talāqī)* encounter

The comment made at the end of paragraph 10 above applies here.

13. Subjunctive of final-weak verbs

Derive the subjunctive of final-weak verbs also from the present tense. Take the present-tense endings and:

- change final ي *-ī* to *-ī/-iya* and و to *-ū/-uwa* (*-iya* and *-uwa* only in short pronunciation before a suffix, and not always then):

  لا يستطيع ان ينفيه. *lā yastaṭī9 'an yánfiyahu*/yanfī́hi.*

  ‹*mā yiqdar yinfī́.*› He cannot deny it.

  لا يستطيع ان يرجوه. *lā yastaṭī9 'an yárjuwahu**.

  ‹*mā yiqdar yirjū́*› He cannot request it.

  *Where appropriate, the stress moves back.

- change ين *-īna,* ان *-āni* and ون *-ūna/-awna* respectively to ي *-ī,* ا *-ā* and وا *-ū/aw* (spelt و before a suffix):

  يمكن ان ينسوا. *yumkin 'an yansaw/yansū.*

  ‹*yumkin yinsū*› They may forget.

- leave other endings unchanged:

  لن ننساه. *lan nansāhu.* We shall not forget it.

14. Use of the dictionary

When using a root-based dictionary, remember that the final root letter of a final-weak root must be و *wāw* or ي *yā'*; it will not be listed as *'alif.* Some final-weak verbs have alternative roots or principal parts in Form I, with either و *-ū* or ي *-ī*.

15. Pronoun suffixes

See paragraphs 8 and 9 above. The final-weak verb-endings ي *-ī* and *-iya* are not *'alif maqṣūra*, so the *yā'* is retained before a suffix:

لقينا *láqiyana* يرميه *yarmīhi**

* *-hu* becomes *-hi* also after verb-endings *-i*, *-ī* or *-ay* (19/14, 16).

16 التمارين

1. Read aloud:

e.g.: نرجو منكم القيام بدراسة الوثائق قبل بحوثنا.

narjū minkum al-qiyām bi dirāsat al-wathā'iq qabla buḥūthina.

(a) ان دراستنا لا تزال تجري قدما وسننشر النتائج في الشهر المقبل.

(b) تلقى اللجنة اعضاء الحكومة بعد البحوث الجارية.

(c) لا يبقى الا عدد صغير من التفاصيل يجب ان نشرحها.

(d) يسعى مدراء البنك الى ان ينشروا تقريرهم قبل رأس السنة.

(e) علينا ان نستغني عن تعاون هذا المأمور.

2. Write:

e.g.: kama sharaḥ al-mushrif, al-mawḍū9 laysa basīṭan.

كما شرح المشرف الموضوع ليس بسيطا.

(a) tas9a l-ḥukūma 'ila tanðīm al-mu'támar fi 'aqrab waqt mumkin.

(b) tajri l-mufāwaḍāt allátī qāmat biha l-ḥukūmatān járyan ghayr murḍin.

(c) man alládhī da9a l-mandūbīn li l-ijtimā9 al-istithnā'ī?

(d) mā hiya l-ma9lūmāt allátī ṭalabat-ha l-'amāna minna?

(e) nasi 'a9ḍā' al-wafd 'ahamm shay' fī barnāmajihim.

3. Put into the present tense:

e.g.: رضي مندوبو الشركة باقتراحنا فورا.

← يرضى مندوبو الشركة باقتراحنا فورا.

(a) نادت الحكومة مسؤولين عرفوا ماذا حدث.

(b) اشتروا مهما احتاجوا اليه.

(c) ما تمكنا من برهان على قوله.

(d) ما زال هذا ادعاءً شديدًا ضد احزاب المعارضة.
(e) نفوا كل ما ادعينا.

4. Join the two sentences as a relative expression:

e.g.: سيشير الرئيس الى الوضع في السوق. هذا مهم جدًا.
← سيشير الرئيس الى الوضع في السوق (الأمر) الذي مهم جدًا.

(a) لماذا لا ينشرون التقرير؟ حضره المتخصص.
(b) ادعاه. هل تصدق؟
(c) دعا المدير المشرف. كان المشرف ينتظر خارج المكتب.
(d) لا يمكن الاعتماد عليه. يقول مثل هذا.
(e) ما صار للبناية؟ كان يسكن فيها.

5. Give the root under which each word is found in a root-based dictionary:

e.g.: ادعاء ← دعو

(a) جارٍ
(b) الساعون
(c) مرضٍ
(d) الباقية
(e) يتلقون

الدرس الرابع والعشرون
ad-dars ar-rābi9 wa l-9ishrūn – Lesson 24
المراسلة al-murāsala – Correspondence

NB.: In the reading passage of this lesson we read the style of writing known as رقعة *ruq9a*. This is a common educated style of handwriting which you need to be able to read. The text is shown in a printed form of *ruq9a*, with some handwriting. Note especially these final/isolated *ruq9a* forms:

ش   ض   ق   ن

1. للقراءة

(a)

حديث حداث	*ḥadīth ḥidāth*	modern
حدّ يحدّ	*ḥadda yaḥuddu* I	to limit
محدود	*maḥdūd*	limited
١٩		19
تحية	*taḥīya*	greeting
تحية طيّبة وبعد	*taḥīya ṭayyiba wa ba9du*	Dear ... (see para. 2 below)
موفّق	*muwaffaq*	successful

السيد بيتر براون
شركة المواصلات الحديثة المحدودة في عمان

عمان في ١٩ شباط

تحية طيبة وبعد
اشكركم قلبيا على الزيارة التي قمتم بها خلال الأسبوع الماضي وأعتبر انه ستكون هناك فرصة للتعاون التدريبي الموفق بيننا وبين شركتكم.

as-sayyid Peter Brown, sharikat al-muwāṣalāt al-ḥadītha l-maḥdūda fī 9ammān. 9ammān fī tis9at9ashr shubāṭ. taḥīya ṭayyiba wa ba9du. ’ashkurukum qalbīyan 9ala z-ziyāra llátī qumtum biha khilāla l-’usbū9 al-māḍī wa ’a9tábir ’annahu sa takūn furṣa li t-ta9āwun at-tadrībī l-muwaffaq baynana wa bayna sharikatikum.

Mr Peter Brown, Modern Communications Ltd., Amman. Amman, 19 February. Dear Mr Brown, My sincere (‘cordial’) thanks for the visit which you made last week. I consider that there will be opportunity for successful training cooperation between your company and ourselves.

شكّل	*shakkala* II	to form, to constitute
حاليًا	*ḥālīyan*	at present
درّب	*darraba* II	to train
مدرّب	*mudarrib*	trainer, instructor
قطع يقطع النظر عن	*qaṭa9a yaqṭa9u* I *an-naðar 9an*	to overlook, to neglect, to lose sight of
قصد	*qaṣd*	purpose
اساسي	*'asāsī*	(also:) essential

انني اعتقد ان مثل هذا التعاون يشكل فرصةً ممتازةً لتقوية الاتصال بين القطاع الخاص والقطاع التعليمي وهذا هو ما تحتاج اليه صناعتنا احتياجا كبيرا الآن وصناعتنا تمر حاليا بأوقات صعبة ومن الجانب الآخر من الممكن ان مدربينا يقطعون النظر عن قصدنا الأساسي وهو تأييد صناعتنا.

'innanī 'a9táqid 'anna mithla hādha t-ta9āwun yushakkil furṣa mumtāza li táqwiyat al-ittiṣāl bayna l-qiṭā9 al-khāṣṣ wa l-qiṭā9 at-ta9līmī wa hādha huwa mā taḥtāj 'ilayhi ṣinā9atuna ḥtiyājan kabīran al-'ān wa ṣinā9atuna tamurr ḥālīyan bi 'awqāt ṣa9ba wa min al-jānib al-'ākhar min al-mumkin 'anna mudarribīna yaqṭa9ūna n-naðar 9an qaṣdina l-'asāsī wa huwa ta'yīd ṣinā9atina.

I believe that such cooperation is ('constitutes') an excellent opportunity to strengthen the contact between the private and the educational sectors. This is what our industry greatly needs at the moment. Our industry is passing through difficult times at present. On the other hand it is possible that our instructors lose sight of our essential purpose which is support for ('of') our industry.

اشارة	*'ishāra*	(also:) reference
بالإشاره الى	*bi l-'ishāra 'ila*	with reference to
تالٍ (التالي)	*tālin (at-tālī)*	(the) following
دراسي	*dirāsī*	academic
٣٤، ٢٨، ٢٥		34, 28, 25
مجموع	*majmū9*	total
٨٧، ٨٩٪		87, 89%

وبالإشارة الى الأرقام التي سألتموني عنها هي التالية:

اولا: عدد المتخرجين في السنة الدراسية الماضية

أ: بالكهربا	٣٤
ب: بالتبريد و التكييف	٢٨
ج: بالمكانيك	٢٥
المجموع	٨٧ أي ٨٩٪

wa bi l-'ishāra 'ila l-'arqām allátī sa'altumūnī 9anha hiya t-tāliya:
'awwalan: 9adad al-mutakharrijīn fi s-sana d-dirāsīya l-māḍiya:
'alif: bi l-kahraba 'arba9a u thalāthīn.
bā': bi t-tabrīd wa t-takyīf thamāniya u 9ishrīn.
jīm: bi l-mikānīk khamsa u 9ishrīn.
al-majmū9: sab9a u thamānīn, 'ay tis9a u thamānīn bi l-mīya.

With reference to the figures about which you asked me, these ('they') are the following:
1. Number of graduates last academic year:
(a) in electricity: 34
(b) in refrigeration and airconditioning: 28
(c) in mechanics: 25
Total: 87, i.e. 89%.

خطّط	*khaṭṭaṭa* II	to plan
٣٦، ٣١، ٢٢، ٨٩		36, 31, 22, 89

ثانيا: عدد المرشحين المخطط للسنة الدراسية المقبلة:

أ: بالكهربا	٣٦
ب: بالتبريد و التكييف	٣١
ج: بالمكانيك	٢٢
المجموع	٨٩

thāniyan: 9adad al-murashshaḥīn al-mukhaṭṭaṭ li s-sana d-dirāsīya l-muqbila:
'alif: bi l-kahraba sitta u thalāthīn.
bā': bi t-tabrīd wa t-takyīf wāḥid u thalāthīn.
jīm: bi l-mikānīk ithnayn u 9ishrīn.
al-majmū9: tis9a u thamānīn.

1. Number of candidates planned for next academic year:
(a) in electricity: 36
(b) in refrigeration and airconditioning: 31
(c) in mechanics: 22
Total: 89

قبول	*qabūl*	acceptance
فاق يفوق	*fāqa yafūqu* I	to excel
وتفضلوا بقبول فائق الاحترام	*wa tafaḍḍalū bi qabūl fā'iq al-iḥtirām*	(see para. 2 below)
اخلص	*'akhlaṣa* IV	to be sincere
مخلص	*mukhliṣ*	sincere

وتفضلوا بقبول فائق الاحترام

المخلص

احمد

احمد هاشم

مدير المدرسة الثانوية الفنية

يا سيد بيتر: يمكن ان تحتاج الى معلومات او ارقام
اكثر تفصيلاً وفي هذه الحالة ارجو الّا تتردد ان
تتصل بي وفي الانتظار اظل مخلصا
احمد

wa tafaḍḍalū bi qabūl fā'iq al-iḥtirām.	Best wishes,
al-mukhliṣ, 'aḥmad hāshim,	Yours sincerely, Ahmad Hashim,
mudīr al-madrasa th-thānawīya l-fannīya.	Director, Technical Secondary School.
yā sayyid Peter, yumkin 'an taḥtāj 'ila ma9lūmāt 'aw 'arqām 'akthar tafṣīlan wa fī hādhihi l-ḥāla 'arjū 'allā tataraddad 'an tattáṣil bī wa fī l-intiðār 'aðall mukhliṣan 'aḥmad.	Mr Brown: Perhaps you need more detailed information or figures; in that case please ('I request') do not hesitate to contact me. In the meantime, I remain Yours sincerely, Ahmad.

(b)

منشور	*manshūr*	memorandum, circular
اداري	*'idārī*	administrative
٤٦		46
١٣\٢\٢٠--		13/2/20...
كذا وكذا	*kadha u kadha*	such-and-such
وكذا وكذا	*wa/u kadha u kadha*	and so on

منشور اداري رقم ٤٦
من: مدير شؤون الموظفين **الى: جميع العمال**
التاريخ: ١٣/٢/٢٠-- الموضوع: دفع الشغل الإضافي

manshūr 'idārī raqm sitta u 'arba9īn.	Administrative Circular No. 46.
min: mudīr shu'ūn al-muwaððafīn.	From: Personnel Manager.
'ila: jamī9 al-9ummāl.	To: All Operatives ('workmen').
at-tārīkh: thalatt9ashr shubāṭ 'alfayn u kadha u kadha.	Date: 13/2/20...
al-mawḍū9: daf9 ash-shughl al-'iḍāfī.	Subject: Payment of Overtime.

دائرة دوائر	*dā'ira dawā'ir*	directorate
اعلان	*'i9lān*	announcement, notice
عام اعوام	*9ām 'a9wām*	year
٢٠--		20...
محاسبات	*muḥāsabāt*	accounts
رفض يرفض رفض	*rafaḍa yarfiḍu* I, *rafḍ*	to reject
حمل يحمل حمل	*ḥamala yaḥmilu* I, *ḥaml*	to carry, to bear
وقّع	*waqqa9a* II	to sign

مذكور	*madhkūr*	(afore)mentioned
لوحة	*lawḥa*	board (for notices etc.)

تشير دائرة شؤون الموظفين الى الإعلان رقم ٢٢ من ١ كانون الثاني من عام ٢٠-- وتذكر جميع العمال بأن قسم المحاسبات يقوم بدفع اجر الشغل الإضافي على اساس شهادة المشرف او المدير المناسب فقط وسيرفض اي طلب دفع لا يحمل توقيع المسؤول المذكور.

فؤاد

فؤاد عبدالرحمن
مدير شؤون الموظين
نسخة الى: جميع الدوائر
لوحات الإعلان

tushīr dā'irat shu'ūn al-muwaðDafīn 'ila l-'a9lān raqm ithnayn u 9ishrīn min 'awwal kānūn ath-thānī min 9ām 'alfayn u kadha u kadha wa tudhakkir jamī9 al-9ummāl bi 'anna qism al-muḥāsabāt yaqūm bi daf9 'ajr ash-shughl al-'iḍāfī 9ala 'asās shahādat al-mushrif 'aw al-mudīr al-munāsib faqaṭ wa sa yarfiḍ 'ayy ṭalab daf9 lā yaḥmil tawqī9 al-mas'ūl al-madhkūr.
fu'ād 9abdarraḥmān, mudīr shu'ūn al-muwaðDafīn.
nuskha 'ila: jamī9 ad-dawā'ir, lawḥāt al-'i9lān.

Personnel Directorate refers to Notice No. 22 of 1 January 20... and reminds all operatives that Accounts Department will pay overtime wages only on the basis of the attestation ('certificate') of the appropriate supervisor or manager. It will reject any claim for payment not bearing the signature of the aforementioned authority ('responsible person').
Fuad Abdarrahman, Personnel Manager. Copy: all directorates; notice boards

النحو

2. Correspondence

Formal letters commonly begin the text with with تحية طيبة وبعد *taḥīya ṭayyiba wa ba9du* which is not directly translatable. The message of the letter then starts immediately; the addressee is not usually greeted by name or appointment.

In the text, we often use the 2nd person plural. Formal closures include:

وتفضلوا بقبول فائق الاحترام *wa tafaḍḍalū bi qabūl fā'iq al-iḥtirām*
('Please accept outstanding respect') Yours faithfully/Best wishes

ارجو ان تتقبلوا وافر الشكر *'arjū 'an tataqabbalū wāfir ash-shukr*
('I ask you to accept abundant thanks') Please accept my warmest thanks.

(تقبّل *taqabbala* V to accept; وفر يفر *wafara yafiru* I to abound)

A briefer, but still polite, closure is simply:

المخلصة\المخلص *al-mukliṣ(a)* ('the sincere')
Yours sincerely

3. Office memoranda usually have neither salutation nor closure; like their European counterpart, they may open with, e.g.:

من : *min:* الى : *'ila:*
التاريخ : *at-tārīkh:* الإشارة : *al-'ishāra:*
الموضوع : *al-mawḍū9:*

4. Informal letters may have a personal salutation such as

اخي العزيز\اختي الكريمة *'akhi l-9azīz/'ukhtī l-karīma* Dear ... (m./f.)

(عزيز أعزّاء *9azīz 'a9izzā'* dear)

or, with more respect but still cordial:

استاذي المحترم *'ustādhi l-muḥtáram* Dear ('Respected') Tutor
زميلي المحترم *zamīli l-muḥtáram* } Dear
زميلتي المحترمة *zamīlati l-muḥtárama* } Colleague

each of which is followed by تحية طيبة وبعد .

Informal letters also close with المخلصة\المخلص, possibly preceded by

تحية للجميع *taḥīya li l-jamī9* Greetings to all
or ويسلمك\يسلمكم قلبيًا *wa yusallimuka/ki/kum qalbīyan*
وتسلمك\تسلمكم قلبيًا *wa tusallimuka/ki/kum qalbīyan*
With cordial greetings from ...

5. Numbers

The written numerals are:

١	٢	٣	٤	٥	٦	٧	٨	٩	٠
1	2	3	4	5	6	7	8	9	0

Numerals 2 and 3 have alternative handwritten forms:

٢ 2 ٣ or ٣ 3

The numerals are assembled from left to right, as in European numbers:

١٤٥٣ 1453 ٢٠٨.٦٩٧ 208,697

Moroccans, Algerians and Tunisians use the European numerals, which are now increasingly used throughout the Arab world.

6. The numbers as words are more complicated in written than in spoken Arabic. Many Arabs have difficulty with the written forms, and prefer to use the spoken forms even when reading aloud from a text. You are strongly advised to use the spoken form for pronouncing the numbers, and the numerals for writing them. From the written language we do need, however, to know the form of the noun used after the number. We study this below.

7. Numbers 2 to 10

See 4/11. Everything said there about the form and position of the noun is valid in writing, except that a noun following a number 3-10 is in the *genitive* plural, irrespective of its function in the sentence. This fact is, however, visible and audible only in the sound m. pl.:

وصل ٤ مهندسين. *waṣal 'arba9a muhandisīn.*

مع ٤ مهندسين *ma9a 'arba9a muhandisīn*

Further, the rules for the written dual (19/9, 10) apply.

8. Numbers 11 to 19, and multiples of ten from 20 to 90

See 5/12. Everything said there about the form and position of the noun is valid in writing, except that a noun following a number 11-99 is in the *accusative* singular, irrespective of its function in the sentence. This fact is, however, visible and audible only with ً *fatḥa tanwīn*:

وصل ١١ طالبًا. *waṣal 'iḥd9ashr ṭāliban.*

خلال ١٥ سنةً *khilāla khamst9ashr sanatan*

٩٠ دولارًا *tis9īn doulāran*

9. When reading, you may encounter numbers written as words. Be prepared for the following phenomena:

- so-called 'polarity' or reverse agreement, i.e. the number has an apparently feminine form (with final ة *tā' marbūṭa*) before a masculine noun, and an apparently masculine form (no ة *tā' marbūṭa*) before a feminine noun:

  اربعة طلاب، اربع طالبات

- multiples of ten from 20 to 90: these follow the pattern of a sound m. pl. (ون\ين *-ūn/-īn*): عشرون مهندسا، مع عشرين مهندسا
- a dual number loses its final ن *-n* before a noun, as in construct:

  مع الفي شخص

- the spelling of *mīya/mīt*: مئة, less commonly مائة.

10. Ordinal numbers

The ordinal numbers 1st to 10th are as in spoken Arabic, except that 2nd ثانٍ\الثاني *thānin/ath-thānī* follows the pattern of ماشٍ etc. (23/10).

Written Arabic has ordinal numbers above 'tenth'. The pronunciation given below is an acceptable educated spoken variant for these words. Ordinals 11th to 19th agree in gender with the noun

11th m.	الحادي عشر	*al-ḥādī 9ashar*
f.	الحادية عشرة	*al-ḥādiya 9ashara*
12th m.	الثاني عشر	*ath-thānī 9ashar*
f.	الثانية عشرة	*ath-thāniya 9ashara*
13th m.	الثالث عشر	*ath-thālith 9ashar*
f.	الثالثة عشرة	*ath-thālitha 9ashara*

(etc.). From 20th upwards, the tens, hundreds, thousands and millions have a form identical with the cardinal number.

20th m./f.	العشرون \ين	*al-9ishrūn/-īn*
21st m.	الحادي والعشرون \ين	*al-ḥādī wa l-9ishrūn/-īn*
f.	الحادية والعشرون \ين	*al-ḥādiya wa l-9ishrūn/-īn*
100th	المائة\المئة	*al-mīya*
101st	المئة والواحد(ة)	*al-mīya wa l-wāḥid(a)*
1000th	الألف	*al-'alf*

The press sometimes uses alternative forms for 100th and 1000th:

المئوي\المئوية *al-mīyawī(ya)* الألفي\الألفية *al-'alfī(ya)*

The ordinal numbers can be represented thus in abbreviated form:

الدرس ال٤\ال ٤ *ad-dars ar-rābi9*

11. *'abjad*

أبجد *'abjad* means 'alphabet'. Every letter of the Arabic alphabet has a numerical value; this is equivalent to our use of Roman numerals to number a series. The numerical values do not follow the alphabetical order. We need to know only the first ten:

109 8 765 4 321
أبجد هوّز حطي

for which the mnemonic is the three words *'abjad hawwaz ḥuṭī*. The last two words have no meaning other than their use here. Examine:

*أ I, i, a) ب II, ii, b) ج III, iii, c) د IV, iv, d)

* with *hamza* to distinguish it from figure ١.

12. Time

In written Arabic we use the ordinal number for all hours except 'one o'clock':

الساعة الواحدة *as-sā9a l-wāḥida*

but: الساعة الثانية *as-sā9a th-thāniya*

'half-past' is والنصف *wa n-niṣf,* and all fractions have the article. For the rest the forms correspond to those of the spoken language:

الساعة الخامسة والنصف *as-sā9a l-khāmisa wa n-niṣf* 5.30

في الساعة السادسة والربع *fi s-sā9a s-sādisa wa r-rub9* at 6.15

قبل الساعة الحادية عشرة الا الثلث *qabla s-sā9a l-ḥādiya 9ashra 'illa th-thulth* before 10.40

بعد الساعة الثانية عشرة وخمس دقائق *ba9da s-sā9a th-thāniya 9ashra wa khams(a) daqā'iq* after 12.05

13. Calendar

Here is the spelling of the days of the week:

(يوم) الجمعة، السبت، الأحد، الاثنين، الثلاثاء*، الأربعاء*، الخميس

* formal pronunciation *ath-thalāthā', al-'arba9ā'*. Little used.

14. Decades

Decades are expressed so:

التسعينات\التسعينيات *at-tis9īnāt/at-tis9īnīyāt* the 90's

15. Vocative

In addition to the vocative particle يا *yā* known to you, written Arabic has أيّها (m.) *'ayyuha* and أيّتها *'ayyatuha* (f.), which are used before a noun with the article:

أيّها المستمعون\المشاهدون الأعزاء *'ayyuha l-mustami9ūn/ l-mushāhidūn al-'a9izzā'* Dear listeners/viewers

(the standard formula used by radio or television announcers, most of whom pronounce the middle word as in spoken Arabic):

‹*'ayyuha l-mustami9**īn**/l-mushāhid**īn** al-'a9izzā'*›

16. Anomalous nouns and adjectives

Certain nouns and adjectives have irregular case-endings. We need to know only those features which are written with letters of the alphabet, and are hence sounded in short pronunciation.

17. The first group is those nouns and adjectives having no اً form (indefinite accusative). They are:

- all nouns and adjectives, m. or f., sing. or pl., having the ending* اء *-ā'*:

  سفراء *sufarā'* حمراء *ḥamrā'*
- all nouns and adjectives on the pattern *'akbar*:

  أسود *'aswad* أكثر *'akthar*
- broken plurals on the patterns *makātib* or *mafātīḥ*:

  اوامر *'awāmir* مدارس *madāris*

  اسابيع *'asābī9* تلاميذ *talāmīdh*

  نرسل لكم كتبا من اجل المكتب. *nursil lakum kutuban min 'ajl al-maktab.*

  but: نرسل لكم وثائق من اجل المكتب. *nursil lakum wathā'iq min 'ajl al-maktab.*

The grammatical term for these words is 'diptote'. There are other diptote forms, but they are too rare to concern us.

*NB: ending, not final root letter. Where either ا *'alif* or ء *hamza* is a root letter, the word is regular. Note also that the indefinite accusative of such a word is written with *fatḥa tanwīn* only, not *'alif-fatḥa-tanwīn*:

ابتداءً *ibtidā'an* اجراءً *'ijrā'an*

18. The second group is the *'ab* group. When used as the theme of a construct, or when carrying a possessive suffix other than ي *-ī*, the nouns اب *'ab* 'father' and اخ *'akh* 'brother' form their singular cases with written vowels which are always pronounced:

nom. ابو\اخو *'abū/'akhū*; acc. ابا\اخا *'abā/'akhā*; gen. ابي\اخي *'abī/'akhī*

كتب لنا ابو\اخو هذا ا طالب. *katab lana 'abū/'akhū hādha ṭ-ṭālib.*

هل تعرف ابا\اخا الطالب؟ *hal ta9rif 'aba/'akha ṭ-ṭālib?*

مع ابي\اخي هذا الطالب *ma9a 'abī/'akhī hādha ṭ-ṭālib*

مع ابيه\اخيه *ma9a 'abīhi/'akhīhi*

When not in construct or when suffixed with ي *-ī*, or when carrying no possessive suffix, these nouns have regular case-endings:

كتب الأب. *katab al-'ab.*

هل تعرف الأخ؟ *hal ta9rif al-'akh?*

19. ذو ***dhū*** **etc.**

The noun ذو *dhū* means 'possessor of' or 'characterised by'. It has a masculine and a feminine form. The m. s. has case-endings like those of اب *'ab*:

		Singular	Dual	Plural
m.	nom.	ذو *dhū*	ذوا *dhawā*	ذوو *dhawū*
	acc.	ذا *dha*	ذوي *dhaway*	ذوي *dhawī*
	gen.	ذي *dhī*		
f.	nom.	ذات *dhāt*	ذواتا *dhawātā*	ذوات *dhawāt*
	acc./gen.		ذواتي *dhawātay*	

This noun is used exclusively in (definite or indefinite) construct. The whole construct works as a compound adjective, the ذو *dhū* (etc.) agreeing in all respects with the qualified noun:

رجل ذو مال *rajul dhū māl* a man of property
مسألة ذات اهمية *mas'ala dhāt 'ahammīya* a matter of importance
مع اشخاص ذوي ثقافة *ma9a 'ashkhāṣ dhawī thaqāfa* with cultured people
طلمبة ذات قوة كبيرة *ṭulumba dhāt qūwa kabīra* a powerful pump

Note how the definite form is made. It is always only the *attribute* of the construct which can carry the article:

في البيت ذي الملحق *fi l-bayt dhi l-mulḥaq* in the house with the annex

(For the record, in full pronunciation ذات *dhāt* has the usual endings *-u*, *-a* and *-i* for the nom., acc. and gen. respectively, and ذوات *dhawāt* has the usual sound endings *-u* [nom.] and *-i* [acc./gen.]. They are very rarely heard.)

Note also:

- the noun ذات ذوات *dhāt dhawāt* 'essence', 'identity'
- the use of this noun as a synonym for نفس *nafs* in the meanings 'the same' and '-self':

ذات\نفس الشيء *dhāt/nafs ash-shay'*
لذاتي\لنفسي *li dhātī/li nafsī*
الاعتماد على الذات\النفس *al-i9timād 9ala dh-dhāt/n-nafs*

20. *-in* and *-an*

Certain final-weak participles (23/10, 11) are more often used as nouns than as adjectives. Important examples are:

قاضٍ (القاضي) *qāḍin (al-qāḍī)* judge, pl. قضاة *quḍā*
محامٍ (المحامي) *muḥāmin (al-muḥāmī)* lawyer,
pl. محامون\محامين *muḥāmūn/muḥāmīn*
مستشفىً (المستشفى) *mustashfan (al-mustashfa)* hospital,
pl. مستشفيات *mustashfayāt*

A few other anomalous nouns follow a similar pattern:

يد اياد (الأيادي) *yad 'ayādin (al-'ayādī) ‹'īd 'ayād›*
ارض أراضٍ (الأراضي) *'arḍ 'arāḍin (al-'arāḍī) ‹'arḍ 'arāḍ›*
ميناء موانٍ (الموانى) *mīnā' mawānin (al-mawānī) ‹mīna mawānī›*
مقهىً (المقهى) *maqhan (al-maqha)* coffee-house,
pl. مقاهٍ (المقاهي) *maqāhin (al-maqāhī)*

Words with the pattern *-an/-a* have no case-endings in the singular.

Remember that the theme of a construct also has definite form:

قاضي المحكمة العليا *qāḍi l-maḥkama l-9ulya* the High Court judge

21. التمارين

1. Read aloud:

e.g.: ١٨ مدينة thamant9ashr madīna

(a) ٢٥ طالبا
(b) ٢٠٠ دينار
(c) من اجل ٤ مشاريع هامة
(d) ١٠ ريالات
(e) ٦ سنوات
(f) لمدة ٦ اسابيع
(g) ٣٦٥ يوما
(h) بين ١٠٠٠ و٢٠٠٠ دينار
(j) ٩٤٪ من السكان
(k) بعد ٤٨ ساعة

2. Rewrite with the ordinal number in full:

e.g.: الطالب الـ ٤ ← الطالب الرابع

(a) المرة الـ ٢
(b) الدرس الـ ٦
(c) الطلمبة الـ ٥
(d) المناسبة الـ ١
(e) اليوم الـ ٢٨

3. Put the correct form of ذو (etc.):

e.g.: قضية ... اهمية ← قضية ذات اهمية

(a) شركة ... رأس مال كبير
(b) في حقل ... احتياطي عظيم
(c) في وكالة ... اكثر من ٢٠ ممثلا
(d) مع اشخاص ... ثقافة
(e) بطلمبة ... قوة كبيرة جدا

4. Here is the handwritten draft of the office memorandum which we studied in paragraph 1(b) above. Read it aloud, then check your answer against the typescript and transcription:

تشير دائرة شؤون الموظفين الى الإعلان رقم ٢٢ من ١ كانون الثاني من عام ٢٠٠- وتذكر جميع العمال بأن قسم المحاسبات يقوم بدفع اجر الشغل الإضافي على اساس شهادة المشرف او المدير المناسب فقط وسيرفض اي طلب دفع لا يحمل توقيع المسؤول المذكور.

فهد

نسخة الى: جميع الدوائر
لوحات الإعلان

5. Look again at the dialogue of Lesson 11. Write a brief letter to the General Manager of the Jordanian Plastics (البلاستيك) Company, thanking him for receiving you on the 19th of February. Say that you had a long discussion with the Production Supervisor, and that the visit to the shop floor was very useful. Ask the GM to express your thanks to the staff whom you met. You believe that the possibilities for cooperation are very good, and you will be in touch again shortly. Tell the GM that he should not hesitate to call you again if he thinks that there is any help which you can give him. Read your letter aloud.

الدرس الخامس والعشرون
ad-dars al-khāmis wa l-9ishrūn – Lesson 25
تحويل التكنولوجيا taḥwīl at-tiknulujīya
The Transfer of Technology

1. للقراءة

حوّل	*ḥawwala* II	to transfer
تحويل	*taḥwīl*	transfer
تكنولوجيا	*tiknulujīya*	technology
بحث يبحث في\على	*baḥatha yabḥathu* I *fī/9ala*	to examine
خبير خبراء	*khabīr khubarā'*	expert
اخيرًا	*'akhīran*	recently
اسّس	*'assasa* I	to establish/set up
تأسيس	*ta'sīs*	establishment, setting-up
فولاذ	*fūlādh*	steel

تجري الآن دراسة امكانية تحويل التكنووجيا من عدة بلدان صناعية الى البلدان المنتجة للنفط في الشرق الأوسط. وبحث اخيرا عدد من الخبراء في امكانية تأسيس مصانع ذات استهلاك كميات كبيرة من الطاقة كمصانع الفولاذ والأسمدة.

tajri l-'ān dirāsat 'imkānīyat taḥwīl at-tiknulujīya min 9iddat buldān ṣinā9īya 'ila l-buldān al-muntija li n-nafṭ fī sh-sharq al-'awsaṭ. wa baḥath 'akhīran 9adad min al-khubarā' fī 'imkānīyat ta'sīs maṣāni9 dhāt istihlāk kammīyāt kabīra min aṭ-ṭāqa ka maṣāni9 al-fūlādh wa l-'asmida.

The possibility is now being studied of the transfer of technology from some industrialised countries to the oil-producing countries of ('in') the Middle East. Recently a number of experts examined the possibility of setting up factories with high energy consumption, such as steel and fertiliser factories.

عُلم	*9ulim*	it was learned
قلّ يقلّ عن	*qalla yaqillu* I *9an*	to be less than
شارك في	*shāraka* III *fī*	to participate in
مشاركة	*mushāraka*	participation

عُلم من تلك الدراسات الاقتصادية ان تكاليف اللازمة لنقل الغاز والبترول للبلدان الصناعية لا تقل عن تكاليف تحويل الصناعة الى موارد الطاقة. فتنوي الحكومات العربية ان تصرّ في المفاوضات على مشاركة هامة في تأسيس مثل هذه المصانع تحت شروط مقبولة لها.

9ulim min tilka d-dirāsāt al-iqtiṣādīya 'anna t-takālīf al-lāzima li naql al-ghāz

It was learned from these economic studies that the cost necessary for

wa l-bitroul li l-buldān aṣ-ṣinā9īya lā taqill 9an takālīf taḥwīl aṣ-ṣinā9a 'ila mawārid aṭ-ṭāqa. fa tanwi l-ḥukūmāt al-9arabīya 'an tuṣirr fī l-mufāwaḍāt 9ala mushāraka hāmma fī ta'sīs mithl hādhihi l-maṣāni9 taḥt shurūṭ maqbūla laha.

transporting the gas and petroleum to the industrialised countries is not less than the cost of transferring the industry to the sources of the energy. The Arab governments intend to insist, in the negotiations, on a significant ('important') participation in the setting-up of such factories under conditions acceptable to them.

خبرة	*khibra*	expertise
وجهة نظر	*wujhat naðar*	point of view
ضمن يضمن ضمان	*ḍamina yaḍmanu* I, *ḍamān*	to guarantee
مضمون	*maḍmūn*	guaranteed
معقول	*ma9qūl*	reasonable
لا شكّ في	*lā shakka fī*	there is no doubt
حلّ يحلّ محلّ	*ḥalla yaḥullu* I *maḥall*	to take the place (of)
كفى يكفي كفاية	*kafa yakfī* I, *kifāya*	to suffice

ان البلدان المنتجة للنفط لا تحتاج الى رأس مال الدول الغربية بل الى خبرتها. ومن وجهة نظر البلدان الصناعية يشكل الحصول على مصادر مضمونة من الطاقة شرطا معقولا لتقديم المساعدة اللازمة للبلدان العربية ولا شك في ان دول الشرق الأوسط تبحث عن اسس اقتصادية تحل محل الغاز والبترول في السنوات المقبلة. لا تكفي لهذا الغرض الاستثمارات العربية في الغرب.

'inna l-buldān al-muntija li n-nafṭ lā taḥtāj 'ila ra's māl ad-duwal al-gharbīya bal 'ila khibratiha. wa min wujhat naðar al-buldān aṣ-ṣinā9īya yushakkil al-ḥuṣūl 9ala maṣādir maḍmūna min aṭ-ṭāqa sharṭan ma9qūlan li taqdīm al-musā9ada l-fannīya al-lāzima li l-buldān al-9arabīya, wa lā shakka fī 'anna duwal ash-sharq al-'awsaṭ tabḥath 9an 'usus iqtiṣādīya taḥull maḥall al-ghāz wa l-bitroul fī s-sanawāt al-muqbila. lā takfī li hādha l-gharaḍ al-istithmārāt al-9arabīya fī l-gharb.

The oil-producing countries do not need western countries' capital, but rather their expertise. From the industrialised countries' point of view, access to guaranteed sources of energy is a reasonable condition for offering the necessary technical assistance to the Arab countries, and doubtless the Middle Eastern countries are looking for economic bases to replace gas and petroleum in future years. Arab investments in the west will not suffice for this purpose.

ترى	*tara*	they see
خطوة	*khuṭwa*	step

واجب	*wājib*	necessary
تجاه	*tujāha*	opposite, facing, towards
حدّة	*ḥidda*	sharpness
توتّر	*tawattara* V	to be tense
توتّر	*tawattur*	tension
تخفيف حدّة التوتّر	*takhfīf ḥiddat at-tawattur*	reduction of tension

في نفس الوقت يفهم رؤساء الحكومات ان لا بد من اخذ اجراءات تحضيرية من اجل تغيير اقتصاد بلادهم. وترى الحكومات في هذه الإجراءات خطوة واجبة تجاه تخفيف حدة التوتر في المنطقة بصورة عامة.

fī nafs al-waqt yafham ru'asā' al-ḥukūmāt 'anna lā budda min 'akhdh 'ijrā'āt taḥḍīrīya min 'ajl taghyīr iqtiṣād bilādihim. wa tara l-ḥukūmāt fī hādhihi l-'ijrā'āt khuṭwa wājiba tujāha takhfīf ḥiddat at-tawattur fī l-minṭaqa bi ṣūra 9āmma.

At the same time, the heads of government understand that it is indispensable to take preparatory measures for changing the economy of their countries ('country'). The governments see in these measures a necessary step towards the reduction of tension in the region in general.

النحو

2. Auxiliaries with the present tense

Some verbs, when used as auxiliaries, are followed by the present tense without a conjunction, similarly to the pattern of spoken Arabic. Common examples are found among the complemented verbs (21/4), some with a modified meaning:

ما زال لا يزال	*mā zāla lā yazālu* I	to continue (to do)
دام يدوم	*dāma yadūmu* I	still (to do)
عاد يعود	*9ada ya9ūdu* I	to (do) again
ظلّ يظلّ	*ḍalla yaḍallu* I	to remain (doing)
صار يصير	*ṣāra yaṣīru* I	to begin (doing)
and other verbs: استمرّ	*istamarra* X	to continue (doing)
كاد يكاد (كدت)	*kāda yakādu (kidt^u)* I	almost (to do)
بدأ يبدأ	*bada'a yabda'u* I	to begin (doing)

ما زلنا نذكّره بأن... *mā zilna nudhakkiruhu bi 'anna ...*
We continued to remind him that ...

عدنا نشير الى... *9udna nushīr 'ila ..*

We referred again to ...

ظللنا ننتظر. *ḍalalna nantaḍir.* We continued to wait.

استمررنا نحاول ان... *istamrarna nuḥāwil 'an ...*

We continued to try to ...

This usage is identical to one of the circumstantial verb constructions.

The verb أعاد *'a9āda* IV followed by the verbal noun is an alternative to عاد يعود *9ada ya9ūdu* I with the present tense:

عدنا نقرأ تقرير اللجنة. *9udna naqra' taqrīr al-lajna.*

أعدنا قراءة تقرير اللجنة. *'a9adna qirā'at taqrīr al-lajna.*

We re-read ('repeated the reading of') the committee's report.

3. *‹mā fī›*

One written equivalent of *‹mā fī›* is لا *lā* with the accusative *-a* of the noun. This is used for general or abstract statements, many of which are set expressions:

لا شكّ من ان... *lā shakka min 'anna ...*

لا بدّ من... *lā budda min ...*

لا شيء اهم من ذلك. *lā shay'a 'ahamm min dhālika.*

لا حياة على القمر. *lā ḥayāta 9ala l-qamar.*

The accusative *-a* is always pronounced in this expression.

For concrete statements, a better expression is ليس هناك *laysa* (etc.) *hunāka,* which requires the nominative as the subject of ليس *laysa* (etc.):

ليس هناك مهندسون في القسم. *laysa hunāka muhandisūn fī l-qism.*

4. Time conjunctions

Here are the main written conjunctions used to introduce clauses of time:

لمّا	*lamma*	عندما	*9indama ‹lamma›*
قبل ان	*qabla 'an ‹qabl mā›*	بعد ان	*ba9da 'an ‹ba9d mā›*
حتّى	*ḥatta*	طالما	*ṭālamā* as long as

بعد ان *ba9da 'an* and لما *lamma* are followed by the past tense:

بعد ان\لما وصل *ba9da 'an/lamma waṣal* after/when he arrives/arrived

5. Doubly weak verbs

A doubly weak verb root has two weak root letters.

When the doubly weak verb has middle root letter و *wāw* or ي *yā'* and final root letter ي *yā'*, the middle root letter stabilises:

نوى ينوي *nawa yanwī* I *‹nawa yinwī›*

حيّ\حيي يحيا *ḥayya yaḥya* I to live (be alive)

In all other cases, each root letter of the verb follows its own typical pattern. The simplest way to learn the verbs is from tables.

Look again at 23/6. The comment concerning the pronunciation of the weak final root letter (*ī/ū* for *ay/aw*) applies also to these verbs.

Common doubly weak verbs are given below, Form I first:

Root ولي , ولي يلي *wáliya yalī* I to be next. Commonest uses:

(في) ما يلي *(fī) mā yalī* (in) what follows

كما يلي *kama yalī* as follows (see 12/9)

Root حيّ \ حيي , حيّ \ حيي يحيا, *ḥayya yaḥya* I to live (be alive):

Past:	حييت	*ḥayītᵘ*	حيينا	*ḥayīna*
	حييت	*ḥayītᵃ*	حييتم	*ḥayītum*
	حييت	*ḥayīti*		
	حيّ\حيي	*ḥayyᵃ*	حيوا	*ḥayū*
	حيّت	*ḥayyat*		

3rd person dual: m. حيّا *ḥayyā*, f. حيّتا *ḥayyatā*

Present:	احيا	*'aḥya**	نحيا	*naḥya**
	تحيا	*taḥya**	تحيون	*taḥyawna*
	تحيين	*taḥyayna*		
	يحيا	*yaḥya**	يحيون	*yaḥyawna*
	تحيا	*taḥya**		

3rd person dual: m. يحيان *yaḥyāni*, f. تحيان *taḥyāni*

*final root letter written as *'alif*, since *'alif maqṣūra* cannot folllow *yā'*.

6. *hamza* in doubly weak verbs

Verbs with *hamza* and a weak final root letter, or with one weak root letter and final *hamza*, are classed as doubly weak. Each root letter again follows its own rules. Important examples are:

Root جيء , جاء يجيء *jā'a yajī'u* I ‹*'aja yījī*›:

Past:	جئت	*ji'tᵘ*	جئنا	*ji'na*
	جئت	*ji'ītᵃ*	جئتم	*ji'tum*
	جئت	*ji'ti*		
	جاء	*jā'ᵃ*	جاؤوا	*jā'ū*
	جاءت	*jā'at*		

3rd person dual: m. جاءا *jā'ā*, f. جاءتا *jā'atā*

Present:	اجيء	*'ajī'^u*	نجيء	*najī'^u*
	تجيء	*tajī'^u*	تجيؤن	*tajī'ūna*
	تجيئين	*tajī'īna*		
	يجيء	*yajī'^u*	يجيؤن	*yajī'ūna*
	تجيء	*tajī'^u*		

3rd person dual: m. يجيئان *yajī'āni*, f. تجيئان *tajī'āni*

جاء يجيء ب *jā'a yajī'u* I *bi* is the written equivalent (and the origin) of ‹*jāb yijīb* I›. In this context, note also تقدّم ب *taqaddama* V *bi* 'to advance' (e.g. a proposal).

Root رأي , رأى يرى *ra'a yara* I to see:

Past:	رأيت	*ra'ayt^u*	رأينا	*ra'ayna*
	رأيت	*ra'ayt^a*	رأيتم	*ra'aytum*
	رأيت	*ra'ayti*		
	رأى	*ra'a*	رأوا	*ra'aw*
	رأت	*ra'at*		

3rd person dual: m. رأيا *ra'ayā*, f. رأتا *ra'atā*

Present: irregular; middle root letter *hamza* dropped entirely:

ارى	*'ara*	نرى	*nara*
ترى	*tara*	ترون	*tarawna*
ترين	*tarayna*		
يرى	*yara*	يرون	*yarawna*
ترى	*tara*		

3rd person dual: m. يريان *yarayāni*, f. تريان *tarayāni*

This verb replaces ‹*shāf yishūf* I› in the meaning 'to see'.

The comments made in 23/6, 14 are valid also here.

7. Increased forms

Important increased forms of doubly weak verbs are:

II	ولّى يولّي	*walla yuwallī* to appoint
III	ساوى يساوي	*sāwa yusāwī* to be/make equal
	والى يوالي	*wāla yuwālī* to be constant
IV	أرى يري	*'ara yurī* to show

Root letter *hamza* is dropped in both tenses in Form IV of this root.

V	تولّى يتولّى	*tawalla yatawalla* to be appointed
X	استولى يستولي	*istawla yastawlī* to take possession of

In roots with final root letter و *wā* or ي *yā'*, this root-letter follows the final-weak verb rule (8/10) in the increased forms.

8. Participles

To make the participles of a doubly weak verb, apply the rules dictated by each root letter, but treating also final root letter *hamza* as a weak letter in Form I:

Root نوي , نوى ينوي *nawa yanwī* I:

active m.	ناوٍ (الناوي)	*nāwin (an-nāwī)*
f.	ناوية	*nā́wiya*
passive m.	منويّ	*manwīy*

Root جيء , جاء يجيء *jā'a yajī'u* I:

active m.	جاءٍ (الجائي)	*jā'in (al-jā'ī)*
f.	جائية	*jā́'iya*

Root سوي , ساوى *sāwa* III:

active m.	مساوٍ (المساوي)	*musāwin (al-musāwī)*
f.	مساوية	*musā́wiya*
passive m.	مساوىً (المساوى)	*musāwan (al-musāwa)*
f.	مساواة	*musāwā́*

9. Verbal nouns and subjunctive

For these derivatives, throughout Forms I to X, the doubly weak verb follows the rules dictated by its final root letter:

Verbal nouns:

I Root نوي	(irregular)	نية	*nīya* intention
II سوي		تسوية	*táswiya* settlement
III سوي		مساواة	*musāwā́** equality
ولي		موالاة	*muwālā* constancy
V ولي		تولٍّ (التولّي)	*tawallin (at-tawallī)* assumption of office

*identical to the f. passive participle (see paragraph 8 above).

Subjunctive: see 22/4 and 23/13 (sound/final-weak verbs).

10. التمارين

1. Read aloud:

e.g.: ان الحكومة لا ترى امكانية لتمويل هذه المشاريع.

'inna l-ḥukūma lā tara 'imkānīya li tamwīl hādhihi l-mashārī9.

(a) ما زلنا ندرس المشروع.

(b) رئيس الوفد لا ينوي ان يساعدنا.
(c) استمررنا نساعده لأن اقتراحه كان مفيدا.

2. Write:
e.g.: mādha tanwi l-lajna t-tanfīdhīya ’an ta9mal min ’ajl ta’yīd iqtirāḥina?
ماذا تنوي اللجنة التنفيذية من اجل تأييد اقتراحنا؟
(a) ’innana na9tábir hādha l-iqtirāḥ ’ashadd ta9qīdan.
(b) ’inna ḥall mushkilat at-tánmiya tuhimm jamī9 ad-duwal al-muḥibba li s-salām ihtimāman ’asāsīyan.
(c) tabda’ al-ḥukūma tadrus mushkilat ziyādat al-mustawradāt.
(d) lā budda min ’i9ādat kitābat at-taqrīr.
(e) kayfa yumkin al-ḥukūma l-9amal fī hādhihi ḍ-ḍurūf?

3. Repeat the sentences of Ex. 2 in spoken Arabic:
e.g.: mādha tanwī l-lajna t-tanfīdhīya ’an ta9mal min ’ajl ta’yīd iqtirāḥina?
– ‹shū tinwī l-lajna t-tanfīdhīya ti9mal min ’ajl ta’yīd iqtirāḥna?›

4. Rewrite the sentence, adding the auxiliary verb indicated:
e.g.: يصرون على تطبيق شروط مقبولة. (ما زالوا)
← ما زالوا يصرون على تطبيق شروط مقبولة.
(a) ايدوا اقتراحنا. (بدأوا)
(b) يضيفون ارقام جديدة الى التقرير. (يحاولون)
(c) مولوا المشروع بمساعدة البنك. (يريدون)
(d) يحفرون بئرا في ظروف صعبة جدا. (يبدأون)
(e) يؤيد القطاع الخاص الحكومة في سياستها الاقتصادية. (يجب)

5. Give the root under which each of the following words is found in a root-based dictionary:
e.g.: يرون ← رأي
(a) منظرة (b) مكتشف (c) يلي
(d) يحيا (e) جاء

الدرس السادس والعشرون
ad-dars as-sādis wa l-9ishrūn – Lesson 26
الأمم المتّحدة al-'umam al-muttáḥida
The United Nations

1. للقراءة

قرن قرون	*qarn qurūn*	century
أسّست	*'ussisat*	it was established/founded
على أثر	*9ala 'athar*	following
راجع	*rāja9a* III	to review, revise
مراجعة	*murāja9a*	review, revision
دور ادوار	*dawr 'adwār*	rôle
لعب يلعب لعب	*la9iba yal9abu* I, *lu9b*	to play
حفظ السلام	*ḥifð as-salām*	peace-keeping

اكثر من نصف قرن بعد ان أُسّست هيئة الأمم المتحدة على اثر الحرب العالمية الثانية يجب ان تقوم المنظمة بمراجعة الدور الذي تلعبه في ما يتعلق بمهام مثل عمليات حفظ السلام وتسوية الخلافات بين الدول الأعضاء.

'akthar min niṣf qarn ba9da 'an 'ussisat hay'at al-'umam al-muttáḥida 9ala 'athar al-ḥarb al-9ālamīya th-thāniya yajib 'an taqūm al-munaððama bi murāja9at ad-dawr alladhī tal9abuhu fī mā yata9allaq bi mahāmm mithla 9amalīyāt ḥifð as-salām wa tásfiyat al-khilāfāt bayna d-duwal al-'a9ḍā'.

More than half a century after the United Nations Organisation was founded following the Second World War, it needs to review the rôle which it plays in areas ('in what is') related to tasks such as peace-keeping operations and settling disputes between member states.

عُبّر عن	*9ubbir 9an*	was expressed
انتقد على	*intáqada* VIII *9ala*	to criticise
انتقاد على	*intiqād 9ala*	criticism of
فاعلية	*fā9ilīya*	effectiveness, efficiency
يشار الى	*yushār 'ila*	it is pointed out
لم تنجح	*lam tanjaḥ*	= ما نجحت
بحث بحوث عن	*baḥth buḥūth 9an*	search for
عدل	*9adl*	justice
مكافحة	*mukāfaḥa* (in construct)	fight against

وبالفعل عُبر عن انتقاد على عدم فاعلية المنظمة ويشار الى انها لم تنجح في عدد من محاولاتها مثلا البحث عن السلام والعدل في الشرق الأوسط وحروب اقليمية مختلفة ومكافحة الإرحاب وغيرها.

wa bi l-fi9l 9ubbir 9an intiqād 9ala 9adam fā9ilīyat al-munaððama wa yushār 'ila 'annaha lam tanjaḥ fī 9adad min muḥāwalātiha mathalan al-baḥth 9an as-salām wa l-9adl fi sh-sharq al-'awsaṭ wa ḥurūb 'iqlīmīya mukhtálifa wa mukāfaḥat al-'irhāb wa ghayriha.

And indeed criticism has been expressed of the organisation's effectiveness. It was pointed out that it has not succeeded in a number of its attempts such as the search for peace and justice in the Middle East, various regional wars, the fight against terrorism, and others.

نوعًا ما	*naw9an mā*	somewhat
مثال امثلة	*mithāl 'amthila*	example
صرّح ب	*ṣarraḥa* II *bi*	to declare
نادٍ (النادي) اندية	*nādin (an-nādī) 'ándiya*	club, circle
سيطر على	*sayṭara* IQ *9ala*	to dominate
مجلس الأمن	*majlis al-'amn*	Security Council
ضمّ يضمّ	*ḍamma yaḍummu* I	to comprise, include
تركّز	*tarakkaza* V	to be concentrated
غير ان	*ghayr 'anna*	whereas, however
فعلي	*fi9lī*	real, actual, factual
دائم العضوية	*dā'im al-9uḍwīya*	with permanent membership

ان نجاح الأمم المتحدة في عدة حقول قد خفف نوعا ما هذه الانتقادات ولكن هذه النتائج الناجحة تشكل في رأي عدد كبير من الحكومات امثلة استثنائية. صرح ناتق بلسان الدول النامية بأن الأمم المتحدة ما زالت ناديا خاصا يسيطر عليه مجلس الأمن الذي يضم ١٥ عضوا غير ان القوة الفعلية فيه تتركز في ايادي الدول الخمس الكبرى الدائمة العضوية.

'inna najāḥ al-'umam al-muttáḥida fī 9iddat huqūl qad khaffaf naw9an mā hādhihi l-intiqādāt walākinna hādhihi n-natā'ij an-nājiḥa tushakkil fī ra'ī 9adad kabīr min al-ḥukūmāt 'amthila stithnā'īya. ṣarraḥ nāṭiq bi lisān ad-duwal an-nấmiya bi 'anna l-'umam al-muttáḥida mā zālat nấdiyan khāṣṣan yusayṭir 9alayhi majlis al-'amn alládhī yaḍumm khamst9ashr 9uḍwan ghayr 'anna l-quwa l-fi9līya fīhi

The success of the UN in some fields has somewhat softened these criticisms, but in the opinion of many governments these successful results are exceptional cases ('examples'). A spokesman for the developing countries declared that the UN is still a private club dominated by the Security Council which comprises fifteen members,

tatarakkaz fī 'ayādi d-duwal al-khams al-kubra d-dā'ima l-9uḍwīya.

while the actual power ('in it') is concentrated in the hands of the five big states with permanent membership.

اعادة التنظيم	*'i9ādat at-tanðīm*	reorganisation
نظام انظمة	*niðām 'anðima*	order, system
بحث بحوث على	*baḥth buḥūth 9ala*	examination of
لم يظهر	*lam yaðhar*	= ما ظهر

ذكر كثير من الأعضاء انه يجب اعادة تنظيم ادارة المنظمة الدولية على ضوء الوضع الجديد. ويعبرون عن الرأي ان النظام الاقتصادي الجديد الذي كان البحث عليه في السبعينيات لم يظهر قابلا للإنجاز في ذلك الوقت،

dhakar kathīr min al-'a9ḍā' 'annahu yajib 'i9ādat tanðīm 'idārat al-munaððama d-duwalīya 9ala ḍaw' al-waḍ9 al-jadīd. wa yu9abbirūna 9an ar-ra'ī 'anna n-niðām al-iqtiṣādi l-jadīd alládhī kān al-baḥth 9alayhi fi s-sab9īnīyāt lam yaðhar qābilan li l-'injāz fī dhālika l-waqt,

Several of the members have mentioned that a reorganisation of the international body's administration is needed in the light of the new situation. They express the view that the new economic order, examined in the 70's, did not seem capable of implementation at that time,

حقّق	*ḥaqqaqa* II	to realise
تحقيق	*taḥqīq*	realisation
حيث ان	*ḥaythu 'anna*	given that
توازن	*tawāzana* VI	to be balanced
توازن	*tawāzun*	equilibrium, balance
استقرّ	*istaqarra* X	to be stable, settled
استقرار	*istiqrār*	stability, steadiness

ولكن الوضع الجديد قد يمكن من تحقيقه حيث ان عدم التوازن بين الشمال (يعني الدول الصناعية) والجنوب (اي الدول النامية) هو اهم سبب لعدم الاستقرار الدولي.

walakinna l-waḍ9 al-jadīd qad yumakkin min taḥqīqihi, ḥaythu 'anna 9adam at-tawāzun bayna sh-shimāl (ya9ni d-duwal aṣ-ṣinā9īya) wa l-janūb ('ay ad-duwal n-nāmiya) huwa 'ahamm sabab li 9adam al-istiqrār ad-duwalī.

but the new situation might make its realisation possible, given that the imbalance between the north (that is, the industrialised countries) and the south (i.e. the developing countries) is the most important cause of international instability.

تشكيل	*tashkīl*	formation, constitution
اعادة التشكيل	*'i9ādat at-tashkīl*	reform, reconstitution

لم يأخذ	*lam ya'khudh*	= ما اخذ
واجح	*wājaḥa* III	to face
افلس	*'aflasa* IV	to be/go bankrupt
افلاس	*'iflās*	bankruptcy
دين ديون	*dayn duyūn*	debt
انتهج	*intáhaja* VIII	to pursue (a policy etc.)

ولهذا الشأن يطلبون اعادة تشكيل دور المنظمة ومراجعة علاقاتها الداخلية. مع الأسف لم يأخذ هذا المطلب بعين الاعتبار وضع المنظمة المالي ومن المعروف ان الأمم المتحدة تواجه الإفلاس بديون عظيمة. ان الأمم المتحدة يعتمد على تأييد الولايات المتحدة بينما تنتهج الولايات المتحدة نفسها سياسة مستقلة.

wa li hādha ash-sha'n yaṭlubūna 'i9ādat tashkīl dawr al-munaðða̱ma wa murāja9at 9alāqātiha d-dākhilīya. ma9a l-'asaf lam ya'khudh hādha l-maṭlab bi 9ayn al-i9tibār waḍ9 al-munaðða̱ma l-mālī wa min al-ma9rūf 'anna l-'umam al-muttáḥida tuwājah al-'iflās bi duyūn 9aðīma. 'inna al-'umam al-muttáḥida ta9támid 9ala ta'yīd al-wilāyāt al-muttáḥida baynamā tantáhij al-wilāyāt al-muttáḥida nafsuha siyāsatan mustaqilla.

To this end, they are asking for a reconstitution of the organisation's rôle and a review of its internal relationships. Unfortunately this request has not taken into account the organisation's financial situation. It is well known that the UN is facing bankruptcy, with enormous debts. The UN depends on the support of the United States, whereas the United States herself pursues an independent policy.

النحو

2. *lam*; jussive tense

Examine the expressions in the text:

لم تنجح	*lam tanjaḥ* it did not succeed
لم يظهر	*lam yaðhar* it did not seem
لم يأخذ	*lam ya'khudh* it did not take

لم *lam* is a negative particle, not used in spoken Arabic, which is followed by a tense called the 'jussive'. لم تنجح *lam tanjaḥ* is synonymous with ما نجحت, but in written Arabic the structure with *lam* + jussive is mostly preferred to *mā* + past tense.

3. The jussive is easily formed, as follows:

Sound, hamzated and initial-*w* verbs. For these verbs the jussive is identical to the subjunctive without its fully-pronounced endings; another way of expressing the formula for these verbs is that the jussive has the endings of the spoken Arabic present, plus the dual ending ا -ā. Examine:

	subjunctive			jussive
يكتبه	yáktubahu	→	يكتبه	yaktúbhu
نأخذها	ná'khudhaha	→	نأخذها	na'khúdhha
اجده	'ájidahu	→	اجده	'ajíd-hu

Hollow verbs. For hollow verbs the jussive ending is the same as for sound verbs, but the weak middle root letter is shortened under the hollow verb rule (Lesson 6/4), also when there is no ending at all:

		subjunctive			jussive
	يقول	yaqū́la	→	يقل	yáqul
	يبيع	yabī́9a	→	يبع	yábi9
but:	يبيعوا	yabī́9ū	=	يبيعوا	yabī́9ū

Doubled verbs. Forms II and V of these verbs behave like sound verbs. In all other forms (including I), the jussive is identical to the subjunctive:

	نجدّده	nujáddidahu II	→	نجدّده	nujaddíd-hu
but:	نحتلّه	naḥtállahu VIII	=	نحتلّه	naḥtállahu

Final-weak verbs. Like the subjunctive, except that whenever the final weak root letter is the last written letter in the subjunctive, drop that root letter and substitute the corresponding short vowel (ُ -u for و -ū, ِ -i for ي -ī, َ -a for ى -a):

ينفي	yánfī/iya	→	ينف	yánfi
نبقى	nábqa	→	نبق	nábqa

Doubly weak verbs. Each root letter follows its own rule. We apply the guidelines given above, includening the shortening of a weak root letter under the hollow and final-weak verb rules where appropriate:

يجيء	yajī́'a	→	يجئ	yáji'

For all verb classes, the stress moves if necessary, to follow the rule.

4. Other uses of the jussive

In addition to the important لم construction, the jussive is used:

- with لم ... بعد *lam ... ba9d* or لما *lamma* 'not ... yet':

  لم يصل بعد\ لما يصل. *lam yaṣil ba9d/lamma yaṣil.*
  He has not arrived yet.

  Do not confuse with the conjunction لما *lamma* 'when', used in writing only with the past tense.

- to express wishes and intentions, always preceded by:
  ل *li* 'let ...' or فل\ول *fa l/wa l* 'so/then let ...':

لنذهب. *li nadhhab.* Let us go.

فلنذهب. *fa l nadhhab.* Let us go, then.

- with لا *lā* to express the negative imperative:

لا تردد ان تتصل بي. *lā tataraddad 'an tattáṣil bī́.*

5. Some, some-

The indefinite form of certain nouns followed by ما *mā* is used to indicate 'some' or 'some-' with indefinite meaning, often adverbial:

نوعًا ما *naw9an mā* somewhat

يومًا ما *yawman mā* some day, some time

لأمرٍ ما *li 'amrin mā* for some reason

The case-ending is always pronounced in such expressions.

6. Conditional sentences

The rules for conditional sentences, both real and unreal, studied in 11/14, are all valid for written Arabic, except for what follows.

After إذا *'idha,* used for real conditions, traditional grammar requires the past tense in both clauses; but modern usage permits a choice for the main verb:

اذا جاءوا ذهبنا\نذهب معًا. *'idha jā'aw/jā'ū, dhahabna/nadhhab ma9an.* If they come, we shall go together.

However, if the main clause begins with anything other than a past- or present-tense verb, the clause must be introduced with ف *fa*:

اذا رفضته انا فهو سيرفضه ايضًا. *'idha rafaḍtuhu 'ana, fa huwa sa yarfiḍuhu 'ayḍan.* If I reject it, he will too.

اذا طلبوه فلن نسمعهم. *'idha ṭalabūhu fa lan nasma9ahum.* If they request it, we shall not hear them.

The conditional clause has verbal-sentence structure. The main clause may have either verbal-sentence or nominal-sentence structure, in which latter case it is introduced by فإنّ *fa 'inna*:

اذا رفضته انا فإنّه سيرفضه ايضًا. *'idha rafaḍtuhu 'ana, fa 'innahu sa yarfiḍuhu 'ayḍan.*

The conjunction إنْ *'in* is also used, much less frequently, for real conditions. It is mostly found in set expressions such as إن شاء الله *'in shā' 'allāh* ‹'inshalla› and إن وجد(ت) *'in wujid(at),* for which see paragraph 10 below.

The conjunction لو *law* introduces unreal conditions as in spoken Arabic, except that we do not use the continuous past in either clause; and a following main clause is usually introduced by the particle لـ *la*:

لو عرفنا لقد ايدناكم. *law 9arafna la qad 'ayyadnākum.*
If we had known, we would have supported you.

The time-sequence of the whole conditional sentence often has to be inferred from the context. However, in affirmative sentences, present or future sequence can be indicated either with the main verb in the future tense (as above); while past sequence can often be underlined by using قد *qad* or كان *kāna* (i.e. the pluperfect) in either clause:

اذا سمعوا (سـ)يفهمون. *'idha sami9ū (sa) yafhamūna.*
If they listen, they will understand.

لو (كانوا\قد) سمعوا لكانوا فهموا\الفهموا. *law (kānū/qad) sami9ū la kānū fahimū/la fahimū.* Had they listened, they would have understood.

In all conditional clauses we use لم *lam* + the jussive, not *mā* or *lā*, to negate the verb:

اذا لم ندفع اضربوا\يضربون. *'idha lam nadfa9 'aḍrabū/yuḍribūna.*
If we do not pay, they will strike.

لو لم ندفع لقد اضربوا. *law lam nadfa9 la qad 'aḍrabū.*
If we had not paid, they would have struck.

Finally, note that, less frequently, the main clause may precede the condition:

نؤيدهم اذا كانت سياستهم سالمة. *nu'ayyiduhum 'idha kānat siyāsatuhum sālima.* We support them if their policy is sound.

7. Passive

Look again at 15/5. The rules which you find there for the passive tenses are those of written Arabic, in short pronunciation. We can represent the vowel pattern graphically (sound verbs, 3rd person m. sing.):

		Past				Present				
2 syllables	+ *full*		*u*	*i*	*a*	*u*		*a*		*u*
3 syllables	*personal*	*u*	*u*	*i*	*a*	*u*	*a*	*a*		*u*
4 syllables	*ending*					*u*	*a*	*a*	*a*	*u*

Three passive verbs occur in tenses in the passage, following this pattern. Two are from verbs with sound root letters:

أُسِّست *'ussisat* it was founded (from اسّس *'assasa* II)

عُبِّر عن *9ubbir 9an* it was expressed (عبّر عن *9abbara* II *9an*)

The third is from a hollow verb:

يشار الى *yushār 'ila* it is pointed out (اشار الى *'ashāra* IV *'ila*)

in which the vocalised middle root letter follows the hollow verb rule.

Note that in verbs beginning with و (whether initial-*w* class or doubly weak), the present tense of Form I has او\تو\يو\نو *'aw/tū/yū/nū* as its prefix, and the past of Form III starts with وو... *wū-*:

(وجد I)	يوجد	*yūjad*
(ولي I)	يولى	*yūla*
(وافق على III)	ووفق على	*wūfiq 9ala*

8. Passive participles, imperative and verbal noun

You know the participles. The passive has no imperative and no verbal noun.

9. Use of the passive

For verbs able to have a direct object, the passive can be used for all persons; it agrees in the usual manner:

كُتبت الرسالة امس. *kutibat ar-risāla 'ams.*

For verbs with a prepositional object, the verb is always m. sing.:

ووفق على الوثيقة. *wūfiq 9ala l-wathīqa.*

The document was agreed upon. ('There was agreement on ...')

See 10/8 for the same phenomenon with the participle.

10. Three useful expressions with passive forms of وجد يجد *wajada yajidu* I:

ان وجد\وجدت	*'in wujid/wujidat* if (there is/are) any
يوجد\توجد	*yūjad/tūjad* there is/are
لا يوجد\توجد	*lā yūjad/tūjad* there is/are no/none

سنشارك بالأرباح ان وجدت. *sa nushārik bi l-'arbāḥ, 'in wujidat.*

We shall participate in the profits, if (there are) any.

يوجد متظاهرون في الشارع. *yūjad mutaẓāhirūn fi sh-shāri9.*

There are demonstrators in the street.

اصغره مع الأسف لا يوجد. *'aṣgharuhu ma9a l-'asaf lā yūjad.*

Unfortunately no smaller one exists.

لا تبحث عن شرح لا يوجد. *lā tabḥath 9an sharḥ lā yūjad.*

Do not search for an explanation which does not exist.

The first expression is always in the past because it is conditional; the second and third expressions are in the present tense.

لا يوجد\توجد *lā yūjad/tūjad* also expresses 'nil' in statistics.

11. In spoken Arabic, Form VII is often used to express the passive, avoiding the complications of the written passive. Of the verbs listed in 13/4, the following are not used in writing:

‹*inkátab, inzār, inqāl, in9add, inláqa*›

The others shown can all be written.

Make full use of the structures تمّ\تمّت *tamm/tammat* I + definite verbal noun, and جرى يجري *jara yajrī* I + definite verbal noun (15/6), which are easy devices commonly used in written Arabic.

12. Improper agreement

Examine the expression in the passage

الدول الدائمة العضوية *ad-duwal ad-dā'ima l-9uḍwīya*
the states with permanent membership

In this expression, the adjective دائم *dā'im* agrees not with عضوية *9uḍwīya* but with دول *duwal,*. i.e. the wrong noun. This is 'improper agreement', a common stylistic device. Examine also:

جامعة كثيرة المال *jāmi9a kathīra l-māl* a wealthy university
الأصدقاء الكرماء القلب *al-'aṣdiqā' al-kuramā' al-qalb*
the kind-hearted friends

Note how the definite form is made, in the last example.

We can instead use a construction with ذو *dhū* (etc., 24/19):

الدول ذات العضوية الدائمة *ad-duwal dhāt al-9uḍwīya d-dā'ima*
جامعة ذات مال كثير *jāmi9a dhāt māl kathīr*
الأصدقاء ذوو القلب الكريم *al-'aṣdiqā' dhawu l-qalb al-karīm*

in which the adjective agrees normally.

Another improper agreement occurs in 23/1:

للاجتماعات ... المقررة عقدها *li l-ijtimā9āt ... al-muqarrara 9aqduha*
to the meetings ... which it has been decided to hold

where the participial phrase could be re-expressed with a relative pronoun + clause with normal agreement:

للاجتماعات التي قُرّر عقدها *li l-ijtimā9āt allátī qurrir 9aqduha*
the holding of which was decided

13. Second person dual, and feminine plural

These forms are very infrequently met and have therefore been omitted from the grammar descriptions. They are shown here for reference:

	2nd m./f. dual		2nd f. pl.		3rd f. pl.	
Pronoun:						
subject	انتما	*'antuma*	انتنّ	*'antunna*	هنّ	*hunna*
suffix*	كما	*-kumā*	كنّ	*-kunna*	هنّ	*-hunna*

* also possessive suffix

	2nd m./f. dual		2nd f. pl.		3rd f. pl.	
Verb:						
past	تما	*-tuma*	تنّ	*-tunna*	ن	*-na*
present	ت...ان	*t...āni*	ت...ن	*t...na*	ي...ن	*y...na*
subjunctive + jussive	ت...ا	*t...ā*	ت...ن	*t...na*	ي...ن	*y...na*
imperative	ا	*-ā*	ن	*-na*	ن	*-na*

14. Equivalent expressions

Some equivalent expressions in spoken and written Arabic which we have learned:

‹*ḥaka yiḥkī*›	تكلّم	‹*wayn*›	اين
‹*aja yījī*›	جاء يجيء	‹*laysh*›	لماذا
‹*jāb yijīb*›	جاء يجيء ب	‹*mīn*›	مَن
‹*rāḥ yirūḥ*›	ذهب يذهب	‹*shū*›	ما، ماذا
‹*rāyiḥ, rāḥ-*›	س، سوف	‹*illī*›	الذي...
‹*shāf yishūf*›	نظر ينظر (الى)	‹*qabl/ba9d mā*›	قبل\بعد أنْ
‹*qidir yiqdar*›	استطاع انْ	‹*hadhāk*› (etc.)	ذلك...
‹*lāzim*›	يجب انْ	‹*'inn*›	أنّ (قال إنّ)
‹*fī*›	يوجد\توجد، هناك	‹*kwayyis*›	طيب
‹*mā fī*›	{ ليس، لا يوجد\توجد، / لا + acc.	‹*mish*›	غير، ليس
		‹*mish rāyiḥ*›	لن + subjunctive
‹*mā*› + present	لا + present	‹*mā*› + past	لم + jussive

15. التمارين

1. Read aloud:

e.g.: عُلم من مصادر رسمية انه تم الاتفاق على العقد امس .

9ulim min maṣādir rasmīya 'annahu tamm al-ittifāq 9ala al-9aqd 'ams.

(a) تم افتتاح المفاوضات امس.

(b) اذا تحسن الطقس كان مفيدا للفلاحين.

(c) ظروف الاستثمار الحالية غير مرضية.

(d) ماذا عُلم من التقرير؟

2. Write:

e.g.: yubḥath 9an ḥall al-mashākil al-muta9alliqa bi taṣnī9 9iddat buldān nāmiya.

يُبحث عن حل المشاكل المتعلقة بتصنيع عدة بلدان نامية.

(a) fa l nashraḥ lahum al-mashākil, 'in wujidat.

(b) lā yūjad shay' 'ajmal fī l-9ālam.

(c) 'a9lan nāṭiq bi lisān al-ḥukūma 'anna l-9aqd qad quddim li l-majlis.

(d) kānat mushkila fī l-mīzānīya 9indamā 'ukhbir al-wazīr bi fashal al-mufawaḍāt at-tijārīya d-duwalīya..

(e) lā tadfa9 ash-sharika mablaghan 'iḍāfīyan; 'innaha tadfa9 9ala 'asās 'as9ār thābita faqaṭ.

3. Join the two sentences into one conditional sentence:

e.g.: عرفنا هذا. ساعدناكم. ← لو عرفنا هذا لساعدناكم.

(a) جاء. كان اسهل علينا.

(b) ترفض الحكومة. نطلب من المحكمة.

(c) تقول له هذا. سيجاوب جوابا واضحا.

(d) ارسلنا لك الرسوم. كانت عندنا.

(e) تعرف اللغة العربية. تستفيد اكثر من اقامتك.

4. Write the following sentences in correct written form:

e.g.: ‹lāzim niḥkī ma9 muwaẓẓafīn ash-sharika bukra.›

يجب ان تتكلم مع موظفي الشركة غدا.

(a) ‹mīn illī kān yiḥkī 9an hadhoul al-'ashkhāṣ?

(b) ‹mish wāḍiḥ shū tinwi l-ḥukūma ti9mal fī hal-ḥāla.›

(c) ‹mā niqdar inqarrir al-youm; khallīna nistanna ḥatta l-'usbū9 al-jāī.›

(d) ‹laysh mā turīd tiqra r-risāla qabl mā njāwib?›

(e) ‹'aẓunn 'innhum mish moujūdīn ba9d as-sā9a th-thalātha.›

5. Read each sentence aloud, then re-express it in spoken Arabic:

e.g.: عندما تجتمع اللجنة يجب ان تأخذ هذه الأسئلة بعين الاعتبار.

9indama tajtámi9 al-lajna yajib ’an ta’khudh hādhihi al-’as’ila bi 9ayn al-i9tibār.

‹lamma tijtámi9 al-lajna lāzim tākhudh hādhi l-’as’ila bi ʿayn al-i9tibār.›

(a) لن اذهب الى المؤتمر الا اذا جئت معي.

(b) لم افهم الوضع الذي شرحه لنا.

(c) ان هذه المشكلة صارت لنا اشد تعقيدا.

(d) تصل غدا.

(e) ان الستات كن حاضرات طول الفترة كلها.

Key to exercises

Lesson 1

1. (a) mabsū́ṭ, ḥamdílla. (b) shúkran. (c) ṣabā́ḥ an-nū́r. (d) mabsū́ṭa ḥamdílla. (e) marḥabtáyn.

2. (a) kayf ḥā́lik? (b) law samáḥti. (c) 'ínti mabsū́ṭa? (d) márḥaba. (e) 'áhlan bī́ki.

3. (a) kayf ḥā́lkum? (b) law samáḥtū. (c) 'íntū mabṣūṭī́n? (d) márḥaba. (e) 'áhlan bī́kum.

4. (a) kayf ḥā́lak? (b) 'áhlan bī́k. (c) ṣabā́ḥ al-kháyr. (d) tfáḍḍal. (e) 9áfwan.

5. (a) mu9állima miṣrī́ya. (b) 'ínti 'amayrkī́ya? (c) mabsū́ṭa jíddan, shúkran. (d) 'ána 'inglīzī́ya. (e) híya min al-'úrdun.

6. (a) mu9allimī́n miṣrīyī́n. (b) 'íntū 'amayrkā́n? (c) mabsūṭī́n jíddan, shúkran. (d) 'iḥna/níḥna 'inglī́z. (e) hum min al-'úrdun.

7. (a) húwa sū́rī. (b) mu9állim 'inglī́zī (c) 'int lubnā́nī? (d) fā́ḍī. (e) fā́ḍī.

8. (a) la', húwa ṭabī́b. (b) húwa 'úrdunī. (c) ná9am, húwa mabsū́ṭ. (d) ná9am, fā́ḍī, tfáḍḍal. (e) mabsū́ṭ, al-ḥamdílla.

9. (a) nushkurálla (b) fā́ḍī fā́ḍīya fāḍīyī́n (c) mabsūṭī́n (d) 9árabī 9arabī́ya 9árab (e) ṭā́lib 'inglī́zī

Lesson 2

1. (a) al-maṭā́r (b) az-ziyā́ra ṭ-ṭawī́la (c) ar-rā́kib al-'amáyrkī (d) al-kīs aṣ-ṣghī́r (e) aṭ-ṭabī́b al-míṣrī

2. (a) sayyārít-hum (b) shantátkum (c) 9índ-hum (d) warā́na (e) ṣandū́qkum

3. (a) fī sayyā́ra (b) 'aghrā́ḍ shakhṣī́ya (c) tádhkara (d) shánta

4. (a) 9índ-hum tádhkara. (b) 9índ-ha shánta ṣghī́ra. (c) 9índik fulū́s. (d) aṭ-ṭā́lib, 9índu kam kitā́b. (e) aṭ-ṭabī́b, 9índu waqt.

5. (a) kitā́bī (b) tadhkártu, tadhkarít-ha (c) fulū́sak, fulū́sik (d) 'amā́mu, 'amā́mha (e) warā́, warā́ha (f) fī́nī, fī́ya (g) 'iláy, 'iláyha (h) 9aláyk, 9aláyki (j) 9ánnu, 9ánha (k) mínnak, mínnik

6. (a) rukkā́b lubnānīyī́n (b) ṭayyā́ra muta'ákhkhira (c) al-mu9állim as-sū́rī (d) ṣúḥufī 9árabī (e) dīnā́r kuwáytī

Lesson 3

1. (a) shantā́t al-musā́fir (b) sayyā́rat mudī́rna (c) miftā́ḥ 'óuḍat fu'ā́d (d) jádwal aṭ-ṭayyārā́t (e) jawā́z ar-rā́kib

2. (a) shántat aṭ-ṭā́lib (b) shantā́t aṭ-ṭā́lib (c) 'aghrā́ḍ aṭ-ṭā́lib (d) tádhkarat aṭ-ṭā́lib (e) ghúrfat aṭ-ṭā́lib

3. (a) mu9allimī́n (b) sayyārā́t (c) mu9allimā́t (d) maṭārā́t (e) musāfirī́n

4. (a) dákhalū. (b) nizílna. (c) shū 'amártū? (d) mā dafá9tū. (e) aṭ-ṭayyārā́t ṭíli9at 9ala l-waqt.

5. (a) mu9állima (b) maṭā́r (c) míṣrī (d) muhándis (e) 9árabī

6. (a) mā wajádt as-sayyā́ra. (b) mā dakhált al-ghúrfa?

(c) mā́ fī rukkā́b ikthī́r. (d) at-táksī mā wíṣil 'ílak.
(e) al-musāfirī́n mā nízilū min aṭ-ṭayyā́ra.
7. (a) nizílt min at-táksī. (b) khā́rij al-júmruk (c) aṭ-ṭayyā́ra ṭili9at.
(d) taḥt al-fársha (e) min al-bálad
8. (a) sayyā́ra 'urubbī́ya (b) sayyārā́t 'urubbī́ya (c) 'iḥna 'urubbīyī́n.
(d) rukkā́b 'urubbīyī́n (e) 'ínti 'urubbī́ya.

Lesson 4

1. (a) hādha sh-shurṭī (b) hādha l-madkhal (c) wazīr al-9amal hādha
(d) hādha t-timthāl (e) hādhi s-sayyāra l-'amayrkīya
2. (a) 9irifnā́. (b) mā katabnāha. (c) simi9nī. (d) ṭalabū minnak
(e) shū sa'altū́?
3. (a) mā dakhalt al-bank. (b) hādha mish ikthīr 9alayk.
(c) mā́ fī 9indak fakka? (d) mā katabu kwayyis. (e) shughlu mish kwayyis.
4. (a) sayyārtayn (b) sayyārtayn 'amayrkān (c) al-baladayn (d) ṣuḥufīyayn
(e) kitābáy
5. (a) shanta wāḥida (b) 'arba9a muhandisīn (c) rākibayn (d) sitta shurṭīyīn
(e) al-mustashfayāt al-khamsa

Lesson 5

1. (a) daras yudrus (b) wiṣil yūṣal (c) 9irif ya9raf (d) shakar yushkur
(e) 'akal yākul
2. (a) 'ukhruj, 'ukhrujī, 'ukhrujū; lā tukhruj, lā tukhrujī, lā tukhrujū
(b) 'inzil, 'inzilī, 'inzilū; lā tinzil, lā tinzilī, lā tinzilū
(c) khudh, khudhī, khudhū; lā tākhudh, lā tākhudhī, lā tākhudhū
(d) 'ismaḥ, 'ismaḥī, 'ismaḥū; lā tismaḥ, lā tismaḥī, lā tismaḥū
(e) 'uktub, 'uktubī, 'uktubū; lā tuktub, lā tuktubī, lā tuktubū
3. (a) nuṭlub (b) lā tirkabū. (c) yushkurū (d) khallīna ninzil. (e) mā ta9rafū?
4 (a) mā yisma9ūna. (b) ya9rafha. (c) khallīna nushkurhum. (d) sa'altak.
(e) mā 'akaltu.
5. (a) khallīhum yuṭlubū. (b) khallīha tukhruj. (c) khallīnī 'ajlis.
(d) khallī́ yinzil huna. (e) khallīna nidfa9 'ujrat at-taksī.
6. (a) sa'alt laysh mā 'akhadht al-fulūs. (b) sa'alt 'idha dafa9u l-ḥisāb.
(c) sa'alt mata tūṣal as-sayyāra. (d) sa'alt wayn al-mudīr.
(e) sa'alt li mīn hādha l-milaff.
7. (a) 'arba9tashr shakhṣ (b) mīt musāfir
(c) al-musāfirīn al-mīya u sab9a u 9ishrīn (d) thamā́niya risālāt
(e) thalāthīn muwaẓẓaf

Lesson 6

1. (a) shuft, shufna (b) ṭirt, ṭirna (c) sa'alt, sa'alna (d) nimt, nimna
2. (a) kunna nudkhul al-bayt. (b) kānū yūṣalū li l-balad.
(c) kānū yūṣalū 9indna. (d) kānū yuktubu l-jawāb. (e) kan yuskun huna.
3. (a) kutub hal-mu9allim (b) haṭ-ṭullāb (c) fī hal-waqt (d) 9ind han-nās
(e) hal-maktab
4. (a) buyūt (b) ṭuruq (c) zumalā' (d) niswān (e) banāt

5. (a) ṭullāb shuṭṭār u mujtahidīn (b) makhāzin ikbīra (c) nusakh wāḍiḥa (d) 'ashkhāṣ luṭafā' (e) ṣanādīq thaqīla
6. (a) kán fī 9indna waqt ikthīr. (b) kam ṭālib kán fī huna? (c) aṭ-ṭabīb kān 9ind al-marīḍ. (d) mā kunna mabsūṭīn. (e) huwa kān moujūd al-youm.
7. (a) ṭālibayn (b) ithn9ashr 'ouḍa (c) sitta ṣuwar (d) 'arba9a musāfirīn (e) shakhṣ wāḥid

Lesson 7

1. (a) shāf yishūf (b) ṭalab yuṭlub (c) nām yinām (d) ṭār yiṭīr (e) bā9 yibī9
2. (a) 'ashūfu l-youm. (b) wayn yirūḥ? (c) nṣīr 'aghniyā'. (d) yibī9ū bayt-hum fī bayrūt. (e) tjību l-fulūs ma9kum?
3. (a) kān lāzim inrūḥ li l-balad. (b) kān lāzim 'ashūfu bukra. (c) kān lāzim yizūru l-mudīr. (d) kān lāzim yijību l-kutub? (e) kān lāzim nuṭlub minnu.
4. (a) kūn, kūnī, kūnū; lā tkūn, lā tkūnī, lā tkūnū
(b) khāf, khāfī, khāfū; lā tkhāf, lā tkhāfī , lā tkhāfū
(c) 'ukhruj, 'ukhrujī, 'ukhrujū; lā tukhruj, lā tukhrujī, lā tukhrujū
(d) qūl, qūlī, qūlū; lā tqūl, lā tqūlī, lā tqūlū
(e) jīb, jībī, jībū; lā tjīb, lā tjībī, lā tjībū
5. (a) 'ams kān youm al-jum9a. (b) ba9d bukra yikūn youm al-ithnayn. (c) na9am, fí 9indī/la', má fī 9indī shughl al-youm. (d) 'awwal 'ams kān youm al-khamīs. (e) fí sab9at 'ayyām fi l-'usbū9.
6. (a) ṭalabt minha 'innha tshūf kitābha.
(b) ṭalabt minnu 'innu yijīb al-fulūs ma9u.
(c) ṭalabt minnu 'innu yirūḥ 9a l-madrasa.
(d) ṭalabt minhum 'innhum yudkhulū 9indī.
(e) ṭalabt minhum 'innhum yirkabu t-taksī.
7. (a) as-sā9a 'arba9a u rub9 (b) as-sā9a sitta u nuṣṣ (c) as-sā9a 9ashra u 'arba9t9ashr daqīqa (d) as-sā9a ḥd9ashr u thulthayn (e) as-sā9a wāḥida u thamániya u thalāthīn daqīqa/as-sā9a wāḥida u nuṣṣ u thamániya daqāyiq
8. (a) mitayn (b) 'arba9at 'alāf u thalāth mīya u thamániya u thalāthīn (c) thalāth mīya u tis9a u sittīn u nuṣṣ (d)'arba9a malāyīn u nuṣṣ/'arba9a malāyīn u khams mīt 'alf (e) sabi9 mīya u thnayn u sab9īn
9. (a) ithn9ashr youm (b) 'usbū9ayn (c) sittat 'ashhur (d) 'arba9at 'imkānīyāt (e) khamsa u 'arba9īn thániya

Lesson 8

1. (a) bada yibda (b) shakk yishukk (c) 'aja yījī (d) nisī yinsa (e) ẓann yiẓunn
2. (a) dill, dillī, dillū; lā tdill, lā tdillī, lā tdillū
(b) 'ibqa, 'ibqī, 'ibqū; lā tibqa, lā tibqī, lā tibqū
(c) ta9āl, ta9ālī, ta9ālū; lā tījī, lā tījī, lā tījū

(d) ḥuṭṭ, ḥuṭṭī, ḥuṭṭū; lā tḥuṭṭ, lā tḥuṭṭī, lā tḥuṭṭū
(e) 'iḍḥak, 'iḍḥakī, 'iḍḥakū; lā tiḍḥak, lā tiḍḥakī, lā tiḍḥakū
3. (a) tinsa (b) yimurr (c) mā yījū (d) shū tinwū? (e) yibda yiqra
4. (a) niqdar nimshī ḥatta l-mafraq. (b) tiqdar tiḥkī 9arabī?
(c) yiqdarū yidillū lana ṭ-ṭarīq. (d) mā yiqdar yibda l-youm.
(e) 'aqdar 'asma9ak kwayyis.
5. (a) thāni, thā́niya (b) 'awwal, 'ūla (c) thāmin, thāmina (d) rābi9, rābi9a
6. (a) ta9raf al-mu9allim illī katab hādha t-taqrīr?
(b) fī́ thānī su'āl nisīt 'as'alu.
(c) 'ishraḥ lī l-mushkila llī kuntū tiḥkū ḥawlha.
(d) wayn al-milaff illī ḥaṭṭaytu 'amāmak yā 'akhū́ī?
(e) bā9ū bayt sakanū fī́ min 9ishrīn sana.

Lesson 9

1. (a) faḍḍal yifaḍḍil (b) waqqaf yiwaqqif (c) ḥabb yiḥibb (d) rabba yirabbī
(e) ṣaddaq yiṣaddiq
2. (a) baqara (b) tuffāḥa, ḥabbat tuffāḥ (c) balāṭa (d) mouza, ḥabbat mouz
(e) bayḍa
3. (a) 'aṭwal, al-'aṭwal (b) 'aḥsan, al-'aḥsan
(c) ḍarūrī 'akthar, ḍarūrī al-'akthar
(d) 'arkhaṣ, al-'arkhaṣ (e) muthaqqaf 'akthar, muthaqqaf al-'akthar
4. (a) huwa mu9allim dāyiman yishraḥ kwayyis.
(b) mā qidir yiwaqqif as-sayyāra llī kān yisūqha.
(c) kān yisūq sayyāra mā qidir yiwaqqifha.
(d) 9allamtu shī mish lāzim yinsā́ 'abadan.
(e) qarrarū mas'ala t-himmna kullna.
5. (a) al-kitāb al-'aṭwal (b) as-sayyāra l-'ajmal (c) ash-shajara l-9ulya
(d) al-'ab al-'akram (e) al-'umm al-'akram

Lesson 10

1. (a) bāyi9, mabī9 (b) mujaddid, mujaddad (c) muṣaddiq, muṣaddaq
(d) kātib, maktūb (e) mudabbir, mudabbar
2. (a) shāf yishūf (b) waqqaf yiwaqqif (c) ṭalab yuṭlub
(d) kawwan yikawwin (e) ḥaḍḍar yiḥaḍḍir
3. (a) qirā'a (b) tárbiya (c) taḥḍīr (d) dirāsa (e) ma9rifa
4. (a) daras yudrus (b) darras yidarris (c) kān yikūn (d) kawwan yikawwin
(e) dabbar yidabbir
5. (a) bi sabab al-'arqām al-mashkūk fīha
(b) musawwadāt muḥaḍḍara 'ams
(c) al-'umūr al-maktūb bi khuṣūṣha (d) min an-nās as-sākinīn huna
(e) li s-sikritayra l-mas'ūla 9an hādha sh-shughl
6 (a)'awwal kānūn ath-thānī/yanāyir, 'alf u tisi9 mīya u thamā́niya u tis9īn
(b) khamst9ashr ḥazīrān/yūniyū, 'alfayn u 9ashra
(c) khamsa u 9ishrīn tishrīn al-'awwal/'oktōbir, 'alf u thamān mīya u thamānīn
(d)'iḥd9ashr 'āb/'aghusṭus, 'alf u tisi9 mīya u sitta u tis9īn

(e) thalātha u 9ishrīn shubāṭ/fibrāyir, 'alf u tisi9 mīya u thamániya u sab9īn

Lesson 11

1. (possible answers:) (a) kān yurīd yiqābil kam mumaththil aṣ-ṣinā9a l-khafīfa.
(b) huwa mushrif qism al-'intāj.
(c) kānū yintijū qiṭa9 blāstikīya min sha'n al-kahraba wa l-muwāṣalāt.
(d) kān yintij min sha'n as-sūq ad-dākhilīya.
(e) mudīr al-mālīya kān mas'ūl 9an as-siyāsa l-mālīya.
2. (a) 'adhā9 yudhī9, 'idhā9a (b) jāwab yijāwib, jawāb
(c) kharaj yukhruj, khurūj (d) rabba yirabbī, tárbiya
3. (a) kawwan yikawwin (b) 'arsal yursil (c) waẓẓaf yiwaẓẓif
(d) 'afād yufīd (e) rikib yirkab
4. (a) mish musāfir bukra. (b) shāyifīn? (c) mish 9ārifīn
(d) jāyīn ma9na?
5. (a) law 9iriftu, kunt 'aqūl lak 'iyyá.
(b) idha huwa muwāfiq, khallí yisā9idna.
(c) law wiṣilū 'ams, kunt shuft-hum. (d) idha mish munāsib, 'akhbirnī.
(e) law mā kān munāsib, kunt 'akhbartak.
6. (a) 'arsalna laha yyāha. (b) qūl lahum iyyāha. (c) 9allamu yyāha.
(d) kunt 'urīd 'as'alu yyá. (e) 'uktubu min sha'nhum.
7. (a) mā dhakarū lana l-'akhbār al-jadīda.
(b) musāfirīn hassa? nshūfkum ba9dayn.
(c) fí talāmīdh yurīdū yiqābilūkum.
(d) mish fāhimīn laysh mā turīdū tishraḥū lana yyāha.
(e) hādhi hiya 'akbar mashākil illī lāzim inḥillha.

Lesson 12

1. (a) ḥaka yiḥkī (b) takhaṣṣaṣ yitkhaṣṣaṣ (c) 'awjab yūjib
(d) tadākhal yitdākhal (e) dakhal yudkhul
2. (a) ta'khīr (b) tawassu9 (c) tanāwul (d) wuṣūl (e) tawẓīf
3. (a) taqaddam, taqaddamī, taqaddamū; lā titqaddam, lā titqaddamī, lā titqaddamū
(b) 'a9ṭī, 'a9ṭī, 'a9ṭū; lā ta9ṭī, lā ta9ṭī, lā ta9ṭū
(c) ta9āl, ta9ālī, ta9ālū; lā tījī, lā tījī, lā tījū
(d) ta9āwan, ta9āwanī, ta9āwanū; lā tit9āwan, lā tit9āwanī, lā tit9āwanū
(e) kul, kulī, kulū; lā tākul, lā tākulī, lā tākulū
4. (a) 9aynu ḥamrā' (b) 9aynáy ḥumr (c) al-kitāb 'aḥmar
(d) al-kutub ḥamrā' (e) as-sayyāra ḥamrā'
5. (a) nitalfin lak al-youm. (b) yifarjīnī kitāb jadīd.
(c) yitalfizū kull al-'akhbār. (d) yitḥassan bi sur9a.
(e) mā yitmakkanū min 'injāzu.
6. (a) mumkin, 'imkānīya, yitmakkan, yumkin
(b) 9ilm, mu9allima, ma9lūm, ma9lūmāt, ta9allamat, ta9līmī, yi9allim, 9ulūm
(c) 9irif, ma9rifa, n9arrifu, ta9rīf, ma9rūfa

7. (a) mīn (b) shū (c) 9amma (d) mā (e) mīn

Lesson 13

1. (a) sā9ad yisā9id, musā9ada (b) kān yikūn, kawn
(c) ittákhadh yittákhidh, ittikhādh (d) 'ansha yunshī, 'inshā'
(e) waẓẓaf yiwaẓẓif, tawẓīf
2. (a) ṭab9an nishtárik fi l-mu'támar. (b) yinqāl 'innu marīḍ.
(c) ash-shurṭa tiḥtall al-bināya. (d) tiktáshif shī jadīd?
(e) titwassa9 'imkānīyat at-ta9āwun baynna u baynhum.
3. (a) yūṣilū fi l-layl, 'aftákir. (b) mā na9raf laysh.
(c) huwa kthīr yiḥtāj 'ila musā9adatna.
(d) mīn yuskun huna? (e) tifhamnī yā 'akhūī?
4. (a) munfáṣil (b) mursil (c) māshī (d) muḥtāj (e) muttáḥid
5. (a) idha huwa mish moujūd, 'attáṣil bi zamīlu.
(b) idha mā ndīr bālna, yikǘn fi nfijār shadīd.
(c) law kān yidīr bālu, mā́ kān fī mithl hādha l-infijār.
(d) law kānat al-'as9ār 'aqall, qidirna níshtarī 'akthar.
6. (a) 'ummha mara laṭīfa wa kbīra s-sinn.
(b) aṭ-ṭabība kān itḥāwil itsā9id al-marīḍa.
(c) ta9rafi l-mu9allimāt al-judud? (d) ittáṣalat fīnī 'ams.
(e) laysh mā tiḥtárimha ḥtirām 'akthar?
7. (a) at-ta9āwun (b) fahm (c) l-kitāba (d) al-intikhāb (e) tanẓīm
6. (a) bāb, 'abwāb, buwayb, bawwāb
(b) fataḥ, mafātīḥ, infátaḥat, iftitāḥ, yiftah
(c) 9idda, yin9add, 9adad (d) madd, mumtadd
(e) takallum, mutakallimīn, kalima

Lesson 14

1. (a) fāhim, mafhūm (b) mustawrid, mustawrad (c) muḥtāj, muḥtāj
(d) mursil, mursal (e) mustarīḥ, mustarāḥ
2. (a) fahm (b) istīrād (c) iḥtiyāj (d) 'irsāl (e) istirāḥa
3. (a) istaghnayt, istaghnū (b) inḥalalt, inḥallū (c) nisīt, nisū
(d) istajwabt, istajwabū (e) istaḥqaqt. istaḥaqqū
4. (a) mish lāzim yistashīrū mutakhaṣṣiṣ fī hal-mouḍū9.
(b) mish lāzim tista9mil 'ibāra mish kwayyisa,
(c) mish lāzim huwa dāyiman yikūn musta9idd yit9āwan.
(d) mish lāzim tistannānī khārij al-bayt. (e) mish lāzim yijaddidu 9ala ṭūl.
5. (a) yinqāl 'innu marīḍ. (b) tinḥall al-mushkila.
(c) tistabdil shī fi l-mākīna? (d) yinsū u mā yidfa9u l-ḥisāb.
6. (a) thintayn, istithnā'īya, thānawīya, ithnayn
(b) ta9līm, 9ulūm, 9ilmī, ma9lūm, nista9lim
(c) 9imil, yi9malū, isti9māl, mu9āmala

Lesson 15

1. (a) yista9mil (b) ista9malat (c) yajid (d) iḥtāj 'ila (e) yistaghnī 9an
2. (a) as-sufarā' qālū 'inn al-mushkila mu9aqqada.

(b) katabū risāla t-himmna jamī9na. (c) mā hiya l-mas'ala llī dhakarha? (d) rāḥ 'aktub al-jawāb al-'ān.
3. (a) qāl yiqūl I (b) intákhab yintákhib VIII (c) 'ansha yunshī IV (d) rabba yirabbī II (e) tafāham yitfāham VI
4. (a) li (b) 9ala (c) bayn, bayn (d) 9an/bi khuṣūṣ

Lesson 16

1. (a) bayt (b) thānawīya (c) muhimm (d) al-'athāth (e) li 'annī
2. (a) اهتمام ihtimām (b) التلال at-tilāl (c) ممثلين mumaththilīn (d) آلاتي 'ālātī (e) باللبن bi l-laban
3. (a) بنتي (b) المالية (c) للبيت (d) مهمتي (e) النيل
4. (d) أثبتت
5. (b) بأن
6. (a) بابني، لابني (b) بالتمثال، للتمثال (c) باللبناني، للبناني (d) باللون، للون (e) بأول، لأول
7. (a) ممنونين (b) البيوت (c) الأمهات (d) المهام (e) انابيب

Lesson 17

1. (a) az-zamīl (b) wuṣūl (c) ash-shurṭa (d) al-intikhābāt (e) tadākhal/tadākhul
2. (a) اللازمة al-lāzima (b) ملابس malābis (c) متظاهرين mutaẓāhirīn (d) خرجنا kharajna (e) النظري an-naẓarī
3. (b) اجزاء (c) مسؤول (d) بالطائرة (e) اللاجئ
4. (a) تمويل (b) مرتين (c) بالأمراض (d) النتيجة الإيجابية (e) المستوردات مهمة
5. (a) سؤال\مسألة su'āl/mas'ala (b) اتخاذ ittikhādh (c) طلب\مطلب ṭalab/maṭlab (d) احترام iḥtirām (e) استئجار isti'jār

Lesson 18

1. (a) ghurfa fāḍiya (b) al-bint aṣ-ṣughra (c) ba9īd 9an al-qáriya (d) 'idha kān huna (e) shakarūnī qalbīyan.
2. (a) بالمستشفى bi l-mustashfa (b) الأساتذة al-'asātidha (c) هذا هو الصديق hādha huwa ṣ-ṣadīq (d) مشى masha (e) اجوبة ايجابية 'ajwiba 'ījābīya
3. (a) استثنى istathnayna, istathna (b) استغنى istaghnayt, istaghna (c) اعطى 'a9ṭayt, 'a9ṭa (d) ربى rabbayt, rabba (e) مشى mashayna, masha
4. (a) جديدًا jadīd, jadīdan (b) عادةً 9āda, 9ādatan (c) مثلاً mathal, mathalan (d) خاصةً khāṣṣa, khāṣṣatan (e) رسميًا rasmī, rasmīyan

5. (a) اللغة العربية صعبة.
(b) في هذا البلد
(c) كنّا مسرورين جدًّا، شكرًا.
(d) دفعت اقلّ ممّا دفعنا اليوم.
(e) الأنباء الواردة من بغداد

6. (a) اسم الصّديق ism aṣ-ṣadīq
(b) تتكلّم سريعًا. tatakallam sarī9an. (c) أكبر منّي 'akbar minnī
(d) التّدخّل أشدّ ممّا كان قبلاً. at-tadakhkhul 'ashadd mimma kān qablan. (e) هو موظّف في الجمرك. huwa muwaẓẓaf fī l-jumruk.

Lesson 19

1. (a) ma'mūr min ma'mūrí l-qism al-mālīya (b) sharikatān kabīratān (c) ash-sharika mas'ūla 9an daf9 al-qisṭ. (d) mutakhaṣṣiṣ fī t-ta'mīn (e) fī madrasa btidā'īya
2. (a), (b) مع مفتشي الجمرك الرئيسيين (c) انتهاء العقد
(d) في السنة المقبلة (e) في البوليصتين الشاملتين
3. (a) وثيقتي wathīqatī (b) زملائي zumalā'ī
(c) تخفيف قسطه takhfīf qisṭihi
(d) شروطها المقبولة shurūṭuha l-maqbūla
(e) حسب بوليصته ḥasaba būlīṣatihi
4. (a) عندهم 9indahum (b) خلالها khilālaha (c) معي ma9ī
(d) بينهما baynahuma (e) لديّ ladayya
5. (a) الوكلاء المسؤولون (b) اجتماعات هامة (c) ممثلون مصريون
(d) البواليص المعقدة (e) وكالات اجنبية
6. (a) المخاطرة الأجنبية (b) الممثّل (c) زميلة جديدة
(d) الوثيقة الملحقة (e) العقد المؤرّخ امس

Lesson 20

1. (a) tasallamt risālatakum. (b) al-muwāṣalāt al-lāsilkīya (c) qad qara'na t-taqrīr. (d) 9ala matn ṭā'irat al-yawm (e) 'arsalnāhu bi l-barīd al-jawwī.
2. (a) وجّهوا لي رسالة طويلة مكتوب فيها جدول اسعارهم.
(b) الحكومة تقوم بتمديد شبكة الطرق الثانوية.
(c) ارسال البضائع بالحجم يكلفنا اقلّ ممّا يكلف بالوزن.
(d) تكون بوليصة الشحن على متن باخرة "كوبي مارو" من يوكوهاما.
(e) الوزارة تنشر جداول الصادرات عادةً في الجريدتين الرسميتين.
3. (a) أُنظُروا (b) زاروا (c) نأخذ (d) تقولون\ يقولون (e) دلّوا

4. (a) نبيع (b) يرسلون (c) تحطّون (d) أستجوب (e) نصير
5. (a) وصلوا (b) اخذت (c) اوجب على (d) شككنا في (e) استبدلنا
6. (a) ابتدأ يبتدئ، مبتدئ مبتدأ، ابتداء
(b) ارسل يرسل، مرسِل مرسَل، إرسال
(c) كان يكون، كائن -، كَوْن
(d) استورد يستورد، مستورِد مستورَد، استيراد
(e) سأل يسأل، سائل مسؤول، سؤال\مسألة
7. (a) فيد (b) نظر (c) مدّ (d) ورث (e) خوف (f) ورد (g) سأل
(h) زيد (j) أخذ (k) وفق

Lesson 21

1. (a) ’inna ḥall al-mushkila yaðhar lana ghayr mumkin.
(b) dumna muta’akkidīn min ḍarūrat at-tadakhkhul.
(c) hal turīd al-’idāra sti’nāf al-mufāwaḍāt?
(d) ’innana masrūrūn jiddan bi qtirāḥikum ḥawl muqābil ash-shughl al-’iḍāfī. (e) ’a mā tasallamt at-taqrīr? ’innana ’arsalnāhu qabla ’usbū9ayn.

2. (a) ما رأيك حول جدول الأبدال الجارية؟
(b) هل نظرتم جدول الرواتب للسنة المقبلة؟
(c) ان الشركة لا تريد تطبيق هذه الأرقام الجديدة.
(d) سيستغرق الإضراب وقتًا قصيرًا فقط لعدم تأييد النقابتين.
(e) اننا نعتبر طلب العمال غير مقبول.

3. (a) ‹shū ra’yak ḥawl jadwal al-’abdāl al-jāriya?›
(b) ‹shuftū jadwal ar-rawātib li s-sana l-muqbila?›
(c) ‹ash-sharika mā turīd taṭbīq hādhi l-’arqām al-jadīda.›
(d) ‹al-’iḍrāb rāḥyistaghriq waqt qaṣīr faqaṭ li 9adam ta’yīd an-niqābtayn.›
(e) ‹ni9tábir ṭalab al-9ummāl ghayr/mish maqbūl.›

4. (a) لا يتمكن منه. (b) لا يستقبله. (c) ما استقبلته.
(d) لا يهمنا كثيرًا. (e) زميله ليس مريضًا.

5.(a) لماذا هو غائب؟ (b) هل قمتم بإرسال الجواب؟ (c) ماذا نظرتم؟
(d) كانوا مأمورين في اي قسم؟ (e) لمن باعه؟

6. (a) قرأ المفتّشون الوثيقة بالتفصيل. (b) ذهب الممثّلون الى المؤتمر.
(c) قال ممثلو الشركة ان الاتفاقية مقبولة.
(d) يفهم الوزير تمامًا ان الوضع معقد.
(e) خرج المتظاهرون من المصنع ودخلوا الشارع الرئيسي.

7. (a) ان الممثلين ذهبوا الى المؤتمر.
(b) ان المفتشين قرأوا الوثيقة بالتفصيل.
(c) ان ممثلي الشركة قالوا ان الاتفاقية مقبولة.
(d) ان الوزير يفهم تمامًا ان الوضع معقد.
(e) ان المتظاهرين خرجوا من المصنع ودخلوا الشارع الرئيسي.

Lesson 22

1. (a) ḍananna 'annahu min aḍ-ḍarūrī 'an yastamirr al-baḥth.
(b) ihtamamt bi dirāsat al-wathīqa htimāman kāmilan.
(c) yaqūm qism al-handasa bi dirāsat al-'arqām.
(d) hal tastaṭī9 ash-sharika tajdīd tanḍīm 'aqsāmiha?
(e) yukhbiruna mumaththilí sharikat at-taswīq bi 'annaha lan tuwaẓẓif 'ayy mumaththil 'iḍāfī khilāl aṣ-ṣayf.

2 (a) يجوز للشركة استعمال جهاز حفر ثالث في حالة اكتشاف احتياطيات اضافية في القطاع للجنوبي.
(b) ان التسويق لا تجري بسهولة تحت تلك الظروف الفنية.
(c) يمكن ان يستغرق الحفر التجريبي وقتًا طويلاً.
(d) لقد حاولت البلدان المنتجة للنفط تخفيف انتاجها.
(e) يجوز لنا ان نستهلك اكثر مما استهلكناه في السنة الماضية.

3. (a) يجوز ان يكتبوا الجواب هذا الأسبوع.
(b) لا يستطيع ان يقول لي المبلغ.
(c) تريد الوكالة ان تقوم باستبدال ممثلها بالكويت.
(d) نفضل الا نتعاون في هذا الأمر.
(e) هل يمكننا ان نتكلم مع السلطات بخصوص الموضوع؟

4. (a) اننا مشغولون جدا صباحا.
(b) لا يمكنكم ان تجدوا مشاكل في مثل هذه المسائل.
(c) ما كانوا مستعدين ان يدفعوا المبالغ.
(d) لا تزال الحفرات التجريبية غير منتجة.
(e) ان الجوانب تحاول ان تتعاون.

5. (a) يطلبون منا اننا نتعاون.
(b) لماذا لا يريد ان يستفيد من هذه الفرصة؟
(c) تفضل الشركة ان تطبّق اجراءات اخرى.
(d) ماذا فهمت مما قال؟
(e) يجب عليك ان تعبر عن رأيك.

6.(a) هاتان\تانك (b) هؤلاء\أولئك
(c) مدير البنك هذا\مدير البنك ذلك (d), (e) هذا\ذلك

Lesson 23

1. (a) 'inna dirāsatana lā tazāl tajrī quduman wa sa nanshur an-natā'ij fi sh-shahr al-muqbil. (b) talqa l-lajna 'a9ḍā' al-ḥukūma ba9d al-buḥūth al-jāriya. (c) lā yabqa 'illa 9adad ṣaghīr min at-tafāṣīl yajib 'an nashraḥaha. (d) yas9a mudarā' al-bank 'ila 'an yanshurū taqrirahum qabla ra's as-sana. (e) 9alayna 'an nastaghnī 9an ta9āwun hādha l-ma'mūr.

2. (a) تسعى الحكومة الى تنظيم المؤتمر في اقرب وقت ممكن.
(b) تجري المفاوضات التي قامت بها الحكومتان جريًا غير مرضٍ.
(c) من الذي دعا المندوبين للاجتماع الاستثنائي؟

(d) ما هي المعلومات التي طلبتها الأمانة منا؟
(e) نسي اعضاء الوفد اهم شيء في برنامجهم.
3. (a) تنادي الحكومة مسؤولين يعرفون ماذا يحدث.
(b) يشترون مهما يحتاجون اليه.
(c) لا نتمكن من برهان على قوله.
(d) لا يزال هذا ادعاءً شديدًا ضد احزاب المعارضة.
(e) ينفون كل ما ندعي.
4. (a) لماذا لا ينشرون التقريرالذي حضره المتخصص؟
(b) هل تصدق ما ادعاه؟
(c) دعا المدير المشرف الذي كان ينتظر خارج المكتب.
(d) لا يمكن الاعتماد على من يقول مثل هذا.
(e) ما صار للبناية التي كان يسكن فيها؟
5. (a) جري (b) سعي (c) رضي (d) بقي (e) لقي

Lesson 24

1. (a) khamsa u 9ishrīn ṭāliban (b) mitayn dīnār
(c) min ’ajl ’arba9a mashārī9 hāmma (d) 9ashra rīyālāt (e) sitta sanawāt
(f) li muddat sittat ’asābī9 (g) thalāth mīya u khamsa u sittīn yawman
(h) bayna ’alf u ’alfayn dīnār (j) ’arba9a u tis9īn bi l-mīya min as-sukkān
(k) ba9da thamāniya u ’arba9īn sā9a
2. (a) المرة الثانية (b) الدرس السادس (c) الطلمبة الخامسة
(d) المناسبة الأولى (e) اليوم الثامن والعشرون
3. (a) ذات (b) ذي (c) ذات (d) ذوي (e) ذات

Lesson 25

1. (a) mā zilna nadrus al-mashrū9.
(b) ra’īs al-wafd lā yanwī ’an yusā9idana.
(c) istimrarna nusā9iduhu li ’anna qtirāḥahu kān mufīdan.
2. (a) اننا نعتبر هذا الاقتراح اشد تعقيدا.
(b) ان حل مشكلة التنمية تهم جميع الدول المحبة للسلام اهتماما اساسيا. (c) تبدأ الحكومة تدرس مشكلة زيادة المستوردات.
(d) لا بد من اعادة كتابة التقرير.
(e) كيف يمكن الحكومة العمل في هذه الظروف؟
3.(a) ‹na9tábir hādha l-iqtirāḥ mu9aqqad ’akthar.›
(b) ‹ḥill mushkilat at-tánmiya t-himm jamī9 ad-duwal al-muḥibba li s-salām ihtimām ’asāsī.›
(c) ‹al-ḥukūma tibda tudrus mushkilat ziyādat al-mustawradāt.›
(d) ‹lā budda min ’inna nuktub at-taqrīr marra thāniya/’ukhra.›
(e) ‹kayf al-ḥukūma tiqdar tishtághil fī hādhi ḍ-ḍurūf?›
4. (a) بدأوا يؤيدون اقتراحنا.

(b) يحاولون ان يضيفوا ارقام جديدة الى التقرير.

(c) يريدون ان يمولوا المشروع بمساعدة البنك.

(d) يبدأون يحفرون بئرا في ظروف صعبة جدا.

(e) يجب ان يؤيد القطاع الخاص الحكومة في سياستها الاقتصادية.

5. (a) نظر (b) كشف (c) ولي (d) حيّ\حيي (e) جيء

Lesson 26

1. (a) tamm iftitāḥ al-mufāwaḍāt 'ams.
(b) 'idha taḥassan aṭ-ṭaqs kān mufīdan li l-fallāḥīn.
(c) ḍurūf al-istithmār al-ḥālīya ghayr múrḍiya.
(d) mādha 9ulim min at-taqrīr?

2. (a) فلنشرح لهم المشاكل ان وجدت.
(b) لا يوجد شيء اجمل في العالم.
(c) اعلن ناطق بلسان الحكومة ان العقد قد قُدّم للمجلس.
(d) كانت مشكلة في الميزانية عندما أخبر الوزير بفشل المفاوضات التجارية الدولية.
(e) لا تدفع الشركة مبلغا اضافيا؛ انها تدفع على اساس اسعار ثابتة فقط.

3. (a) اذا جاء كان اسهل علينا.
(b) اذا رفضت الحكومة نطلب من المحكمة.
(c) اذا قلت له هذا فسيجاوب جوابا واضحا.
(d) ارسلنا لك الرسوم لو كانت عندنا.
(e) اذا عرفت اللغة العربية تستفيد اكثر من اقامتك.

4. (a) من الذي كان يتكلم عن هؤلاء الأشخاص؟
(b) ليس واضحا ما تنوي الحكومة ان تعمل في هذه الحالة.
(c) لا نستطيع ان نقرر اليوم؛ لننتظر حتى الأسبوع المقبل.
(d) لماذا لا تريد ان تقرأ الرسالة قبل ان نجاوب؟
(e) اظن انهم ليسوا حاضرين بعد الساعة الثالثة.

5. (a) lan 'adhhab 'ila l-mu'támar 'illa 'idha ji't ma9ī.
‹mish rāyiḥ 'ila l-mu'támar 'illa 'idha tījī ma9ī.›
(b) lam 'afham al-waḍ9 alládhī sharaḥahu lana.
‹mā fihimt al-waḍ9 illī sharaḥ lana yyā.›
(c) 'inna hādhihi l-mushkila ṣārat lana 'ashadd ta9qīdan.
‹hādhi l-mushkila ṣārat lana mu9aqqada 'akthar.›
(d) taṣil ghadan. ‹yūṣal bukra.›
(e) 'in as-sittāt kunna ḥāḍirāt ṭūl al-fatra kulliha.
‹as-sittāt kānū ḥāḍirīn/moujūdīn ṭūl al-fatra kullha.›

Index of words

References indicate the lesson/paragraph with the first or fullest explanation of the word or expression. Nouns and adjectives are shown as indicated in 6/13, and verbs as indicated in 11/12, 12/12 and 20/4 (but without the particle 'to'). Personal and family names are not listed.
The sign → refers you to another entry in the same index. A broken plural or irregular feminine form is referred to its singular form (m. sing. for adjectives), except where the two entries would be adjacent.

Arabic, Part I

The transcription symbols appear in the order *' a/ā b d ḍ dh f g gh h ḥ i/ī j k kh l m n o q r s ṣ sh t ṭ th u/ū v w y z ẓ/ḍ̄ 9*. The sign ~ repeats the headword (or that part of it preceding the hyphen -). Search also under *q* for regional forms *'* and *g*, under *j* for regional forms *g* and *zh*, and under *k* for regional form *ch*.
Words normally used with the article (e.g. *al-qāhira)* are shown with the article, but listed under their own initial symbol. Expressions consisting of a preposition + noun (e.g. *bi khuṣūṣ*) are shown with the preposition but listed under the noun.

'

'ab 'abā' father 6/3, 14, 15
'āb August 10/15
'ābā' → *'ab*
'abadan (n)ever 6/1, 2
'abḥār → *baḥr*
'abnā' → *'ibn*
'abrīl April 10/15
'abwāb → *bāb*
'abyaḍ bayḍā' bīḍ white 12/11; → *baḥr*
'adilla → *dalīl*
'adna → *sharq*
'ádwiya → *dawā'*
'aḍāf yuḍīf IV add, annex 11/6
'aḍḥa: 9īd al-~ see 10/15
'ādhār March 10/15
'adhā9 yudhī9 IV broadcast 11/6
'afād yufīd IV benefit 11/6, 15/1, 2
'afkār → *fikr*
'afrīq-ī African, *~iya* Africa 13/3
'aghlāṭ → *ghalaṭ*
'aghniyā' → *ghanī*
'aghrāḍ possessions 2/1; → *gharaḍ*
'aghusṭus August 10/15
'ahā! ah! 6/1
'ahālī → *'ahl*
'ahamm yihimm IV concern, be important to 11/6
'ahammīya importance 15/1
'ahl 'ahālī people 13/1; ~ *al-mudun* townspeople, ~ *al-qura* country people 13/3; *~an* welcome 1/1; *~an bīk* (etc.) welcome to you (etc.) 1/1, 3, 4, 2/2; *~an wa sahlan* welcome 2/1, 2
'áhwiya → *hawa*
'aḥabb yiḥibb IV love 15/1
'aḥad (some)one 9/16, 17; (m.) one of 13/1; *lā* ~ no one 9/1, 16; *(youm) al-~* Sunday 7/1, 14
'aḥmar ḥamrā' ḥumr red 12/1, 11
'aḥrār → *ḥurr*
'aḥsan better 4/1, 9/13
'aḥwāl → *ḥāl*
'aḥyā' → *ḥayy*
'aḥzāb → *ḥizb*
'aja yījī I come 8/9, 10
'ajadd newer 9/13

'ajānib ⟶ *'ajnabī*
'ajashsh jashshā' jushsh hoarse 12/11
min 'ajl for (the sake of) 15/1
'ajmal more beautiful, *mā ~u!* (etc.) how beautiful! 13/1, 2, 12
'ajnabī 'ajānib foreign(er) 8/1
'ajnās ⟶ *jins*
'ajsām ⟶ *jism*
'ajwiba ⟶ *jawāb*
'akal yākul I, *'akl* eat 3/7, 5/5, 9/1
'akbar bigger 9/13, 14
'ākil eating 10/5
'akl food 9/1, 11
'akram yukrim IV treat with deference 13/2
'akram: mā ~ak (etc.) how kind you are (etc.) 13/12
'akthar more 9/13, 14, 11/21, 12/11
'aktharīya majority 8/1
'akyas ⟶ *kīs*
'akh 'ikhwa/'ikhwān brother 6/1, 3, 14
'akhadh yākhudh I, *'akhdh* take 3/7, 5/2, 5, 13/6; ~ *bi 9ayn al-i9tibār* take into consideration 13/10
'akhaff weaker 9/13
'ākhar 'ukhra ~īn other 6/11, 12
'akhbar yukhbir IV *bi* inform of 11/6
'akhbār ⟶ *khabar*
'akhḍar khaḍrā' khuḍr green 12/11
'akhdh taking 10/11
'akhīr recent 6/12
'ākhir 'awākhir last 6/11, 12; ⟶ *kalima*
'akhkhar II delay 9/10
'akhmās ⟶ *khums*
'akhraj yukhrij IV publicise, expel 11/6
'akhṭiba ⟶ *khiṭāb*
'āla kātiba typewriter 5/3
'alf 'alāf/'ulūf thousand 7/10
'alla: ~ yisallimak (etc.) goodbye 2/1, 2; ~ *yiḥfaẓak* (etc.) God bless you, ~ *ya9fīk* (etc.) well done! 6/1, 2; ~ *yibārik fīk* (etc.) thank you 14/1, 2; *lā samaḥ* ~ God/Heaven forbid 15/10
'almániya Germany 1/2
'alqa yulqī IV deliver (speech) 11/6
'alsina ⟶ *lisān*
'alwān ⟶ *loun*
'amal 'āmal bi hope for 15/1
'amām in front of 2/7
'amān safety, safekeeping 14/1; *fī ~ illā, fī ~ al-karīm* goodbye 14/1, 2
'amar yu'mur I, *'amr* order 3/7, 5/4, 5
'amayrka America 1/2, 15/3
'amayrkī 'amayrkān American 1/1
'amīn 9āmm secretary-general 15/3
'amīr 'umarā' prince, emir 15/3
'āmir ordering 10/5
'amr 'umūr affair 4/3, 10/11; ~ *'awāmir* order 10/11
'amraḍ ⟶ *maraḍ*
'amrīkī American 15/3
'ams yesterday, *'awwal* ~ the day before yesterday 7/3
'amsā' ⟶ *masa*
'amtār ⟶ *mitr*
'amṭār ⟶ *maṭar*
'amthāl ⟶ *mathal*
'an see 15/1
al-'ān now 8/1, 2; *li ḥadd al-ān* until now 11/2
'ana I 1/1, 5
'anābīb ⟶ *'unbūb*
'anbā': tufīd al-~ it is reported 15/1, 2; ⟶ *naba'*
'anfus ⟶ *nafs*
'anhur ⟶ *nahār, nahr*
'anjaz yinjiz IV implement, accomplish 11/6
'anna that 15/1
'ansha yunshī IV construct, create 11/6
'antaj yintij IV produce 11/6
'anwā9 ⟶ *nou9*
'aqālīm ⟶ *'iqlīm*
'aqall less 9/13; *~īya* minority 10/3

'aylūl September 10/15
'ayna9am yes 4/1
'aywa yes 7/1
'ayy what, which 5/15; any/any- see 9/16; ~ *nou9 min* what kind of 5/15; ~ *shakhṣ* anyone, no one, ~ *shī* anything see 9/16; ~ *wāḥid* which one 5/15
'ayyām → *youm*
'azmān → *zamān, zaman*
'azraq zarqā' zurq blue 12/11
'azwāj → *zouj*
'az9aj yiz9ij IV disturb 11/6
'azhar → *zuhr*
'a9dād → *9adad*
'a9ḍā' → *9uḍw*
'a9jab yi9jib IV please 11/6
'a9la higher 9/13
'a9lan yi9lin IV announce 15/1
'a9ma 9amyā' 9umī blind 12/11
'a9mār → *9umr*
'a9nāb → *9inab*
'a9raj 9arjā' 9urj lame 12/11
'a9shār → *9ushr*
'a9ṭa ya9ṭī IV give to 11/6
'a9yād → *9īd*
'ibār → *'ibra*
'ibil camels 9/5
'ibn 'abnā' son 6/3
'ibra 'ibār needle, injection 12/3
'īd 'ayād hand, arm 12/3
'idāra administration 5/3
'iḍāf-a addition 11/10; ~*ī* additional 11/1, 11
'idha whether 5/16; if 9/1, 11/14
'idhā9a broadcasting 11/10
'iḥd-a (f.) one of, ~*āhum* one (f.) of them 13/1
'iḥd9ashr eleven 5/12
'iḥna we 1/5
'ījāb compulsion 11/10; ~*ī* positive 10/1; 11/11
'ijāza leave, holiday 10/15
'ijbārī compulsory 8/3
'ijrā' (administrative) measure 13/1
'ikrām deference; ~*an li* in honour of 13/1, 2
'ikhrāj expulsion 11/10
'ikhwa/'ikhwān → *'akh*
'ikhwāt → *'ukht*
'ila to, for 2/7, 8
'ilay- see 2/8
'ilaykum al-'ān (we bring) to you now 15/1, 2
'iliktrounī → *barīd*
'illa except 2/7, 8; to (an hour) 7/12; (+ negative) only 11/25
'ilqā' delivery (speech etc.) 11/10
'imāra principality, emirate 15/3
'īmayl e-mail 5/3
'imkānīya possibility 7/1
'imma ... 'aw either ... or 8/1
'imshī go 4/1
'ingiltra England, Britain 1/2
'inglīzī 'inglīz English, British 1/1
'inn that 3/1, 4/7, 8, 7/15; → *ka, ma9*
'inna see 15/9
'inshalla I hope 6/1, 2
'inshā' creation, composition 11/10
'int you (m.) 1/1
'intāj production 5/3, 11/10
'inti you (f.) 1/1, 5
'intū you (pl.) 1/5
'īqāf stoppage 11/10
'iqāma stay, residence 2/3
'iqlīm 'aqālīm region 13/3
'irād-a wish 11/10; ~*ī* intentional 11/11
'irhāb terrorism 15/3
'irsāl despatch 11/10
'ism 'asmā' name 1/1
'ismaḥ (etc.) *li* permit 1/1, 3, 4
'isrā'īl Israel 15/1; ~*ī* Israeli 13/1
'iṣrār insistence, persistence 11/10
'ishāra sign(al) 4/1
'īṭāl-ī Italian 1/9; ~*iya* Italy 1/2, 9
'iz9āj disturbance 11/10
'i9ṭā' donation 11/10
'oktōbir October 10/15
'ouḍa 'uwaḍ room 3/1; ~*t ḥammām* bathroom, ~*t noum* bedroom 3/3
'ouḍā9 → *waḍ9*

'oujā9 → *waja9*
'oulād children 6/3; → *walad*
'ouqāt → *waqt*
'ujra fare 2/3; rent 6/3
'ukkid it was confirmed 15/1
'ukhra → *ākhar*
'ukht 'ikhwāt sister 6/3, 14
'ūla → *'awwal*
'ulūf → *'alf*
al-'umam al-muttáḥida United Nations 15/3
'umarā' → *'amīr*
'umm ~ahāt mother 6/3, 14
'umūr affairs 4/3; → *'amr*
'unbūb 'anābīb pipe 11/1
'urdun: al-~ Jordan, ~*ī* Jordanian 1/1
'ūro euro 2/3
'urubb-a Europe 1/2, 9; ~*ī* European 1/9, 15/3; → *ittiḥād, sūq*
'usbū9 'asābī9 week 6/1
'usus → *'asās*
'ustādh 'asātidha professor 6/1
'utayl hotel 3/1
'utubīs bus 2/3
'uwaḍ → *'ouḍa*

a

allátī who, which, that 15/1

b

bāb 'abwāb door 3/1
bada yibda I begin 8/7, 8, 12
bādī beginning 10/5
badāyi9 → *biḍā9a*
badhla suit 14/3
baḥath yibḥath I, *baḥth* discuss 10/3
baḥr 'abḥār sea;
al-~ al-'abyaḍ al-mutawassiṭ Mediterranean Sea,
al-~ al-'aḥmar Red Sea 13/3
baḥrayn Bahrain 6/1
baḥth buḥūth discussion 5/3, 10/11
bal but rather 15/1
bāl: dār yidīr I ~*ak* (etc.) take care 12/1, 2
balad bilād town 3/1; ~*īya* town/village hall, municipality 13/1
balagh yiblagh I amount to 15/1
balāṭ tiles 9/5
banadūra tomatoes 9/1
banāt → *bint*
bank bunūk bank 1/2;
al-~ ad-duwalī World Bank 15/3
banṭaloun trousers 14/3
baqar cattle 9/5; ~*a* cow 9/6
bārak III *fī* bless 14/1, 2
barāmij → *barnāmaj*
barānīṭ → *burnayṭa*
barhan IQ *9ala, burhān* prove 12/12
barīd mail, ~ *'iliktrounī* e-mail 5/3
bārid cold 6/1
barlamān parliament 5/3
barnāmaj barāmij programme 12/1
barrāda refrigerator 6/3
bas only 2/1
basātīn → *bustān*
basīṭ busaṭā' simple 6/11; in poor supply 13/2
baṣ bus 2/3
baṭṭāl → *mish*
baṭṭānīya blanket 3/3
baṭn buṭūn stomach 12/3
bawwāb doorman 3/3
bayḍ eggs 9/5; ~*a* egg 9/6
bayḍā' → *'abyaḍ*
bāyi9 selling 10/5
bayn between, among 2/7, 8
bayrūt Beirut 6/1
bayt buyūt house 6/1
bay9 buyū9 sale 10/11
bā9 yibī9 I, *bay9* sell 6/4, 7/4
ba9d after 2/7, 6/18; ~ *mā* after 3/1, 6/18; ~ *bukra* the day after tomorrow 7/3;
~*ayn* afterwards 4/1;
~ *ishwayy* soon 11/21; → *ẓuhr*
ba9ḍ some 8/1, 17; each other 8/17
ba9īd 9an far from 4/1
bi with, in 2/7, 8;
~ *kam* (for) how much? 14/3
bí with it/him 2/8
bī- see 2/8
bid (*-di* etc.) want see 11/18

bidūn without 2/7
biḍā9a baḍāyi9 merchandise 14/1
bīḍ → *'abyaḍ*
bīk → *'ahlan*
bilād buldān country 6/11; → *balad*
bināya building 3/1
binnī/bunnī brown 12/11
bint banāt girl, daughter 6/3
biqī yibqa I remain 8/9
bīra beer 9/1
bissa bisas cat 9/8
blāstīkī plastic 11/1
blūza blouse 14/3
bouṣṭa post office 4/1
brīṭānī British 4/1
budda: lā ~ (min) there's no escaping 12/1, 2
buḥayra lake 13/3, 17
buḥūth → *baḥth*
bukra tomorrow 7/1; *ba9d* ~ the day after tomorrow 7/3
buldān → *bilād*
būlīs police 4/3
bunnī → *binni*
burhān 9ala proof of 12/12
burnayṭa barānīṭ hat 14/3
burtuqān oranges 9/5; *~a* orange 9/6
busaṭā' → *basīṭ*
bustān basātīn garden 6/3
buṭūn → *baṭn*
buwayb small door 13/17
buyū9 → *bay9*
būẓa/būẓa ice 9/3

d

da this see 6/19
dabbar II arrange 9/10
dafa9 yidfa9 I, *daf9* pay 3/6, 5/4
daf9 madfū9āt payment 10/11
dajāj chicken(s) 9/1, 5; *~a* chicken 9/6
dāk that see 6/19
dakākīn → *dukkān*
dakātira → *duktur*
dakhal yudkhul I, *dukhūl* enter 3/6, 5/4
dākhil inside 2/7; *~īya* Interior, Internal Affairs 4/3
dalīl 'adilla directory 7/3
dall yidill I direct, indicate 8/4, 5
dam blood 12/3
danānīr → *dīnār*
daqīqa daqāyiq minute 4/1, 7/12
dār yidīr I *bāl-* take care 12/1, 2
daraja degree, *~t ḥarāra* temperature 12/1
daras yudrus I, *dirāsa* study 4/1, 5/4
dārij colloquial 8/3
darras II instruct 9/10
dasātīr → *dustūr*
dawā' 'ádwiya medicine 12/1
dawla duwal state 5/3; ~ *kubra* superpower, ~ *nā́miya* developing country, ~ *ṣinā9īya* industrialised country 15/3; → *jāmi9a*
dāyiman always 6/1
di this see 6/19
dibloum diploma 8/3
diblumāsī diplomat(ic) 1/2
difā9 defence 4/3
ad-dijla Tigris 13/3
dīk that see 6/19
diktātūrīya dictatorship 13/11
dimashq Damascus 4/1
dīmuqrāṭīya democracy 13/11
dīnār danānīr dinar 2/3
dirāsa study 8/1, 10/11
disimbir December 10/15
di9āya advertising 10/1
ad-douḥa Doha 5/1
doul these see 6/19
doulār dollar 2/3
dukkān dakākīn shop 4/3
duktur dakātira doctor 1/1, 2/4
dukhūl entry 8/1, 10/11
dulāk those see 6/19
dunya world 13/3
dustūr dasātīr constitution 15/3
duwal → *dawla, jāmi9a*
duwalī international 5/3; → *bank, ṣandūq*

ḍ

ḍaḥak yiḍḥak I, *ḍaḥk* laugh 6/1
ḍarab yuḍrub I strike 7/3;
~ *'ibra* inject 12/3;
~ *tilifoun* telephone 7/3
ḍarība ḍarāyib tax 11/3
ḍarur-a necessity 11/1;
~*ī* necessary 5/1
ḍayf ḍuyūf guest 3/3
ḍa9īf ḍu9afā' weak 12/3
ḍidd against 2/7
ḍiffa ḍifaf bank, shore, coast 13/1
ḍuyūf ⟶ *ḍayf*
ḍu9afā' ⟶ *ḍa9īf*

dh

dhakar yudhkur I mention 9/1
dhakkar II *bi* remind 9/10
dhātī ⟶ *ḥukm*
dhū see 10/15
dhubāb flies 9/5; ~*a dhubbān* fly 9/6

f

fa so, then 4/1, 11/16
fāḍī fāḍiya fāḍīyīn empty, free
1/1, 10, 7/13, 10/5
faḍḍal II favour 9/10
min faḍlak (etc.) please 1/1, 3, 4, 13
faḥaṣ yifḥaṣ I, *faḥṣ* examine 12/1
faḥṣ examination 12/3
fākiha fawākih fruit 9/1
fakka small change 4/1
faks fax 5/3
fallāḥ peasant, farmer 13/3
fanājīn ⟶ *finjān*
fann funūn art 8/3; ~*ī* technical 5/1
faqaṭ only 2/1
faqīr fuqarā' poor 6/11
farans-a France 1/2, 9;
~*āwī* French 1/9
farja yifarjī IQ show 12/12
farsha bed 3/3
fasātīn ⟶ *fustān*
fāṣal III bargain 14/1
al-faṣīḥ literary Arabic 8/3
faṣl fuṣūl season 10/15
fataḥ yiftaḥ I open 3/6, 5/4
fatra fatarāt interval, period 7/13
fattash II *9an* look for 14/1
fāwaḍ III negotiate 15/1
fawākih ⟶ *fākiha*
fi ⟶ *fī*
fī in 2/1, 7, 8; on 10/15
fī́ there is/are 2/1, 11, 6/7, 7/7,
9/16; in him/it 2/8
fibrāyir February 10/15
fihim yifham I, *fahm* understand 11/1
fikra 'afkār idea, thought 5/1, 2;
9ala ~ by the way 6/1, 2
filasṭīn Palestine 1/2
filfil pepper 9/3
finjān fanājīn cup 9/3
fiṣiḥ: 9īd al-~ Easter 10/15
fīsh, mā ~ there is/are no 12/1, 17
fitr: 9īd al-~ see 10/15
fīziya physics 8/3
fouq above 2/7; up 3/1; upstairs 6/3
four boiling, ~*an* immediately 11/19
fulūs (pl.) money 2/3
funūn ⟶ *fann*
fuqarā' ⟶ *faqīr*
furaṣ ⟶ *furṣa*
al-furāt Euphrates 13/3
furṣa furaṣ occasion, opportunity,
~ *sa9īda* pleased to meet you
5/1, 2; ⟶ *intáhaz*
fustān fasātīn dress 14/1
fuṣḥa: al-lugha l-~ literary Arabic 8/3
fuṣūl ⟶ *faṣl*
fuṭūr breakfast 3/1

g

gārāj garage 6/3
gārsoun waiter 9/1
grām gram 14/3
gravāt necktie 14/3

gh

ghadhā' lunch 3/3
ghādar III leave 11/4
ghalaṭ 'aghlāṭ mistake 5/1; error 6/15
ghālī ghāliya ghālīyīn expensive
14/1
ghanī 'aghniyā' rich 6/11
gharaḍ 'aghrāḍ purpose 8/1;
al-~ *min* the purpose of 8/1, 2

gharb west, ~*ī* western 13/1
ghasīl washing 14/3;
  qābil li l-~ washable 14/1, 10
ghassal II wash 14/3
ghayba absence 6/1, 2
ghāyib absent 7/1
ghayr other, not, un- 7/1, 16, 10/7, 14/10; ~ *9ādī* extraordinary 10/3; ~ *mumkin* impossible, ~ *musta9mal* unused, disused, ~ *9arabī* non-Arab, *u ~u/ha* and so on 7/16
ghayyar II change 9/10
ghurfa ghuraf room 3/1; ~*t ḥammām* bathroom, ~*t noum* bedroom 3/3; ~*t tijāra* Chamber of Commerce 10/1

h

ha- this 6/9
hādī Pacific 13/3
hādha this 1/1, 4/1, 4, 5, 6/9, 19; ~ *wa* furthermore 15/1, 2
hadhāk that 4/4
hādhi this, these 4/1, 4, 5
hadhīk those 4/4
hadhoul these 4/4
hadhulāk those 4/4
halóu hello (on the telephone) 7/1
hamm yihimm I be important 8/4, 5
handasa geometry, engineering 8/3
hassa now 5/1
hawa 'áhwiya air 8/3, 13/3
hay here is/are 2/1, 4/10
hay'a organisation 15/3
hayāna (etc.) here we are (etc.) 4/1, 10
hayk so, therefore, thus 8/1
hiya she, it, they 1/5
hijrī see 10/15
al-hind India 1/2, 9; ~*ī hunūd* Indian 1/9, 13/3
huwa he, it 1/5
hum they 1/5
huna here 4/1
hunāk there 2/1
hunūd → *hind*

ḥ

ḥabb yiḥibb I like, love 8/4, 5, 12
ḥabb grains, seeds 9/5; ~*a ḥubūb* grain, seed, ~*at tīn* (etc.) see 9/7
ḥadath yaḥduth I happen 15/1
ḥadd ḥudūd limit 11/1; *li ~ al-ān* until now 11/2
ḥādith ḥawādith event 15/1
ḥaḍar yuḥḍur I attend 10/3
ḥaḍḍar II prepare 9/10
ḥāḍir present 7/13; ready, present, certainly 9/1; *fi l-waqt al-~* at present 10/2
ḥaḍirtak (etc.) you (etc.) 2/1, 2
ḥafaẓ yiḥfaẓ I keep 6/1, 2
ḥaka yiḥkī I speak 8/7, 8
ḥākī speaking 10/5
ḥāl 'aḥwāl condition 1/1; *kayf ~ak* (etc.,) how are you? (etc.) 1/1, 3, 4; *kayf al~* how are you? 5/2; *ḥusn al-~* good conditions, *sū' al-~* poor conditions 12/15; *9ala kull ~* in any case 11/1, 2
ḥāla case 8/1
ḥālhum (etc.) themselves (etc.) 13/1; see 13/14
ḥalīb milk 9/3
ḥall yiḥill I, *ḥill* solve 8/4, 5
ḥalq ḥulūq throat 12/1
ḥamd: (al-)~illa thank you, thank heavens 1/1, 3; *al-~ulilla* thank you, thank heavens 5/1
ḥammāl porter 3/1
ḥammām bath 3/3
ḥamrā' → *'aḥmar*
ḥaqīqa ḥaqāyiq truth, *fi l-~* in truth 11/20
ḥaql ḥuqūl field 8/1
ḥaraka movement 14/1
ḥarāra heat, fever; *darajat ~* temperature 12/1
ḥarb ḥurūb (f.) war 15/3
ḥārr hot 13/3
ḥāsis sensing 10/5
ḥass yiḥiss I feel 8/4, 5
ḥashara insect 9/8

ḥashd ḥushūd crowd 15/1
ḥatta until, as far as 2/7, 8; so that 5/1; until 8/1, 2; ~ *u law* even if 11/1, 15
ḥāṭiṭ putting 10/5
ḥaṭṭ yiḥuṭṭ I put 8/4, 5
ḥāwal III try 11/4
ḥāwar III dialogue with 11/4
ḥawālay- see 2/8
ḥawālī around, about 2/7, 8
ḥawl around, about 2/7
ḥaya ḥayawāt life 13/1
ḥayawān animal 9/8
ḥayawāt → *ḥaya*
ḥayy 'aḥyā' quarter (of town) 4/1
ḥazīrān June 10/15
ḥaẓẓ: li ḥusn al-~ fortunately 12/1, 2, 15; *li sū 'al-~* unfortunately 12/2, 15
ḥijja see 10/15
ḥikāya narrative 10/11
ḥill ḥulūl solution 9/1, 10/11
ḥilu, f. *ḥilwa* sweet 9/3
ḥilwa → *ḥilu, qahwa* see 9/4
ḥilwiyāt dessert, sweets 9/1
ḥisāb account 3/3; arithmetic 8/3
ḥiṣān ḥuṣun horse 9/8
ḥiwār dialogue 11/9
ḥizb 'aḥzāb (political) party 15/3
ḥubūb → *ḥabb*
ḥudūd → *ḥadd*
ḥukm dhātī autonomy 15/3
ḥukūma government 1/9; *muwaẓẓaf* ~ civil servant 1/2
ḥukūmi governmental 1/9
ḥulūl → *ḥill*
ḥulūq → *ḥalq*
ḥumr → *'aḥmar*
ḥuqūl → *ḥaql*
ḥurr 'aḥrār free, *~īya* freedom 13/11
ḥurūb → *ḥarb*
ḥusn good (noun) 12/2, 15; → *ḥaẓẓ*
ḥusna best 9/14
ḥuṣun → *ḥiṣān*
ḥushūd → *ḥashd*

i

i'támar VIII deliberate 13/6
i'timār deliberation 13/10
ibtáda VIII begin 13/6
ibtidā' beginning 13/1, 10; *~an min* with effect from 13/10; *~ī* primary 8/3; initial, primary 13/10
ibyaḍḍ IX blanch, go white 14/4
iḍṭárab VIII clash 13/7
iḍṭirāb commotion, riot 13/10
iftákar VIII think 13/6
iftátaḥ VIII inaugurate 13/6
iftitāḥ VIII inauguration 13/6; *~ī* inaugural 13/10
ihtamm VIII *bi/fī* be concerned by, look after 13/6
ihtimām concern, attention 13/10; *ghayr qābil li l~* unremarkable 14/10
iḥmarr IX go red, blush 14/4
iḥmirār going red 14/4
iḥtāj VIII *'ila* need 13/6
iḥtall VIII occupy 13/6
iḥtámal VIII tolerate, be probable 13/6
iḥtáram VIII respect 13/6
iḥtilāl occupation 13/10
iḥtimāl tolerance, probability 13/10
iḥtirām respect 13/10
iḥtiyāj need 13/10
ijtáhad VIII exert oneself 13/6
ijtáma9 VIII congregate 13/6
ijtihād zeal 13/10
ijtimā9 meeting 5/3, 13/10; *~ī* social 13/10
ikbīr → *kbīr*
iktáshaf VIII discover 13/6
ikthīr → *kthīr*
ikhḍarr IX go green 14/4
ikhtār VIII choose, select 14/1
ikhtiyārī optional 8/3
illī who, which, that 8/1, 13–15
imtadd VIII be extended 13/6
imtāz VIII be distinguished 13/6
imtidād extension 13/10
imtiḥān examination 8/1

imtiyāz distinction 13/10
inbásaṭ VII enjoy oneself, be pleased 13/4
inḍamm VII join, be annexed 13/4
inḍimām annexation 13/10
infájar VII explode 13/4
infáṣal VII be separated 13/4
infijār explosion 13/10
infiṣāl separation, ~*ī* separatist 13/10; ~*īya* separatism 13/11
inḥall VII be solved 13/4
inkásar VII be broken 13/4
inkátab VII be written 13/4
inláqa VII be encountered 13/4
inqāl VII be said 13/4
inqálab VII be overturned 13/4
inqásam VII be divided 13/4
inqilāb coup d'état 15/3
insáḥab VII (be) withdraw(n) 13/4
insiḥāb withdrawal 13/10
intáha VIII end 13/6
intáhaz VIII: ~ *furṣa* take an opportunity 13/2, 6
intákhab VIII (s)elect 13/6
intáqal VIII move away 13/6
intáðar/intáẓar VIII wait for 13/6
intáðir/intáẓir wait 4/1
intihā' end 13/10
intiðār/intiẓār wait, expectation 13/10
intikhāb election, ~*ī* electoral 13/10
intiqāl transfer 13/10
inzār VII be visited 13/4
in9add VII be counted 13/4
in9áqad VII be convened, assemble 13/4
in9iqād convening 13/10
iqtáraḥ VIII propose, suggest 13/6
iqtirāḥ proposal 13/10
iqtiṣād economy, ~*ī* economic 11/3
irtāḥ VIII rest 13/6
ista'dhan X ask permission 14/5
ista'jar X rent (as tenant) 14/5
ista'naf X resume 14/5
istabdal X exchange, substitute 14/5
istafād X *min* benefit from 14/5
istafham X *9an* enquire about 14/5
istaghfar X *min* apologise for 14/5
istaghna X *9an* do without 14/5
istaghrab X *min* be astonished at 14/5
istaghraq X last 14/5
istaḥaqq X deserve 14/5
istaḥḍar X summon 14/5
istaḥsan X consider good 14/5
istajāb X grant a request 14/5
istajwab X interrogate 14/5
istakbar X be arrogant, consider great 14/5
istakhdam X employ 14/5
istamarr X *fī/9ala* continue 14/5
istankar X reject 14/5
istanna yistanna X wait for 14/5
istaqall X be independent, consider small 14/5
istaqbal X receive 14/5
istarāḥ X rest 14/5
istashār X consult 14/5
istathmar X invest 14/5
istathna X except 14/5
istawrad X import 14/5
istawṣaf X consult (a doctor) 14/5
istawṭan X settle (in a place) 14/5
ista9add X be ready 14/5
ista9lam X *9an* enquire of 14/5
ista9mal X use 14/5
isti'jār tenancy 14/8
isti'nāf resumption 14/8
istibdāl substitution 11/1, 14/8
istighrāb astonishment 14/8
istiḥqāq merit 14/8
istijwāb interrogation 14/8
istikhdām employment 14/8
istimrār continuation 14/8
istinkār rejection 14/8
istiqbāl reception 3/1, 14/8
istiqlāl independence 14/8
istīrād importation 14/8
istirāḥa rest 14/8
istithmār investment 11/3, 14/8
istithnā' exception 14/8; ~*ī* exceptional 8/1

isti9dād readiness 14/8
isti9māl use 14/8
iswadd IX go black 14/4
iṣfarr IX go yellow 14/4
iṣṭána9 VIII manufacture 13/7
iṣṭinā9 manufacture,
~*ī* artificial 13/10
ishtághal VIII work 13/6
ishtára VIII buy 13/6
ishtárak VIII *fī* participate in 13/6
ishtirā' purchase 13/10
ishtirāk participation, ~*ī* socialist 13/10; ~*īya* socialism 13/11
ittáḥad VIII be united 13/6
ittáfaq VIII *9ala* agree on 13/6
ittákhadh VIII take 13/6
ittáṣal VIII *bi/fī* contact 13/6
ittifāq (spoken) agreement, ~*īya* (written) agreement 15/3
ittiḥād unity, union 13/10; *al-~ al-'urubbī* European Union, *al-~ as-sufiyāti/sufiyaytī* Soviet Union 15/3; ~*ī* federal 13/10; ~*īya* federalism 13/11
ittikhādh taking 13/10
ittiṣāl (telephone) call 7/3; contact 13/10
ithnayn two 4/11; *(youm) al-~* Monday 7/14
ithn9ashr twelve 5/12
iyyā- see 11/1, 17
izdād VIII be increased 13/7
izdáwaj VIII be double 13/7
izdiyād increase 13/10
izraqq IX go blue 14/4
i9tábar VIII consider 13/6
i9támad VIII *9ala* rely on 13/6
i9táqad VIII believe 13/6
i9tibār consideration 13/10; ~*an min* starting/with effect from 13/10; ⟶ *'akhadh*
i9timād confidence 8/16; accreditation, ~ *9ala* dependence on, confidence in 13/10; ⟶ *'awrāq*
i9tiqād belief 13/10
i9wajj IX become bent 14/4

j

jāb yijīb I bring 6/4, 7/4
jabal jibāl mountain 13/3
jabr algebra 8/3
jadāwil ⟶ *jadwal*
jaddad II renew, renovate 9/10
jadīd judud new 6/11; ~*an* recently 9/1, 11/19
jadwal jadāwil timetable 2/3; ~ *'a9māl* agenda 10/3
jāhil juhhal ignorant 8/3
jāī next (in time) 7/13
jākayt jacket 14/3
jalas yijlis I sit 8/1
jamal jimāl camel 9/8
jamārik ⟶ *jumruk*
jamb beside 2/7
jamīl beautiful 4/1
jamī9 all 8/19
jāmi9-a university 4/1; ~*at ad-duwal al-9arabīya* League of Arab States 15/3; ~*ī* university (adj.) 8/3
jānib jawānib side 15/1
janūb south, ~ *gharbī* southwest, ~ *sharqī* southeast 13/3
jara yijrī I flow, proceed 8/7, 8; see 15/6
jarāyid ⟶ *jarīda*
jārī jāriya jārīyīn current (adj.) 7/13, 10/5; flowing 9/1
jarīda jarāyid newspaper 11/1
jarrab II try 9/10
jarrāḥ surgeon 12/3
jashshā' ⟶ *'ajashsh*
jawāb 'ajwiba reply 5/1; answer 11/9
jāwab III answer 11/4
jawānib ⟶ *jānib*
jawāz, ~ *safar* passport 2/1
jawla tour 5/1, 2
al-jazāyir Algeria, Algiers 1/2
jazīlan: shukran ~ many thanks 1/1
jazīra juzur island 13/3; *shibih* ~ peninsula 13/3, 16
jibāl ⟶ *jabal*
jibna cheese 9/3

jiddan very 1/1
jimāl ⟶ *jamal*
jinayh pound (£) 2/3
jinayna garden 6/3
jins 'ajnās sort 14/1
jirāḥī surgical 12/3
jism 'ajsām body 12/3
jisr jusūr bridge 4/3
jou9ān jou9a jiyā9 hungry 9/3
judud ⟶ *jadīd*
jughrāfīya geography 8/3
juhhal ⟶ *jāhil*
jumāda see 10/15
jumhūrī republican,
~*ya* republic 15/3
jumruk jamārik customs 2/1
jum9a: (youm) al-~ Friday 7/14
jusūr ⟶ *jisr*
jushsh ⟶ *'ajashsh*
jūwa inside 6/1

k

ka as 6/1; ~ *'inn* as if 11/14
kabīr: 9īd al-~ Easter see 10/15
bi l-kād almost 11/20
kadha thus, so 2/1;
mish ~ isn't that so? 4/1
kaffa II suffice 14/1
kahraba electricity 8/1
kalb kilāb dog 9/8
kalima word 5/1;
'ākhir ~ your best price 14/1, 2
kallaf II cost 9/10
kalsa sock 14/3
kam how much/many, some 2/1, 9, 5/15; ~ *as-sā9a/as-sā9a* ~ what's the time? 7/12
kama as 5/1; ⟶ *yalī*
kamān also 1/1
kambyūtir computer 5/3
kāmil complete, perfect 12/1
kammīya quantity 14/3
kān yikūn I, *kawn* be 6/4, 6, 16, 7/4, 8, 8/12, 11/13; ~ *bid-* wanted 11/19; *kān fī* there was/were 6/7, 9/16; ~ *9āwiz* wanted 6/21; *kayf mā* ~ somehow or other 13/1, 2, 13; *mahma* ~ anything at all, *mata mā* ~ at some/any time, *mīn mā* ~ anybody at all, *wayn mā* ~ somewhere or other, 13/13; *yikūn fī* there will be 7/8
kanādir ⟶ *kundara*
kanīsa kanāyis church 4/3
kānūn: ~ (al-)'awwal December, ~ *(ath-)thānī* January 10/15
karāsī ⟶ *kursī*
karīm kuramā' generous 6/11
kās ku'ūs a glass 9/1
kaslān kasla lazy 8/3
kassar II shatter 9/10
katab yuktub I, *kitāba* write 3/6, 5/4
kātab III write to 11/4, 12/5
kātib writing 10/5;
~ *kuttāb,* ~*a* clerk 10/9; ⟶ *'āla*
kaththar II increase 13/1, 2
kawa yikwī I, *kawī* iron 14/3
kawī ironing 14/3
kawn existence 10/11
kawwan II constitute 9/10
kayf how 1/1; ~ *mā* as 11/15;
⟶ *ḥāl, kān*
kayfīya mode, manner 10/1
kbīr kbār big 3/1; ⟶ *sinn*
kilāb ⟶ *kalb*
kīlou kilogram 14/3
kīmiya chemistry 8/3
kīs 'akyās bag 2/1
kitāb kutub book 2/1
kitāba writing 8/3, 10/11
kthīr kthār much, many 3/1, 17; very 4/1, 2, 14
ku'ūs ⟶ *kās*
kubra biggest 9/14; ⟶ *dawla*
kul, ~ī, ~ū eat see 5/9
kulayb puppy 13/17
kull whole, all 5/1, 8/1, 18, 19;
9ala ~ *ḥāl* in any case 11/1, 2
kullīya faculty, college 8/3
kundura kanādir shoe 14/3
kuramā' ⟶ *karīm*
kursī karāsī chair 6/3
kutayyib booklet 13/17

kuttāb → *kātib*
kutub → *kitāb*
al-kuwayt Kuwait 1/2
kwayyis good 2/1; well 4/14, 11/20

kh

khabar 'akhbār news 6/1; message 7/1, 2
khaḍrā' → *'akhḍar*
khāf yikhāf I *(min), khouf* fear 6/4, 7/4, 12/2
khaffaf II reduce 14/3
khafīf khifāf light(weight) 6/11
khalīj khulūj gulf, *al-~ al-9arabī* Arabian Gulf 13/3
khalla II let (go), release 9/10, 11
khallaṣ II finish 9/10
khallī- let see 5/11, 8/12
khamīs: (youm) al-~ Thursday 7/14
khāmis fifth 8/20
khams mīya five hundred 7/10
khams-a five 4/1, 11; *~īn* fifty 5/12; *~t9ashr* fifteen 5/1, 12
kharaj yukhrij I *min, khurūj* come/go out 3/1, 6, 5/4
kharbān defective 7/1
kharīf autumn 10/15
khārij outside 2/7; *~īya* Foreign Affairs 4/3
kharūf khirāf sheep 9/8
khasāra khasāyir loss 11/3
khasāyir (pl.) damage 15/1
khasir yikhsar I, *khasāra* lose 11/3
khāṣṣ special, private 5/3
khāṣṣa khawāṣṣ particularity 11/19; *~tan* especially 11/1, 19
khāṭ yikhīṭ I, *khayṭ* sew 14/1
khaṭir dangerous 12/1
khaṭṭ khuṭūṭ line 7/1
khawāṣṣ → *khāṣṣa*
khāyif fearing 10/5
khayl horses 9/5
khayr khuyūr good (noun) 13/1; *masa/ṣabāḥ al-~* good evening/ morning 1/1, 3; *tiṣbiḥ* (etc.) *9ala ~* goodnight 9/1, 2; *wa 'int* (etc.) *bi ~* goodnight 9/1, 2; *yikaththir ~ak* (etc.) God bless you 13/2
khayṭ sewing 14/1
khayyāṭ tailor, *~a* dressmaker 8/23
khidm-a service 10/1; *qiṭā9 al-~āt* services sector 11/3
khifāf → *khafīf*
khilāl during 2/7; *fī ~* in the course of 15/1
khirāf → *kharūf*
khiṭāb 'akhṭiba speech 11/6
khiyāṭa sewing 8/1, 23
khouf fear 10/11; *~an min* for fear of 12/2; *~an 9ala* fearing for 12/1, 2
khubz bread 9/3
khuḍr → *'akhḍar*
khuḍra vegetables 9/1
khudh, ~ī, ~ū take see 5/9
khulūj → *khalīj*
khums 'akhmās a fifth 7/11
khurūj exit 10/11
bi khuṣūṣ concerning 2/7
khuṭūṭ → *khaṭṭ*
khuyūr → *khayr*

l

lā not 5/9, 15/1, 10; *~ 'aḥad* no one 9/1, 16; *~ budda* there's no escaping 12/1, 2; *law ~* if not, but for 11/14
la' no 1/1
labas yilbis I wear 14/3
lahja accent 4/1
laḥḥām welder, butcher 8/23
laḥm meat 9/3
lājī refugee 8/1
lajna lijān committee 5/3
lamma when 3/1, 5/15, 6/18
lāqa III find, encounter 11/4
laṭīf luṭafā' kind (adj.) 4/1
law if 11/1, 14–16; *~ lā* if not, but for 11/14; *~ samaḥt* (etc.) please 1/1, 4, 13; → *ḥatta*
layla layālī night 7/3
laysh why 5/15
lāzim necessary 5/1, 7/9; must 7/8
lazīz lizāz pleasant 6/11

li to, for 2/7, 8, 6/8; of 11/27; see 5/13;
~ *'ann* because 14/1, 9;
~ *mīn* whose 5/15
lībiya Libya 1/2
liḥa → *liḥya*
liḥām welding 8/3, 23
liḥya liḥa beard 6/15
lijān → *lajna*
lisān 'alsina (m./f.) tongue 12/1;
→ *nāṭiq*
lissa still, yet, (+ neg.) not yet 6/1
lizāz → *lazīz*
līra lira 2/3
līsta menu 9/1
loun 'alwān colour 14/1
lubnān Lebanon 1/2
lugha language 4/1, 8/3
luṭafā' → *laṭīf*

m

mā do/does/did/will not 3/9, 5/7, 6/5, 19, 12/17, 14/10; what 12/9;
~ *huwa/hiya* what 8/1, 15;
~ *fī shī* there's/it's nothing 4/1, 2;
→ *'ajmal, kān, yalī*
ma'kūl eaten 10/5
ma'mūr official (noun) 2/1; ordered 10/5
mabdū begun 10/5
mabī9 sold 10/5
mabrūk! congratulations! 14/1, 2
mabsūṭ well, pleased 1/1, 3
madākhil → *madkhal*
madāris → *madrasa*
madd yimudd I extend 8/4, 5
mādda mawādd material,
~ *'awwalīya* raw material,
~ *tijārīya* commodity 11/3
maddad II extend 14/10
madfū9āt → *daf9*
madīna mudun city 13/3
madkhal madākhil entrance 4/3
madrasa madāris school 7/1, 8/23
māḍī māḍiya māḍīyīn past 7/13
mafāriq → *mafraq*
mafātīḥ → *miftāḥ*
mafhūm understood 8/1
mafraq mafāriq crossroad 4/3, 8/23
maftūḥ open(ed) 3/3
al-maghrib Morocco 1/2
mahamma mahāmm task, assignment 7/1
mahma, ~ *kān* whatever 11/15;
~ *kān* anything at all 13/13
maḥākim → *maḥkama*
maḥall place 1/1; ~*āt* (pl.) department store 4/3
maḥaṭṭa station 8/23
maḥḍar ijtimā9 minutes (of meeting) 10/3
maḥkama maḥākim law-court 8/23
maḥkī spoken 10/5
maḥsūs sensed, tangible 10/5
maḥṭūṭ put 10/5
majāl baḥth terms of reference 10/3
majālis → *majlis*
majārīḥ → *majrūḥ*
majbūr forced 12/1
majlis majālis council,
~ *an-nuwwāb/ash-shuyūkh* lower/upper house of Parliament,
~ *al-wuzarā'* cabinet (of ministers) 15/3
majrūḥ majārīḥ injured 12/3
makātib → *maktab, maktaba*
makātīb → *maktūb*
mākīna: katab yuktub I *bi l-*~ type 5/1
maktab makātib office 4/3, 8/23
maktaba makātib library, bookshop 4/3, 8/23
maktūb written 5/1, 10/5;
~ *makātīb* letter 10/9
makhārij → *makhraj*
makhātīr → *mukhtār*
makhāzin → *makhzan*
makhlūṭ mixed 9/1
makhraj makhārij exit 4/3
makhūf feared 10/5
makhzan makhāzin warehouse 4/3
māl: shū ~*ak* (etc.) what's wrong with you (etc.) 12/1, 2; → *ra's*
malābis clothes 2/1, 14/3; → *taḥt*

ṃay miyāh water,
~ *ma9danī* mineral water 9/3
maydān mayādīn square (in town) 4/3
māyū May 10/15
māzza hors d'œuvres 9/1
maẓbūṭ correct 4/1; ⟶ *qahwa*
ma9 with 2/7; ~*an* together 11/19; ~ *as-salāma* goodbye 2/1, 2; ~ *'inn* although 11/15
ma9āhid ⟶ *ma9had*
ma9āmil ⟶ *ma9mal*
mā9alaysh no matter 4/1, 2
ma9ārif ⟶ *ma9rifa*
ma9danī mineral (adjective) 9/3
ma9had ma9āhid institute 8/1, 23
ma9īsha life 13/1
ma9lūm known, of course 8/1; ~*āt* (pl.) information 10/1, 9
ma9mal ma9āmil workshop, laboratory 8/23
ma9rifa ma9ārif knowledge, acquaintance 5/1, 10/10, 11
ma9rūf famous 4/1; known 10/5; *'i9mal* (etc.) ~ be so kind 9/1, 2
miftāḥ mafātīḥ key 3/1, 8/23
mikānīk mechanics 8/3
mīlād Christmas, ~*'ī, sana ~īya* AD 10/15
milaff file (of papers) 5/3
miliḥ salt 9/3
mimma than 9/13; from what 12/9
min from 1/1, 2/7, 8; since 3/15; than 9/13; ~ *'ajl* for (the sake of) 15/1; ~ *al-* see 6/17; ~ *faḍilkum* please 1/4; ~ *faḍlak* please 1/1, 3; ~ *faḍlik* please 1/1, 4; ~ *qarīb* recently 11/24; ~ *sha'n* for the sake of 6/1; ~ *zamān* for a long time now 6/2; (in fractions) see 7/11
mīn who, whose 5/15; *li* ~ whose 5/15; ~ *illī* who see 8/15; ~ *mā* whoever 11/15; ~ *mā kān* anyone at all 13/13
mīna mawānī port 13/3
minshafa manāshif towel 3/3, 8/23
minshār manāshīr saw 8/23
minṭaqa manāṭiq region, area 13/1
miqyās maqāyīs measure(ment) 8/23
miriḍ yimraḍ I be/fall ill 12/3
mismār masāmīr nail 8/23
miṣr Egypt 1/2, 9; ~*ī* Egyptian 1/9
mish not 4/1, 13, 6/19, 7/16, 10/7; ~ *baṭṭāl* not bad 1/1, 3; ~ *qalīl* quite a lot 12/2; ~ *kadha* isn't that so? 4/1
mīt ⟶ *mīya*
mitayn two hundred 7/1, 10
mitr 'amtār metre 4/1
mithl like 2/7, 8/22; as ... as 9/15; ~ *mā* as 8/22
mī-ya hundred 5/1; ~*t* hundred 5/12; *fi/bi l-~ya* percent 7/11
miyāh ⟶ *ṃay*
mīzānīya budget 5/3
mnīḥ mnāḥ good 6/11
mouḍū9 mawāḍī9 subject, *shaklan wa ~an* in form and content 11/19
moujūd present, available 5/1, 10/5
moulūd an-nabī the Prophet's birthday 10/15
mouqif: ~ *baṣ* bus stop 4/3; ~ *min* attitude towards 15/1
mousim mawāsim season 10/15
mouz bananas 9/5; ~*a* banana 9/6; *ḥabbat* ~ banana 9/7
mou9id mawā9id appointment 4/1
mu'allif writer 1/2
mu'támar conference 7/1, 13/9
mubahhar spicy 9/3
mubtádī beginner 13/9
mudad ⟶ *mudda*
mudarā' ⟶ *mudīr*
mudarris instructor 8/3, 10/9
mudda mudad period 5/1, 7/13
mudīr mudarā' director 1/2; manager 5/3
mudun: 'ahl al-~ townspeople 13/3; ⟶ *madīna*
muḍāf added 11/8
muḍīfa stewardess 1/1

muḍṭárib agitated 13/9
mudhakkira memorandum 10/1
mudhī9 (radio, TV) announcer 11/8
mufīd useful 11/8
mughādara departure 2/3
muhājara immigration 2/1
muhandis engineer 1/1
muhimm important 5/1, 11/8
muḥaḍḍar prepared 10/6
muḥaḍḍir preparing 10/6
muḥāmī lawyer 1/2
muḥammar roast(ed) 9/3
muḥarram see 10/15
muḥāsib accountant 1/2
muḥāwala attempt 11/9
muḥāwara dialogue 11/9
muḥibb; dawla/duwal ~a li s-salām peace-loving nation(s) ('state(s)') 15/2
muḥīṭ ocean 13/3
muḥmarr reddening 14/4
muḥtāj needy 13/9
muḥtall occupied, occupying 13/9
muḥtámal bearable, probable 13/9
muḥtáram respected 13/9
mūjab obligatory 11/8
mūjib obligating 11/8
mūjaz summary 15/1
mujtáhid industrious 6/1, 13/9
mukātaba correspondence 11/9
mukātib correspondent 11/8
mukawwan constituted 10/6; ~ *min* composed/consisting of 10/1
mukawwin constituting 10/6
mukayyifa (air)conditioner 6/3
mukhadda pillow 3/3
mukhtálif varied, various 8/1
mukhtār makhātīr mayor 13/1
mulāqā encounter 11/9
mulḥaq attaché 6/1
mulūk ⟶ *malik*
mumarriḍ orderly, ~*a* nurse 12/3
mumaththil representative 10/1
mumkin possible 7/1, 9; may, might, can 7/8
mumtadd extended 13/9
mumtāz excellent 5/1; excellent, distinguished 13/9
munāsib suitable 8/1, 11/8
munaẓẓama organisation, body 10/1
mundh since 2/7, 3/15
munfájir explosive 13/9
munfáṣil separate(d) 13/9
munḥall (being) solved 13/9
muntákhab elected 13/9
muntákhib elector 13/9
muntij productive 11/8
muqābala encounter 11/9
muqābil opposite, remuneration 11/8
muqaddam offered, presented 10/6
muqaddim offering, presenting 10/6
muqarrir reporter 10/9
muqātala fight 11/9
muqātil fighter, ~*a* fighter aircraft 11/8
muqbil next 7/13
mur, ~ī, ~ū order see 5/9
murabba jam 9/3; educated 10/6
murabbī educating 10/6; educator 10/9
murashshaḥ candidate 8/1
murḍī múrḍiya murḍīyīn satisfactory 13/1
mursal sent 11/8
mursil sender 11/8
murūr traffic 4/1, 10/11; *ma9 ~ az-zaman* with the passage of time 7/3
musāfir traveller 2/3, 11/8
musā9ada help 11/9
musā9id assistant 7/1, 11/8
musakkar closed 3/3
musakhkhan cooked in spices 9/1
musawwada draft 10/3
musta'jir tenant 14/7
mustaḥiqq deserving 14/7
mustaḥsan approved 14/7
mustajīb 'ila responsive to 14/7
mustakhdam employee 14/7
mustakhdim employer 14/7
mustamirr continuous 14/7
mustankar objectionable 14/7

mustaqbal future 14/7
mustaqbil (radio) receiver 14/7
mustaqill independent 14/7
mustarāḥ lavatory 14/7
mustarīḥ restful 14/7
mustashār counsellor 14/7
mustashfa hospital 4/3
mustathmir beneficiary 14/7
mustathna excepted 14/7
mustawrad import 11/1; imported 14/7
mustawrid importer 14/7
mustawṣaf clinic 14/7
mustawṭin native 14/7
musta9idd ready, prepared 8/1, 14/7
musta9mal used 7/1, 14/7
musta9mil user 14/7
muṣirr persistent, resolute 11/8
muṣṭána9 fabricated 13/9
mushkila mashākil problem 7/1
mushrif supervisor 11/1
mushtárak common, joint 13/9, 15/3
mushtarayāt (pl.) shopping 14/3
mushtárik participant 13/9
muta'akhkhir delayed, late 2/3, 12/7
muta'assif sorry 7/1, 12/7
mutabādal mutual, reciprocal 12/7
mutakallim speaker 12/7
mutakharrij graduate 8/3
mutakhaṣṣiṣ specialising, specialist 5/1, 12/7
mutanāwal available 12/7
mutanāwib alternating 12/7
mutaqaddim foremost 12/7
mutarjam translated 12/12
mutarjim translator 12/12
mutawallī in charge 12/7
mutawaqqa9 expected 12/7
mutawaqqif 9ala conditional/ dependent on 12/7
mutawassiṭ middle, medium (adj.) 8/1; → *baḥr*
mutaẓāhir demonstrator 12/7
muta9allim educated, apprentice 12/7
muta9alliq bi relevant/pertinent to 12/7
muttáḥid united 13/9, 15/3: → *'umam, wilāyāt*
muthaqqaf educated, cultured 8/3
muwāfaq 9ala agreed to 11/8
muwāfiq 9ala agreeing to 11/8
muwāṣalāt communications 11/1
muwaẓẓaf employee, clerk 3/1, 10/9; *shu'ūn al-~īn* personnel matters 5/3; ~ *ḥukūma* civil servant 1/2
muzdáwij double 13/9
muz9ij annoying, *~āt* discomforts 11/8
mu9allam taught 10/6
mu9allim, ~a teacher 1/2, 10/9; teaching 10/6
mu9āmala treatment 11/9, 12/15; → *sū'*
mu9āraḍa opposition 15/3
mu9ayyan certain, definite 10/1
mu9jab admirer 11/8
mu9jib admirable 11/8
mu9támad reliable, accredited 13/9
mu9táqad believed 13/9
mu9ṭa given, *~yāt* data 11/8
mu9ṭī donor 11/8

n

naba' 'anbā' news 15/1
nabī prophet 10/15
nāda III call 11/4
nafs 'anfus self 8/1; self, same 8/16
nahār 'anhur daytime 7/3, 13
nahr 'anhur river 13/3
najaḥ yinjaḥ I, *najāḥ* succeed 8/3, 12
najāḥ success 10/11
najjār carpenter 8/23
nām yinām I, *noum* sleep 6/4, 7/4
nāmiya → *dawla*
naqd → *ṣandūq*
nāqiṣ nuqqaṣ in short supply 14/3
naqqāsh painter 8/23
nār → *'aṭlaq*
nās people 2/1
nāsab III suit 11/4
nasama person (in statistics) 13/1
nashar yunshur I, *nashr* publish 11/1

nāshif dry 14/3
nashra bulletin 15/1
nāṭiq bi lisān spokesman 15/3
nawa yinwī I intend 8/7, 8, 12
nawwa9 II assort, vary 14/1
nazzal II take down 9/10
naẓarī: bi ṣūra ~ya theoretically 8/1, 11/22
naðīf nuðafā' clean 6/11
naððaf II *9ala n-nāshif* dry-clean 14/3
nāyib nuwwāb deputy, member of lower house of parliament 15/3
na9am yes 1/1
nbīdh wine 9/3
niḥna we 1/5
nijāra carpentry 8/3, 8/23
an-nīl Nile 13/3
niqābat 9ummāl trade union 11/3
niqāsha painting 8/23
nīsān April 10/15
nisī yinsa I forget 8/9, 12
niswān women 6/11
niṣf 'anṣāf half 7/11
nizil yinzil I, *nuzūl* get/go down 3/6, 5/4
noum sleep 10/11
nou9 'anwā9 kind (noun), *'ayy ~ min* what kind of 5/15
novimbir November 10/15
nuzūl descent 10/11
nuðafā' ⟶ *naðīf*
numra numar number 7/1
nuqqaṣ ⟶ *nāqiṣ*
nuskha nusakh copy 5/3
nuṣṣ half 7/1, 11; ~ *layl* midnight 7/3
nushkuralla thank God 1/1; thank you 1/3
nuwwāb ⟶ *majlis, nāyib*

q

qābal III meet 11/4
qābil li: ~ l-ghasīl washable 14/1, 10; *~ li t-tajdīd* renewable, *~ li t-tamdīd* extensible 14/10; *~ li l-i9timād* reliable 15/2; ⟶ *ihtimām*
qabl before 2/7, 6/18; ago 3/15; *~ mā* before 6/18; *~an* before(hand) 11/19
qad see 15/11
qaddam II offer, serve, present 9/10
qadīm qudamā' old 6/11
qaḍīya qaḍāya case, cause 15/3
al-qāhira Cairo 5/17
qahwa coffee 1/1; ~ *ḥilwa* very sweet, ~ *sāda* without sugar 9/3; ~ *maẓbūṭ(a)* medium sweet 9/3
qāl yiqūl I, *qawl* say 6/4, 7/4
qalb qulūb heart 12/3; *~īyan* cordially 9/1
qalīl little 9/13; *mish ~* quite a lot 12/2
qām yiqūm I *bi, qiyām* undertake 6/4, 7/4
qamar 'aqmār moon 13/3
qamīṣ qumṣān shirt 14/3
qammāsh draper, cloth merchant 14/1
qanānī ⟶ *qinnīna*
qanāṣil ⟶ *qunṣul*
qara yiqra I, *qirāya* read 8/7, 8
qarār resolution 10/3
qārī reading 10/5
qarīb: ~ min near to 4/1; *~an* soon 11/19; *min ~* recently, *9an ~* soon 11/23
qārra continent 13/3
qarrar II decide, report 9/10
qáriya qura village 13/1
qās yiqīs I measure 14/3
qaṣd see 12/15
qaṣīr qiṣār short 6/11
qaṣṣ yiquṣṣ I cut 14/1
qātal III fight 11/4
qawī 'aqwiyā' strong 9/13
qawl 'aqwāl saying, utterance 10/11
qa9da see 10/15
min qibal by, on the part of 13/15
qidir yiqdar I can, be able 8/1, 12
qinnīna qanānī bottle 9/3
qirāya reading 8/3, 10/5
qism 'aqsām division, department 5/1

qiṣār → *qaṣīr*
qitāl fight 11/9
qiṭa9 → *qiṭ9a*
qiṭā9 sector,
al~ al-khāṣṣ private sector,
al-~ al-9āmm public sector 5/3;
~ *al-khidmāt* services sector 11/3
qiṭ9a qiṭa9 part, component 11/1
qiyām bi undertaking 10/11
qmāsh 'aqmisha cloth 14/1
qudamā' → *qadīm*
quddām in front of 2/7
quduman ahead 9/1, 2
qulūb → *qalb*
qumṣān → *qamīṣ*
qunṣul qanāṣil consul,
~*īya* consulate 4/3
qura: 'ahl al-~ country people 13/3;
→ *qáriya*
qurṣ 'aqrāṣ tablet 12/1
qutil he was killed 15/1

r

ra'-ī 'arā' opinion 7/1; *shū ~yak* (etc.) what do you (etc.) think? 7/2
ra'īs ru'asā' chairman 10/3;
(~ *al-jumhūrīya)* president (of the republic) 15/3;
~ *al-wuzarā'* prime minister 15/3;
~*ī* principal, main 4/3
ra's ru'ūs head 12/3; ~ *as-sana* New Year 10/15; ~ *māl* capital 11/3;
~*mālīya* capitalism 13/11;
9ala ~ī certainly 4/1, 2
rabba II bring up, educate 9/10
rabiḥ yirbaḥ I *min* profit from 11/3
rabī9 spring (season) 10/15;
~ *al-'awwal/ath-thānī* see 10/15
rābi9 fourth 8/20
rádiyo radio 15/1
raghba raghabāt fī wish for 8/1
bi r-raghm min despite 2/7
rāḥ yirūḥ I go 6/4, 7/4
rāḥ- shall, will 10/14, 15/12
raja yarjū I request 8/7, 8
rajab see 10/15
rājī requesting 10/5
rajul rijāl man 6/3
rākib rukkāb passenger 2/3, 10/9
rama yirmī I throw 8/7, 8
ramādī grey 12/11
ramaḍān see 10/15
raml rimāl sand, ~*ī* sand (adj.) 13/3
raqm 'arqām figure, number 4/1, 8/21
rasab yursub I fail (in examination) 8/3
rasmī official 5/3; *bi ṣūra ~ya* officially 11/1; ~*yan* officially 11/19
rashḥ a cold 12/1
rāyiḥ going to, shall, will 10/14, 15/12
rayy irrigation 13/1
riyāḍa sport 8/3
riyāḍīyāt mathematics 8/3
riyāḥ → *rīḥ*
ribḥ 'arbāḥ profit 11/3
rīḥ riyāḥ (f.) wind 13/3
rijāl → *rajul*
riji9 yirja9 I return 5/4
rikib yirkab I mount, get into 3/6, 5/4
rimāl → *raml*
risāla letter 5/1
riyāl rial, riyal 2/3
rkhīṣ rkhāṣ cheap 6/11
ru'asā' → *ra'īs*
ru'ūs → *ra's*
rub9 'arbā9 a quarter 7/11
rujū9 return 10/11
rukkāb → *rākib*
rúsiya Russia 15/3
ruzz rice 9/1

s

sa shall, will 15/12
sa'al yis'al I *su'āl/mas'ala* enquire 3/7, 16, 5/4
bi sabab because of 2/7
sabbab II cause 15/1
sabbāk smelter, plumber 8/23
sābiq former 6/1
sabi9 mīya seven hundred 7/10
sābi9 seventh 8/20
sabt:(youm) as-~ Saturday 7/14

suḥub → *saḥāb*
sukkān: 9adad ~ population 13/2;
→ *sākin*
sukkar sugar 9/3
sukhn hot 9/3
sullam salālim staircase 6/3
sulṭa authority 15/3
sūq 'aswāq (f.) market 11/1;
as-~ al-'urubbīya l-mushtáraka Common Market 15/3
sū́riya Syria 1/2
sur9a speed, *bi* ~ fast 11/20
su9adā' → *sa9īd*

ṣ

ṣabāḥ: ~ al-khayr/an-nūr good morning 1/1, 3;
~an in the morning 11/19
ṣadar yuṣdur I be issued, appear 10/1
ṣaddaq II believe 9/10
ṣaddar II export 11/3
ṣadīq 'aṣdiqā' friend 6/11
ṣādirāt exports 11/3
ṣadr ṣudūr chest 12/3
ṣafar see 10/15
ṣaff ṣufūf (school) class 8/1
ṣafrā' → *'aṣfar*
ṣaghīr: 9īd aṣ-~ see 10/15
ṣahyūnī Zionist 15/3
ṣaḥāra → *ṣaḥra*
ṣāḥib 'aṣḥāb owner,
~ *bayt* landlord 6/3;
~ *al-9amal* employer 11/3
ṣaḥīḥ ṣiḥāḥ true 4/1; healthy 12/3
ṣaḥn ṣuḥūn plate 9/1
ṣaḥrā' ṣaḥāra/ṣaḥrāwāt desert 13/3
ṣāloun living-room 6/3
ṣanādīq → *ṣandūq*
ṣana9 yiṣna9 I manufacture 11/3
ṣandūq ṣanādīq box, trunk 2/3;
~ *an-naqd ad-duwalī* International Monetary Fund 15/3
ṣanna9 II industrialise 9/10
ṣan9/ṣun9 manufacture 10/1
ṣār yiṣīr I become 6/4, 7/4; begin to 9/12; → *yiṣir*; ~ *li* see 6/8
ṣawt 'aṣwāt voice, noise 7/1
ṣawwar II depict, photograph 9/10
ṣaydalīya pharmacy 12/1
ṣayf summer 6/1;
~ī summer (adj.) 14/1
ṣa9b ṣi9āb difficult 6/11
ṣghīr ṣghār small 2/1; → *sinn*
ṣifr zero 4/11
ṣiḥāḥ → *ṣaḥīḥ*
ṣiḥḥa health 4/3
aṣ-ṣīn China, *aṣ-~ ash-sha9bī* People's Republic of China 15/3
ṣinā9-a industry 4/3;
~ī industrial 15/3; → *dawla*
ṣi9āb → *ṣa9b*
ṣubḥ 'aṣbāḥ morning 7/3
ṣudūr → *ṣadr*
ṣufr → *'aṣfar*
ṣufūf → *ṣaff*
ṣughra smallest 9/14
ṣuḥufī journalist 1/2;
~ya journalist 3/13
ṣuḥūn → *ṣaḥn*
ṣun9 → *ṣan9*
ṣūra ṣuwar form, shape, picture 5/1; form, image, *bi* ~ ... in a ... manner 11/21

sh

sha'n shu'ūn matter 6/11; *min* ~ for the sake of 6/1
shabāb → *shābb*
shabābīk → *shubbāk*
shābb shabāb young man 13/1
shadīd 'ashiddā' severe 9/13;
~an severely, vigorously 11/19
shāf yishūf I see, look (at) 6/4, 7/4
shahāda certificate 8/1
shahr 'ashhur month 6/11
shāī tea 1/1
shajar trees 9/5; *~a* tree 9/6
shakar yushkur I *9ala* thank for 5/4
shākik doubting 10/5
shakk yishukk I *fī*, *shakk* doubt 8/4, 5
shakk shukūk doubt 10/11, 11/20;
bi lā ~ doubtless 11/20
shakl 'ashkāl form 11/19; pattern

14/3; *~an wa mouḍū9an* in form and content 11/19
shakhṣ 'ashkhāṣ person 4/1; someone see 9/16; *~ī* personal 2/1; *~īyan* personally 11/1, 19; *'ayy ~* anyone, no one see 9/16
ash-shām Damascus, Syria 6/1
shāmil comprehensive 10/1
shams shumūs (f.) sun 13/3
shanta (suit)case 2/1
shaqqa shiqaq apartment 6/3
sharaf honour 13/1, 2
sharaḥ yishraḥ I, *sharḥ* explain 5/4
sharāshif ⟶ *sharshaf*
sharika company, *mudīr ~* company director 1/2
shāri9 shawāri9 street 4/1
sharq east, *ash-~ al-'adna* Near East, *ash-~ al-'aqṣa* Far East, *ash-~ al-'awsaṭ* Middle East 13/3
sharraf II honour 9/10; *~tūna* see 9/1, 2
sharshaf sharāshif sheet 3/3
sharṭ shurūṭ (pre)condition 8/1
shatawī winter (adj.) 14/3
shāṭir shuṭṭār clever 6/1
shawāri9 ⟶ *shāri9*
shawwāl see 10/15
shāyif seeing 10/5; *~ ḥālu* (etc.) conceited see 13/4
shaykh shuyūkh old man, elder 13/1; senator 15/3
sha9bān see 10/15
sha9bī people's 15/3
shī 'ashyā' thing 4/1; something, nothing see 9/16; *kull ~* everything 6/1; *'ayy ~* anything, nothing see 9/16; *walā ~* nothing 9/1, 17; something 6/1
shibih 'ashbāh resemblance 13/16; *~ jazīra* peninsula 13/3, 16; *~ ḥukūmī* quasi-governmental, *~ qārra* subcontinent, *~ rasmī* semi-official 13/16
shidda vigour, severity, *bi ~* vigorously, severely 11/20
shimāl left 4/1; north, *~ gharbī* northwest, *~ sharqī* northeast 13/3
shiqaq ⟶ *shaqqa*
shirib yishrab I drink 8/1
shita 'áshtiya winter 10/15; snow 13/3
shloun see 8/24
shouka shuwak fork 9/3
shouraba soup 9/1
shū what 2/1, 5/15, 12/9; *~ mālak* (etc.) what's wrong with you (etc.)? 12/1, 2
shu'ūn: ~ al-muwaẓẓafīn personnel (matters) 5/3; ⟶ *sha'n*
shubāṭ February 10/1, 15
shubbāk shabābīk window 6/3
shughl 'ashghāl work 4/3
shukran thank you 1/1, 3
shukūk ⟶ *shakk*
shumūs ⟶ *shams*
shurṭ-a police, *~ī* policeman 4/3
shurūṭ ⟶ *sharṭ*
shuṭṭār ⟶ *shāṭir*
shuwak ⟶ *shouka*
shuyūkh ⟶ *majlis, shaykh*
shuyū9ī communist 15/3
shwayy a little 4/1; *ba9d i~* soon 11/23

t

ta'akhkhar V be delayed 12/4
ta'assaf V be sorry 12/4
ta'khīr delay 2/3, 10/12
tabādal VI exchange with each other 12/5
tabādul exchange 12/8
tabassam V smile 12/4
taba9 belonging to 12/1 see 12/16
tabrīd refrigeration 8/3
tadābīr ⟶ *tadbīr*
tadākhal VI *fī* interfere in 12/5
tadakhkhal V *fī* intervene in 12/4
tadakhkhul intervention 12/8
tadākhul interference 12/8
tadbīr tadābīr/tadbīrāt arrangement 10/12

tádfiya heating 6/3
tadrīb training 8/3
tadrīs instruction 8/3, 10/12
tadhākir ⟶ *tadhkara*
tadhakkar V remember 12/4
tadhkara tadhākir ticket 2/3; (medical) prescription 12/1
tafāhum mutual understanding 12/15
tafāṣīl ⟶ *tafṣīl*
tafalsaf IIQ philosophise 12/12
tafṣīl tafāṣīl detail, *bi t-~* in detail 11/20
taghyīr change 10/12
taḥassan V improve, get better 12/4
taḥassun improvement 12/1
taḥḍīr preparation 10/12; *~ī* preparatory 8/1, 11/11
taḥsīn improvement 10/1
taḥt under 2/7; downstairs 6/3; *malābis ~ānīya* underclothes 14/3
tajārib ⟶ *tajriba*
tajdīd renewal, renovation 10/12; *qābil li t-~* renewable 14/10
tājir tujjār businessman, trader 1/2
tajmī9 (act of) collecting 10/1
tajriba tajārib attempt, experiment 10/12
tajrībī experimental 11/11
takālīf ⟶ *taklīf*
takallam V speak 12/4
takātib VI write to each other 12/5
taklīf takālīf cost 10/12
taksī taxi 2/3
takwīn formation 10/12
takyīf conditioning 8/3
takhaṣṣaṣ V *fī* specialise in 12/4
takhaṣṣuṣ specialisation 8/1, 12/8
takhṭīṭ planning 5/1
talāmīdh ⟶ *tilmīdh*
talāqa VI come together, meet 12/5
talfan IQ telephone 12/12
talfaz IQ, *talfaza* televise 12/12
talfaza television 12/12
tamakkan V *min* be capable of, possess 12/4
tamām complete, perfect, perfection 6/1; *~an* completely 9/1, 11/19
tamāthīl ⟶ *timthāl*
tamdīd extension, *qābil li t-t~* extensible 14/10
tamm yitimm I be completed 8/4, 5; see 15/6
tammūz July 10/15
tamr dates (fruit) 9/1, 5; *~a tumūr* 9/6, *ḥabbat ~* date 9/7
tamwīl financing 10/1, 12
tamyīz discrimination, *~ 9unṣurī* racial discrimination 15/3
tanānīr ⟶ *tannūra*
tanāwab VI alternate 12/5
tanāwal VI reach for, take (food/drink) 12/5
tanāwul intake (food/drink) 12/1, 8
tanfīdh execution, fulfilment 11/1
tánmiya development 4/1
tannūra tanānīr skirt 14/3
tanẓīm organisation 5/1
taqaddam V progress 12/4
taqaddum advance, progress 12/1, 8; *~ī* progressive 12/8
taqārīr ⟶ *taqrīr*
taqāwīm ⟶ *taqwīm*
taqdīm offer(ing) 10/12
taqrīb approximation 11/19; *~an* approximately 2/1, 11/19
taqrīr taqārīr report 8/3, 10/12; *~ taqrīrāt* decision 10/12
taqwīm taqāwīm calendar 10/15
taraddad V hesitate 12/4
taraddud hesitation 12/8
tarājim ⟶ *tarjama*
tarak yutruk I leave 3/6, 5/4
tarashshaḥ V catch a cold 12/4
tarbawī educational 8/3
tárbiya education 4/3, 10/12; education, upbringing 8/3, 10/12
tārīkh tawārīkh history, date 8/3
tarjam IQ, *tarjama tarājim* translate 12/12
tarjama tarājim translation 12/12
tarwīj promotion 10/1
tasallam V receive 12/4

ṭ

ṭayyāra aeroplane 2/3
ṭayyib good 2/1
ṭāẓa fresh 9/3
ṭibākha cookery 8/1, 23
ṭibb medicine (medical science), ~*ī* medical 12/3
ṭifl 'aṭfāl child 13/1
ṭili9 yiṭla9 I, *ṭulū9* go up, rise 3/6, 5/4
ṭiwāl → *ṭawīl*
ṭoub bricks 9/5
ṭūl for the whole (duration) of 2/7; ~ *'aṭwāl* length, height 14/3; *9ala* ~ immediately 9/1
ṭūla longest 9/14
ṭullāb → *ṭālib*
ṭuruq → *ṭarīq*
ṭursh → *'aṭrash*

th

thābit firm, stable 14/1
thalaj yuthluj I snow 13/3
thalāth mīya three hundred 7/10
thalātha three 2/1, 4/11; *(youm) ath-~* Tuesday 7/14
thalāthīn thirty 5/1, 12
thalatt9ashr thirteen 5/12
thālith third 4/1, 8/20; → *9ālam*
thalj ice 9/3; ~ *thulūj* snow 13/3
thaman 'athmān cost 11/3
thamān mīya eight hundred 7/10
thamániya eight 4/11
thamānīn eighty 5/12
thamant9ashr eighteen 5/12
thāmin eighth 8/20
thānawī secondary 7/1
thānī second, other 8/20
thániya thawān a second 7/13
thaqāf-a culture 8/3; ~*ī* cultural 6/1
thaqīl thuqalā' heavy 6/11
thawān → *thániya*
thawra revolution 15/3
thintayn two 4/11
thulth 'athlāth a third 7/1, 11
thulūj → *thalj*
thumn 'athmān an eighth 7/11
thuqalā' → *thaqīl*

u

u and 1/1, 14, 5/12; while, when 6/1, 10; past (an hour) 7/12

v

vīza vīzayāt visa 2/3

w

wa and 1/1
wād widyān valley 13/3
wāḍiḥ clear 6/1; *bi ṣūra ~a* clearly 11/22
waḍ9 'ouḍā9 situation, position 8/1
wāfaq III *9ala* agree on/to 11/4
wāḥa oasis 13/3
wāḥid, ~a one 2/1, 4/11; *al-~* one (pronoun) 9/1, 16; *'ayy* ~ which one 5/15; anyone 9/16
wajad yūjid I find 3/8, 5/6, 9
waja9 'oujā9 pain 12/3
wājid finding 10/5
wakāla agency 4/3
wakīl wukalā' agent 4/3
wala shī nothing 9/1, 17
walad 'oulād child, boy 6/3
walākin but 3/1, 4/8
wālid parent 6/3
wallāhi Good Heavens 4/1, 2
waqqaf II (bring to a) stop 9/10
waqt 'ouqāt time 2/1, 7/13
wara behind 2/1, 7, 8
warad yūrid I come in, arrive 15/1
waraq foliage, paper 9/5; ~*a 'awrāq* (sheet of) paper 5/3
warsha workshop 11/1
wāsi9 wisā9 wide 9/13
wāṣil arriving 10/5
waṣṣal II convey 9/10
waṭan 'awṭān home country, ~*ī* national 5/3
wāṭi9 low 14/1
wathīqa wathā'iq document 10/3
wayn where 2/1, 5/15; ~ *mā* wherever 11/15; ~ *mā kān* somewhere or other 13/13
wazan yūzin I weigh 14/3
wazīr wuzarā' minister 4/3
wazn 'ouzān weight 12/3

wazzaf II recruit 9/10
widyān ⟶ *wād*
al-wilāyāt al-muttáḥida (li 'amayrka/l-'amrīkīya) United States (of America) 15/3
willa or 1/1
wisā9 ⟶ *wāsi9*
wiṣil yūṣal I, *wuṣūl* arrive 3/8, 5/6, 9
wizāra ministry 4/3
wujha direction, aspect 10/1
wujūd existence 12/15
wukalā' ⟶ *wakīl*
wuṣūl arrival 2/3, 10/11
wuzarā' ⟶ *majlis, ra'īs, wazīr*

y

yā see 1/1, 12
al-yābān Japan 1/2
yalī: kama ~ as follows, *mā* ~ what follows 12/9
yamīn right (not left) 4/1
yanāyir January 10/15
ya9fīk: 'alla ~ (etc.) see 6/1, 2
ya9nī that is to say 4/1, 2
ya9ṭīk (etc.) *al-9áfiya* see 6/1, 2
yikaththir khayrak (etc.) God bless you (etc.) 13/2
yisallim: ~ *9alayk* (etc.) he (etc.) sends his regards 6/2; ⟶ *'alla*
yiṣīr it is acceptable 7/1, 6
youm 'ayyām day 6/11, 7/13; *al-*~ today 1/1; ~ *al-'aḥad* Sunday 7/1, 14; ~ *al-'arba9a* Wednesday, ~ *al-ithnayn* Monday, ~ *al-jum9a* Friday, ~ *al-khamīs* Thursday, ~ *as-sabt* Saturday, ~ *ath-thalātha* Tuesday 7/14; ~*ī*, ~*īyan* daily 11/19
yūliū July 10/15
yumkin perhaps 7/1; may, might 7/8, 8/12; perhaps 7/9; see 9/15
yūniū June 10/15
yūro euro 2/3

z

zabūn zabāyin customer 14/3
zād yizīd I, *ziyāda* increase 6/4, 7/4
zāl: mā ~ *lā yazāl* I see 15/13
zalzal IQ, *zilzāl* shake 12/12
zamān/zaman 'azmān time 6/1, 7/13; *ma9 murūr az-*~ with the passage of time 7/3; *min* ~ for a long time now 6/2
zamīl zumalā' colleague 5/3
zār yizūr I, *ziyāra* visit 6/4, 7/4
zara9 yizra9 I, *zar9* farm, plant, cultivate 13/1
zarqā' ⟶ *'azraq*
zawwad II supply 14/3
zawwar II show round 9/10
zayy as, like 9/1, 2
ziyāda increase 10/11
ziyāra visit 2/1
zibda butter 9/3
zilzāl shock, earthquake 12/12
zirā9a agriculture 4/3
zouj 'azwāj husband 5/1; ~*a* wife 6/1
zumalā' ⟶ *zamīl*
zurq ⟶ *'azraq*

ẓ/ḏ̣

ẓabṭ accuracy, exactness 11/1; precision, *bi ẓ-*~ precisely 11/20
ẓahar yiẓhar I appear 5/4
ḏ̣ahr ḏ̣uhūr, ẓahr ẓuhūr back 12/3
ḏ̣all yiḏ̣all, ẓall yiẓall I remain 8/4, 5
ẓann yiẓunn I suppose 8/4, 5
ẓuhr 'aẓhār noon, midday, *ba9d aẓ-*~ afternoon 7/3

9

9a- to see 4/9
9abbar II *9an* express 15/1
9āda habit 11/19; ~*tan* usually 8/1, 11/19
9adad 'a9dād number 13/1; ~ *min* a number of 6/1; ~ *sukkān* population 13/1, 2
9adam lack of 12/1, 15
9ādī ordinary 10/3
9adīm lacking 12/15
9afwan don't mention it/you're welcome 1/1, 3; excuse me 4/1
9áfiya see 6/1, 2
9ala on 2/7, 8; up to see 4/9; ~ *fikra* by the way 6/1, 2; ~ *kull ḥāl* in any

case 11/1, 2; ~ *ra'sī* certainly 4/1, 2; ~ *ṭūl* immediately 9/1; ~ *9aynī* certainly 4/2; ~ *9ilm bi* aware of 7/1, 2; (in fractions) see 7/11
9ālaj III treat (medically) 12/3
9ālam 9awālīm world 13/3; *al-~ ath-thālith* third world 15/3
9alāqa relation(ship) 10/1
9aláy (etc.) see 2/8, 4/1
9ālī high 9/13; *ta9līm* ~ higher education 8/3
9allam II teach 9/10
9amal labour 4/3; *~ī* practical 8/1; *~īya* operation 12/3; *bi ṣūra ~īya* in practice 11/22
9āmal III treat 11/4
9āmil working 10/1
9āmil 9ummāl, ~a worker 10/9; (*~ tilifoun*) (telephone) operator 7/3; ~ *9awāmil* factor 10/9
9āmm general, public 5/1, 3; *bi ṣūra ~a* in general 5/2, 11/22
9amma from what 12/9
9ammān Amman 1/1
9amyā' → *'a9ma*
9an from 2/7, 8; ~ *qarīb* soon 11/24
9anāwīn → *9unwān*
9aqad ya9qid I, *9aqd* tie, hold 15/1
9aqqad II complicate 13/1
9arabī 9arab Arab 1/2; Arabian 13/3; Arab 15/3; *al-lugha l-~ya* Arabic (language) 8/3; → *jāmi9a*
9araq arrack 9/1
9arḍ 9urūḍ width 14/1, 2
9ārif knowing 10/5
9arjā' → *'a9raj*
9arraf II acquaint 9/10
9aṣfūr 9aṣāfīr bird 9/8
9āṣifa 9awāṣif storm, ~ *ramlīya* sandstorm 13/3
9āṣima 9awāṣim capital city 15/1
9aṣīr juice 9/3
9āsh yi9īsh I, *ma9īsha* live 13/1
9ashā' dinner 3/3
9āshir tenth 8/20
9ashra ten 4/1, 11
9aṭshān 9aṭsha 9iṭash thirsty 9/3
9awālim → *9ālam*
9awāṣif → *9āṣifa*
9awāṣim → *9āṣima*
9āwiz wanting 6/19
9ayād → *9īd*
9ayla 9iyāl family 6/3
9ayn 9uyūn eye 4/2, 12/3
9aẓīm 9uẓamā' huge, splendid 6/11
9īd 9ayād holiday 10/15
9idda (in indef. construct) a number of 5/1
9ilāj treatment, cure 12/1
9ilm 9ulūm science, *~ī* scientific 8/1; *9ala ~ bi* informed/aware of 7/1, 2
9imāra building, block 6/3
9imil yi9mal I, *9amal* do, make 5/4
9inab grapes 9/5; *~a 'a9nāb* grape 9/6; *ḥabbat* ~ grape 9/7
9ind at, in the presence of 2/7; with, in the possession of 2/12; at the time of 6/18
9indama when 15/1
al-9irāq Iraq 1/2
9irif ya9raf I, *ma9rifa* know 3/6, 5/4
9ishrīn twenty 5/1, 12
9iṭash → *9aṭshān*
9iyāda clinic, surgery 12/1, 3
9iyāl → *9ayla*
9uḍw 'a9ḍā' member 15/3
9ulūm → *9ilm*
9ulya highest 9/14
9umī → *'a9ma*
9ummāl → *9āmil*
9umr 'a9mār age, life 12/14
9unṣurī: ~ya racism, racialism, *tamyīz* ~ racial discrimination 15/3
9unwān 9anāwīn address 3/1
9urj → *'a9raj*
9urūḍ → *9arḍ*
9ushr 'a9shār/9ushūr a tenth 7/11
9uẓamā' → *9aẓīm*
9uyūn → *9ayn*

English, Parts I and II

The following are not listed here, and can be found through the Contents or the Grammar Index: days, demonstratives, months, numbers, personal pronouns, possessives. The sign ~ repeats the headword (or that part of it preceding the hyphen -); the sign ≈ repeats the headword but with a capital initial letter.

A

able: be ~ *qidir yiqdar* I 8/1, 12; استطاع *istaṭā9a* X 22/5

-able *qābil li* 14/10; see 13/5

abound وفر يفر *wafara yafiru* I 24/2

about *ḥawālī, ḥawl, 9an* 2/7

above *fouq* 2/7

absen-ce *ghayba* 6/1; ~t *ghāyib* 7/1

Abu Dhabi ابو ظبي *'abū ḍabī* 23/1

abundantly *jazīlan* 1/1

academic دراسي *dirāsī* 24/1

accent *lahja* 4/1

accept تقبّل *taqabbala* V 24/2; ~able مقبول *maqbūl* 19/1; it is ~able *yiṣīr* 7/6; ~ance *'akhdh* 10/11, قبول *qabūl* 24/1

access to حصول على *ḥuṣūl 9ala* 20/1

according to حسب *ḥasaba* 19/1

account *ḥisāb* 3/3; ~ant *muḥāsib* 1/2; ~s محاسبات *muḥāsabāt* 24/1

accreditation *i9timād* 13/10

accredited *mu9támad* 13/9

accuracy *ẓabṭ* 11/1

acquaint *9arraf* II 9/10; get ~ed with *ta9arraf* V *bi* 12/4; ~ance *ma9rifa* 5/1, *ta9arruf* 12/8

acquire تلقّى *talaqqa* V 23/9, 12

acquisition (تلقٍّ (التلقّي *talaqqin (at-talaqqī)* 23/12

action فعل افعال *fi9l 'af9āl* 18/4

actual فعلي *fi9lī* 26/1

AD *mīlādī* 10/15

add *'aḍāf yuḍīf* IV 11/6; ~ed *muḍāf* 11/8; ~itional *'iḍāfī* 11/1, 11

address *9unwān 9anāwīn* 3/1

administrat-ion *'idāra* 5/3; ~ive اداري *'idārī* 24/1

admir-able *mu9jib*, ~er *mu9jab* 11/8

advance *taqaddam* V 12/4; تقدّم ب *taqaddam* V *bi* 25/6; ~d *mutaqaddim* 12/7

advertising *di9āya* 10/1

aeroplane *ṭayyāra* 2/3; طائرة *ṭā'ira* 17/10

affair *'amr 'umūr* 4/3, 10/11

affect (have an effect on) *'aththar* II *9ala* 9/10

aforementioned مذكور *madhkūr* 24/1

Africa *'afrīqiya*, ~n *'afrīqī* 13/3

after *ba9d* 2/7, 6/18; *ba9d mā* 3/1, 6/18; بعد انْ *ba9da 'an* 25/4; ~noon *ba9d aẓ-ẓuhr* 7/3; ~wards *ba9dayn* 4/1; Good ~noon *masa l-khayr/n-nūr* 1/1, 3

again: do ~ عاد يعود *9āda ya9ūdu* I 25/2; ~st *ḍidd* 2/7

age *9umr 'a9mār* 12/14

agency *wakāla* 4/3

agenda *jadwal 'a9māl* 10/3

agent *wakīl wukalā'* 4/3

agitated *muḍṭárib* 13/9

ago *qabl* 3/15

agree: ~ to *wāfaq* III *9ala* 11/4, *ittáfaq* VIII *9ala* 13/6; ~d to *muwāfaq 9ala*, ~ing to *muwāfiq 9ala* 11/8; ~ment (spoken) *ittifāq*, (written) *ittifāqīya* 15/3

agriculture *zirā9a* 4/3

AH (Anno hegiræ) *hijrī* 10/15

ah! *'ahā!* 6/1

ahead *quduman* 9/1, 2

air *hawa 'áhwiya* 13/3, (adj.) جوّي *jawwī*, ~line خطّ جوّي *khaṭṭ jawwī* 20/2; ~ conditioner

mukayyifa 6/3; ~ conditioning takyīf al-hawa 8/3; ~ waybill بوليصة شحن būlīṣat shaḥn 20/2
airport maṭār 2/3, 8/23
algebra jabr 8/3
Alg-eria, ~iers al-jazāyir 1/2
all kull 8/1, 18, jamī9 8/19; ~ right ma9alaysh 4/1
alleg-ation ادّعاء iddi9ā', ~e ادّعى iddá9a' VIII 23/1, 9
allowance بدل ابدال badal 'abdāl 21/2
almost bi l-kād 11/21; ~ to (do) كاد يكاد kāda yakādu I 25/2
alphabet ابجد 'abjad 24/11
also kamān 1/1, 'ayḍan 3/1
alternat-e tanāwab VI 12/5; ~ing mutanāwib 12/7
always dāyiman 6/1
ambassador safīr sufarā' 4/3
America 'amayrka 1/2; ~n 'amayrkī 'amayrkān 1/1, امريكي 'amrīkī 23/1
Amman 9ammān 1/1
among bayn 2/7
amount مبلغ مبالغ mablagh mabāligh 18/1; ~ to balagh yiblagh I 15/1
and wa 1/1, u 1/1, 14; ~ so on u ghayru 7/16, وكذا و كذا wa/u kadha u kadha 24/1
animal ḥayawān 9/8
annex 'aḍāf yuḍīf IV 11/6; ملحق mulḥaq 19/1; be ~ed to inḍamm VII 13/4; ~ation inḍimām 13/10; ~ed ملحق mulḥaq 19/1
announce 'a9lan yi9lin IV 15/1; ~ment اعلان 'i9lān 24/1; ~r mudhī9 11/8
annoying muz9ij 11/8
annual sanawī, ~ly sanawīyan 11/19
answer jawāb 'ajwiba 11/9
any 'ayy 5/15; ~one at all mīn mā kān 13/13; ~one 'ayy wāḥid/ shakhṣ, ~thing 'ayy shī 9/16; ~thing at all mahma kān 13/13; ~ way one can kayf mā kān 13/2, 13; at ~ time mata mā kān 13/13; in ~ case 9ala kull ḥāl 11/1
apartment shaqqa 6/3
apologise for istaghfar X min 14/5
appear (seem) ẓahar yiẓhar I 5/4 (be issued) ṣadar yuṣdur I 10/1
apple tuffāḥa 9/1, 6, ḥabbat tuffāḥ 9/7; ~s tuffāḥ 9/5
appl-ication تطبيق taṭbīq, ~y طبّق ṭabbaqa II 21/1
appoint ولّى walla II, be ~ed تولّى tawalla V 25/7; ~ment mou9id mawā9id 4/1
apprentice muta9allim 12/7
appropriate munāsib 8/1
approve رضي يرضى ب ráḍiya yarḍa I bi 23/7; ~d mustaḥsan 14/7
approxim-ately taqrīban 2/1, 11/19; ~ation taqrīb 11/19
Arab 9arabī 9arab 1/2; ~ic al-(lugha l-)9arabīya 8/3; ~ian Gulf al-khalīj al-9arabī 13/3; ~ian Pen-insula al-jazīra/shibih al-jazīra l-9arabīya 13/3, 16
area (region) minṭaqa manāṭiq 13/1
arithmetic ḥisāb 8/3
arm 'īd 'ayād (f.) 12/3
around ḥawl, ḥawālī 2/7
arrack 9araq 9/1
arrange dabbar II 9/10; ~ment tadbīr tadābīr/tadbīrāt 10/12
arriv-al wuṣūl 2/3, 10/11; ~e waṣal yūṣal I, wuṣūl 3/8, 5/6; warad yūrid I 15/1; ~ing wāṣil 10/5; ~ing from قادمًا من qādiman min 23/1
arrogant: be~ istakbar X 14/5
art fann funūn 8/3
article (press) maqāla 11/1
artificial iṣṭinā'ī 13/10
as kama 5/1, ka 6/1, mithl mā 8/22, 9/15; ~ far as ḥatta 2/7; ~ if ka 'inn 11/14; ~ if/though كأنّ ka 'anna 21/8; ~long as طالما ṭālamā 25/4;

~ follows *kama yalī* 12/9
as ... as see 9/15
Asia *'āsiya*, ~n *'āsiyawī* 13/3;
~ Minor آسيا الصغرى *'āsiya ṣ-ṣughra* 22/8
ask (request) *ṭalab yuṭlub* I, *ṭalab/maṭlab maṭālib* 3/6, 16, 5/4; (enquire) *sa'al yis'al* I, *su'āl 'as'ila/mas'ala masā'il* 3/7, 16, 4/6, 5/4; ~ing *sāyil* 10/5; ~ permission *ista'dhan* X 14/5
aspect *wujha* 10/1
assemble *ijtáma9* VIII 13/6; *in9áqad* VII13/4
assignment *mahamma mahāmm* 7/1
assistant *musā9id* 7/1, 11/8
assort *nawwa9* II 14/1
assumption of office تولٍّ (التولّي) *tawallin (at-tawallī)* 25/9
astonish: be ~ed at *istaghrab* X *min* 14/5; ~ment *istighrāb* 14/8
at *9ind* 2/7; ~ all *'abadan* 6/1, 2
Atlantic Ocean *al-muḥīṭ al-'aṭlasī* 13/3
attaché *mulḥaq* 6/1
attempt *tajriba tajārib* 10/12; *muḥāwala* 11/9
attend *ḥaḍar yuḥḍur* I 10/3
attention *ihtimām* 13/10; pay ~ *dār yidīr* I *bālak* (etc.) 12/1, 2
attitude towards *mouqif min* 15/1
authority *sulṭa* 15/3
autonomy *ḥukm dhātī* 15/3
autumn *kharīf* 10/15
available *mutanāwal* 12/7
await *tawaqqa9* V 12/4
aware of *9ala 9ilm bi* 7/1

B

back *ẓahr ẓuhūr, ḍahr ḍuhūr* 12/3
bad: ~ luck *sū' al-ḥaẓẓ* 12/15; not ~ *mish baṭṭāl* 1/1
bag *kīs 'akyās* 2/1
Bahrain *baḥrayn* 6/1
balance توازن *tawāzun*, be ~d توازن *tawāzana* VI 26/1
banana *mouza* 9/5, *ḥabbat mouz* 9/8; ~s *mouz* 9/5
bank (financial) *bank bunūk* 1/2; (shore) *ḍiffa ḍifāf* 13/1; → World; ~ruptcy افلاس *'iflās*, be/go ~rupt افلس *'aflasa* IV 26/1
bargain *fāṣal* III 14/1
barrel برميل براميل *barmīl barāmīl* 22/2
basi-c *'asāsī* 8/1, ~cally *bi l-'asās* 10/1, 2; ~s *'asās 'usus* 8/1
bath *ḥammām*, ~room *'ouḍat/ghurfat ḥammām* 3/3
bay *khalīj khulūj* 13/3
be see 1/6; *kān yikūn* I, *kawn* 6/4, 6, 7/4; كان يكون *kāna yakūnu* I 21/4; → no, not, still
bear حمل يحمل حمل *ḥamala yaḥmilu* I, *ḥaml* 24/1; ~able *muḥtámal* 13/9
beard *liḥya liḥa* 6/15
beautiful *jamīl* 4/1
because *li 'annu* 14/1, 9; لأنّ *li 'anna* 21/8; ~ of *bi sabab* 2/7; *min sha'n* 6/1
become *ṣār yiṣīr* I 6/4, 7/4; صار يصير *ṣāra yaṣīru* I 24/4
bed *farsha*, ~room *'ouḍat/ghurfat noum* 3/3
beer *bīra* 9/1
before (place) *'amām, quddām,* (time) *qabl* 2/7, 6/18; *qabl mā* 6/18; قبل انْ *qabla 'an* 25/4; ~hand *qablan* 11/19
begin *bada yibda* I 8/7, 8, 12; see 9/1, 12; *ibtáda* VIII 13/6; صار يصير *ṣāra yaṣīru* I, بدأ يبدأ *bada'a yabda'u* I 25/2; ~ner *mubtádī* 13/9; ~ning *bādī* 10/5, *ibtidā'* 13/1; 10 see 6/11
begun *mabdū* 10/5
behind *wara* 2/1, 7
Beirut *bayrūt* 6/1
belief *i9tiqād* 13/10
believe *ṣaddaq* II 9/10; *i9táqad* VIII 13/6; ~d *mu9táqad* 13/9
belonging to *taba9* 12/1; see 12/16

beneficiary *mustathmir* 14/7
benefit *'afād yufīd* IV 11/6; ~ from *istafād* X *min* 14/5
bent: become ~ *i9wajj* IX 14/4
beside *jamb* 2/7; ~s *ghayr* 7/16
best see 9/14
better *'aḥsan* 4/1, 9/13; get ~ *taḥassan* V 12/4
between *bayn* 2/7, 8
beyond عبر *9abra* 19/15
big *kbīr kbār* 3/1; ~ger *'akbar* 9/13; ~gest see 9/14
bill *ḥisāb* 3/3; ~ of lading بوليصة شحن *būlīṣat shaḥn* 20/2
bird *9aṣfūr 9aṣāfīr* 9/8
Birthday: Prophet's ~ *moulūd an-nabī* 10/15
bitumen زفت *zift* 22/1
black *'aswad sawdā' sūd* 12/11; go ~ *iswadd* IX 14/4
blanch *ibyaḍḍ* IX 14/4
blanket *baṭṭānīya* 3/3
bless *bārak* III 14/1, 2; God ~ *'alla yiḥfaẓ* 6/1, 2
blind *'a9ma 9amyā' 9umī* 12/11
block (of buildings) *9imāra* 6/3
blood *dam* 12/3
blouse *blūz* 14/3
blue *'azraq zarqā' zurq* 12/11; go ~ *izraqq* IX 14/4
blush *iḥmarr* IX 14/4
board: ~of directors مجلس ادارة *majlis 'idāra* 21/1; (notice etc.) ~ لوحة *lawḥa* 24/1; on ~ على متن *9ala matn* 20/2
body *jism 'ajsām* 12/3; (organisation) *hay'a* 15/3
boil-ed *maslūq* 9/3; ~ing (noun) *four* 11/19
book *kitāb kutub* 2/1; ~let *kutayyib* 13/17; ~shop *maktaba makātib* 4/3, 8/23
both كلا *kila* 18/5
bottle *qinnīna qanāni* 9/3
box *ṣandūq ṣanādīq* 2/3
boy *walad 'oulād* 6/3
bravo! see 6/2
bread *khubz* 9/3
breakfast *fuṭūr* 3/1
bricks *ṭoub* 9/5
bridge *jisr jusūr* 4/3
bring *jāb yijīb* I 6/4, 7/4; جاء يجيء ب *jā'a yajī'u* I *bi* 25/6; ~ about احدث *'aḥdatha* IV 20/1; ~up (educate) *rabba* II 9/10
Brit-ain *'ingiltra* 1/2; ~ish *'inglīzī inglīz* 1/1; *briṭānī* 4/1
broadcast *'adhā9 yudhī9* IV 11/6; ~ing *'idhā9a* 11/10
broadening *tawsī9* 11/1
broken: be ~ *inkásar* VII 13/4
broker سمسار سماسير *simsār samāsīr* 19/2
brother *'akh 'ikhwa/'ikhwān* 6/3, 14
brown *bunnī, binnī* 12/11
Brussels بروكسل *bruksil* 18/6
budget *mīzānīya* 5/3
building *bināya* 3/1; *9imāra* 6/3
bulk حجم حجوم *ḥajm ḥujūm* 20/1
bulletin *nashra* 15/1
bus *'utubīs, bāṣ* 2/3; ~ stop *mouqif bāṣ* 4/3
businessman *tājir tujjār* 1/2
busy *mashghūl* 5/3
but *walākin* 3/1, 4/8; (و)لكنّ *(wa)lākinna* 21/8; ~ for *law lāk* (etc.) 11/14; ~ rather *bal* 15/1
butcher *laḥḥām* 8/23
butter *zibda* 9/3
buy *ishtára* VIII 13/6
by *min qibal* see 13/15; ~ the way *9ala fikra* 6/1

C

cabinet (of ministers) *majlis al-wuzarā'* 15/3
Cairo *al-qāhira* 5/17
calendar *taqwīm taqāwīm* 10/14
call (name) *samma* II 9/10; (summon) *nāda* III 11/4; telephone ~ *ittiṣāl* 7/3
camel *jamal jimāl* 9/8; ~s *'ibil* 9/5
can (be able) *mumkin* 7/8; *qidir*

yiqdar I 8/1, 12; استطاع *istaṭā9a* X 22/5
candidate *murashshaḥ* 8/1
capable: be ~ of *tamakkan* V *min* 12/4
capacity: in the ~ of *ka* 6/1
capital (city) *9āṣima 9awāṣim* 15/1; (money) *ra's māl* 11/3
capitalism *ra'smālīya* 13/11
car *sayyāra* 2/3
care: take ~ *dār yidīr* I *bālak* (etc.) 12/1, 2
carpent-er *najjār* 8/23; ~ry *nijāra* 8/3, 23
carry حمل يحمل حمل *ḥamala yaḥmilu* I, *ḥaml* 24/1
case (abstract) *ḥāla* 8/1; *qaḍīya qaḍāya* 15/3; in any ~ *9ala kull ḥāl* 11/1, 2; (suit~) *shanta* 2/1
cat *bissa bisās* 9/8
catch a cold *tarashshaḥ* V 12/4
cattle *baqar* 9/5
cause *sabbab* II 15/1; سبب اسباب *sabab 'asbāb* 21/1; (case) *qaḍīya qaḍāya* 15/3
cease *zāl yazāl* I see 15/13
centimetre *santimitr* 14/1
centre *markaz marākiz* 4/3
century قرن قرون *qarn qurūn* 26/1
certain *mu9ayyan* 10/1; ~ly *tikram* (etc.) 3/1, 2; *9ala ra'sī* 4/1, 2; *9ala 9aynī* 4/2; *ḥāḍir* 9/1
certificate *shahāda* 8/1
chair *kursī karāsī* 6/3; ~man *ra'īs ru'asā'* 10/3; ~manship رئاسة\رياسة *ri'āsa/riyāsa* 17/5
Chamber of Commerce *ghurfat tijāra* 10/1
change *ghayyar* II 9/10; *taghyīr* 10/12; (small ~) *fakka* 4/1
characterised by ذو *dhū* (etc.) see 24/19
charge: be put in ~ *tawalla* V 12/4; in ~ *mutawallī* 12/7
cheap *rkhīṣ rkhāṣ* 6/11; ~er *'arkhaṣ* 9/1, 13
cheese *jibna* 9/3
chemistry *kīmiya* 8/3
chest (breast) *ṣadr ṣudūr* 12/3
chicken *dajāja* 9/1, 6; ~s *dajāj* 9/5
Chief Engineer مدير الهندسة *mudīr al-handasa* 19/1
child *walad 'oulād* 6/3; *ṭifl 'aṭfāl* 13/1
China: People's Republic of ~ *aṣ-ṣīn ash-sha9bī* 15/3
choose *ikhtār* VIII 14/1
Christian *masīḥī* 13/1
Christmas *(9īd al-)mīlād* 10/15
church *kanīsa kanāyis* 4/3
cigarette *sīgāra sagāyir* 2/1
circle → club
circular (memorandum) منشور *manshūr* 24/1
circumstance ظرف ظروف *ẓarf ẓurūf* 21/1
city *madīna mudun* 13/3
civil servant *muwaẓẓaf ḥukūma* 1/2
claim طلب *ṭalab* 19/2; ادّعى *iddá9a* VIII, ادّعاء *iddi9ā'* 23/1
clash *iḍṭárab* VIII 13/7
class (school) *ṣaff ṣufūf* 8/1
clean *naẓīf nuẓafā'* 6/11; dry-~ *naẓẓaf 9ala n-nāshif* 14/3
clear *wāḍiḥ* 6/1; ~er *'awḍaḥ* 9/13; ~ly *bi ṣūra wāḍiḥa* 11/21
clerk *muwaẓẓaf* 3/1; *kātib kuttāb, kātiba, muwaẓẓaf* 10/9
clever *shāṭir shuṭṭār* 6/1
clinic *9iyāda* 12/3; *mustawṣaf* 14/7
clock *sā9a* 7/1
close: be ~ to (doing) *'awshak yūshik* IV *9ala* 11/6
closed *musakkar* 3/3
cloth *qmāsh 'aqmisha,* ~ merchant *qammāsh* 14/1
clothes *malābis* 2/1
cloud *saḥāba suḥub,* ~s *saḥāb* 13/3
club (circle) نادٍ (النادي) اندية *nādin (an-nādī) 'ándiya* 26/1
coast *ḍiffa ḍifāf* 13/1; ساحل سواحل *sāḥil sawāḥil* 22/1
coat *jākayt* 14/3

coffee *qahwa* 1/1; see 9/1, 3; بنّ *bunn* 16/19; -~house (المقهى) مقهًى (المقاهي) مقاهٍ *maqhan (al-maqha) maqāhin (al-maqāhī)* 24/20
cold *bārid* 6/1; (noun) *rashsh* 12/1; catch a ~ *tarashshaḥ* V 12/4
colleague *zamīl zumalā'* 5/3
collection *tajmī9* 10/1
college *kullīya* 8/3
colloquial Arabic *al-lugha l-9arabīya/al-9arabīya d-dārija, ad-dārij* 8/3
colour *loun 'alwān* 14/1
come *'aja yījī* I 8/9, 10; جاء يجيء *jā'a yajī'u* I 25/6; ~ in *warad yūrid* I 15/1; ~ out *kharaj yukhruj* I, *khuruj* 3/6, 5/4; ~ together *talāqa* VI 12/5
command *'amr 'awāmir* 10/11
Commerce → Chamber
commissioner *mandūb* 15/3
committee *lajna lijān* 5/3
commodity *mādda tijārīya* 11/3
common *mushtárak* 13/9; ≈ Market *as-sūq al-'urubbīya l-mushtáraka* 15/3
commotion *iḍṭirāb* 13/10
communications *muwāṣalāt* 11/1
communist *shuyū9ī* 15/3
company *sharika* 1/2
compensation تعويض *ta9wīḍ* 19/1
complaint شكوة شكوات *shakwa shakawāt* 21/1
complete *kāmil* 12/1; تامّ *tāmm* 16/24; اتمّ *'atamma* IV 23/1; ~ly *tamāman* 9/1, 11/19; be ~d *tamm yitimm* I 8/4, 5
complicate *9aqqad* II 13/1
component *qiṭ9a qiṭa9* 11/1
composed of *mukawwan min* 10/1
composition *'inshā'* 10/10
comprehensive *shāmil* 10/1
comprise ضمّ يضمّ *ḍamma yaḍummu* I 26/1
compulsion *'ījāb* 10/10
compulsory *'ijbārī* 8/3
computer *kambyūtir* 5/3
conceited *shāyif ḥālu* (etc.) see 13/14
concentrated: be ~ تركّز *tarakkaza* V 26/1
concern *'ahamm yihimm* IV 11/6; *ihtimām* 13/10; be ~d by *ihtamm bi/fī* VIII 13/6; ~ing *bi khuṣūṣ* 2/7
conclude اتمّ *'atamma* IV 23/1
condition (state) *ḥāl 'aḥwāl* 1/1; (pre~) *sharṭ shurūṭ* 8/1; ~al on *muta9alliq bi* 12/7; (circumstance) ظرف ظروف *ḍarf ḍurūf* 21/1; good/poor ~s *ḥusn/sū' al-ḥāl* 12/15
conference *mu'támar* 7/1, 13/9
confidence (in) *i9timād (9ala)* 13/10
confirmed: it was ~ *'ukkid* 15/1
congratulations! *mabrūk!* 14/1, 2
congregate *ijtáma9* VIII 13/6
consider *i9tábar* VIII 13/6; ~ good *istaḥsan* X, ~ great *istakbar* X, ~ small *istaqall* X 14/5; ~ation *i9tibār* 13/10; → take
consisting of *mukawwan min* 10/1
constancy موالاة *muwālā* 25/9
constant: be ~ والى *wāla* III 25/7
constitut-e *kawwan* II 9/10; شكّل *shakkala* II 24/1; ~ed *mukawwan*, ~ing *mukawwin* 10/6
constitution تشكيل *tashkīl* 26/1; (political) *dustūr dasātīr* 15/3
construct *'ansha yunshī* IV 11/6
consul *qunṣul qanaṣīl*, ~ate *qunṣulīya* 4/3
consult *istashār* X, (doctor) *istawsaf* X 14/5
consum-e استهلك *istahlaka* X, ~ption استهلاك *istihlāk* 22/2
contact *ittáṣal* VIII *bi/fī* 13/6; *ittiṣāl* 13/10
container مستودع *mustawda9* 20/1
content: in form and ~ *shaklan wa mouḍū9an* 11/19
continent *qārra* 13/3
continuation *istimrār* 14/8

continue *istamarr* X 14/5; *mā zāl lā yazāl* I 15/1 see 15/13; استمرّ *istamarra* X 25/2; ما زال لا يزال *mā zāla lā yazālu* I 25/2
continuous *mustamirr* 14/7
contract (agreement) عقد عقود *9aqd 9uqūd* 19/2
convened: be ~ *in9áqad* VII 13/4
convening *in9iqād* 13/10
convey *waṣṣal* II 9/10
convinced of متأكّد من *muta'akkid min* 21/1
cook *ṭabbākh* 8/23; ~ery *ṭibākha* 8/1, 23; ~ed in spices *musakhkhan* 9/1
cooperate *ta9āwan* VI 12/5
cooperation *ta9āwun* 8/1, 12/8; non~ *9adam at-ta9āwun* 12/15
cooperative *ta9āwunī* 12/8; un~ *9adīm at-ta9āwun* 12/15
cooperativism *ta9āwunīya* 13/11
copy *nuskha nusakh* 5/3
cordially *qalbīyan* 9/1
corps (diplomatic etc.) *hay'a* 15/3
correct *maẓbūṭ* 4/1
correspond: ~ with *kātab* III 11/4 ~ence *mukātaba* 11/9, مراسلة *murāsala* 24/1; ~ent *mukātib* 11/8
cost *kallaf* II 9/10; *taklīf takālīf* 10/12; *thaman 'athmān* 11/3
council *majlis majālis* 15/3: → security
counsellor *mustashār* 14/7
counted: be ~ *in9add* VII 13/4
country *bilād buldān* 6/1; ~ people *'ahl al-qura* 13/3; home ~ *waṭan 'awṭān* 5/3; → developing, industrialised
coup d'état *inqilāb* 15/3
course: of ~ *ṭab9an* 4/1, *ma9lūm* 8/1; in the ~ of *fī khilāl* 15/1
court (law) *maḥkama maḥākim* 8/23
cow *baqara* 9/6
creat-e *'ansha yunshī* IV 11/6; ~ion *'inshā'* 10/10
credentials (diplomatic) *'awrāq al-i9timād* 13/10
criticis-e انتقد على *intáqada* VIII *9ala*, ~m of انتقاد على *intiqād 9ala* 26/1
crossroad *mafraq mafāriq* 4/3, 8/23
crowd *ḥashd ḥushūd* 15/1
crude oil نفط\زيت خام *nafṭ/zayt khām* 22/1
cubic مكعّب *muka99ab* 20/2
cultivate *zara9 yizra9* I, *zar9* 13/1
cultur-al *thaqāfī* 6/1; ~e *thaqāfa*, ~ed *muthaqqaf* 8/3
cup *finjān fanājīn* 9/3
cure *9ilāj* 12/1
current (adjective) *jārī jắriya jārīyīn* 7/13, 10/5
customer *zabūn zabāyīn* 14/3
Customs *jumruk jamārik* 2/1
cut *qaṣṣ yiquṣṣ* I 14/1; ~ off (telephone) *maqṭū9* 7/3

D

daily *youmī(yan)* 11/20
Damascus *dimashq* 4/1, 5/17; *ash-shām* 6/1
damage *khasāyir* (pl.) 15/1
dangerous *khaṭir* 12/1
data *mu9ṭayāt* 11/8
date (calendar) *tārīkh tawārīkh* 8/3; ~d مؤرّخ *mu'arrakh* 19/1; (fruit) *tamra tumūr* 9/6, *ḥabbat tamr* 9/7; ~s *tamr* 9/1, 5
daughter *bint banāt* 6/3
day *youm 'ayyām* 6/11, 7/13, 14; ~time *nahār 'anhur*, the ~ after tomorrrow *ba9d bukra*, the ~ before yesterday *'awwal 'ams* 7/3; → next
deaf *'aṭrash ṭarshā' ṭursh* 12/11
dear عزيز اعزّاء *9azīz 'a9izzā'* 24/4
debt دين ديون *dayn duyūn* 26/1
deci-de *qarrar* II 9/10; ~sion *taqrīr* 10/12
declare صرّح ب *ṣarraḥa* II *bi* 26/1
defective *kharbān* 7/1
defence *difā9* 4/3
deference *'ikrām* 13/1, 2; treat with ~

'akram yukrim IV 13/2
definite *mu9ayyan* 10/1
degree *daraja* 12/1
delay *ta'khīr* 2/3, 10/12; *'akhkhar* II 9/10; ~ed *muta'akhkhir* 2/3, 12/7; be ~ed *ta'akhkhar* V 12/4
delegat-e *mandūb* 10/1; ~ion وفد وفود *wafd wufūd* 23/1
deliberat-e *i'támar* VIII 13/6; ~ion *i'timār* 13/10
deliver (speech etc.) *'alqa yulqī* IV 11/6; ~y (of a speech etc.) *'ilqā'* 10/10
democracy *dimuqrāṭīya* 13/11
demonstrat-e *taẓāhar* VI 12/5; ~ion *taẓāhur* 12/8; ~or *mutaẓāhir* 12/7
den-ial نفي *nafy* 23/1; ~ied منفيّ *manfīy* 23/10
deny نفى ينفي نفي *nafa yanfī* I, *nafy* 23/1, 7, 8
department *qism 'aqsām* 5/1; ~ store *maḥallāt* 4/3
departure *mughādara* 2/3
depend on *ta9allaq* V *bi*, *tawaqqaf* V *9ala* 12/4; ~ence (on) *i9timād (9ala)* 13/10; ~ent on *mutawaqqif 9ala* 12/7
depict *ṣawwar* II 9/10; ~ion *taṣwīr* 10/12
deput-ising for نيابةً عن *niyābatan 9an* 23/1; ~y *nāyib nuwwāb* 15/3
descent *nuzūl* 10/11
desert *ṣaḥra ṣaḥāra/ṣaḥrāwāt* 13/3
deserv-e *istaḥaqq* X 14/5; ~ing *mustaḥiqq* 14/7
despatch *'irsāl* 10/10
despite *bi r-raghm min* 2/7
dessert *ḥilwīyāt* 9/1
detail *tafṣīl tafāṣīl*, in ~ *bi t-tafṣīl* 11/20
detention *tawqīf* 10/12
determined مصمّم *muṣammim* 17/3
develop طوّر *ṭawwara* II 23/1; ~ing country *dawla nāmiya* 15/3; ~ment *tánmiya* 4/1; *taṭawwur* 12/8; تطوير *taṭwīr* 23/1
dialogue *ḥiwār*, *muḥāwara* 11/9; ~ with *ḥāwar* III 11/4
dictatorship *diktāturīya* 13/11
did not *mā* 3/9; لم *lam* (+ jussive) 26/2, 3
diesel ديزل *dīzil* 22/1
different *ghayr* 7/16
difficult *ṣa9b ṣi9āb* 6/11
dinar *dīnār danānīr* 2/3
dining table *sufra sufar* 9/3
dinner *9ashā'* 3/3
diploma *dibloum* 8/3
diplomat *diblumāsī* 1/2
direct *dall yidill* I 8/4, 5
direction *wujha* 10/1
director *mudīr mudarā'* 1/2; ~ate دائرة دوائر *dā'ira dawā'ir* 24/1; ~y *dalīl 'adilla* 7/3
disaster كارثة كوارث *kāritha kawārith* 19/2
discomforts *muz9ijāt* (pl.) 11/8
discover *iktáshaf* VIII 13/6
discrimination: racial ~ *tamyīz 9unṣurī* 15/3
discuss *baḥath yibḥath* I, *baḥth* 10/3; ~ion *baḥth buḥūth* 5/3, 10/11
dismiss عزل يعزل *9azala ya9zilu* I, ~al عزل *9azl* 21/2
dispute خلاف *khilāf* 21/1
distance بعد ابعاد *bu9d 'ab9ād* 22/1
distil قطّر *qaṭṭara* II 22/2
distinction *imtiyāz* 13/10
distinguished *mumtāz* 13/9; be ~ed *imtāz* VIII 13/6
disturb *'a9aj yiz9ij* IV 11/6; ~ance *'iz9āj* 11/10
disused *ghayr/mish musta9mal* 7/16
divided: be ~ *inqásam* VII 13/4
divis-ible see 13/5; ~ion *qism 'aqsām* 5/1
do *9imil yi9mal* I, *9amal* 5/4; ~ not *mā* 5/7, 21/5; *lā* 5/9, 15/10, 21/5; ~ without *istaghna* X *9an* 14/5
doctor *ṭabīb 'aṭibba* 1/1, 6/11; (title) *duktur* 1/1, 2/4
document *wathīqa wathā'iq* 10/3

does not *mā* 5/7, *lā* 15/10
dog *kalb kilāb* 9/8
Doha *ad-douḥa* 5/1
dollar *doulār* 2/3
dominate سيطر على *sayṭara* IQ *9ala* 26/1
don-ation *'i9ṭā'* 10/10; ~or *mu9ṭī* 11/8
door *bāb 'abwāb* 3/1; ~man *bawwāb* 3/3; small ~ *buwayb* 13/17
double ثنائي *thunā'ī* 17/5; be ~ *izdáwaj* VIII 13/7; ~d *muzdáwij* 13/9
doubt *shakk yishukk* I, *fī shakk* 8/4, 5, 10/11, 11/20; ~ed *maskūk fī*, ~ing *shākik* 10/5, شاكّ *shākk* 20/9; ~less *bi lā shakk* 11/21
downstairs *taḥt* 6/3
draft *musawwada* 10/3
drag *saḥab yisḥab* I 13/14
draper *qammāsh* 14/1
drawing رسم رسوم *rasm rusūm* 19/1
dress (woman's) *fustān fasātin* 14/1
dressmak-er *khayyāṭa* 8/23; ~ing *khiyāṭa* 8/1, 23
drill حفر يحفر حفر *ḥafara yaḥfiru* I, *ḥafr* 22/1; ~er حفّار *ḥaffār*, ~ing rig جهاز حفر *jihāz ḥafr* 22/2
drink *shirib yishrab* I 8/1; *mashrūbāt* 2/1, 9/3; *mashrūb* 10/9
drive *sāq yisūq* I 6/4, 7/4; ~r *sawwāq* 3/1
dry-clean *naðḍaf* II *9ala n-nāshif* 14/3
duration: for the ~ of *ṭūl* 2/7
during *khilāl* 2/7
dying مائت *mā'it* 17/5

E

each *kull* 8/18; ~ other see 8/17
early see 6/11
earthquake *zilzāl* 12/12
eas-e *suhūla*, ~ily *bi suhūla* 11/20
east *sharq* 13/3; ⟶ Far, Middle, Near
Easter *9īd al-fisiḥ*, *al-9īd al-kabīr* 10/15
easy *sahil* 13/3
eat *'akal yākul* I, *'akl* 3/7, 5/5; ~en *ma'kūl*, ~ing *'ākil* 10/5
econom-ic *iqtiṣādī*, ~y *iqtiṣād* 11/3
educate *rabba* II 9/10; ~d *muthaqqaf* 8/3; *murabba* 10/6; *muta9allim* 12/7
educating *murabbī* 10/6
education *tárbiya* 4/3, 8/3, 10/12; *ta9līm* 8/1; ~al *ta9līmī* 8/1, *tarbawī* 8/3; ⟶ high
educator *murabbī* 10/9
effect: with ~ from *ibtidā'an min*, *i9tibāran min* 13/10
effectiveness فاعلية *fā9ilīya* 26/1
efficiency فاعلية *fā9ilīya* 26/1
egg *bayḍa* 9/6; ~s *bayḍ* 9/5
Egypt *miṣr* 1/2, 9; ~ian *miṣrī* 1/9
either ... or *'imma* ... *'aw* 8/1
elder *shaykh shuyūkh* 13/1
elect *intákhab* VIII 13/6; ~ed *muntákhab* 13/9; ~ion *intikhāb* 13/10; ~or *muntákhib* 13/9; ~oral *intikhābī* 13/10
electricity *kahraba* 8/1
e-mail *barīd 'iliktrounī*, *'īmayl* 5/3
embassy *sifāra* 4/1
emir *'amīr 'umarā'*, ~ate *'imāra* 15/3; ⟶ United
employ *istakhdam* 14/5; ~ee *muwaẓẓaf* 3/1, 10/9; ~ed *mustakhdam* 14/7; ~er *ṣāḥib* (pl. *'aṣḥāb*) *al-9amal* 11/3; *mustakhdim* 14/7; ~ment *istikhdām* 14/8
empty *fāḍī fāḍiya fāḍīyīn* 1/1, 10
encounter *lāqa* III 11/4, *mulāqā*, *muqābala* 11/9; تلاقى *talāqa* VI, تلاقٍ (التلاقي) *talāqin (at-talāqī)* 23/10; be ~ed *inláqa* VII 13/4
end see 6/11; *intáha* VIII 13/6; *intihā'* 13/10
energy طاقة *ṭāqa* 23/1
engineer *muhandis* 1/1; ~ing

handasa 8/3; ⟶ Chief
Engl-and *'ingiltra* 1/2; ~ish *'inglīzī 'inglīz* 1/1
enjoy oneself *inbásaṭ* VII 13/4
enquire *sa'al yis'al* I 3/7, 16, 5/4; ~about *istafham* X *9an*, ~ of *ista9lam* X 14/5
enter *dakhal yudkhul* I, *dukhūl* 3/6, 5/4
entr-ance, ~y *madkhal madākhil* 4/3; *dukhūl* 8/1, 10/11
equal: be/make ~ ساوى *sāwa* III 25/7; ~ity مساواة *musāwā* 25/9
equilibrium توازن *tawāzun* 26/1
error *ghalaṭ 'aghlāṭ* 6/15
escaping: there's no ~ *lā budda min* 12/1; see 12/2
especially *khāṣṣatan* 11/1, 20
essen-ce ذات ذوات *dhāt dhawāt* 24/19; ~tial *ḍarūrī* 5/1; اساسي *'asāsī* 24/1
establish استّس *'assasa* II, ~ment تأسيس *ta'sīs* 25/1
Euphrates *al-furāt* 13/3
euro *'ūro, yūro* 2/3
Europe *'urubba* 1/2; ~an *'urubbī* 1/9; ~an Union *al-ittihād al-'urubbī* 15/3
even: ~if *ḥatta u law* 11/1, 15; ~ though *ma9 'inn* 11/15
evening مساء امساء *masā' 'amsā'* 17/6; ⟶ good
event *ḥāditha ḥawādith* 15/1
ever *'abadan* 6/1, 2
every *kull* 8/18; ~thing *kull shī* 6/1, 8/18, 9/16
evolution *taṭawwur*, ~ary *taṭawwurī* 12/8
evolve *taṭawwar* V 12/4
exactness *ẓabt* 11/1
exaggerated: it is ~ *tubālagh* 15/1
examin-e (medically) *faḥaṣ yifḥaṣ* I, *faḥṣ* 12/1; بحث يبحث في\على *baḥatha yabḥathu* I *fī/9ala* 25/1; ~ation (academic) *imtiḥān* 8/1, (medical) *faḥṣ ṭibbī* 12/3; ~ation of بحث بحوث على *baḥth buḥūth 9ala* 26/1
example *mathal 'amthāl* 11/19; مثال امثلة *mithāl 'amthila* 26/1; for ~ *mathalan* 8/1, 11/19
excel فاق يفوق *fāqa yafūqu* I 24/1
Excellency (title) *sīyāda* 7/1, 2
excellent *mumtāz* 5/1, 13/9
except *istathna* X 14/5; ~ (for) *'illa* 2/7; *ghayr* 7/16; ~ed *mustathna* 14/7; ~ion *istithnā'* 14/8; ~ional *istithnā'ī* 8/1
exchange *tabādal* VI 12/5; *tabādul* 12/8; *istabdal* X 14/5; بدّل *baddala* II, تبديل *tabdīl* 23/1; (telephone ~) *markaz marākiz* 7/1
excuse عفا يعفو ل *9afa ya9fū* I *li* 23/7; ~ me *'ismaḥ lī* 1/1, 3; *9afwan* 4/1
execution (of a task) *tanfīdh* 11/1
exert oneself *ijtáhad* VIII 13/6
existence *kawn* 10/11; *wujūd* 12/15
exit *makhraj makhārij* 4/3; *khurūj* 10/11
expand *tawassa9* V 12/4
expansion *tawsī9* 11/1; *tawassu9* 12/8; ~ism *tawassu9īya* 13/11; ~ist *tawassu9ī* 12/8
expect *tawaqqa9* V 12/4; ~ation *intiẓar/intiḍār* 13/10; ~ed *mutawaqqa9* 12/7
expel *'akhraj yukhrij* IV 11/6
expensive *ghālī ghāliya ghālīyīn* 14/1
experiment *tajriba tajārib* 10/12; ~al *tajribī* 11/11
expert خبير خبراء *khabīr khubarā'*, ~ise خبرة *khibra* 25/1
expiry انتهاء *intihā'* 19/2
explain *sharaḥ yishraḥ* I, *sharḥ* 5/4
explode *infájar* VII 13/4
exploitation *istithmār* 14/8
explor-ation استكشاف *istikshāf*, ~e استكشف *istakshafa* X 22/1
explos-ion *infijār* 13/10; ~ive *munfájir* 13/9

export *ṣaddar* II, ~s *ṣādirāt* 11/3
express *9abbar* II *9an* 15/1
expulsion *'ikhrāj* 10/10
extend *madd yimudd* I 8/4, 5; *maddad* II 14/10; ~ed *mumtadd* 13/9; be ~ed *imtadd* VIII 13/6
extens-ible *qābil li t-tamdīd* 14/10; ~ion *imtidād* 13/10
extraordinary *ghayr 9ādī* 10/3
eye *9ayn 9uyūn* (f.) 12/3

F

fabricated *muṣṭana9* 13/9
face *wujha* 10/1; واجه *wājaha* III 26/1
facing (opposite) *muqābil* 11/8; تجاه *tujāha* 25/1
factor *9āmil 9awāmil* 10/9
factory *maṣna9 maṣāni9* 8/23
factual فعلي *fi9lī* 26/1
faculty (academic) *kullīya* 8/3
fail (examination) *rasab yursub* I *fī* 8/3; ~ure فشل *fashal* 19/1
fall *saqaṭ yusquṭ* I 13/3
family *9ayla 9iyāl* 6/3
famous *ma9rūf* 4/1
far: ≈ East *ash-sharq al-'aqṣa* 13/3; ~ from *ba9īd 9an* 4/1; as ~ as *ḥatta* 2/7
fare *'ujra* 2/3
farm *zara9 yizra9* I, *zar9* 13/1; ~er *fallāḥ* 13/3
fast *sarī9 sirā9, bi sur9a* 11/20, سريعًا *sarī9an* 22/9; ~er *'asra9* 9/13, بصورة اسرع *bi ṣūra 'asra9* 22/9
father *'ab 'ābā'* 6/3, 14
fax *faks* 5/3
fear *khāf yikhāf* I, *khouf* 6/4, 7/4; *khouf* 10/11; for ~ of *khoufan min* 12/2; ~ed *makhūf*, ~ing *khāyif* 10/5; ~ing for *khoufan 9ala* 12/1,2
federal *ittiḥādī* 13/10; ~ism *ittiḥādīya* 13/11
feel *ḥass yiḥiss* I 8/4, 5
fertiliser *samād 'asmida* 13/1
festival *9īd 'a9yād* 10/15
fever *ḥarāra* 12/1
field *ḥaql ḥuqūl* 8/1
fig *tīna* 9/6, *ḥabbat tīn* 9/7; ~s *tīn* 9/5
fight *qātal* III 11/4; *qitāl, muqātala* 11/9; ~er *muqātil*, (aircraft) *muqātila* 11/8; ~ against مكافحة *mukāfaḥa* 26/1
file (of papers) *milaff* 5/3
financ-e *mālīya* 4/3; *mawwal* II 9/10; ~ing *tamwīl* 10/1, 12
find *wajad yūjid* I 3/8, 5/6; *lāqa* III 11/4; وجد يجد *wajada yajidu* I 20/6; ~ing *wājid* 10/4
finish *khallaṣ* II 9/10; be ~ed انقضى *inqáḍa* VII 23/9
fire حريقة حرائق *ḥarīqa ḥarā'iq* 19/1; to open ~ *'aṭlaq yiṭlaq* IV *an-nār* 15/1
firm (stable) *thābit* 14/1
first *'awwal 'ūla 'awā'il* 6/11; ~ly *'awwalan* 8/1
fish *samak* 9/1, 5; *samaka* 9/6
flies *dhubāb* 9/5
flow *jara yijrī* I 8/7, 8; see 15/6; جرى يجري جري *jara yajrī* I, *jary* 23/1, 7; ~ing *jārī jāriya jārīyīn* 9/1
fluid *sāyil sawāyil* 12/1
fly *ṭār yiṭīr* I 6/4, 7/4; (insect) *dhubāba dhubbān* 9/6
foliage *waraq* 9/5
follow-ing على اثر *9ala 'athar* 26/1; as ~s *kama yalī*, the ~ing, what ~s *mā yalī* 12/9; the ~ing تالٍ (التالي) *tālin (at-tālī)* 24/1
food *'akl* 9/1, 10/11
for *li* 2/7; (~ the sake of) *min sha'n* 6/1, *min 'ajl* 15/1
forbid-den *mamnū9* 8/1; ⟶ God, Heaven
forced *majbūr* 12/1
forecast تنبّؤ *tanabbu'* 17/6
foreign, ~er *'ajnabī 'ajānib* 8/1; ≈ Affairs *khārijīya* 4/3
foremost *mutaqaddim* 12/7

for-get *nisi yinsa* I 8/9, 12; نسي ينسى *násiya yansa* I 23/7; ~gotten منسيّ *mansīy* 23/10
fork *shouka shuwak* 9/3
form *ṣūra ṣuwar* 5/1; *shakl 'ashkāl* 11/19; شكّل *shakkala* II 24/1; in ~ and substance *shaklan wa mouḍū9an* 11/19
formation *takwīn* 10/12; تشكيل *tashkīl* 26/1
former *sābiq* 6/1
fortunately *li ḥusn al-ḥaẓẓ* 12/1, 15; see 12/15
found-ation *'asās 'usus* 8/1; ~ed مؤسّس *mu'assas*, ~er مؤسّس *mu'assis* 17/5
fraction كسر كسور *kasr kusūr* 22/1
France *faransa* 1/2
free *fāḍī fāḍiya fāḍīyīn* 1/1, 9; *ḥurr 'aḥrār*, ~dom *ḥurrīya* 13/11
freighter ناقلة *nāqila* 20/1
French *faransāwī* 1/9
fresh *ṭāza* 9/3
fried *maqlī* 9/1
friend *ṣadīq 'aṣdiqā'* 6/1
from *min* 1/1; *min, 9an* 2/7; ~ whom ممّن *mimman* 16/20; ~ what *mimma, 9amma* 12/9
front: in ~ of *'amām, quddām* 2/7
frontier حدود *ḥudūd* (pl.) 20/1
fruit *fākiha fawākih* 9/1
fulfilment *tanfīdh* 11/1
full *malān* 12/1
furniture *'athāth* 6/3
furthermore *hādha wa* 15/1, 2
future *mustaqbal* 14/7

G

garage *gārāj* 6/3
garden *jinayna, bustān basātīn* 6/3
gas غاز *ghāz* 22/1
gasolene بنزين *binzīn* 22/1
general *9āmm* 5/1; in ~ *bi ṣūra 9āmma* 5/1, 2. 11/21; ≈ Manager *mudīr 9āmm* 5/3; ~ly *bi ṣūra 9āmma* 11/21
generous *karīm kuramā'* 6/11
gentleman *sayyid sāda* 1/1
geography *jughrāfīya* 8/3, 13/3
geometry *handasa* 8/3
Germany *'almāniya* 1/2
get: ~down/off *nizil yinzil* I, *nuzūl* 3/6, 5/4; ~ in *rikib yirkab* I 3/6, 5/4; ~ out *nizil yinzil* I, *nuzūl* 3/6; ~ up *ṭili9 yiṭla9* I 5/4, *qām yiqūm* I 6/4, 7/4 ; ~ well *salāmtak* (etc.) 12/1, 2; → married
girl *bint banāt* 6/3
give *'a9ṭa ya9ṭī* IV see 11/6; ~n *mu9ṭa* 11/8; ~n that (since) حيث أنّ *ḥaythu 'anna* 26/1
glass: (a ~) *kās ku'ūs* 9/1
go *rāḥ yirūḥ* I 6/4, 7/4, ذهب يذهب *dhahaba yadhhabu* I 20/11; ~ing *rāyiḥ* 10/5; ~ing to see 10/14; ~ down *nizil yinzil* I, *nuzūl*, ~ out *kharaj yukhruj* I, *khurūj*, ~ up *ṭili9 yiṭla9* I 3/6, 5/4
God: thank ~ *nushkuralla*, ~ be praised *(al-)ḥamdilla* 1/1, *al-ḥamdulilla* 5/1; ~ keep/bless *'alla yiḥfaẓ* 6/1, 2; ~ forbid *lā samaḥ 'alla* 15/10
good *kwayyis, ṭayyib* 2/1; *kwayyis* 4/14; *mnīḥ mnāḥ* 6/11; (noun) *khayr khuyūr* 13/1; ~ afternoon/evening *masa l-khayr/n-nūr* 1/1; ~bye *ma9 as-salāma, 'alla yisallimak* (etc.) 2/1, 2, *fī 'amān illa/al-karīm* 14/1, 2; ≈ Heavens *wallāhi* 4/1, 2, *māshalla* 6/1, 2; ~ morning *ṣabāḥ al-khayr/an-nūr* 1/1, 3; ~night see 9/1, 2; ~ conditions *ḥusn al-ḥāl*, ~ luck *ḥusn al-ḥaẓẓ*` ~will *ḥusn al-qaṣd* 12/15; be so ~ as to *'i9mal* (etc.) *ma9rūf* 9/2; consider ~ *istaḥsan* X 14/5
government *ḥukūma*, ~al *ḥukūmī* 1/9
grade درجة *daraja* 21/2
graduate *mutakharrij* 8/3
grain *ḥabba ḥubūb* 9/7; ~s *ḥabb* 9/5
gram *grām* 14/3; غرام\جرام *grām*

18/6
grant a request *istajāb* X 14/5
grape *9inaba 'a9nāb* 9/6, *ḥabbat 9inab* 9/7; ~s *9inab* 9/5
grateful *mamnūn* 4/1
great-ly كثيراً *kathīran* 22/9; to consider ~ *istakbar* X 14/5
green *'akhḍar khaḍrā' khuḍr* 12/11; go ~ *ikhḍarr* IX 14/4
greeting تحية *taḥīya* 24/1
grey *ramāḍī* 12/11
group (corps etc.) *hay'a* 15/3
guarantee ضمان *ḍamān* 19/2, ضمن يضمن ضمان *ḍamina yaḍmanu* I, *ḍamān*, ~d مضمون *maḍmūn* 25/1
guest *ḍayf ḍuyūf* 3/3
gulf *khalīj khulūj*, Arabian ≈ *al-khalīj al-9arabī* 13/3

H

habit *9āda* 11/19
hall: town/village ~ *baladīya* 13/1
Hamburg هامبورج *hamburg* 18/6
hand *'īd 'ayād* (f.) 12/3; يد اياد ٍ(الأيادي) *yad 'ayādin (al-'ayādī)* (f.) 24/20
happen *ḥadath yaḥduth* I 15/1
happy *sa9īd* 5/1
hardly *bi l-kād* + neg. 11/21
hat *burnayṭa barānīṭ* 14/3
have see 2/12, 4/1, 9; ~ to *lāzim* 7/8; يجب *yajib* I see 22/5
head *ra's ru'ūs* 12/3; قاد يقود *qāda yaqūdu* I, ~ing for متوجّهًا الى *mutawajjihan 'ila*, ~quarters مقرّ مقارّ *maqarr maqārr* 23/1; ~ for توجّه الى *tawajjaha 'ila* 23/1
health *ṣiḥḥa* 4/3, 12/3; ~y *ṣaḥīḥ ṣiḥāḥ* 12/3; ⟶ world
hear *simi9 yisma9* I 4/1, 5/4
heart *qalb qulūb* 12/3; ~ily *qalbīyan* 9/1
heat *ḥarāra* 12/1; ~ing *tádfiya* 6/3
Heaven: Good ~s *wallāhi* 4/1, 2; *mashalla* 6/1, 2; ~ forbid *lā samaḥ 'allah* 15/10
heavy *thaqīl thuqalā'* 6/11
height *ṭūl 'aṭwāl* 14/3
hello *marḥaba/marḥabtayn* 1/1, 2; (on the telephone) *halóu* 7/1
help *sā9ad* III 11/4; *musā9ada* 11/9; it can't be ~ed *lā budda* 12/2
here *huna* 4/1; ~ are/is *hay* 2/1; ~ we are (etc.) *hayāna* (etc.) 4/1, 10
hesitat-e *taraddad* V 12/4; ~ion *taraddud* 12/8
high *9ālī*, ~er *'a9la* 9/13; مرتفع *murtáfi9* 21/1; ~est see 9/14; ~er education *at-ta9līm al-'9ālī* 8/3
hill تلّ تلال *tall tilāl* 16/19
history *tārīkh tawārīkh* 8/3
hoarse *'ajashsh jashshā' jushsh* 12/11
hold (conference etc.) *9aqad ya9qid* I, *9aqd* 15/1
holiday *9īd 'a9yād, 'ijāza* 10/15
home country *waṭan 'awṭān* 5/3
honour *sharraf* II 9/10; *sharaf* 13/1; be ~ed *tasharraf* V 12/4; ~ing *tashrīf* 10/12; in ~ of *'ikrāman li* 13/1, 2
hope: ~ for *'amal 'āmal bi* 15/1; I ~ *'inshalla* 6/1, 2
horse *ḥiṣān ḥuṣn* 9/8; ~s *khayl* 9/5
hospital *mustashfa* 4/3; مستشفىً (المستشفى) *mustashfan (al-mustashfa)* 24/20
hot *sukhn* 9/3; *ḥārr* 13/3
hotel *'utayl* 3/1
hour *sā9a* 7/1, 13
house *bayt buyūt* 6/1
how *kayf* 1/1, 5/15; ~ are you? *kayf ḥālak* (etc.) 1/1, *kayf al-ḥāl* 5/2; ~ beautiful it is (etc.) *mā 'ajmalu* (etc.) 13/1, 12; ~ever *kayf mā* 11/15, ~ many/much *kam* 2/1, 9, 5/15, 14/3
huge *9aẓīm 9uẓamā'* 6/11; ضخم ضخام *ḍakhm ḍikhām* 20/1
hungry *jou9ān jou9a jiyā9* 9/3
husband *zouj 'azwāj* 5/1

I

-ible see 13/5, 14/10
ice *thalj,* ~-cream *būza, būẓa* 9/3
idea *fikr 'afkār* 5/1
identity ذاتد ذوات *dhāt dhawāt* 24/19
i.e. أي *'ay* 21/6
if *'idha* 9/1, 11/14; *law* 11/1, 14, 15; ~ any (إنْ وجد(ت *'in wujid(at)* 26/10
ignorant *jāhil juhhal* 8/3
ill: ~-treatment *sū' al-mu9āmala,* ~ will *sū' al-qaṣd* 12/15; be/fall ~ *miriḍ yimraḍ* I 12/3
immediately *9ala ṭūl* 9/1, *fouran* 11/19
immigration *muhājara* 2/1
implement *'anjaz yinjiz* IV 11/6
import *mustawrad* 11/1; *istawrad* X 14/5
importance *'ahammīya* 15/1
important *muhimm* 5/1, 11/8; هامّ *hāmm* 16/22; be ~ *hamm yihimm* I 8/4, 5; *'ahamm yihimm* IV 11/6
import-ation *istīrād* 14/8; ~ed *mustawrad,* ~er *mustawrid* 14/7
impose *'awjab yūjib* IV *9ala* 11/6
impossible *ghayr/mish mumkin* 7/16
improve *taḥassan* V 12/4; ~ment *taḥsīn* 10/1, *taḥassun* 12/1
in *fī* 2/1, 7; *bi* 2/7
inaugur-al *iftitāḥī* 13/10; ~ate *iftátaḥ* VIII 13/6; ~ation *iftitāḥ* 13/10
incidentally *9ala fikra* 6/1
include ضمّ يضمّ *ḍamma yaḍummu* I 26/1
increase *zād yizīd* I, *ziyāda* 6/4, 7/4, 10/11, *izdiyād* 13/10; *kaththar* II 13/1; be ~d *izdād* VIII 13/7
indeed *fi l-ḥaqīqa* 11/21
independen-ce *istiqlāl* 14/8; ~t *mustaqill* 14/7; be ~t *istaqall* X 14/5
India *al-hind* 1/2; ~n *hindī hunūd* 1/9; ~n Ocean *al-muḥīṭ al-hindī* 13/3
indicate *dall yidill* I 8/4, 5; *'ashār yushīr* IV *'ila* 12/1
indubitably *bi lā shakk* 11/20
industrialis-ation *taṣnī9* 10/12; ~e *ṣanna9* II 9/10; ~ed country *dawla ṣinā9īya* 15/3
industr-ious *mujtáhid* 6/1, 13/9; ~y *ṣinā9a* 4/3
inform *'akhbar yukhbir* IV *bi* 11/6; *'afād yufīd* IV *bi* 15/1; ~ation *ma9lūmāt* 10/1, 9, *naba' 'anbā'* 15/1; ~ed of *9ala 9ilm bi* 7/1
inhabitant *sākin sukkān* 13/1
inherit ورث يرث *waritha yarithu* I 20/6
initial (adjective) *ibtidā'ī* 13/10
inject *ḍarab yuḍrub* I *'ibra,* ~ion *'ibra 'ibār* 12/3
injured *majrūḥ majārīḥ* 12/3
insect *ḥashara* 9/8
inside *dākhil* 2/7, *jūwa* 6/1
insist: ~ on *'aṣarr yiṣirr* IV *9ala* 11/6; ~ence *'iṣrār* 10/10
inspect-ion تفتيش *taftīsh* 20/1; ~or مفتّش *mufattish* 18/4
instal-lation جهاز اجهزة *jihāz 'ajhiza* 22/1; ~ment قسط اقساط *qisṭ 'aqsāṭ* 19/1
institute *ma9had ma9āhid* 8/1, 23
instruct *darras* II 9/10; ~ion *tadrīs* 8/3, 10/12; ~ional *ta9līmī* 11/11; ~ions *ta9līmāt* 10/1, 12; ~or *mudarris* 8/3, 10/9, مدرّب *mudarrib* 24/1
insur-ance تأمين *ta'mīn,* ~ed مؤمّن عليه *mu'amman 9alayhi,* ~er مؤمّن *mu'ammin* 19/1
intake (food, drink) *tanāwul* 12/1, 8
intend *nawa yinwī* I 8/7, 8, 12; نوى ينوي *nawa yanwī* I 25/5
intention نية *nīya* 25/9; ~al *'irādī* 11/11
interest (legal/political) *maṣlaḥa maṣāliḥ* 15/3
interfer-e *tadākhal* VI 12/5; ~ence *tadākhul* 12/8

interior *dākhilīya* 4/3
international *duwalī* 5/3;
≈ Monetary Fund *ṣandūq an-naqd ad-duwalī* 15/3
interrogat-e *istajwab* X 14/5; ~ion *istijwāb* 14/8
interval *fatra fatarāt* 7/13
interven-e *tadakhkhal* V 12/4; ~tion *tadakhkhul* 12/8
invest *istathmar* X 14/5; ~ment *istithmār* 11/3, 14/8
Iraq *al-9irāq* 1/2
iron (clothes) *kawa yikwi* I, *kawī* 14/3
irrigation *rayy* 13/1
island *jazīra juzur* 13/3
isn't that so? *mish kadha?* 4/1
Israel *'isrā'īl* 15/1; ~i *'isrā'īlī* 13/1
issued ⟶ appear
it is reported *tufīd al-'anbā'* 15/2
Ital-ian *'īṭālī* 1/9; ~y *'īṭāliya* 1/2

J

jacket *jākayt* 14/3
jam *murabba* 9/3
Japan *al-yābān* 1/2
job وظيفة وظائف *waẓīfa waẓā'if* 21/2
join *inḍamm* VII 13/4
joint *mushtárak* 13/9
Jordan *'urdun*, ~ian *'urdunī* 1/1
journalist *ṣuḥufī* 1/2, *ṣuḥufīya* 3/13
judge قاضٍ (القاضي) قضاة *qāḍin (al-qāḍī) quḍā* 24/20
juice *9aṣīr* 9/3
junior صغير صغار *ṣaghīr ṣighār* 21/1
justice عدل *9adl* 26/1

K

keep *ḥafaẓ yiḥfaẓ* I 6/1, ~ it up! *ya9ṭīk al-9āfiya* 6/1, 2
key *miftāḥ mafātīḥ* 3/1, 8/23
kerosene كيروسين *kirusīn* 22/1
killed: he was ~ *qutil* 15/1
kilo-gram *kīlou* 14/3; ~metre كيلومتر *kīlumitr* 22/1
kind (noun) *nou9 'anwā9* 5/15, *jins 'ajnās* 14/1; (adj.) *laṭīf luṭafā'* 4/1; ~ness *ma9rūf* 9/1
king *malik mulūk*, ~dom *mamlaka mamālik* 15/3
kitchen *maṭbakh maṭābikh* 6/3, 8/23
knife *sikkīn sakākīn* 9/3
know *9irif ya9raf* I, *ma9rifa* 3/6, 5/4; ~ing *9ārif* 10/5; ~ledge *ma9rifa ma9ārif* 5/1, 10/10, 11; ~n *ma9lūm* 8/1, *ma9rūf* 10/5
Kuwait *al-kuwayt* 1/2

L

laboratory *ma9mal ma9āmil* 8/23
labour *9amal, shughl* 4/3
lack: ~ of *9adam* 12/1, 15; ~ing *9adīm* 12/15
lading: bill of ~ بوليصة شحن *būlīṣat shaḥn* 20/2
lady *sayyida* 4/1
lake *buḥayra* 13/3, 17
lame *'a9raj 9arjā' 9urj* 12/11
land *'arḍ 'arāḍī* (f.) 13/1; أرض اراضٍ(الأراضي) *'arḍ 'arāḍin (al-'arāḍī)* (f.) 24/20; (adj.) برّي *barrī* 20/2; ~lord *ṣāḥib bayt* 6/3
language *lugha* 4/1
last (adj.) *'ākhir 'awākhir* 6/11; (verb) *istaghraq* X 14/5
Latakia اللاذقية *al-lādhiqīya* 20/1
late *muta'akhkhir* 2/3, 12/7; see 6/11
laugh *ḍaḥak yiḍḥak* I, *ḍaḥk* 6/1
laundry *ghasīl* 14/3
lavatory *mustarāḥ* 14/7
law قانون قوانين *qānūn qawānīn* 21/1; ~court *maḥkama maḥākim* 8/23; ~yer *muḥāmī* 1/2; محامٍ (المحامي) *muḥāmin (al-muḥāmī)* 24/20
lazy *kaslān kasla* 8/3
lead قاد يقود *qāda yaqūdu* I 23/1; ~ing كبير كبار *kabīr kibār* 21/1
League of Arab States *jāmi9at ad-duwal al-9arabīya* 15/3
learn *ta9allam* V 12/4; it was ~ed عُلم *9ulim* 25/1
least see 9/14; at ~ على الأقلّ *9ala l-'aqall* 20/1

leave *tarak yatruk* I 3/6, 5/4, *ghādar* III 11/4; (noun) *'ijāza* 10/15
Lebanon *lubnān* 1/2
left (not right) *shimāl* 4/1
length *ṭūl 'aṭwāl* 14/3
less *'aqall* 9/13; be ~ than قلّ يقلّ عن *qalla yaqillu* I *9an* 25/1
let *khalla* II 9/10; ~ me (etc.) *khallīnī* (etc.) 5/1, 11. 8/12, ل *li* see 26/4
letter *risāla* 5/1; *maktūb makātīb* 10/9
library *maktaba makātib* 4/3, 8/23
Libya *lībiya* 1/2
life *9umr 'a9mār* 12/14; *ḥaya ḥayawāt, ma9īsha* 13/1
lift *'asansayr* 3/3
light (adj.) *khafīf khifāf* 6/11; ~er *'akhaff* 9/13
light (noun) ضوء اضواء *ḍaw' 'aḍwā'* 17/6
like *mithl* 2/7, 8/22; *zayy* 9/1; *ḥabb yiḥibb* I, *ḥubb* 8/4, 5, 12
limit *ḥadd ḥudūd* 11/1; حدّ يحدّ *ḥadda yaḥuddu* I 24/1; ~ed محدود *maḥdūd* 24/1
line *khaṭṭ khuṭūṭ* 7/1
link رابطة روابط *rābiṭa rawābiṭ* 20/1; ~ed مربوط *marbūṭ* 20/2
liquid *sāyil sawāyil* 12/1
liquor *mashrūbāt* 2/1
lira *līra* 2/3
listener مستمع *mustámi9* 24/15
literary Arabic *(al-lugha) (a)l-9arabīya l-fuṣḥa, al-faṣīḥ* 8/3
little: a ~ (some) *kam* 2/9, *shwayy* 4/1, قليلاً *qalīlan* 22/9
live (reside) *sakan yuskun* I 6/3; (be alive) *9āsh yi9īsh* I, *ma9īsha* 13/1, حيّ يحيا *ḥayya yaḥya* I 25/5
living-room *ṣāloun* 6/3
load شحن *shaḥn* 20/1
London لندن *landan* 18/6
long *ṭawīl ṭiwāl* 2/1; ~er *'aṭwal* 9/13, → no; ~est see 9/14; as ~ as طالما *ṭālamā* 25/4
look (at) *shāf yishūf* I 6/4, 7/4, نظر ينظر (الى) *naḍara yanḍuru* I *('ila)* 20/11; ~after *ihtamm* VIII *bi/fī* 13/6; ~ for *fattash* II *9an* 14/1
lose *khasir yikhsar* I, *khasāra khasāyir* 11/3; ~ sight of قطع يقطع النظر عن *qaṭa9a yaqṭa9u* I *an-naḍar 9an* 24/1
lot: quite a ~ *mish qalīl* 12/1, 2
love *ḥabb yiḥibb* I 8/4, 5; *'aḥabb yiḥibb* IV 15/1
low *wāṭi'* 14/1
lubricat-e شحّم *shaḥḥama* II, ~ion تشحيم *tashḥīm* 22/1
luck: bad ~ *sū' al-ḥaẓẓ*, good ~ *ḥusn al-ḥaẓẓ* 12/15
lunch *ghadhā'* 3/3

M

machine آلة *'āla* 16/23
mad مجنون مجانين *majnūn majānīn* 17/8
mail *barīd* 5/3
main *ra'īsī* 4/3
majority *'aktharīya* 8/1
make *9imil yi9mal* I 5/4; ~ for توجّه الى *tawajjaha* V *'ila* 23/1
man *rajul rijāl* 6/3; old ~ *shaykh shuyūkh*, young ~ *shābb shabāb* 13/1
manager *mudīr mudarā'* 1/2; → general
management → personnel
manner *kayfīya* 10/1
manufactur-e *ṣana9 yiṣna9* I, *ṣan9/ṣun9* 11/3; *iṣtána9* VIII 13/6; *iṣtinā9* 13/10; ~ing *ṣan9/ṣun9* 10/1
many *kthīr(a), kthār* 3/1, 17; → how
market *sūq 'aswāq* (f.) 11/1; سوّق *sawwaqa* II 22/2; → common; ~ing *taswīq* 10/1
married: get ~ to *tazawwaj* V *bi* 13/1
material *mādda mawādd*, raw ~ *mādda 'awwalīya* 11/3
mathematics *riyāḍīyāt* 8/3
matter *mas'ala masāyil* 8/1, 10/11; *'amr 'umūr* 10/11
may *mumkin, yumkin* 7/8; يمكن\يجوز *yumkin/yajūz* 22/5

mayor (of a village) *mukhtār makhātīr* 13/1
maza (hors d'œuvres) *māzza* 9/1
means: by ~ of بواسطة *bi wāsiṭat* 20/1; it ~ *ya9nī* 4/1
measure *miqyās maqāyīs* 8/23; *qās yiqīs* I 14/3; (administrative) *tadbīr tadābīr* 10/12; *'ijrā'* 13/1; ~ment *miqyās maqāyīs* 8/23
meat *laḥm* 9/3
mechanics *mikānīk* 8/3
medi-cal *ṭibbī* 12/3; ~cine (drug) *dawā' 'ádwiya* 12/1; (medical science) *ṭibb* 12/3
Mediterranean Sea *al-baḥr al-'abyaḍ al-mutawassiṭ* 13/3
medium (adjective) *mutawassiṭ* 8/1; ~ sweet (coffee) *maẓbūṭ* 9/1, 3
meet *qābal* III 11/4, *talāqa* VI 12/5, لقي يلقى *láqiya yalqa* I 23/7; ~ing *ijtimā9* 5/3, 13/10
member *9uḍw 'a9ḍā'* 15/3; ~ship عضوية *9uḍwīya* 26/1
memorandum *mudhakkira* 10/1, منشور *manshūr* 24/1
mention *dhakar yudhkur* I 9/1; ~ed مذكور *madhkūr* 24/1; don't ~ it *9afwan* 1/1
menu *līsta* 9/1
merchandise *biḍā9a baḍāyi9* 14/1
merit *istiḥqāq* 14/8
message *khabar 'akhbār* 7/1, 2
metre *miṭr 'amtār* 4/1; cubic ~ متر مكعّب *mitr muka99ab* 20/2
midday *ẓuhr 'aẓhār* 7/3
middle (adjective) *mutawassiṭ* 8/1; ≈ East *ash-sharq al-'awsaṭ* 13/3
midnight *nuṣṣ layl* 7/3
might (verb) *(kān) mumkin/yumkin* 7/8; (كان) يمكن\يجوز *(kān) yumkin/yajūz* 22/5
milk *ḥalīb* 9/3, لبن *laban* 16/19
mind: never ~ *ma9alaysh* 4/1, 2
mineral water *may ma9danī* 9/3
minist-er *wazīr wuzarā'*, ~ry *wizāra* 4/3; ~erial وزاري *wizārī* 23/1; prime ~ *ra'īs al-wuzarā'* 15/3
minority *'aqallīya* 10/3
minute *daqīqa daqāyiq* 4/1, 7/12; ~s (of meeting) *maḥḍar ijtimā9* 10/3
mismanagement *sū' al-'idāra* 12/15
Miss *sitt* 1/12
mission (delegation) وفد وفود *wafd wufūd* 23/1
mistake *ghalaṭ 'aghlāṭ* 5/1
misunderstanding → mutual
mixed *makhlūṭ* 9/1
mode *kayfīya* 10/1
modern حديث حداث *ḥadīth ḥidāth* 24/1
money *fulūs* (pl.) 2/3
month *shahr 'ashhur* 2/1
moon *qamar 'aqmār* 13/3
more *'akthar* 9/13
morning *ṣubḥ 'aṣbāḥ* 7/3; good ~ *ṣabāḥ al-khayr/an-nūr* 1/1, 3; in the ~ *ṣabāḥan* 11/19
Morocco *al-maghrib* 1/2
mosque *masjid masājid* 4/3
mother *'umm 'ummahāt* 6/3, 14
mount *rikib yirkab* I 3/6, 5/4
mountain *jabal jibāl* 13/3
move (administrative) *tadbīr tadābīr* 10/12; ~ away *intáqal* VIII 13/6; ~ment *ḥaraka* 14/1
Mr *sayyid sāda* 1/1, 12
Mrs, Ms *sitt* 1/12
much *kthīr* 3/1, 17, 9/13; → how, very
mud طين *ṭīn* 22/2
municipality *baladīya* 13/1
must *lāzim* 7/8; يجب *yajib* 22/5
mutual *mutabādal* 12/7; ~ misunderstanding *9adam at-tafāhum* 12/15

N

nail *mismār masāmīr* 8/23
name *'ism 'asmā'* 1/1; *samma* II 9/10
narrat-e حكى يحكي *ḥaka yaḥkī* I 23/7; ~ive *ḥikāya* 10/11

national *waṭanī* 5/3; ~isation تأميم *ta'mīm* 16/20
native *mustawṭin* 14/7
natural طبيعي *ṭabī9ī* 19/2; ~ly *ṭab9an* 4/2
near: ~ to *qarīb min* 4/1; ≈ East *ash-sharq al-'adna* 13/3
necess-ary *lāzim* 5/1, 7/9; واجب *wājib* 25/1; ~ity *ḍarūra* 11/1
need *iḥtāj* VIII *'ila* 13/6; *iḥtiyāj* 13/10; ~y *muḥtāj* 13/9
needle *'ibra 'ibar* 12/3
neglect قطع يقطع النظر عن *qaṭa9a yaqṭa9u* I *an-naḍar 9an* 24/1
negotiate *fāwaḍ* III 15/1
network شبكة شباك *shabaka shibāk* 20/2
never *'abadan* (+ neg.) 6/1, 2; ~ mind *ma9alaysh* 4/1, 2
new *jadīd judud* 6/11; ~er *'ajadd* 9/13; ≈ Year's Day *ra's as-sana* 10/15
news *khabar 'akhbār* 6/1, 15/1; *naba' 'anbā'* 15/1; ~paper *jarīda jarāyid* 11/1, صحيفة صحف *ṣaḥīfa ṣuḥuf* 18/4
next (in time) *jāī, muqbil* 7/13; ~day *thānī youm* 8/20; be ~ ولي يلي *wáliya yalī* I 25/5
night *layla layālī* 7/3; ⟶ good
nil (in statistics) لا يوجد\توجد *lā yūjad/tūjad* 26/10
Nile *an-nīl* 13/3
'nineties التسعينات\التسعينيات *at-tis9īn(īy)āt* 24/14
no *la'* 1/1; ~body *lā 'aḥad* 9/1; ~ one see 9/16, 17; ~ thank you *salāmtak* (etc.) 9/1, 2; be ~ longer ما عاد لا يعود *mā 9āda lā ya9ūdu* I 21/4; ⟶ there
noise *ṣawt 'aṣwāt* 7/1
non-Arab *ghayr 9arabī* 7/16
non-cooperation *9adam at-ta9āwun* 12/15
none ⟶ there
noon *ẓuhr 'aẓhār*, after~ *ba9d aẓ-ẓuhr* 7/3
north *shimāl*, ~east *shimāl sharqī*, ~west *shimāl gharbī* 13/3
not *mish* 4/1; ~ at all *'abadan* (+ neg.) 6/1, 2; ~ bad *mish baṭṭāl* 1/1; am/is/are ~ *mish* 4/13, ليس *laysa* I 21/5; ~ yet *lissa* (+ neg.) 6/1, لم ... بعد *lam ... ba9d*, لمّا *lamma* 26/4; ⟶ did, do
nothing *wala shī* 9/1, 17; it's ~ *mā fī shī* 4/1, 2
notice إعلان *'i9lān*, ~board لوحة *lawḥa* 24/1
now *hassa* 5/1, *al-'ān* 8/1; ~ that *u* see 6/10; up to ~ *li ḥadd al-'ān* 11/2
number *raqm 'arqām* 4/1; *9adad 'a9dād* 13/1; *numra numar* 7/1; a ~ of *9idda* (in indef. construct) 5/1, *9adad min* 6/1
nurse *mumarriḍa* 12/3

O

oasis *wāḥa* 13/3
objectionable *mustankar* 14/7
obligat-ory *mūjab*, ~ing *mūjib* 11/8
occasion *furṣa furaṣ* 5/1; *marra* 7/13
occup-ation *iḥtilāl* 13/10; ~ied, ~ying *muḥtall* 13/9; ~y *iḥtall* VIII 13/6
ocean *muḥīṭ* 13/3
o'clock *as-sā9a* see 7/12, 13
offer *qaddam* II 9/10; *taqdīm* 10/12; ~ed *muqaddam*, ~ing *muqaddim* 10/6
office *maktab makātib* 4/3, 8/23; ~r ضابط ضبّاط *ḍābiṭ ḍubbāṭ* 17/11; ⟶ assumption, post
official (noun) *ma'mūr* 2/1, 10/9; *mas'ūl* 5/3; (adj.) *rasmī* 5/3; ~ly *bi ṣūra rasmīya* 11/1; *rasmīyan* 11/20
oil بترول *bitroul* 20/1; نفط *nafṭ*, زيت *zayt* 22/1
old (things) *qadīm qudamā'* 6/11; (people) *kbīr as-sinn* 12/14; ~ man *shaykh shuyūkh* 13/1
on *9ala* 2/7; ~ the part of *min qibal*

13/15
one (indef. pronoun) *al-wāḥid* 9/1, 16
one of *'aḥad, 'iḥda* 13/1 see 5/14; احدى *'iḥda* (f.) 18/2, 3
only *faqaṭ* 2/1; *'illa* + negative 11/25
OPEC → organisation
open *maftūḥ* 3/3; *fataḥ yiftaḥ* I 3/6, 5/4; ~ fire *'aṭlaq yiṭlaq* IV *an-nār* 15/1
operation *9amalīya* 12/3
operator (telephone) *9āmil 9ummāl, 9āmila* 7/3
opinion *ra'ī 'arā'* 7/1, 2
opportunity *furṣa furaṣ* 5/1
opposite-e *muqābil* 11/8; تجاه *tujāha* 25/1; ~ion (political) *mu9āraḍa* 15/3
optional *ikhtiyārī* 8/3
or *willa* 1/1; *'aw* 2/1; → either
orange *burtuqāna* 9/6; ~s *burtuqān* 9/5
order *'amar yu'mur* I, *'amr* 3/7, 5/4, 5; *'amr 'awāmir* 10/11; (system) نظام انظمة *niḍām 'anḍima* 26/1; ~ed *ma'mūr*, ~ing *'āmir* 10/5
orderly (hospital) *mumarriḍ* 12/3
ordinary *9ādī* 10/3
organisation (act) *tanẓīm* 5/1; (body) *munaẓẓama* 10/1; ≈ of Petroleum Exporting Countries (OPEC) منظّمة الدول المصدّرة للنفط (أوبيك) *munaḍḍamat ad-duwal al-muṣaddira li n-nafṭ ('oubek)* 23/1; → world
other *'ākhar 'ukhra 'ākharīn* 6/11, 12; *thānī* 8/20; *ghayr* see 7/16
outside *khārij* 2/7
overlook قطع يقطع النظر عن *qaṭa9a yaqṭa9u* I *an-naḍar 9an* 24/1
overthrown: be ~ *inqálab* VII 13/4
overtime (work) شغل إضافي *shughl 'iḍāfī* 21/2

P

Pacific Ocean *al-muḥīṭ al-ḥādī* 13/3
pain *waja9 'oujā9* 12/3
painter *naqqāsh* 8/23
painting (activity) *niqāsha* 8/23
Palestine *filasṭīn* 1/2
paper *waraqa* 5/3, *waraq* 9/5
paraffin كيروسين *kirusīn* 22/1
parent *wālid* 6/3
parking *tawqīf* 10/12
parliament *barlamān* 5/3; lower house of ~ *majlis an-nuwwāb*, upper house of ~ *majlis ash-shuyūkh* 15/3
part *qiṭ9a qiṭa9* 11/1; جزء اجزاء *juz' 'ajzā'* 17/8; → on
particip-ant *mushtárik* 13/9; ~ate in *ishtárak* VIII *fī* 13/6; شارك في *shāraka* III *fī* 25/1
participation *ishtirāk* 13/10; مشاركة *mushāraka* 25/1; ~ (in profits) مساهمة (في الأرباح) *musāhama (fī l-'arbāḥ)* 19/2
particularity *khāṣṣa khawāṣṣ* 11/19
party (political) *ḥizb 'aḥzāb* 15/3; → third
pass (examination) *najaḥ yinjaḥ* I 8/3; ~ by *marr yimurr* I *bi/9ala* 8/4
passage of time *murūr az-zaman/zamān* 7/3
passenger *rākib rukkāb* 2/3, 10/9
passport *jawāz (safar)* 2/1
past *māḍī māḍiya māḍīyīn* 7/13
pattern *shakl 'ashkāl* 14/3
pay *dafa9 yidfa9* I 3/6, 5/4; ~ scale جدول رواتب *jadwal rawātib* 21/2; ~ment *daf9 madfū9āt* 10/11; ~ attention *dār yidīr* I *bālak* (etc.) 12/1
peace *salām* 15/1; ~keeping حفظ السلام *ḥifḍ as-salām* 26/1; ~-loving *muḥibb li s-salām* 15/2
peasant *fallāḥ* 13/3
peninsula *shibih jazīra* 13/3, 16
people *nās* 2/1; *'ahl 'ahālī* 13/1;

→ China, country, town
pepper *filfil* 9/3
perfect *kāmil* 12/1; *tamām* 6/1, 12/1; ~ion *tamām* 6/1
perhaps *yumkin* 7/1, 9; قد *qad* (+ present) 22/9
period *mudda mudad* 5/1, 7/13; *zaman/zamān 'azmān, fatra fatarāt* 7/13
permanent دائم *dā'im* 26/1
permission: ask ~ *ista'dhan* X 14/5
permit me (etc.) *'ismaḥ lī* (etc.) 1/1, 3; *samaḥ yismaḥ* I *li* 5/4, 8/12
persist: ~ in *'aṣarr yiṣirr* IV *9ala* 11/6; دام يدوم *dāma yadūmu* I 21/4; ~ence *'iṣrār* 11/10; ~ent *muṣirr* 11/8
person *shakhṣ 'ashkhāṣ* 4/1; (in statistics) *nasama* 13/1; ~al *shakhṣī* 2/1; ~ally *shakhṣīyan* 11/1, 19
personnel: ~ management ادارة شؤون الموظّفين *'idārat shu'ūn al-muwaḍḍafīn* 21/1; ~ matters *shu'ūn al-muwaẓẓafīn* 5/3
per-tain to *ta9allaq* V *bi* 12/4; ~tinent to *muta9alliq bi* 12/7
petrochemicals بتروكيميائيات *bitrukīmīyā'īyāt* 22/1
petrol بنزين *binzīn* 22/1; ~eum بترول *bitroul* 20/1
pharmacy *ṣaydalīya* 12/1
philosophise *tafalsaf* IIQ 12/12
photograph *ṣawwar* II 9/10; ~y *taṣwīr* 10/12
physics *fīziya* 8/3
picture *ṣūra ṣuwar* 5/1
pilgrimage حجّ *ḥajj* 17/8
pillow *mukhadda* 3/3
pipe *'unbūb 'anābīb* 11/1
place *maḥall* 1/1; *ḥaṭṭ yiḥuṭṭ* I 8/4, 5; → take
plain (noun) *sahil suhūl* 13/3; (adj., invariable) *sāda* 9/3
plan خطّط *khaṭṭaṭa* II 24/1; ~ning *takhṭīṭ* 5/1
plant *zara9 yizra9* I, *zar9* 13/1; (industrial) جهاز اجهزة *jihāz 'ajhiza* 22/1
plastic *blāstikī* 11/1
plate *ṣaḥn ṣuḥūn* 9/1
play لعب يلعب *la9iba yal9abu* I, *lu9b* 26/1
pleasant *lazīz lizāz* 6/11
please *'a9jab yi9jib* IV 11/6; *min faḍlak* (etc.), *tfaḍḍal* (etc.) 1/1, 3, 4; *law samaḥt* (etc.) 1/1, 4; see 1/13; ~d *mabsūṭ* 1/1, سرور *masrūr* 17/2; be ~d *inbásaṭ* VII 13/4; ~d to meet you *furṣa sa9īda, mabsūṭ bi ma9riftak* (etc.) 5/1, 2
pleasure سرور *surūr* 17/2; it was a ~/the ~'s mine (etc.) see 9/1, 2
plentiful: be ~ *tawaffar* V 14/3
plumb-er *sabbāk* 8/23; ~ing *sibāka* 8/3, 23
point: ~ of view وجهة نظر *wujhat naḍar* 25/1; ~out *'ashār yushīr* IV *'ila* 12/1; be on the ~ of *'awshak yūshik* IV *'inn* 11/6
police *shurṭa, būlīs,* ~man *shurṭī* 4/3
policy (insurance) بوليصة بواليص *būlīṣa bawālīṣ* 19/1
poli-cy, ~tics *siyāsa,* ~tical *siyāsī* 5/3
pool: → swimming-~
poor *faqīr fuqarā'* 6/11; ~ conditions *sū' al-ḥāl* 12/15; in ~ supply *basīṭ busaṭā'* 13/2
population (in statistics) *9adad sukkān* 13/2
port *mīna mawānī* 13/3; ميناء موانٍ (الموانى) *mīnā' mawānin (al-mawānī)* 24/20
porter *ḥammāl* 3/1
position (situation) *waḍ9 'ouḍā9* 8/1
positive *'ījābī* 10/1, 11/11
possess *tamakkan* V *min* 12/4
possession-s *'aghrāḍ* 2/1; take ~ of استولى *istawla* X 25/7
possessor of ذو *dhū* (etc.) see 24/19
possibility *'imkānīya* 7/1
possible *mumkin* 7/1, 9; as ... as ~

see 9/15
post office *bouṣṭa* 4/1
pound (£) *jinayh* 2/3
power قوة *qūwa* 22/2
practical *9amalī* 8/1
practice: in ~ *bi ṣūra 9amalīya* 11/21
precis-ely *bi ẓ-ẓabṭ* 11/20; بالضبط *bi ḍ-ḍabṭ* 17/10, 22/9; ~ion *ẓabṭ* 11/20; ضبط *ḍabṭ* 22/9
prefer *faḍḍal* II 9/10
premium (insurance) قسط اقساط *qisṭ 'aqsāṭ* 19/1
prepar-ation *taḥḍīr* 10/12; ~atory *taḥḍīrī* 8/1, 11/11; ~e *ḥaḍḍar* II 9/10; ~ed *muḥaḍḍar* 10/6; *musta9idd* 8/1; ~ing *muḥaḍḍir* 10/6
prescription (medical) *tadhkara tadhākir (ṭibbīya)* 12/1
presence: in the ~ of *9ind* 2/7; لدى *lada* 19/15
present (actual) *ḥāḍir* 7/13; (not absent) *moujūd* 5/1, 10/5; at ~ *fi l-waqt al-ḥāḍir* 10/2; حاليًا *ḥālīyan* 24/1
present *qaddam* II 9/10; ~ed *muqaddam*, ~ing *muqaddim* 10/6
presiden-cy رئاسة\رياسة *ri'āsa/ riyāsa* 17/5; ~t *ra'īs (al-jumhūrīya)* 15/3
pressure ضغط *ḍaghṭ* 22/1
price *si9r 'as9ār* 11/3; best/last ~ *'ākhir kalima* 14/1, 2
primary *ibtidā'ī* 8/3, 13/10
prince *'amīr 'umarā'* 15/3
principal (adjective) *ra'īsī* 4/3
principality *'imāra* 15/3
private *khāṣṣ* 5/3
probab-ility *iḥtimāl* 13/10; ~le *muḥtámal* 13/9; be ~le *iḥtámal* VIII 13/6
problem *mushkila mashākil* 7/1
procedure إجراءات *'ijrā'āt* (pl.) 21/1
proceeding *jārī/jāriya quduman* 9/2
produce *'antaj yintij* IV 11/6
product منتوج *mantūj* 22/1; ~ion *'intāj* 5/3, 11/10; ~ive *muntij* 11/8
profess-ion *mihna mihan* 1/2; ~or *'ustādh 'asātidha* 6/1
profit from *rabiḥ yirbaḥ* I *min, ribḥ 'arbāḥ* 11/3
programme *barnāmaj barāmij* 12/1
progress *taqaddum* 12/1, 8; *taqaddam* V 12/4; ~ive *taqaddumī* 12/8
prohibited *mamnū9* 8/1
project *mashrū9 mashārī9* 10/1
promot-e رقّى *raqqa* II 21/1; ~ion *tarwīj* 10/1; ترقية *tárqiya* 21/1
proof of *burhān 9ala* 12/12
Prophet's Birthday *moulūd an-nabī* 10/15
propos-e *iqtáraḥ* VIII 13/6; ~al *iqtirāḥ* 13/10
property مال اموال *māl 'amwāl* 16/20
protection وقاية *wiqāya* 19/2
protocol *tashrīfāt* (pl.) 10/12
prove *barhan* IQ *9ala* 12/12; اثبت *'athbata* IV 16/9
provisional موقّت\مؤقّت *muwaqqat/mu'aqqat* 19/1
public *9āmm* 5/1, 3; ~ation *nashra* 15/1; ~ise *'akhraj yukhrij* IV 11/6
publish *nashar yunshur* I 11/1
pull *saḥab yisḥab* I 13/4
pump ضخّ يضخّ *ḍakhkha yaḍukhku* I, طلمبة *ṭulumba* 22/1
pupil *tilmīdh talāmīdh* 6/1
puppy *kulayb* 13/17
purchase *ishtirā'* 13/10
purpose *gharaḍ 'aghrāḍ* 8/1; قصد *qaṣd* 24/1
pursue (policy etc.) انتهج *intáhaja* VIII 26/1
put *ḥaṭṭ yiḥuṭṭ* I 8/4, 5; *maḥṭūt* 10/5; ~ting *ḥāṭiṭ* 10/5

Q

quak-e *tazalzal* IIQ, ~ing *tazalzul* 12/12
qualif-ications مؤهّلات *mu'ahhilāt*,

~ied مؤهّل *mu'ahhal* 21/2
quality *jins 'ajnās* 14/1
quantity *kammīya* 14/3
quarter (part of town) *ḥayy* 4/1
quasi- *shibih* see 13/15
question *su'āl 'as'ila* 5/1, 10/11

R

rac-ial discrimination *tamyīz 9unṣurī*, ~ialism, ~ism *9unṣurīya* 15/3
radio *rādiyo* 15/1; (adj.) لاسلكي *lāsilkī* 20/1
railway سكّة سكك حديدية *sikka sikak ḥadīdīya* 20/1
rain *maṭar 'amṭār* 13/1; *maṭar yumṭur* I, it's ~ing *yumṭur, as-sama tumṭur, yusquṭ al-maṭar* 13/3
rather (but instead) *bal* 15/1
reach for *tanāwal* VI 12/5
read *qara yiqra* I *qirāya* 8/7, 8; *maqrū* 10/5
readiness *isti9dād* 14/8
reading *qirāya* 8/3, 10/11; قراءة *qirā'a* 16/1, 20/9; *qārī* 10/5
ready *musta9idd* 8/1; *ḥāḍir* 9/1; be ~ *ista9add* X 14/5; ~ for *musta9idd 9ala* 14/7
real فعلي *fi9lī* 26/1; ~isation تحقيق *taḥqīq*, ~ise حقّق *ḥaqqaqa* II 26/1
reason: for some ~ or other لأمرٍ ما *li 'amrin mā* 26/4
reasonable معقول *ma9qūl* 25/1
receive *tasallam* V 12/4; *istaqbal* X 14/5; تلقّى *talaqqa* V 23/9; ~er (radio/TV) *mustaqbil* 14/7
recent *'akhīr* 6/12; ~ly *jadīdan* 9/1, 11/19; *min qarīb* 11/23; اخيراً *'akhīran* 25/1
reception *istiqbāl* 3/1, 14/8
reciprocal *mutabādal* 12/7
recommendation *táwṣiya* 10/3
reconstitution إعادة التشكيل *'i9ādat at-tashkīl* 26/1
recover (in health) *ta9āfa* VI 12/5
recruit *waẓẓaf* II 9/10; ~ment *tawẓīf* 10/1, 11
red *'aḥmar ḥamrā' ḥumr* 12/1, 11; ≈ Sea *al-baḥr al-'aḥmar* 13/3; go ~ *iḥmarr* IX 14/4
reduce *khaffaf* II 14/3
reduction of tension تخفيف حدّة التوتّر *takhfīf ḥiddat at-tawattur* 25/1
reference إشارة *'ishāra* 24/1; with ~ to بالإشاره الى *bi l-'ishāra 'ila* 24/1
refin-e كرّر *karrara* II, ~ing تكرير *takrīr* 22/1
reform إعادة التشكيل *'i9ādat at-tashkīl* 26/1
refrigera-tion *tabrīd* 8/3; ~tor *barrāda* 6/3
refugee *lājī* 8/1
regards: give my (etc.) ~ *sallim 9aláy* (etc.) 6/1, 2
region *minṭaqa manāṭiq* 13/1; *'iqlīm 'aqālīm* 13/3
regist-er سجّل *sajjala* II; ~ration تسجيل *tasjīl* 21/1
regret *'asaf* 7/1
reinforcement تقوية *táqwiya* 19/1
reject *istankar* X 14/5; رفض يرفض رفض *rafaḍa yarfiḍu* I, *rafḍ* 24/1; ~ion *istinkār* 14/8; رفض *rafḍ* 24/1
relation(ship) *9alāqa* 10/1
release *khalla* II 9/10
relevant to *muta9alliq bi* 12/7
reliable *mu9támad* 13/9; *qābil li l-i9timād* 15/2
rely on *i9támad* VIII *9ala* 13/6
remain *ḍall yiḍill/ẓall yiẓill* I 8/4, 5; *biqi yibqa* I 8/9; ظلّ يظلّ *ḍalla yaḍallu* I 21/4, 25/2; بقي يبقى *báqiya yabqa* I 23/7
remember *tadhakkar* V 12/4
remind *dhakkar* II *bi* 9/10
remuneration *muqābil* 11/8
renew *jaddad* II 9/10; ~able *qābil li t-tajdīd* 14/10; ~al *tajdīd* 10/12
renovat-e *jaddad* II 9/10; ~ation

scale → pay
school *madrasa madāris* 7/1, 8/23
scien-ce *9ilm 9ulūm*, ~tific *9ilmī* 8/1
sea *baḥr 'abḥār* 13/3; (adj.) بحري *baḥrī* 20/2; → Mediterranean, red
search for بحث عن *baḥth 9an* 26/1
season *faṣl fuṣūl, mousim mawāsim* 10/15
second (of time) *thāniya thawān* 7/13; ~ary *thānawī* 7/1
secretar-iat امانه *'amāna* 23/1; ~y *sikritayra* 5/1; ~y-general *'amīn 9āmm* 15/3
sector *qiṭā9* 5/3; services ~ *qiṭā9 al-khidmāt* 11/3
security امن *'amn* 19/1; ≈ Council مجلس الأمن *majlis al-'amn* 26/1; → social
see *shāf yishūf* I 6/4, 7/4; نظر ينظر *naðara yanðuru* I 20/10, 11; رأى يرى *ra'a yara* I 25/6; ~ing *shāyif* 10/5
seed *ḥabba ḥubūb* 9/7; ~s *ḥabb* 9/5
seen *mashūf* 10/5
seismic زلزالي *zilzālī* 22/2
seize an opportunity *intáhaz furṣa* VIII 13/6
select *ikhtār* VIII 14/1
-self *nafs 'anfus* 8/1, 16; ذات *dhāt* see 24/19; *ḥālu* (etc.) see 13/14
self-confidence *i9timād 9ala n-nafs* 8/16
sell *bā9 yibī9* I, *bay9* 6/4, 7/4; ~ing *bāyi9* 10/5
semi- *shibih*, ~official *shibih rasmī* 13/16
senator *shaykh shuyūkh* 15/3
send *'arsal yursil* IV 11/6; وجّه *wajjaha* II 20/2; ~er *mursil* 11/8
senior كبير كبار *kabīr kibār* see 21/11
sens-ed *maḥsūs*, ~ing *ḥāsis* 10/5
sent *mursal* 11/8
sentence جملة جمل *jumla jumal* 17/8
separate جزّأ *jazza'a* II 22/1; ~d *munfáṣil* 13/9; be ~d *infáṣal* VII 13/4
separation *infiṣāl* 13/10
separatis-m *infiṣālīya* 13/11; ~t *infiṣālī* 13/10
servant: civil ~ *muwaẓẓaf ḥukūma* 1/2
serve *qaddam* II 9/10
service *khidma* 10/1; → sector
set: ~ up أسّس *'assasa* II, ~ting up تأسيس *ta'sīs* 25/1
settle (in a place) *istawṭan* X 14/5; be ~d استقرّ *istaqarra* X 26/1
settlement (of dispute) تسوية *táswiya* 21/1, 25/9
severe *shadīd 'ashiddā'*, more ~ *'ashadd* 9/13; ~ly *shadīdan* 11/19; *bi shidda* 11/20
severity *shidda* 11/20
sew *khāṭ yikhīṭ* I 14/1; ~ing *khiyāṭa* 8/1, 23
shake *zalzal* IQ 12/12
shall *rāyiḥ/rāḥ-* 10/14; سوف\س *sawfa/sa* 15/12, 21/11; ~ not لن *lan* see 22/4
shape *ṣūra ṣuwar* 5/1
sharpness حدّة *ḥidda* 25/1
shatter *kassar* II 9/10
sheep *kharūf khirāf* 9/8
sheet *sharshaf sharāshif* 3/3
shift (work) نوبة نوب *nawba nuwab* 19/1
ship سفينة سفن *safīna sufun* 20/1; باخرة بواخر *bākhira bawākhir* 20/2
shirt *qamīṣ qumṣān* 14/3
shock *zilzāl* 12/12
shoe *kundura kanādir* 14/3
shop *dukkān dakākīn* 4/3; ~ping *mushtarayāt* (pl.) 14/3; ~floor *warsha* 11/1
shore *ḍiffa ḍifaf* 13/1; ساحل سواحل *sāḥil sawāḥil* 22/1
short *qaṣīr qiṣār* 6/11; ~er *'aqṣar* 9/13; in ~ supply *nāqiṣ nuqqaṣ*

14/3
show *farja* IQ 12/12; اری يري *'ara yurī* IV 25/7; ~ round *zawwar* II 9/10
shut *sakkar* II 9/10
sick *marīḍ marḍa* 6/11; ~ness *maraḍ 'amrāḍ* 12/3
side *jānib jawānib* 15/1
sign وقّع *waqqa9a* II 24/1; ~, ~al *'ishāra* 4/1; ~ature *tawqī9* 10/3
simple *basīṭ busaṭā'* 6/11
since *mundh, min* 2/7
sincere مخلص *mukhliṣ*, to be ~ اخلص *'akhlaṣa* IV 24/1, 2; Yours ~ly see 24/2
sir *yā sīdna* 3/1; *yā sidī* 7/1
sister *'ukht 'ikhwāt* 6/3, 6/14; ~(-state) شقيق شقائق *shaqīq shaqā'iq* see 23/1
sit *jalas yijlis* I 8/1
situation *waḍ9 'ouḍā9* 8/1
skirt *tannūra tanānīr* 14/3
sky *sama samāwāt* (m./f.) 13/3
sleep *nām yinām* I, *noum* 6/4, 7/4; *noum* 10/11
small *ṣghīr ṣghār* 2/1; ~ door *buwayb* 13/7; ~er *'aṣghar* 9/13; ~est *'aṣghar, ṣughra* 9/14; → change, consider
smelt-er *sabbāk*, ~ing *sibāka* 8/23
smile *tabassam* V 12/4
snow *shita 'áshtiya, thalj thulūj, thalaj yuthluj* I, it's ~ing *yuthluj, as-sama tuthluj, yusquṭ ath-thalj* 13/3
so *kadha* 2/1; *hayk* 8/1, *fa* 4/1; ~ let me (etc.) فل *fa l* 26/4; ~ that *ḥatta* 5/1; انْ *'an,* ل *li,* لأنْ *li 'an,* كي *kay,* لكي *li kay,* حتّى *ḥatta,* ~ that ... not لئلاّ *li'allā* 22/4; and ~ on *u ghayru* 7/16, وكذا وكذا *wa/u kadha u kadha* 24/1
social *ijtimā9ī* 13/10; ~ security الضمان الاجتماعي *aḍ-ḍamān al-ijtimā9ī* 19/2
social-ism *ishtirākīya* 13/11; ~ist *ishtirākī* 13/10
sock *kalsa* 14/3
sold *mabī9* 10/5
solution *ḥill ḥulūl;* 9/1, 10/11
solve *ḥall yiḥill* I, *ḥill* 8/4, 5; be ~d *inḥall* VII 13/4; ~d *munḥall* 13/9
some *kam* 2/1, 9; ~ day/time يومًا ما *yawman mā* 26/5; ~ of *ba9ḍ* 8/1, 17; ~how or other *kayf mā kān* 13/1, 2, 13; ~one see 9/16; ~thing *shī* 6/1; see 9/16; ~what نوعًا ما *naw9an mā* 26/1, 5; ~where or other *wayn mā kān,* at ~ time *mata mā kān* 13/13; for ~ reason or other لأمرٍ ما *li 'amrin mā* 26/5
son *'ibn 'abnā'* 6/3
soon *qarīban* 11/19; *9an qarīb, ba9d ishwayy* 11/23; as ~ as possible see 9/15
sorry *muta'assif* 7/1, 12/7; be ~ *ta'assaf* V 12/4
sort *jins 'ajnās* 14/1
sound (adj.) سالم *sālim* 21/1
soup *shouraba* 9/1
source *maṣdar maṣādir* 15/1
south *janūb*, ~east *janūb sharqī*, ~west *janūb gharbī* 13/3
Soviet Union *al-ittiḥād as-sufiyātī/ sufiyaytī* 15/3
speak *ḥaka yiḥkī* I 8/7, 8; *takallam* V 12/4; تكلّم *takallama* V 23/7; ~er *mutakallim* 12/7; ~ing *ḥākī* 10/5
special *khāṣṣ* 5/3
specialisation *takhaṣṣuṣ* 8/1, 12/8
specialis-e in *takhaṣṣaṣ* V *fī* 12/4; ~ing *mutakhaṣṣiṣ* 5/1, 12/7; ~t *mutakhaṣṣiṣ* 5/1, 12/7
speech (oration) *khiṭāb 'akhṭiba* 10/6;
speed *sur9a* 11/20
spices → cooked
spicy *mubahhar* 9/3
splendid *9aẓīm 9uẓamā'* 6/11
spoken *maḥkī* 10/5
spokesman *nāṭiq bi lisān* 15/3
spoon *mal9aqa malā9iq* 9/3

sport *riyāḍa* 8/3
spring (season) *rabī9* 10/15
square (open place) *sāḥa, maydān mayādīn* 4/3
stab-le (adj.) *thābit* 14/1; be ~ استقرّ *istaqarra* X, ~ility استقرار *istiqrār* 26/1
staircase *sullām salālīm* 6/3
stand up *qām yiqūm* I 6/4, 7/4
starting from *ibtidā'an min, i9tibāran min* 13/10
state (country) *dawla duwal* 5/3; → united
station *maḥaṭṭa* 8/23
statue *timthāl tamāthīl* 4/3
stay *'iqāma* 2/3
steadiness استقرار *istiqrār* 26/1
steel فولاذ *fūlādh* 25/1
step خطوة *khuṭwa* 25/1
stewardess *muḍīfa* 1/1
still *lissa* 6/1; ~ to be دام يدوم *dāma yadūmu* I 21/4;
~ to be/do ما زال لا يزال *mā zāla lā yazālu* I 21/4, 25/2
Stockholm استكهولم *istok-holm* 18/6
stomach *baṭn buṭūn* 12/3
stop *waqqaf* II 9/10; *'awqaf* IV 11/6; وقف يقف *waqafa yaqifu* I 20/6; قف *qif* 20/10; (bus etc.) ~ *mouqif* 4/3; ~page *'īqāf* 11/10
storage تخزين *takhzīn* 19/1
store: department ~ *maḥallāt* (pl.) 4/3
storm *9āṣifa 9awāṣif* 13/3
street *shāri9 shawāri9* 4/1
strength قوة *qūwa* 22/2
strike *ḍarab yuḍrub* I 7/3; (from work) اضرب *'aḍraba* IV, اضراب *'iḍrāb* 21/1
strive for سعى يسعى الى *sa9a yis9a* I *'ila* 23/7
strong *qawī 'aqwiyā'* 9/13; ~er *'ashadd* 9/1; *'aqwa* 9/13
student *ṭālib ṭullāb, ṭāliba* 1/2, 10/9
study *daras yudrus* I, *dirāsa* 4/1, 5/4; *dirāsa* 8/1, 10/11
subcontinent *shibih qārra* 13/16
subject *mouḍū9 mawāḍī9* 11/19
substance → form
substitut-e *istabdal* X 14/5; ~ion *istibdāl* 11/1; 14/8
succeed *najaḥ yinjaḥ* I, *najāḥ* 8/12
success *najāḥ* 10/11; ~ful موفّق *muwaffaq* 24/1
such *kadha* 2/1; ~ a *mithl* see 8/22
such-and-such كذا و كذا *kadha wa/u kadha* 24/1
Sudan *as-sūdān* 1/2
suffice *kaffa* II 14/1; كفى يكفي كفاية *kafa yakfī* I, *kifāya* 25/1
sugar *sukkar* 9/3
suggest *iqtáraḥ* VIII 13/6
suit *nāsab* III 11/4; ~able *munāsib* 8/1, 11/8
suit (of clothes) *badhla* 14/3
suitcase *shanta* 2/1
summar-ise *'awjaz yūjiz* IV, ~y *mūjaz* 15/1
summer *ṣayf* 6/1; (adj.) *ṣayfī* 14/1
summon *nāda* III 11/4, *istaḥḍar* X 14/5; دعا يدعو *da9a yad9ū* I 23/7
sun *shams shumūs* (f.) 13/3
super-power *dawla kubra* 15/3; ~tanker ناقلة ضخمة *nāqila ḍakhma* 20/1
supervisor *mushrif* 11/1
supplement *'iḍāfa* 11/10; ~ary *'iḍāfī* 11/11
supply *zawwad* II 14/3; poor ~ *basīṭ busaṭā'* 13/2; → short
support ايّد *'ayyada* II, تأييد *ta'yīd*, in ~ of تأييدًا لِ *ta'yīdan li* 21/1
suppose *ẓann yiẓunn* I 8/4, 5
sure of متأكّد من *muta'akkid min* 21/1
surg-eon *jarrāḥ* 12/3; ~ery (clinic) *9iyāda* 12/1, 3; ~ical *jirāḥī* 12/3
sweet *ḥilū*, f. *ḥilwa* 9/3; ~s *ḥilwīyāt* 9/1
swimming-pool *masbaḥ masābiḥ* 3/3

Syria *sūriya* 1/2; *ash-shām* 6/1
system نظام انظمة *niẓām 'anẓima* 26/1

T

table *ṭarabayza, ṭābla, ṭawla* 6/3; dining ~ *sufra sufar* 9/3; (of data) جدول جداول *jadwal jadāwil* 19/1
tablet *qurṣ 'aqrāṣ* 12/1
tailor *khayyāṭ* 8/23
take *'akhadh yākhudh* I, *'akhdh* 3/7, 5/5, 9; *ittákhadh* VIII 13/6; (food, drink) *tanāwal* VI 12/5; ~ down *nazzal* II 9/10; ~ into consideration *'akhadh yākhudh* I *bi 9ayn al-i9tibār* 13/10; ~ place *ḥadath yaḥduth* I 15/1; ~ the place of حلّ يحلّ محلّ *ḥalla yaḥullu* I *maḥall* 25/1
taking *'akhdh* 10/11; *ittikhādh* 13/10
talk *ḥaka yiḥkī* I 8/7, 8
tangible *maḥsūs* 10/5, *malmūs* 12/1
tank صهريج صهاريج *ṣahrīj ṣahārīj* 19/1; ~er ناقلة *nāqila* 20/1
tar زفت *zift* 22/1
task *mahamma mahāmm* 7/1
taught *mu9allam* 10/6
tax *ḍarība ḍarāyib* 11/3
taxi *taksī* 2/3
tea *shāī* 1/1
teach *9allam* II 9/10; ~er *mu9allim(a)* 1/2, 10/6, 9; ~ing *ta9līm* 8/1, 3, 10/10, 12
techn-ical *fannī* 5/1; ~ology تكنولوجيا *tiknulujīya* 25/1
telephone *tilifoun* 7/1, 3; *ḍarab yuḍrub* I *tilifoun* 7/3; *talfan* IQ 12/12; by ~ *tilifonīyan* 7/3
televis-e *talfaz* IQ, *talfaza*, ~ion *talfaza* 12/12
temperature *darajat ḥarāra* 12/1
temporary موقّت\مؤقّت *muwaqqat/mu'aqqat* 19/1
tenan-cy *isti'jār* 14/8; ~t *musta'jir* 14/7
tens-e: be ~ توتّر *tawattara* V, ~ion توتّر *tawattur* 25/1
terms of reference *majāl baḥth* 10/3
terrorism *'irhāb* 15/3
test *tajrīb* 10/12
than *min, mimma* 9/13
thank: ~ for *shakar yushkur* I *9ala, shukr* 5/4; ~ God *nushkuralla*, ~ you *shukran* 1/3; *'alla ya9fīk* (etc.) see 6/1, 2; *'alla yibārik fīk* (etc.) see 14/1, 2; ~ you/Heavens *(al-)ḥamdilla* 1/1, 3; *(al-)ḥamdulilla* 5/1; → no
that (conjunction) *'inn* 3/1, 4/7; أنّ *'anna* 21/8, 22/4; إنّ *'inna* 21/12; أنْ *'an*, ~ ... not ألاّ *'allā* 22/4; (relative) *illī* 8/1, 13; الّذي *alládhī* (etc.) 23/1; ~ is to say *ya9nī* 4/1, 2; → so
theft سرقة *sariqa* 19/2
then (afterwards) *ba9dayn* 4/1; (so) *fa* 4/1; see 11/16; ف *fa* 26/4
theoretically *bi ṣūra naẓarīya* 8/1, 11/21
there *hunāk* 2/1; ~ are/is *fī* 2/1, 11; يوجد\توجد *yūjad/tūjad* 26/10; ~ is no/none لا يوجد\توجد *la yūjad/tūjad* 26/10; لا...َ *lā ... -a* see 25/3; ~'s nothing *mā fī shī* 4/1, 2; ~ was/were *kān fī* 6/7; ~ will/won't be *(mā) yikūn fī* 7/7
therefore *hayk* 8/1
thing *shī 'ashyā'* 4/1
things (possessions) *'aghrāḍ* 2/1
think *iftákar* VIII 13/6
third: ~ party طرف ثالث *ṭaraf thālith* 19/2; ~ world *al-9ālam ath-thālith* 15/3
thirsty *9aṭshān 9aṭsha 9iṭash* 9/3
thought *fikra 'afkār* 5/1
throat *ḥalq ḥulūq* 12/1
through عبر *9abra* 19/15
throw *rama yirmī* I 8/7, 8; رمى يرمي *rama yarmī* I 23/7
thus *kadha* 2/1; *hayk* 8/1
ticket *tadhkara tadhākir* 2/3
tie *9aqad ya9qid* I, *9aqd* 15/1;

(neck~) *gravāt* 14/3
Tigris *ad-dijla* 13/3
tiles *balāṭ* 9/5
time *waqt 'ouqāt* 2/1, 7/13; *zaman/ zamān 'azmān* 6/1, 7/3, 13; a ~ *marra* 7/13; at the ~ of *9ind* 6/18; for a long ~ now *min zamān* 6/1, 2
timetable *jadwal jadāwil* 2/3
tired *ta9bān* 9/1
to *'ila, li* 2/7; *9a* see 4/9; أنْ *'an* see 22/4
today *al-youm* 1/1
together *ma9an* 11/19; *sawa* 13/1
toler-ance *iḥtimāl* 13/10; ~ate *iḥtámal* VIII 13/6
tomatoes *banadūra* 9/1
tomorrow *bukra* 7/1; غداً *ghadan* 18/11; the day after ~ *ba9d bukra* 7/3
ton(ne) طنّ اطنان *ṭunn 'aṭnān* 20/2
tongue *lisān 'alsina* (m./f.) 12/1
too (also) *kamān* 1/1
tooth *sinn 'asnān* 12/3
total مجموع *majmū9* 24/1
tour *jawla* 5/1, 2
towards تجاه *tujāh* 25/1
towel *minshafa manāshif* 3/3, 8/23
town *balad bilād* 3/1; ~ hall *baladīya* 13/1; ~speople *'ahl al-mudun* 13/3
trade *tijāra* 4/3; ~r *tājir* 1/2; ~ union *niqābat al-9ummāl* 11/3
traffic *murūr* 4/1, 10/11
train درّب *darraba* II 24/1; (noun) قطار قطر *qiṭār quṭur* 20/2; ~er مدرّب *mudarrib* 24/1; ~ing *tadrīb* 8/3
transfer *intiqāl* 13/10; حوّل *ḥawwala* II, تحويل *taḥwīl* 25/1
translat-e *tarjam* IQ, *tarjama tarājim,* ~ed *mutarjam,* ~ion *tarjama tarājim,* ~or *mutarjim* 12/12
transport نقل *naql* 20/1
travel *safra safarāt* 2/3; *sāfar* III 11/4; ~ler *musāfir* 2/3, 11/8
treat *9āmal* III 11/4; (medically) *9ālaj* III 12/3
treatment *mu9āmala* 11/9; (medical) *9ilāj* 12/1; ⟶ ill
treaty *ittifāqīya* 15/3
tree *shajara* 9/6; ~s *shajar* 9/5
Tripoli طرابلس *ṭrāblus* 23/1
trousers *banṭaloun* 14/3
true *ṣaḥīḥ* 4/1
trunk *ṣandūq ṣanādīq* 2/3
truth *ḥaqīqa ḥaqāyiq,* in ~ *fi l-ḥaqīqa* 11/20
try *jarrab* II 9/10; *ḥāwal* III 11/4; حاول *ḥāwala* III 22/5
tube *'unbūb 'anābīb* 11/1
Tunis, ~ia *tūnis* 1/2
turn نوبة نوب *nawba nuwab* 19/1
type *katab yuktub* I *bi l-mākina* 5/1; ~writer *mākīna* 5/1, *'āla kātiba* 5/3

U

unclear see 11/21
uncooperative *9adīm at-ta9āwun* 12/15
uncountable see 13/5
under *taḥt* 2/7; ~clothes *malābis taḥtānīya* 14/3
under-stand *fihim yifham* I 11/1; ~stood *mafhūm* 8/1
undertak-e *qām yiqūm* I *bi* 6/4; ~ing *qiyām bi* 10/11
unfortunately *li sū' al-ḥaẓẓ* 12/2, 15
union *ittihād* 13/10; ⟶ trade, Europe
united *muttáḥid* 13/9; ≈ Arab Emirates الإمارات العربية المتّحدة *al-'imārāt al-9arabīya l-muttáḥida* 23/1; ≈ Nations (Organisation) *(hay'at) al-'umam al-muttáḥida,* ≈ States of America *al-wilāyāt al-muttáḥida l-'amrīkīya/li 'amayrka* 15/3; be ~ *ittáḥad* VIII 13/6
unity *ittiḥād* 13/10
university *jāmi9a* 4/1; (adj.) *jāmi9ī* 8/3
unless *'idha* + negative 11/14
unofficially *mish/ghayr rasmīyan* 11/19

'*idha* 21/3
which *'ayy* 5/15, 8/15; ~ one *'ayy wāḥid* 5/15
which (relative) *illī* 8/1, 13, 15; ٱلّذي *alládhī* (etc.) 23/1; الأمر ٱلّذي *al-'amr alládhī* 23/2
while *u* see 6/1, 10
white *'abyaḍ bayḍā' bīḍ* 12/11; go ~ *ibyaḍḍ* IX 14/4
who *mīn* 5/15; من *man* 16/20, 21/6
who (relative) *illī* 8/1, 13; *mīn illī* 8/15; ٱلّذي *alládhī* (etc.) 23/1
whoever *mīn mā* 11/15
whole *kull* 5/1, 8/18; for the ~ (duration) of *ṭūl* 2/7
whose *(li) mīn* 5/15; (ل)من *(li) man* 16/20, 21/6
why *laysh* 5/15; لماذا\لما *li mādha/li mā* 21/6
wid-e *wāṣiḥ*, ~er *'awṣaḥ* 9/13; ~th *9arḍ 9urūḍ* 14/1
wife *zouja* 6/1
will *rāyiḥ/rāḥ-* 10/14; سوف\س *sawfa/sa-* 15/12, 21/11; ~ not لن *lan* see 22/4; ⟶ good, ill
wind *rīḥ riyāḥ* 13/3
window *shubbāk shabābīk* 6/3
wine *nbīdh* 9/3
winter *shita* 10/15; (adj.) *shatawī* 14/3
wire سلك اسلاك *silk 'aslāk*, ~less لاسلكي *lāsilkī* 20/1
wish *'irāda* 11/10; ~ for *raghba fī* 8/1
with *bi, ma9* 2/7
withdraw *insáḥab* VIII 13/4; ~al *insiḥāb* 13/10
without *bidūn* 2/7; to do ~ *istaghna* X *9an* 14/5
woman *mara niswān* 6/3
word *kalima* 5/1
work *shughl 'ashghāl* 4/3; *ishtághal* VIII 13/6; ~man *9āmil 9ummāl* 10/9; ~ing *9āmil* 10/1; ~shop *mashghal mashāghil* 8/23; *ma9mal ma9āmil* 8/1, 23; *warsha* 11/1
world *9ālam 9awālim, dunya* 13/3; ≈ Bank *al-bank ad-duwalī* 15/3; ≈ Health Organisation منظّمة الصحّة العالمية *munaḍḍamat aṣ-ṣiḥḥa l-9ālamīya* 23/1; ⟶ third
writ-e *katab yuktub* I, *kitāba* 3/5, 6, 5/4; ~e to *kātab* 11/4; ~e to each other *takātab* VI 12/5; ~er *mu'allif* 1/2; ~ing *kātib* 10/5; *kitāba* 8/3, 10/11; ~ten *maktūb* 5/1, 10/5; be ~ten *inkátab* VII 13/4
wrong: what's ~ with *shū malu* (etc.) 12/1, 2

Y

year *sana snīn/sanawāt* 4/1; عام اعوام *9ām 'a9wām* 24/1
yellow *'aṣfar ṣafrā' ṣufr* 12/11; go ~ *iṣfarr* IX 14/4
yes *na9am* 1/1; *'ayna9am* 4/1; *'aywa* 7/1
yesterday *'ams*, the day before ~ *'awwal 'ams* 7/3
yet ⟶ not
yoghurt لبن *laban* 16/19
young *sghīr as-sinn* 12/14; ~ man *shābb shabāb* 13/1

Z

zeal *ijtihād* 13/10
Zionist *ṣahyūnī* 15/3

Arabic, Part II

Words normally used with the article (e.g. اللاذقية *al-lādhiqīya*) are shown with the article, but listed under their own initial letter. Expressions consisting of a preposition + noun (e.g. بواسطة *bi wāsiṭat*) are listed under the noun. If you do not find your word in this index, look under its transcribed form in the Arabic Part I index.

بالإشارة الى *bi l-'ishāra 'ila* with reference to 24/1

اضافي: شغل اضافي *shughl 'iḍāfī* overtime (work) 21/2

اضراب *'iḍrāb* strike (from work) 21/1

اضرب *'aḍraba* IV strike (from work) 21/1

ضوء → اضواء

طنّ → اطنان

اعاد *'a9āda* IV (do) again 25/2

اعادة التشكيل *'i9ādat at-tashkīl* reform, reconstitution 26/1

اعادة التنظيم *'i9ādat at-tanẓīm* reorganisation 26/1

عزيز → اعزّاء

اعلان *'i9lān* announcement, notice 24/1

عام → اعوام

فعل → افعال

افلاس *'iflās* bankruptcy 26/1

افلس *'aflasa* IV be/go bankrupt 26/1

قسط → اقساط

علي الأقلّ *9ala al-'aqall* at least 20/1

ألاّ *'allā́* that ... not 22/4

إلاّ *'illa* except 19/15

الألف\الألفي *al-'alf(ī)* thousandth 24/10

الإمارات (العربية) المتّحدة *al-'imārāt (al-9arabīya) al-muttáḥida* United Arab Emirates 23/1

التّي *allátī* see 23/2

الّذي *alládhī* see 23/1, 2, 26/14

الّذين *alladhīna* see 23/2

اللتان *allatāni* see 23/2

اللتين *allatayni* see 23/2

اللذان *alladhāni* see 23/2

اللذين *alladhayni* see 23/2

اللواتي *allawātī* see 23/2

آلة *'āla* machine 16/24

امانة *'amāna* secretariat 23/1

مثال → امثلة

امر: الأمر الذي *al-'amr alládhī* see 23/2; لأمرٍ ما *li 'amrin mā* for some reason or other 26/5

امريكي *'amrīkī* American 23/1

مساء → امساء

الأمم المتّحدة *al-'umam al-muttáḥida* United Nations 26/1

امن *'amn* safety, security 19/1; → مجلس

مال → اموال

أنْ *'an* (so) that, to, see 22/4

أنّ *'anna* that 21/8, 26/14

إنْ *'in* if see 26/6

إنّ *'inna* see 21/8, 26/14

إنْ شاء الله *'in shā' 'allāh* see 26/6

إنْ وجد(ت) *'in wujid(at)* if any 26/10

انت *'anta* (m.) *'anti* (f.) you 20/3

انتقد على *intáqada* VIII *9ala* criticise 26/1

انتقاد على *intiqād 9ala* criticism of 26/1

انتم *'antum* you (pl.) 20/3

انتما *'antuma* both of you 26/13

انتنّ *'antunna* you (f. pl.) 26/13

انتهاء *intihā'* expiry 19/2

انتهج *intáhaja* VIII pursue (e.g. a policy) 26/1

تخفيف حدّة التوتّر *takhfīf ḥiddat at-tawattur* reduction of tension 25/1

ترقية *tárqiya* promotion 21/1

تركّز *tarakkaza* V be concentrated 26/1

تسجيل *tasjīl* registration 21/1

التسعينات \ التسعينيات *at-tis9īnāt/ at-tis9īnīyāt* the 'nineties 24/14

تسوية *táswiya* settlement (of a dispute) 21/1, 25/9

تشحيم *tashḥīm* lubrication 22/1

تشكيل *tashkīl* formation, constitution 26/1

تطبيق *taṭbīq* application 21/1

تطوير *taṭwīr* development 23/1

تعويض *ta9wīḍ* compensation 19/1

تفتيش *taftīsh* inspection 20/1

تقبّل *taqabbala* V accept 24/2

تقدّم ب *taqaddama* V *bi* advance (e.g. a proposal) 25/6

تقوية *táqwiya* reinforcement 19/1

تكرير *takrīr* refining 22/1

تكلّم *takallama* V speak 23/7, 26/14

تكنولوجيا *tiknulujīya* technology 25/1

تلّ تلال *tall tilāl* hill 16/19

تلاقى *talāqa* VI encounter 23/12

تلاقٍ (التلاقي) *talāqin (at-talāqī)* encounter 23/12

تلّ→ تلال

تلقّى *talaqqa* V acquire, receive 23/9, 12

تلقٍّ (التلقّي) *talaqqin (at-talaqqī)* acquisition 23/12

تلك *tilka* see 22/3

تنبّؤ *tanabbu'* forecast 17/6

توازن *tawāzana* VI be balanced, توازن *tawāzun* equilibrium, balance 26/1

توتّر *tawattara* V be tense, *tawattur* tension 25/1

توجد *tūjad* there is/are; لا توجد *lā tūjad* there is no/none, nil (in statistics) see 26/10

توجّه الى *tawajjaha* V *'ila* make for, head for 23/1

توقيع *tawqī9* signature 24/1

تولّى *tawalla* V be appointed 25/7

تولٍّ (التولّي) *tawallin (at-tawallī)* assumption of office 25/9

تينك *taynika* see 22/3

ث

الثالث عشر *ath-thālith 9ashar* thirteenth 24/10

ثانٍ (الثاني) *thānin (ath-thānī)* second 24/10

الثاني عشر *ath-thānī 9ashar* twelfth 24/10

ثنائي *thunā'ī* double 17/5

ج

جاء يجيء *jā'a yajī'u* I come, جاء يجيء ب *jā'a yajī'u* I *bi* bring 25/6, 26/14

جدول جداول *jadwal jadāwil* table (of data) 19/1

جدول رواتب *jadwal rawātib* pay scale 21/2

جرام *grām* gram 18/6

جرى يجري جري *jara yajrī* I, *jary* flow 23/1, 7

جزّأ *jazza'a* II separate 22/1

جزء اجزاء *juz' 'ajzā'* part 17/8
جملة جمل *jumla jumal* sentence 17/8
جهاز اجهزة *jihāz 'ajhiza* installation, plant, rig 22/1; جهاز حفر *jihāz ḥafr* drilling rig 22/2
جوّي *jawwī* air (adj.) 20/2

ح

الحادي عشر *al-ḥādī 9ashar* eleventh 24/10
الحادي والعشرين *al-ḥādī wa l-9ishrīn* twenty-first 24/10
حاليًا *ḥālīyan* at present 24/1
حاول *ḥāwala* III try 22/5
حتّى *ḥatta* so that 22/4; until 25/4
حجّ *ḥajj* pilgrimage 17/8
حجم حجوم *ḥajm ḥujūm* volume, bulk 20/1
حدّ يحدّ *ḥadda yaḥuddu* I limit 24/1
حديث → حداث
حدّة *ḥidda* sharpness 25/1; → تخفيف
حديث حداث *ḥadīth ḥidāth* modern 24/1
حدود *ḥudūd* (pl.) frontier 20/1
حريقة حرائق *ḥarīqa ḥarā'iq* fire 19/1
حسب *ḥasaba* according to 19/1
حصول على *ḥuṣul 9ala* access to 20/1
حطي *ḥuṭī* see 24/11
حفّار *ḥaffār* driller 22/2
حفر يحفر حفر *ḥafara yaḥfiru* I, *ḥafr* drill 22/1
حفظ السلام *ḥifẓ as-salām* peace-keeping 26/1
حقّ حقوق *ḥaqq ḥuqūq* right (noun) 18/4
حقّق *ḥaqqaqa* II realise 26/1
حقّ → هقوق
حكى يحكي *ḥaka yaḥkī* I narrate 23/7
حلّ يحلّ محلّ *ḥalla yaḥullu* I *maḥall* ... take the place of ... 25/1
حمل يحمل حمل *ḥamila yaḥmilu* I, *ḥaml* carry, bear 24/1
حوّل *ḥawwala* II transfer 25/1
حيّ\حيي يحيا *ḥayya yaḥya* I live 25/5
حيث انّ *ḥaythu 'anna* given that 26/1

خ

زيت ,نفط → خام
خبير → خبراء
خبرة *khibra* expertise 25/1
خبير خبراء *khabīr khubarā'* expert 25/1
خطّ جوّي *khaṭṭ jawwī* airline 20/2
خطّط *khaṭṭaṭa* II plan 24/1
خطوة *khuṭwa* step 25/1
خلاف *khilāf* dispute 21/1

د

دام يدوم *dāma yadūmu* I persist, still to be 21/4; still to (do) 25/2
دائرة دوائر *dā'ira dawā'ir* directorate 24/1
دائم *dā'im* permanent 26/1
دراسي *dirāsī* academic 24/1
درّب *darraba* II train 24/1
درجة *daraja* grade 21/2

دعا يدعو *da9a yad9ū* I summon 23/7
دائرة → دوائر
دور ادوار *dawr 'adwār* rôle 26/1
ديزل *dīzil* diesel 22/1
دين ديون *dayn duyūn* debt 26/1

ذ

ذا *dhā* see 24/19
ذات *dhāt* see 24/19
ذانك *dhānika* see 22/3
ذات ذوات *dhāt dhawāt* essence, identity, same, -self 24/19
ذلك *dhālika* see 22/3, 26/14
ذهب يذهب *dhahaba yadhhabu* I go 20/11, 26/14
ذو *dhū* see 24/19
ذوا *dhawā* see 24/19
ذوات *dhawāt* see 24/19; → ذات
ذواتا *dhawātā* see 24/19
ذواتي *dhawātay* see 24/19
ذوو *dhawū* see 24/19
ذوي *dhaway/dhawī* see 24/19
ذي *dhī* see 24/19
ذينك *dhaynika* see 22/3

ر

رابطة روابط *rābiṭa rawābiṭ* link 20/1
راتب رواتب *rātib rawātib* salary 21/2
راجع *rāja9a* III review, revise 26/1
رأى يرى *ra'a yara* I see 25/6
رجا يرجو *raja yarjū* I request 23/7
رسم رسوم *rasm rusūm* drawing 19/1
رضي يرضى ب *rāḍiya yarḍa* I *bi* approve of, be satisfied with 23/7
رفض يرفض رفض *rafaḍa yarfiḍu* I, *rafḍ* reject 24/1
رقّى *raqqa* II promote 21/1
رمى يرمي *rama yarmī* I throw 23/7
رابطة → روابط
راتب → رواتب
رئاسة\رياسة *ri'āsa/riyāsa* chairmanship, presidency 17/5

ز

ما زال لا يزال :زال *mā zāla lā yazālu* I still to be 21/4; continue to (do) 25/2
زفت *zift* bitumen, tar 22/1
زلزالي *zilzālī* seismic 22/2
زيت زيوت *zayt zuyūt* oil, زيت خام *zayt khām* crude oil 22/1

س

س *sa* shall, will 21/11, 26/14
ساحل سواحل *sāḥil sawāḥil* shore, coast 22/1
سالم *sālim* sound (adj.) 21/1
ساوى *sāwa* III be/make equal 25/7
سبب اسباب *sabab 'asbāb* cause 21/1
سجّل *sajjala* II register 21/1
بسرعة اكثر *bi sur9a 'akthar* faster 22/9
سرقة *sariqa* theft 19/2
سرور *surūr* pleasure 17/2
سريعًا *sarī9an* fast 22/9
سعادة *sa9āda* see 23/1
سعى يسعى الى *sa9a yas9a* I *'ila* strive for 23/7
سفينة سفن *safīna sufun* ship 20/1
سكّة سكك حديدية *sikka sikak*

19/2
طلب *ṭalab* claim 19/2
طلمبة *ṭulumba* pump 22/1
طنّ اطنان *ṭunn 'aṭnan* ton(ne) 20/2
طوّر *ṭawwara* II develop 23/1
طيّب *ṭayyib* good 16/14
طين *ṭīn* mud 22/2

ظ

ظرف ظروف *ḍarf ḍurūf* condition, circumstance 21/1
ظلّ يظلّ *ḍalla yaḍallu* I remain 21/4; remain (doing) 25/2

ع

عاد عود *9āda ya9ūdu* I (do) again 25/2; ما عاد لا يعود *mā 9āda lā ya9ūdu* I be no longer 21/4
منظّمة ← عالمي
عام اعوام *9ām 'a9wām* year 24/1
عبر *9abra* through, beyond 19/15
عبّر عن *9abbara* II *9an* express 26/7
عدل *9adl* justice 26/1
عزل *9azl* dismissal 21/2
عزل يعزل *9azala ya9zilu* I dismiss 21/2
عزيز اعزّاء *9azīz 'a9izzā'* Dear ... 24/4
العشرين *al-9ishrīn* twentieth 24/10
عضوية *9uḍwīya* membership 26/1
عفا يعفو ل *9afa ya9fū* I *li* excuse 23/7
عقد عقود *9aqd 9uqūd* contract 19/2
عندما *9indama* when 25/4

غ

غاز *ghāz* gas 22/1
غدًا *ghadan* tomorrow 18/11
غرام *grām* gram 18/6
غير *ghayr* see 26/14
غير انّ *ghayr 'anna* whereas 26/1

ف

ف *fa* see 26/4, 6
فاعلية *fā9ilīya* effectiveness, efficiency 26/1
فاق يفوق *fāqa yafūqu* I excel 24/1
فإنّ *fa 'inna* see 26/6
فشل *fashal* failure 19/1
فعل افعال *fi9l 'af9āl* action 18/4
فعلي *fi9lī* real, actual 21/1; factual 26/1
فولاذ *fūlādh* steel 25/1
ڤيزا *vīza* visa 18/6

ق

قاد يقود *qāda yaqūdu* I lead, head 23/1
قادمًا من *qādiman min* arriving from 23/1
قاضٍ (القاضي) قضاة *qāḍin (al-qāḍī) quḍā* judge 24/20
قانون قوانين *qānūn qawānīn* law 21/1
قبل انْ *qabla 'an* before 25/4, 26/14
قبول *qabūl* acceptance 24/1
قد *qad* (+ present) perhaps 22/10
قراءة *qirā'a* reading 16/1, 20/9
قرن قرون *qarn qurūn* century 26/1
قسط اقساط *qisṭ 'aqsāṭ* premium, instalment 19/1
قصد *qaṣd* purpose 24/1
قاضٍ ← قضاة
قطار قطر *qiṭār quṭur* train 20/2
قطّر *qaṭṭara* II distil 22/2
قطع يقطع النظر عن *qaṭa9a*

لئلاّ *li'allā* so that ... not see 22/4

م

ما *mā* did not 21/5; what 21/6, 14

ما اذا *mā 'idha* whether 21/13

ماذا *mādha* what 21/6, 26/14

مال اموال *māl 'amwāl* property 16/20

مائت *mā'it* dying 17/5

مائة *mīya* hundred 24/9

مبلغ مبالغ *mablagh mabāligh* amount 18/1

متأكّد من *muta'akkid min* convinced/sure of 21/1

على متن *9ala matn* on board 20/2

متوجّهًا الى *mutawajjihan 'ila* (heading) for 23/1

مثال امثلة *mithāl 'amthila* example 26/1

مجنون ← مجانين

مجلس ادارة *majlis 'idāra* board of directors 21/1

مجلس الأمن *majlis al-'amn* Security Council 26/1

مجموع *majmū9* total 24/1

مجنون مجانين *majnūn majānīn* mad 17/8

محاسبات *muḥāsabāt* accounts 24/1

محامٍ (المحامي) *muḥāmin (al-muḥāmī)* lawyer 24/20

محدود *maḥdūd* limited 24/1

حلّ ← محلّ

مخاطرة *mukhāṭara* risk 19/2

مخلص *mukhliṣ* sincere 24/1, 2

مدرّب *mudarrib* trainer, instructor 24/1

مدير الهندسة *mudīr al-handasa* Chief Engineer 19/1

مذكور *madhkūr* (afore-)mentioned 24/1

مراجعة *murāja9a* review, revision 26/1

مراسلة *murāsala* correspondence 24/1

مربوط *marbūṭ* linked 20/2

مرتفع *murtafi9* high 21/1

مرجوّ *marjūw* requested 23/10

مساء امساء *masā' 'amsā'* afternoon, evening 17/6

مساهمة *musāhama* participation 19/2

مساواة *musāwā* equality 25/9

مستشفىً (المستشفى) *mustashfan (al-mustashfa)* hospital 24/20

مستمع *mustámi9* listener 24/15

مستودع *mustawda9* container 20/1

مسرور *masrūr* pleased 17/2

مشاركة *mushāraka* participation 25/1

مشاهد *mushāhid* viewer 24/15

مشى يمشي *masha yamshī* I walk 23/7

منظّمة ← مصدّر

مصمّم *muṣammim* determined 17/3

مضمون *maḍmūn* guaranteed 25/1

معقول *ma9qūl* reasonable 25/1

مفتّش *mufattish* inspector 18/4

مقرّ ← مقارّ

مقهًى ← مقاهٍ (المقاهي)

مقبول *maqbūl* acceptable 19/1

مقرّ مقارّ *maqarr maqārr* headquarters 23/1

المقرّرة عقدها *al-muqarrara 9aqduha* see 23/1, 26/12

مقهًى (المقهى) مقاهٍ (المقاهي) *maqhan (al-maqha) maqāhin (al-maqāhī)* coffee-house 24/20
مكافحة *mukāfaḥa* fight against 26/1
مكعّب *muka99ab* cubic 20/2
ملحق *mulḥaq* annex(ed) 19/1
ممّن *mimman* from whom 16/20
من *man* who 16/20, 21/6, 26/14
منتوج *mantūj* product 22/1
منسيّ *mansīy* forgotten 23/10
منشور *manshūr* memorandum, circular 24/1
منظّمة الدول المصدّرة للنفط (اوبيك) *munaḍḍamat ad-duwal al-muṣaddira li n-nafṭ ('oubek)* Organisation of Petroleum Exporting Countries (OPEC) 23/1
منظّمة الصحّة العالمية *munaḍḍamat aṣ-ṣiḥḥa l-9ālamīya* World Health Organisation (WHO) 23/1
منفيّ *manfīy* denied, repudiated 23/10
مهنة مهن *mihna mihan* profession 21/2
مورد ← موارد
مواصلات *muwāṣalāt* communications 20/1
موالاة *muwālā* constancy 25/9
ميناء ← موانٍ (الموانى)
مؤرّخ *mu'arrakh* dated 19/1
مورد موارد *mawrid mawārid* resource 23/1
مؤسّس *mu'assas* founded, *mu'assis* founder 17/5
موفّق *muwaffaq* successful 24/1
موقّت\مؤقّت *muwaqqat/mu'aqqat* provisional, temporary 19/1
موم *mūm* wax 16/21
مؤمّن *mu'ammin* insurer 19/1
مؤمّن عليه *mu'amman 9alayhi* insured 19/1
مؤهّل *mu'ahhal* qualified 21/2
مؤهّلات *mu'ahhilāt* qualifications 21/2
ميناء موانٍ (الموانى) *mīnā' mawānin (al-mawānī)* port 24/20
مئة *mīya* hundred 24/9
المئة\المئوي *al-mīya(wī)* hundredth, المئة والواحد *al-mīya wa l-wāḥid* 101st 24/10

ن

نادٍ (النادي) اندية *nādin (an-nādī) 'ándiya* club, circle 26/1
ناقلة *nāqila* freighter, tanker, ناقلة ضخمة *nāqila ḍakhma* supertanker 20/1
نتيجة نتائج *natīja natā'ij* result 17/8
نحن *naḥnu* we 20/3
نسي ينسى *násiya yansa* I forget 23/7
نظام انظمة *niḍām 'anḍima* order, system 26/1
وجهة ← نظر
نظر ينظر *naḍara yanḍuru* I see, نظر ينظر الى *naḍara yanḍuru* I *'ila* look at 20/11, 26/14
نظرًا ل *naḍaran li* in view of 20/1
نفط *nafṭ* oil, نفط خام *nafṭ khām* crude oil 22/1
نفي *nafy* denial, repudiation 23/1

نفى ينفي نفي *nafa yanfī* I, *nafy* deny, repudiate 23/1, 7

نقل *naql* transport 20/1

نوبة نوب *nawba nuwab* shift, turn 19/1

نوعًا ما *naw9an mā* somewhat 26/1, 5

نوى ينوي نية *nawa yanwī* I, *nīya* intend 25/5

نيابةً عن *niyābatan 9an* deputising for 23/1

نية *nīya* intention 25/9

ه

هامّ *hāmm* important 16/22

هامبورج *hamburg* Hamburg 18/6

هاتان\هاتين *hātāni/hātayni* see 22/3

هذان *hādhāni* see 22/3

هذه *hādhihi* see 22/3

هذين *hādhayni* see 22/3

هل *hal* see 21/13

هما *huma* both of them 20/3

هنّ *hunna* they (f.) 26/13

مدير ← هندسة

هوّز *hawwaz* see 24/11

هؤلاء *hā'ulā'i* see 22/3

و

واجب *wājib* necessary 25/1

واجه *wājaha* III face 26/1

بواسطة *bi wāsiṭat* by means of 20/1

واشنطن *wāshinṭun* Washington 18/6

والى *wāla* III be constant 25/7

إنْ ← وجد (ت)

وجّه *wajjaha* II send 20/2

وجهة نظر *wujhat naḍar* point of view 25/1

وزاري *wizārī* ministerial 23/1

وظيفة وظائف *waḍīfa waḍā'if* job 21/2

وفد وفود *wafd wufūd* delegation, mission 23/1

وفر يفر *wafara yafiru* I abound 24/2

وفد ← وفود

وقاية *wiqāya* protection 19/2

وقّع *waqqa9a* II sign 24/1

(و)لكنّ *(wa)lākinna* but 21/8

ولّى *walla* II appoint 25/7

ولي يلي *wáliya yalī* I be next 25/5

ي

يجب *yajib* must see 22/5, 26/14

يجوز *yajūz* may see 22/5

يد اياد (الأيادي) *yad 'ayādin (al-'ayādī)* hand 24/20

(في) ما يلي :يلي *(fī) mā yalī* (in) what follows, كما يلي *kama yalī* as follows 25/5

يمكن *yumkin* may see 22/5

يوجد *yūjad* there is/are 26/10, 14; لا يوجد *lā yūjad* there is no/none, nil (in statistics) see 26/10

يومًا ما *yawman mā* some day, some time (in the future) 26/5

Grammar index

References indicate Lesson no./paragraph no. The sign → refers you to another entry in the index.